THEORY AND PRACTICE
OF EARLY READING
Volume 2

THEORY AND PRACTICE
OF EARLY READING
Volume 2

Edited by   **LAUREN B. RESNICK**
University of Pittsburgh

PHYLLIS A. WEAVER
Harvard University

LEA LAWRENCE ERLBAUM ASSOCIATES, PUBLISHERS
1979   Hillsdale, New Jersey

Copyright© 1979 by Lawrence Erlbaum Associates, Inc.
All rights reserved. No part of this book may be reproduced in
any form, by photostat, microform, retrieval system, or any other
means, without the prior written permission of the publisher.

Lawrence Erlbaum Associates, Inc., Publishers
365 Broadway
Hillsdale, New Jersey 07642

Library of Congress Cataloging in Publication Data

Main entry under title:

Theory and practice of early reading.

Based on papers presented at a series of 3
conferences, held at the Learning Research and Development Center, University of Pittsburgh, 1976.
Bibliography: p.
Includes indexes.
1. Reading (Elementary) I. Resnick, Lauren B.
II. Weaver, Phyllis A. III. Pittsburgh.
University. Learning Research and Development
Center.
LB1573.T46   372.4   79-23784
ISBN 0-89859-010-8 (v. 2)

Printed in the United States of America

Contents

Preface

Concern for the pedagogy of reading is almost as old as the history of the written word. Yet never before the present century has reading instruction commanded so much attention on the part of so many. A society that aspires to universal literacy must necessarily be fascinated with the question of how people read and how they learn to read. When everyone must be literate, problems that once could be solved by attrition and dropping out must now be solved by instruction. Not only those who learn easily but those who are hard to teach and even those who are reluctant to learn must be taught. Every resource, theoretical and practical, must be brought to bear on the problem of reading instruction.

These volumes explore the range and depth of our theoretical and practical knowledge about early reading instruction. Contributors—psychologists, linguists, instructional designers, reading and special education experts—were asked to address three questions: (1) What is the nature of skilled reading? (2) How is reading skill acquired? (3) What do the nature of skilled reading and the process of acquiring reading skill jointly suggest for reading instruction? In this context, issues such as the centrality of decoding in early reading, "stages" in learning to read, the role of "automatic" word recognition in reading comprehension, the role of oral language in acquiring reading skill, the effect of cultural and linguistic differences on reading acquisition and performance, and the nature of individual differences in learning to read are addressed and debated. Several major instructional programs are analyzed, and there is considerable discussion of the possible and appropriate role of theory and experimental research in guiding the course of reading instruction. Taken together, the chapters of these three volumes suggest clearly where reading research and practice stand with respect to the key questions of skilled performance, acquisition sequences, and early instruction. Accordingly, these volumes should be of interest to reading educators, psychologists, and other theorists of reading.

Many of the chapters in these volumes are based on papers that were presented and discussed at a series of three conferences held at the Learning Research and Development Center, University of Pittsburgh, in 1976. The conferences were supported by the National Institute of Education as part of the Compensatory Education Evaluation Study. Organization of the volumes is by conference, with discussion chapters appearing at the end of each volume. The thematic content of each volume and of the series as a whole is outlined in some detail in the introductory chapter.

We gratefully acknowledge those many individuals who assisted in planning and conducting the conferences and preparing these volumes. Cathlene Hardaway and Barbara Haky Viccari assisted in many details of planning and running the conferences; they and Carol Evans had responsibility for many aspects related to preparing these volumes. Shirley Tucker prepared the subject indexes to the three volumes. Charles Teggatz was technical editor for most chapters in the three volumes; his substantive suggestions and editoral assistance were invaluable. During a major part of the preparation of these volumes, one of us (Lauren Resnick) was a Fellow at the Center for Advanced Study in the Behavioral Sciences, Palo Alto, California, supported in part by a grant from the Spencer Foundation. This support is gratefully acknowledged.

LAUREN B. RESNICK

PHYLLIS A. WEAVER

THEORY AND PRACTICE
OF EARLY READING
Volume 2

The Theory and Practice of Early Reading: An Introduction

Phyllis A. Weaver
Harvard University

Lauren B. Resnick
University of Pittsburgh

> *There is a kind of idle theory which is antithetical to practice;*
> *but genuinely scientific theory falls within practice as the agency*
> *of its expansion and its direction to new possibilities.*
>
> John Dewey (1932)

Never before the present century has reading instruction commanded so much attention on the part of so many. The sources of this concern and attention lie in a combination of social and scientific developments that set the context in which these volumes and the positions on reading taken in them can best be understood and evaluated. In the social sphere, standards of literacy have been rising during the course of the past century. Virtually everyone is now expected to become literate, and the criteria for assessing literacy are more stringent today than at any previous time. The result is increased public concern for reading and increased attention to reading on the part of educators. In the scientific sphere, meanwhile, there has been a continuing press to apply scientific knowledge to practical affairs, with the result that attention has been directed most to those aspects of educational practice about which science has the most to say. Together, these social and scientific developments have shaped both the extent and the direction of current work on reading, work that is reported and debated in these volumes. In this chapter, we begin by considering how theory and practice in reading instruction have been influenced by these forces. We then outline the specific issues that are dominant in today's debates about early reading; these issues are directly addressed in the chapters of these volumes.

1

THE SOCIAL PRESS FOR LITERACY

The Expectation of Universal Literacy

A short story by Somerset Maugham helps to illustrate the ways in which social perceptions of literacy have changed. "The Verger" (Maugham, 1937) is about a man, Albert Edward Foreman, who has held the position of verger in a fashionable church (St. Peter's, Neville Square) for many years. He is illiterate, a fact that has just been discovered by the current vicar and churchwardens. The discovery leads to a request for the verger's resignation, although all involved freely admit that he performs his duties quite acceptably. Nevertheless, they find it inappropriate for a man who cannot read or write to be their verger:

> "It's the most amazing thing I ever heard," cried the [warden]. "Do you mean to say that you've been verger of this church for sixteen years and never learned to read or write?"
>
> "I went into service when I was twelve, sir. The cook in the first place tried to teach me once, but I didn't seem to 'ave the knack for it, and then what with one thing and another I never seemed to 'ave the time. I've never really found the want of it. I think a lot of these young fellows waste a rare lot of time readin' when they might be doin' something useful."

The story relates how the verger, faced with the need to earn a living in some new way, opens a tabacconist's shop, then a second, then several more. Eventually he owns a string of shops, and he is making weekly bank deposits so large that his holdings total over thirty thousand pounds. Noting this, a bank officer suggests that the funds might better be invested and offers to make out a list of securities so that all the verger-turned-businessman would need to do is to sign the necessary papers:

> "I could do that all right," said Albert uncertainly. "But 'ow should I know what I was signin'?"
>
> "I suppose you can read," said the manager a trifle sharply.
>
> Mr. Foreman gave him a disarming smile.
>
> "Well, sir, that's just it. I can't. I know it sounds funny like, but there it is, I can't read or write, only me name, an' I only learnt to do that when I went into business."
>
> The manager was so surprised that he jumped up from his chair.
>
> "That's the most extraordinary thing I ever heard."
>
> "You see, it's like this, sir, I never 'ad the opportunity until it was too late and then some'ow I wouldn't. I got obstinate like."
>
> The manager stared at him as though he were a prehistoric monster.
>
> "And do you mean to say that you've built up this important business and amassed a fortune of thirty thousand pounds without being able to read or write? Good God, man, what would you be now if you had been able to?"

"I can tell you that, sir," said Mr. Foreman, a little smile on his still aristocratic features. "I'd be verger of St. Peter's, Neville Square."

The story's ironic ending helps to illustrate the profound ways in which society's demands for literacy have changed. The story takes place in a time when an expectation of widespread literacy was just developing. The astonishment of both church and bank officials serves to highlight the expectation. Both groups seem to believe that literacy is required for satisfactory performance of the work in question; in fact, the deepest source of their astonishment is not that Albert Edward cannot read or write but that he has been performing his jobs successfully in spite of being illiterate. Albert Edward's experiences might serve to demonstrate to these people that literacy is not essential to successful performance, at least in many jobs and social functions. But that is not their interpretation. The church officials, offering the excuse of a possible accident in the church, treat literacy, even that of the verger, as a necessary status symbol for members of their organization. The bank official assumes that Albert Edward might have succeeded even more brilliantly had he been literate. Albert Edward, however, understands that his success does not depend on literacy and seems also to recognize that his inability to read is not linked to intelligence but to the accidents of birth in a period in which opportunity and expectation for learning to read were tied to social class.

Maugham wrote "The Verger" in the 1930s, an ironic commentary on an already changing scene in which formal credentials of literacy were beginning to replace functional performance and inherited status as a criterion for access to certain positions. The shifts Maugham noted fifty years ago are all the more marked now. Moreover, it is unlikely that Albert Edward today could be successful as a tabacconist. Opportunities for small business have shrunk, and even these depend heavily on obtaining credit and negotiating other formalities that require at least minimum literacy. Furthermore, it is unlikely that Albert Edward today would be so serenely accepting of his state of illiteracy, juding himself neither incompetent nor lazy for being unable to read.

The Rising Criteria for Literacy

At the same time as we have expected more people to be literate, our criteria for literacy have been rising, placing double pressures on the instructional system. Our definitions of reading competence have changed markedly over the past century, and neither our methods of teaching nor our understanding of the reading process has caught up with our social aspirations. Reviewing the history of literacy standards in Western Europe and America, Resnick and Resnick (1977) noted that until well into the present century, knowing "how to read" meant being able to recognize and respond to highly familiar texts, such as those of catechisms or other religious or civil tracts. Given this criterion, teaching reading meant teaching people to translate printed words into spoken ones—that is, to read aloud. During the 19th century, an able reader—according to the definition used in most schools—was one who could give a good public rendition of a text, declaiming it with appropriate phrasing and emphasis. Although readers undoubtedly needed to grasp at least the gist of what they were reading to achieve such a performance, there is little evidence that schools were expected to *teach* anything having to do with the comprehension of written texts. In fact, there is evidence to the contrary, suggesting that most schools explicitly understood their reading instruction mandate to end with the development of fluent oral reading skill. A description of the pedagogical aims and practices of a well-known Scottish school, drawn from an American teachers' journal of 1831, highlights this understanding (from Mathews, 1966):

> English reading, according to the prevailing notion, consists of nothing more than the power of giving utterance to certain sounds, on the perception of certain figures; and the measure of progress and excellence is the facility and continuous fluency with which those sounds succeed each other from the mouth of the learner. If the child gathers any knowledge from the book before him, beyond that of color, form, and position of the letters, it is to his own sagacity he is indebted for it, and not to his teacher [p. 55].

It is only during the present century that reading for the purpose of gaining information has become a virtually universal goal, an expectation applied in ordinary elementary schools to the entire population of students. This shift in the criteria for literacy has direct bearing on the state of our knowledge regarding reading instruction. To the extent that reading instruction is concerned with the ability to declaim print, it has a long history of pedagogical thought and effort on which to draw. Over several centuries, considerable ingenuity and thoughtfulness have been brought to bear on the problem (see Mathews, 1966, for a review), and there is a great deal of richness and depth in past discussions both of how people manage to translate print to sound and how this skill can best be taught. However, insofar as reading instruction is concerned with the process of drawing meaning from print, it has only a brief history of scientific work to draw on; and there is little richness in the range of instructional practices that have been tried. As a result, there is comparatively little in the way of empirical evidence to support competing conceptions of the nature of skilled comprehension or of how it develops. This difference in historical depth accounts in great part for the difference in how much we are able to say about decoding texts and understanding them—a difference that will become apparent to the readers of these volumes. It also suggests why professionals and scientists concerned with reading are in a position to make some meaningful prescriptive judgments about how people learn and use alphabetic codes but are able to say relatively little, with assurance, about how they develop and enhance their ability to comprehend written text.

THE FOCUS ON EARLY READING

It is in recognition of the differential state of scientific knowledge about decoding and comprehension that we chose to limit the focus of these volumes to early reading. Early reading has often been defined as learning the code, being able to recognize words, or translating print to sound. As we have just suggested, this is a definition with considerable historical tradition: Learning the code *was* learning to read for many centuries. As a result, we know more about how people use the code during both beginning and skilled stages of reading than we do about how they use the semantic or syntactic aspects of texts. If there is a part of the total process of becoming literate in which science and professional practice have an opportunity to interact fruitfully at this time, it is with respect to learning the code. A great deal of research has been conducted on recognizing printed words and translating them into oral language, and a significant amount is known about the processes involved in word recognition and how to teach this aspect of reading to young children. Research provides some knowledge of the relations between word recognition and comprehension, although this knowledge is still limited. Moreover, far less is known about the processes involved in constructing meaning from written or spoken language, and very little is known about how to facilitate the development of these processes in young learners. In fact, the study of natural language processes as part of reading is only now emerging as a major focus of scholarly research.

Code and Meaning

A decision to focus on early reading and thus on learning the code, however well justified in terms of our past history and current knowledge, immediately and inevitably raises the question of whether the equation of early reading and code learning is necessary and proper. The question is central in these volumes, for by no means all of our authors agree that the code should be central to the definition of reading or in research on reading instruction. Concern about the relationship between code and meaning is not new to reading pedagogy. In fact, our present views with respect to the roles of code and meaning in reading instruction can be understood best in light of a dialectic relation in which code and meaning emphases successively challenge, and thereby refine, one another.

Challenge to the code emphasis began in this country in the 19th century and gathered force toward the end of that century as the progressive education movement began to emphasize function and meaning over drill and stylized performance in education. But it was probably not until after World War I that reading comprehension, rather than oral reading, became a central concern of reading pedagogy. Two factors seem to have influenced the direction of this shift. One was the increasing recognition that large numbers of people who had been to school and could read certain texts aloud, although haltingly, could not gather meaning from print. This recognition was given impetus by the World War I army testing program in which about 25% of recruits were insufficiently literate to take the written form of the test (Army Alpha) used to assign men to training and jobs in the army. The other factor was the findings of early research on reading processes. Psychologists such as Cattell (1886), Huey (1908/1968), and Buswell (1920) found that people read in units at least as large as words and that meaningful phrases were the most common units of processing.

Around 1920, the combination of the emphasis on comprehension of text as the goal of reading instruction and the finding that attention to meaningful units rather than to letters and sounds characterized the reading of skilled individuals led to a radical change in reading pedagogy. Reading educators argued that if extraction of meaning is the goal of instruction and the strategy of skilled readers, then the focus from the very outset of reading instruction should be on meaning. This was to be accomplished by teaching children to recognize words as wholes, thereby allowing them—very early in their reading experience—to read sentences and stories about characters and topics of interest to them.

To make this new pedagogy work, new instructional materials were needed. If words were to be learned and read as wholes, ignoring the alphabetic principle, only a limited vocabulary could be taught. From this need grew the idea and practice of "basal readers," graded series of books in which a few words at a time are introduced and extensively reviewed in story contexts. Accompanying the readers were detailed suggestions to teachers for how to teach children to read them. The basal approach with words chosen for their relatively high frequency of occurrence rather than for their spelling-to-sound regularity, gradually replaced most of the older approaches. By the 1950s, it was the established way to teach reading. Virtually all teachers were trained in basal approaches and knew how to manage classes using such approaches. Massive publishing efforts made it possible for schools and teachers to buy varied, attractive, and complete "systems" for teaching reading, all based on the controlled vocabulary, sight recognition principle. A new "establishment" was clearly in place.[1]

---

[1] In earlier times the terms *basal* and *whole word* were used synonymously, whereas today basal reading series may stress code as well as meaning.

Inevitably, reactions to this new orthodoxy developed. Challenges to sight-word methods began to be heard in both scholarly and lay circles in the 1950s and early 1960s (see, e.g., Flesch, 1955; Fries, 1962). In 1967 Chall published a book reviewing research evidence on early reading instruction and concluded that code approaches were generally superior to whole-word and other meaning-oriented approaches in the earliest years of instruction. However, those who advocated a reemphasis on the code in the 1950s and 1960s were not suggesting a return to alphabetic drills stripped of meaning; instead, they were proposing programs of direct code instruction in the context of meaningful reading material. The proposed new code emphasis, in other words, would be systematically refined to incorporate some of the more successful and appealing aspects of basal-style instruction.

In a sense, these volumes are a reexamination of issues considered by Chall a decade ago. Somewhat modified basal reading approaches are still dominant in today's instructional practice, and they are even less favorably viewed by our contributors than they were by Chall. In both theoretical and practical chapters, there is more attention paid to aspects of teaching, learning, and using the code than to comprehending written language. Yet an interest in meaning is not absent. Indeed, a number of the contributors to these volumes express concern that in a return to code approaches to teaching reading, the heart of reading may again be lost. But most of those proposing meaning-oriented initial instruction are not suggesting that the code be abandoned in a return to a 1930s style of basal readers. Instead, emerging theories of how people understand language and how language functions in social communication are being used to refine views of what a new meaning-oriented approach to early reading instruction might become. It is in this general context of debate that a number of specific issues about the nature of reading and of early reading instruction are addressed by the contributors to these volumes. We outline next some of the major themes to be found in the chapters that follow.

THE ISSUES

In inviting contributions to these volumes, we asked each author to consider three sets of questions:

1. What is the nature of skilled reading; that is, what is the goal of reading instruction?
2. How is reading skill acquired? What are the "stages" or steps in competence in the process of going from being a nonreader to being a skilled reader, and how does one pass from one stage to the next?
3. What do the nature of skilled reading and the process of acquiring reading skill jointly suggest for reading instruction?

To answer these questions, we brought together theorists and practitioners, some who were almost exclusively concerned with documenting the nature of skilled reading and some who were largely concerned with reading acquisition and development. We defined our task as relating what is known about skilled reading performance to what is being learned about the development of that performance capability. In so doing, our hope was to shed some light on instruction. What is needed for improving reading instruction is not only a description of skilled performance but also a theory of *propaedeutics*—a theory that does not assume that processes performed early in learning will directly match those performed later but instead, suggests what kind of early preparatory instruction will help people learn subsequent more complex capabilities.

Few of the chapters in these volumes, considered individually, draw explicit connections between the three questions of skilled performance, acquisition sequences, and instruction. Yet taken together, these volumes suggest clearly where reading research and practice stand with respect to these questions. Attention to the questions emerges in the context of a number of specific issues raised by the authors, and we outline some of them here. Table 1.1 depicts these issues, the viewpoints related to them, and which contributors address the various issues. The headings in the table match those in the discussion that follows here. Therefore, the table is useful both as a summary of our discussion and as a guide to the volumes for readers with particular interests.

The Centrality of Decoding to Early Reading

Should beginning reading instruction emphasize the relationship between sounds and graphic symbols, or should it stress getting meaning from print? Although an emphasis on one aspect of reading does not necessarily exclude the other, the question of balance between them has occupied educators and researchers since at least the beginning of the 20th century. Individuals who address this issue tend to take one of several positions that vary along a continuum from: (a) learning to decode (i.e., using knowledge of phoneme-grapheme correspondences to recognize words) *is* early reading; to (b) learning to decode (through phonics instruction or some similar approach) is important because it helps develop sensitivity to orthographic regularity (i.e., recurrent spelling patterns), which is important in the transition from early to skilled reading; to (c) learning to decode is at best incidental to becoming literate and at worst, may interfere with acquiring reading skill. We examine each position briefly.

Early Reading Is Decoding. At one end of the continuum are those who contend that reading is, to use Liberman and Shankweiler's (Vol. 2) term, *parasitic* on spoken language. That is, learning to read is viewed as learning to map graphic symbols onto speech. Once this skill is learned, the established processes of understanding spoken language "take over." This position is represented centrally in the chapters by Liberman and Shankweiler and by Perfetti and Lesgold (Vol. 1). Liberman and Shankweiler propose that children need to be taught the alphabetic principle and skills of phonemic segmentation before they are taught to read. They suggest specific strategies and sequences of instruction that include preparing children for phonemic analysis and teaching them to associate the shape of the letter with its name and sound.

Perfetti and Lesgold contend that comprehension in reading depends on highly skilled generation and manipulation of language codes. They argue that even in skilled reading, there is a form of phonological encoding, albeit an abbreviated one, that precedes comprehension; and they recommend that decoding expertise should be the basic goal of early reading instruction. They offer suggestions for developing coding skills that include games and computer-assisted instruction.

Several other chapters suggest the importance of a code emphasis in early reading instruction or discuss commercially available programs with such an emphasis. Among them are the chapters by Beck and Block and by Chall in Volume 1, by Bartlett and by Fletcher in Volume 2, and by Popp, Wallach and Wallach, and Williams in Volume 3.

Reading and Orthographic Regularity. A less extreme position regarding the role of decoding suggests that although skilled reading may not involve phonological recoding, it involves attention to recurring letter patterns in written language. Furthermore, because direct code instruction necessarily involves attention to this orthographic detail, learning to decode helps develop the awareness of orthographic regularity that is necessary for skilled reading. This position is developed in detail by Venezky and Massaro (Vol. 1). They advocate an early phonics emphasis for both traditional reasons (e.g., it allows independence for beginning readers) and because it provides a vehicle for developing awareness of orthographic regularity. That is, phonics programs introduce almost all the orthographic patterns and do so "by procedures that give overt attention to the relevant spelling units for orthographic regularity." Thus, phonics instruction helps develop skills that are required for obtaining information from written text. A similar position is held by Juola, Schadler, Chabot, McCaughey, and Wait (Vol. 2), who discuss the development of visual search strategies and their relation to word recognition. In this context they suggest that although phonemic encoding plays a minor role in skilled reading, phonic knowledge and knowledge of English orthography are important for developing reading skill.

TABLE 1.1

	Chall	Perfetti – Lesgold	Venezky – Massaro	Fisher	Goodman – Goodman	Frederiksen	Shuy	Sticht	Bateman	Holland	Beck – Block	Kintsch	Posner	Samuels	Gordon
VOLUME 1															
	WORD RECOG				LANGUAGE				INSTR		DISCUSSION				
Centrality of Decoding															
Early reading is decoding	●	●									●				
Reading and orthographic regularity			●												
Decoding not central					●	●									
Nature of Skilled Reading															
Bottom-up or top-down		●	●	●	●	●	●	●						●	
Direct or mediated access		●	●		●	●									
Automaticity		●												●	
Word recognition			●												
Units of processing				●											
Lexical knowledge		●				●									
Reading and Language															
Oral language transfers to written		●						●			●				
Functional language emphasis					●		●								
Richness and variety in reading materials											●				
Factors Interfering with Learning to Read															
Cultural and linguistic differences							●								●
Individual differences			●						●						
Acquiring Reading Competence															
Developmental theory and research	●											●			
Reading instruction and reading acquisition										●	●				
Assessing reading progress					●			●							
Teacher as an instructional variable					●		●		●		●				
Time engaged in reading										●	●				
Relations Between Theory and Practice												●	●		●

● = This topic is discussed or emphasized in the chapter

VOLUME 2															VOLUME 3															
F. Smith	Chomsky	E. Smith – Kleiman	Juola et. al.	Liberman – Shankweiler	Rosner	Clay	Calfee – Drum	Johnson	Bartlett	Fletcher	Venezky	White	Gordon	Resnick	LaBerge	Gregg – Farnham-Diggory	McConkie	Danks – Fears	Simons	Natalicio	Guthrie–Martuza–Seifert	Williams	Wallach – Wallach	Popp	Trabasso	Cazden	Glaser	Carroll – Walton	Resnick
LANGUAGE AND READING					INSTRUCTION						DISCUSSION				PROCESSES OF READING			LANG DIFF & READ			INSTRUCTION				DISCUSSION				

Decoding Is Not Central to Reading.   At the far end of the continuum is the position that decoding is secondary, even in early reading, to the task of getting meaning from print. Goodman and Goodman (Vol. 1) hold this position in its most extreme form. They suggest that written language is an alternative form of linguistic communication and like spoken language, can and should be learned in the context of its functional uses. Therefore, if appropriate experiences occur or are arranged, there is no need for explicit decoding instruction. Not only is there no need for it, Goodman and Goodman argue, but providing such instruction can actually interfere with the natural extension of general language skills to understanding the printed form. They offer suggestions for alternative learning experiences designed to promote the development of children's knowledge of language functions and to facilitate reading acquisition.

Smith (Vol. 2) also questions the value of instruction in decoding. He argues that reading is not guided by letter-by-letter or even word-by-word analysis; instead, it begins in the head with a prediction of meaning and ends with selective attention to only parts of the written text. He characterizes this as an "inside-out" process and says that children learn to read by "making sense" of written language. Therefore, he views decoding letters and combining them into words as the most difficult way to learn to read, because it does not match the processes of skilled performance. A focus on decoding, he argues, does not make sense to children and is therefore a hindrance to learning. Danks and Fears (Vol. 3) review some of the research that might provide evidence on the question of whether a hypothesis about meaning always precedes attention to the written text; they conclude that this depends on an interaction between the capability of the reader, the difficulty of the text, and the reader's purpose. The suggestion is that decoding skills are needed in at least some "skilled" reading performances.

The position held by Frederiksen (Vol. 1) reflects this sense of variability in the reading process. He contends that the primary goal in early reading instruction should be to teach children to comprehend written discourse in the same way that they comprehend oral discourse. However, because reading does involve attention to graphemic information, teaching the code is a necessary subgoal of instruction. Nevertheless, Frederiksen recommends that if achieving efficiency in the subgoal interferes with the primary goal of comprehension, then inefficiency in decoding must be tolerated.

The Nature of Skilled Reading

Many chapters in these volumes focus on the issue of how skilled readers process written discourse. Several aspects of the nature of skilled reading processes are discussed, including: (a) whether discourse processing is controlled in a "bottom-up" or "top-down" manner; (b) whether meaning is accessed directly from the graphic display or is mediated by a phonolgical recoding; and (c) what role automaticity of word recognition processes plays.

Bottom-Up or Top-Down?   In a bottom-up processing view of reading, lower level processes (e.g., letter and word recognition) are thought to occur prior to and independent of higher level processes. First words are recognized, then a syntactic processing occurs, and finally a semantic interpretation is made based on the sentence syntax. Furthermore, these processes are controlled by textual input; word recognition precedes comprehension of meaning. By contrast, in a top-down conception, reading is not controlled exclusively by the textual input; instead, higher level cognitive processes (e.g., making inferences) control the system, and lower processes are called into play only as they are needed. Hypotheses regarding the meaning of the text are generated from prior knowledge of the topic, knowledge of the specific textual content, and a minimal syntactic parsing and sampling of visual cues. According to the extreme top-down view, comprehension of meaning precedes recognition of words, and complete encoding of separate words may not occur at all. (See Frederiksen, Vol. 1, for a more detailed discussion of these concepts.)

Although most researchers would not characterize skilled reading as an exclusively bottom-up or top-down process, the authors who discuss this issue tend to do so with one or the other "direction" predominating.[2] Smith and Kleiman (Vol. 2) are the main proponents of reading as predominantly a bottom-up process. Several other authors imply a bottom-up view in the context of discussions of other aspects of reading (see the chapters by Sticht, Perfetti and Lesgold, and Fisher in Vol. 1). The chapters by Frederiksen (Vol. 1) and by Smith (Vol. 2) discuss skilled reading as a top-down controlled process ("inside-out" in Smith's terms), and this position is implied in the chapters by Goodman and Goodman and by Shuy in Volume 1.

It is important to note that several authors distinguish between skilled and novice readers in this respect. They view the skilled reading process as one that is controlled from the top down but see the *development* of reading skill proceeding from the bottom up. This position is represented by Samuels, Shuy, Venezky and Massaro (all in Vol. 1), LaBerge (Vol. 3), and to a certain

---

[2]It is noteworthy that when these volumes went to press, views about this issue had already changed. The nature of this change is captured by Adams and Collins (1977) in their schema theoretic account of reading. They suggest and attribute to Rumelhart (in press) that "top-down and bottom-up processing should be occurring at all levels of analysis simultaneously.... Bottom-up processing insures that the reader will be sensitive to information that is novel or that does not fit his on-going hypotheses about the content of the text; top-down processes help him to resolve ambiguities or to select between alternative possible interpretations of the incoming data [p. 9]."

extent by Frederiksen. On the other hand, Goodman and Goodman and Smith view *both* early and skilled reading as a top-down controlled process.

Direct or Mediated Access?   Several chapters address the issue of whether there is phonological recoding during skilled reading. On one side of this issue are those who hold that even in skilled reading, graphic information is recoded into phonological information before meaning is accessed. Viewpoints on this issue are often related to those on the bottom-up versus top-down conception of skilled reading. That is, those who view reading as a bottom-up process usually hold that there is a phonolgical recoding stage, even in skilled reading (e.g., Liberman & Shankweiler; Perfetti & Lesgold); whereas those who view reading as a top-down process tend to believe that meaning is accessed directly (e.g., Frederiksen; Goodman & Goodman; Smith). Exceptions to this correlation can be found in the chapters of Venezky and Massaro and of Smith and Kleiman, both of which propose a generally bottom-up view of the skilled reading process that does not depend on phonological recoding. Danks and Fears, as we have noted, suggest that whether access is direct or mediated depends on the individual reader and the task.

The Role of Automaticity.   One argument often used to support a direct-access-to-meaning view is that skilled reading proceeds at a rate that precludes the possibility of phonological recoding. A common reply to the argument is that in high-speed skilled reading, word recognition or phonological recoding takes place in an automatic fashion. That is, words are recognized rapidly, accurately, and with minimal attentional resources. Therefore, although it appears that meaning is obtained without actually recognizing words or recoding them, it is possible that these recognition processes are present but highly automatized and abbreviated. This position is central to the discussion by Perfetti and Lesgold, and it is supported by LaBerge (Vol. 3) in his chapter on perceptual units in the reading process and by Samuels in his discussion of the chapters in Volume 1.

Other Aspects Related to Skilled Reading.   A number of other topics related to skilled reading are considered by various authors. There is now a considerable body of research literature on word (and letter-string) recognition processes in skilled reading. For reviews and discussions of this literature, see the chapters by Smith and Kleiman, Venezky and Massaro, Juola et al., and Danks and Fears. Smith and Kleiman review this literature in the context of an information-processing model of skilled reading, whereas Venezky and Massaro consider it in supporting their claims for the importance of orthographic regularity in word and letter-string recognition. Juola et al. (Vol. 2) review research on "word superiority" (faster and more accurate recognition of real words than of pseudowords that follow the rules of conventional English spelling) in their discussion of the development of visual search performance. And Danks and Fears (Vol. 3) review a selected body of literature on oral reading errors, eye–voice span, and effects of text alteration in their discussion of oral production in a decoding-comprehension model of reading.

The question of perceptual units in reading is discussed in the chapters by McConkie, Fisher, and LaBerge. McConkie (Vol. 3) reports eye-movement research related to the perceptual span in reading; Fisher (Vol. 1) discusses the effects on reading of limited peripheral-visual processing; and LaBerge (Vol. 3) discusses functions of units for perceptual processing, selection of units for specific tasks, and learning of new units.

Finally, the skilled reader makes use of an extensive body of knowledge about words and what they represent during skilled reading. The extent of this network of lexical and semantic knowledge and the effectiveness of strategies for accessing it determine in part the reader's level of proficiency. Issues related to the lexicon and lexical access are explored in the chapters by Frederiksen, Smith and Kleiman, Perfetti and Lesgold, and Gregg and Farnham-Diggory (Vol. 3).

Reading and Language

We have mentioned the question of the relation between reading and general language skills in the course of discussing other issues. As we noted, some authors argue that reading is a matter of translating print to sound and then using established language skills to derive meaning; others argue that understanding written language is a unique process, more than the sum of decoding plus understanding spoken language. Regardless of which position on the nature of the relations between oral language and reading is held, most authors seem to agree that general language competence is essential to reading skill. Differences of opinion arise, however, over when and how language skills should be taught in the context of reading.

One position is that the development of language skills should be promoted in the oral mode while initial reading (coding) skills are being taught. In this way, language skills of increasing complexity can be transferred to the written language form. Sticht (Vol. 1) develops this argument most explicitly and extensively. His "audread" model implies the need for early code teaching and assumes that training in the oral mode will transfer to reading once the learner is past the decoding stage. He defines individuals' reading potentials in terms of the discrepancy between what they can comprehend aurally and what they can comprehend in written form. A similar position on the relation of aural to written comprehension skills is espoused by Beck and Block (Vol. 1), Perfetti and Lesgold, Liberman and Shankweiler, and by Rosner (Vol. 2).

A contrasting position holds that written language is an alternative functional form of language and that skill in using it does not transfer directly from oral competence as a result of learning the code. Instead, children should be taught reading in the context of the various functional modes that are relevant to them. In this way, written language can become a form of communication that is as useful as oral language. The functional language approach to reading is discussed extensively by Goodman and Goodman and by Shuy in Volume 1, and it is implicit in the chapters by Smith (Vol. 2), by Cazden (Vol. 3), and by Simons (Vol. 3). It is worth noting that whereas a functional language emphasis is usually accompanied by an anticode stance in instruction, this negative relation between functional language and code orientations is not a necessary one. Shuy, for example, recognizes a need for direct code teaching while emphasizing functional aspects of language in reading instruction.

A concern for richness of content and form of language within code-oriented instruction characterizes Bartlett's chapter (Vol. 2) comparing the *Distar* and *Open Court* beginning reading programs. Bartlett speculates that literary forms, or genres, can function as cognitive structures, serving to organize verbal information and to aid comprehension and memory. Both reading programs, Bartlett notes, are organized to facilitate code learning, but they provide a different range of literary experience. Bartlett suggests that the relative literary limitation of one of the programs may foster an impoverished kind of literacy. The need for phonics teaching in a semantically rich context is also acknowledged in the other chapters in which instructional programs are analyzed (Beck & Block in Vol. 1, Fletcher in Vol. 2, and Popp in Vol. 3). Similar concerns are expressed by Clay (Vol. 2), who suggests that reading programs that focus only on word attack and have tightly controlled vocabularies may actually be counterproductive to developing independent reading skills. She advocates programs rich in many aspects of language that may support, to use Clay's term, a *self-improving system* of language development.

Factors That Interfere With Learning to Read

The motivation for extended research in reading, and especially for the present attempt to explore the implications of theory and research for instructional practice, derives from the fact that large numbers of people in our society are not achieving expected standards of literacy. The efforts of many researchers and educators are directed at improving or preventing this situation. Children who fail to learn to read or who do so slowly and with extreme difficulty are therefore a major concern of many of the contributors to these volumes. In discussing those who have difficulty learniing to read, it is possible to distinguish between students who encounter difficulty because the expectations and habits of their social-cultural group do not match those of the schools and students who have difficulty because of individual differences in ability. These groups have overlapping memberships, even in the most elegant and theoretical classifications, and they are often very difficult to distinguish in practice. Despite this, it is important, for purposes of analysis, to consider separately these different sources of reading difficulty.

Cultural and Linguistic Differences.   The chapters that focus explicitly on social-cultural origins of reading difficulty are those by Shuy, Simons, Natalicio (Vol. 3), Wallach and Wallach (Vol. 3), and Gordon (Vols. 1 & 2). Shuy discusses the mismatch between the language that children bring to school and the language used by teachers and in texts. He suggests that for children who are culturally and linguistically different from the majority, the language mismatch is not so much a phonological or grammatical one as it is a mismatch of functional language competence—the ways in which language is used for various communication purposes. Shuy suggests that research in the area of language functions may be the most promising of all for determining causes of reading difficulty and failure.

Simons reviews the literature on phonological and grammatical inter- ference in reading among speakers of a black dialect. Like Shuy, Simons concludes that there is little evidence to suggest that speaking a dialect interferes with comprehending written texts once basic skills have been mastered. However, according to Simons, the evidence on the role of dialect speech in *acquiring* reading skill is inconclusive, and speaking a dialect may indeed interfere. Simons proposes to study the question by examining reading instruction as it actually occurs in the classroom; he describes several studies that examine reading interference and classroom interaction by analyzing videotaped instructional sequences.

Natalicio reviews the existing literature on reading and the bilingual child. Although there is currently considerable pressure among Hispanics and others to teach reading in the child's native language, Natalicio suggests that there is little empirical evidence for such an approach. She calls for more research on bilingualism and second-language learning to resolve what have become largely political arguments regarding the best way to teach reading to bilingual children. Trabasso (Vol. 3), in discussing Natalicio's paper, suggests that parallel teaching of reading in both English and the home language should also be considered, in the spirit of what has been called by Riegel and Freedle (1976) "independent bilingualism." It is not surprising that we know less about the problems of bilingual children than about those of bidialectic children. As Natalicio points out, the recognition of reading problems among bilinguals is relatively new in the United States, and they have only recently gained the attention of researchers.

Gordon (Vol. 2) addresses issues of social-cultural differences and reading from a broader perspective. He discusses compensatory education, characteristics of the groups served by compensatory education, and the effects of various compensatory educational programs. His comments on the teaching and learning of reading are set in this broader context.

Individual Differences. The chapters by Fisher and by Bateman in Volume 1, by Johnson and by Rosner in Volume 2, and by Wallach and Wallach and by Williams in Volume 3 are concerned primarily with individuals—rather than members of social or ethnic groups—who have difficulty learning to read. Fisher and Johnson focus on individuals who are from a clinical population, those with severe learning or reading disabilities; the other authors focus on individuals whose reading difficulties are less severe and for whom instruction can take place in a regular classroom setting.

Fisher discusses the visual-neurological origins of severe reading disability and describes experiments that show sharply reduced peripheral-visual processing among the severely reading disabled. He discusses the importance of the visual periphery in obtaining information and guiding eye movements, and he suggests that instruction for the severely disabled should compensate for these difficulties. Johnson discusses a variety of factors as possible sources of learning or reading disabilities, and she proposes a systems analysis approach to diagnosis and remediation. By this, she means identifying the various psychosensory systems and processes that are involved in reading and determining which are intact and which are impaired. She stresses that the population of children with learning disabilities is heterogeneous and that children with learning disabilities require individual remedial instruction. Examples of these individual remedial strategies are described in her chapter.

The chapters by Bateman, Rosner, Wallach and Wallach, and Williams are concerned with classroom instructional procedures for the hard to teach, whether they are labeled disabled, retarded, or culturally different. Although there are differences in the approaches recommended, a common thread in these chapters is an assumption that those who have difficulty learning to read require a structured curriculum that attends to the phonemic nature of the language and to the relationship of the phonemic to the graphemic code. Bateman recommends using principles of applied behavioral analysis and task analytic programming. Operationally, according to Bateman, this means direct practice with many trials to ensure acquisition and development of the decoding aspect of reading. She suggests that *Distar* is an exemplary program for teaching beginning reading (but cf. Bartlett, Vol. 2). Wallach and Wallach and Williams report on programs they designed and implemented to teach certain beginning reading skills to children who are at high risk for reading failure. The Wallachs report an apparently successful attempt at teaching phoneme identification and segmentation skills to inner-city children in

Chicago. Williams designed and is testing a program with learning disabled children from inner-city neighborhoods in New York City. Like Bateman, she recommends that the cognitive and perceptual skills necessary for reading be taught in the context of reading rather than apart from it. Her program follows a sequence in which segmentation and blending of syllables are taught before segmentation and blending of phonemes. Both the Wallachs' program and Williams', then, teach the kinds of skills Liberman and Shankweiler stress as necessary for learning the code. Rosner, discussing the general problem of teaching poor-prognosis children, outlines the components of an instructional system in which he believes it is possible to match student traits with instruction so as to optimize learning. His suggestions are slated for children he views as hard to teach, but his outline appears to be for an instructional system that would benefit all students.

Acquiring Reading Competence

As we have noted earlier, it is important in discussing reading and reading instruction to distinguish between descriptions of the skilled reading process and accounts of how reading skill is acquired. In reading as in other skills, it is probable that the novice performs differently from the expert. Novice readers probably are not only slower, but they probably also attend to different features of text, perceive text in different-sized units, and bring knowledge that is both less extensive and less well structured to the reading activity. Therefore, for example, the skilled reader may read in phrase or clause units, whereas the novice may attend to every word or even to every letter. Despite growing knowledge of the processes involved in skilled reading, much less is known about the ways in which the reading process changes in the course of its development (see Gibson & Levin, 1975, for a discussion of developmental research related to reading), and there is virtually nothing that can reliably be said about how transitions from one stage of competence to another occur. Several authors in these volumes call for additional developmental research on reading; others have begun such investigations. Still others have analyzed existing early reading programs and offer comments on the sort of literacy skill that may result from different instructional procedures.

Developmental Theory and Research.   In several chapters, preliminary models or schemes of reading and its development are offered. Chall (Vol. 1) offers a theory of the stages of reading development that can serve to organize much of the subsequent discussion in these volumes. The first three of Chall's stages include a prereading stage; a decoding stage, during which the learner acquires the elements of the code; and a confirmation and fluency stage, during which the code is mastered through the reading of largely familiar material. Following these are stages in which the reader focuses primarily on meaning: first reading for learning from one viewpoint, then reading from multiple viewpoints, and finally reading with what Chall terms a "world view." A stage theory of this kind is of potentially great significance for organizing and focusing the debate over the proper role of the code in reading acquisition. It poses the question of *when* rather than *whether* the code should be emphasized, and it also stresses the role of practice on meaningful and familiar texts. Chall clearly places the code emphasis at the beginning of the acquisition process, but her scheme also emphasizes high levels of comprehension as central to the full cycle of reading development. Other authors would order the emphases differently. What is important is that a stage-oriented theory provides a framework for empirical studies that are both developmental in nature and attentive to the instructional environment in which acquisition proceeds (cf. Kintsch, Vol. 1).

Gregg and Farnham-Diggory (Vol. 3) view reading as a special case of information processing and see the processing system as having three major parts: the perceptual system, the semantic system, and the operations and programs for performing reading tasks. Each of these systems develops greater capability with age and experience. They also offer a taxonomy of reading tasks that is arranged along two dimensions: size of unit and number of operations. The authors suggest that as the processing systems mature, tasks involving larger units and more operations can be performed. Trabasso (Vol. 3), in his discussion chapter, calls for more work on such a taxonomy (and suggests some possible modifications), because it contains an implicit developmental model of reading from prereading to skilled levels with a potential focus on task demands. This, he feels, would force researchers to concentrate on the mechanisms by which skills required for reading are *acquired*. That such schemes have begun to be formulated is promising for our eventual understanding of reading acquisition and development.

The chapters by Chall and by Gregg and Farnham-Diggory offer a relatively macroscopic view of the development of reading skill. By contrast, the chapters by LaBerge (Vol. 3), Juola et al., Liberman and Shankweiler, and Chomsky (Vol. 2) examine aspects of reading acquisition more micro-scopically. A focus of LaBerge's chapter is on how readers acquire the cognitive structures necessary for recognizing a word, with an emphasis on units of processing. Juola et al.'s chapter examines the appearance and changes over time of visual search strategies in reading and the development of a word superiority effect. Liberman and Shankweiler examine the relation between spoken and written language and describe the phonemic segmenta-tion skills learners need to acquire (on their own or through direct instruction) to be able to map written onto spoken language. Theirs is a developmental theory with explicit implications for instruction. Chomsky offers evidence to support the view that the ability to construct written language (i.e., to write and spell) developmentally precedes the ability to read, at least in some children. She suggests that children can be introduced to reading through a form of creative writing where they are not formally taught spelling but use a spelling system that they themselves invent.

Reading Instruction and Reading Acquisition.   Instructional implications have been considered throughout our discussion of issues in reading. However, a few instructional topics did not lend themselves to discussions in other contexts, and we mention them briefly here. Attention should perhaps first be directed to several chapters that address matters related to reading acquisition in the course of describing and assessing instructional programs. The chapters by Beck and Block and by Holland in Volume 1, by Fletcher and by Bartlett in Volume 2, and by Popp in Volume 3 analyze a number of early reading programs. Each is interspersed with comments on the processes of reading acquisition. These chapters are major sources for information on the current state of the art in American reading instruction and the kinds of questions that skilled analysts are raising about this practice.

Assessing Reading Progress.   Several chapters stress the importance of assessment as an integral component of the reading instructional process. In order to "deliver" instruction at the proper pace and level of difficulty, the teacher must be able to measure every child's progress in an ongoing way and incorporate the results in daily instruction. This is the major focus of the chapter by Calfee and Drum (Vol. 2), who discuss the goals, methods, and criteria for assessment in the context of instruction. Their emphasis is on measurement of specific skills for short-term instructional decisions rather than on long-term placement decisions. The other chapters that include discussion of assessment are those by Frederiksen, Sticht, and Danks and Fears. Frederiksen suggests that a taxonomy of inference types could be used to construct achievement-test items to measure aspects of discourse processing and that the methods he uses for analyzing children's recall of stories could be adapted for classroom instructional decisions. Sticht describes a procedure for assessing the reading potential of adults. The Literacy Assessment Battery measures the "gap" between auding and reading abilities and reveals the degree to which reading problems are indicative of problems with the printed language specifically or of low levels of general language ability. Danks and Fears offer an experimental task that may be applicable to classroom assessment procedures. They propose a hierarchy of processing levels in reading and describe a series of experiments with texts that have been systematically altered or disrupted. By building the disruptions into the text according to the level in the processing hierarchy that one wishes to study, they argue, it is possible to analyze oral reading behavior to determine if the text is processed at least to the level of the disruption.

The Teacher as an Instructional Variable.   The importance of the teacher both as the deliverer of instruction and as a creator of the learning environment is stressed in several chapters. All authors explicitly or implicitly recognize that the quality of instruction depends in great part on the teacher. Those authors whose chapters emphasize the importance of the teacher are Bateman (Vol. 1), Clay and Rosner (Vol. 2), and Simons, Cazden, and Glaser (Vol. 3). Many other chapters discuss the role of the teacher in the context of other topics (e.g., Beck & Block, Goodman & Goodman, Natalicio, and Shuy). A point that can be drawn from all these discussions is that we know more about the reading process and reading instruction than is currently being used. The teacher is of course pivotal in this matter. Bateman, for example, claims that we already know how to teach the decoding aspect of reading. What we need to do is help teachers to apply the proper methods.

Both Simons and Cazden implicate the teacher and the social interactions in the classroom as possible sources of reading difficulty for some children. They describe observational reasearch suggesting that the quality of instruction may vary for different children even within the same classroom. Rosner describes the traits that teachers must have to be able to teach reading effectively to children who are hard to teach. They must be familiar with basic concepts of reading (many are not), able to be precise and repetitive, able to perform in a structured, relatively nondynamic environment, and able to sustain efforts even when progress is slow and results are small.

Clay describes a program of instructional change in New Zealand. She, like Rosner, emphasizes the importance of teachers' knowledge of reading and reading instruction. She refers also to the importance of teachers as sensitive observers of reading progress, suggesting that observation is itself an assessment technique. She includes an interesting account of in-service training designed to make teachers better informed regarding reading theory and research and more able to apply this knowledge to their teaching.

Time Engaged in Reading.   The importance of time spent in direct instruction in reading is touched on in many of the chapters that analyze and compare different reading instructional approaches. These discussions are found in the chapters by Beck and Block; Bartlett; Fletcher; Guthrie, Martuza, and Seifert (Vol. 3); and Popp. The most direct consideration of this issue is found in the chapter by Guthrie et al., who reanalyzed data collected by the Educational Testing Service on compensatory reading programs. Using that data, they examined the impacts of instructional time in reading on reading achievement among middle- and low-socioeconomic-status (SES) groups. They concluded that amount of time spent in formal reading instruction influenced achievement more than the specific approach used to teach reading. Their findings suggest that a large amount of instructional time benefited sixth graders from low-SES groups but not those from middle- and high-SES groups. Findings at the second-grade level suggest that the amount of instructional time in reading affected achievement but that different SES groups were not affected differently. The authors stress that it is not time itself that affects achievement but the specific events that occur during that time, and they conclude with a recommendation that we improve the measures of instructional intensity by quantifying the events that occur among students and teachers.

Holland focuses explicitly on issues related to the quality rather than the quantity of time spent on reading. Proceeding from a behavioral engineering point of view, he suggests the importance of arranging sequences of contingent interrelations among materials and of clear consequences contingent upon students' responses to details of the materials. Resnick's review chapter (Vol. 2) summarizes and evaluates research on engaged time and instructional programs and suggests that for several reasons, decoding approaches to instruction have probably been correlated with high amounts of time engaged in reading and with more tightly engineered instructional programs. She argues that at least until meaning-oriented instruction can be organized to promote heavy engagement in the actual tasks of reading, code approaches to instruction will best serve the needs of hard-to-teach populations.

On the Relations Between Theory and Practice

We noted earlier that certain chapters—primarily the discussion chapters at the end of each volume—focus on the actual and potential relationships between theory and research on one hand and practice of reading instruction on the other. Other authors also discuss issues of theory and practice relationships in the context of their specific substantive concerns. Belief in the power of scientific pedagogy is far from universal, as a reading of these volumes will amply demonstrate. Practitioners succeed in teaching reading to many children without being informed of or directly influenced by the results of research. And psychologists themselves are not always convinced that current theory and research can improve educational practice. Depending partly on how individuals became interested in the study of reading and partly on their experiences in applying scientific theory and knowledge to social needs and practices, expectations for the relation between theory and practice differ. All agree, however, that drawing instructional implications directly from current laboratory-based experimental findings is extremely difficult.

Of the several discussants, Venezky (Vol. 2) and Kintsch (Vol. 1) are the least optimistic about the possibility of a direct link between laboratory research and classroom practice. Venezky claims that applying theory to practice is not only difficult but at times has actually led to poor instruction.

He argues, not for the direct application of laboratory research, but instead for a "separate but equal" discipline of applied research that is grounded in classroom experimentation. Kintsch, on the other hand, sees a need for more, rather than less, interaction between laboratory and classroom. He holds that although work on reading instruction and basic research in reading are both flourishing, the interaction between them is insufficient. Furthermore, he argues that the lack of a serious theory of reading is a main source of the problem: Instruction is based more on intuition than on research, and research often circumvents important instructional issues.

Kintsch directs attention toward increased efforts in the theoretical realm as an eventual basis for scientifically grounded practice. He perhaps would be joined in this judgment by Posner (Vol. 1), who in addition, points out the ways in which theory can limit as well as expand our work in reading instruction. Posner characterizes theory as both a lens and a set of blinders for practitioners and curriculum developers. He suggests that theory tends to magnify those aspects of a problem on which scientists have worked (the lens), making them more understandable. At the same time, the existence of well-elaborated theory tends to reduce attention to other important aspects of a problem on which there has been little work (the blinders). Posner's chapter elaborates this lens–blinders metaphor with reference to specific issues discussed in the papers on which he comments.

Two discussants, Glaser (Vol. 3) and White (Vol. 2), offer more positive views of actual and potential theory–practice relations. Glaser contends that we know enough now from theory and research to produce positive changes in the outcomes of reading instruction. He suggests that although psychological knowledge is imperfect, it can and should be applied, in an artful and heuristic fashion. White goes a step further. Not only does he think that theory and research can and should change practice; he also suggests a scheme for effecting a more successful change. He argues that the traditional approach of researchers conducting experiments in laboratories and then shipping the results to the classroom has not worked. Instead, he proposes that researchers leave the laboratory to conduct their research in classroom settings and allow their hypotheses to be formulated from actual instructional problems. He argues convincingly that his new scheme may be as important for theory as for education.

It is noteworthy that although Glaser, White, and others seem to be generally satisfied with the state of theory with respect to reading instruction, they all point to a need for more elaborated theories of reading acquisition. The discrepancy between theories of skilled reading and those of reading acquisition and development is discussed by Gordon (Vol. 1), Venezky (Vol. 2), and Trabasso (Vol. 3). Regardless of disagreements on other issues, all contributors whose discussion focuses on this topic unite in calling for more research on reading acquisition. The need for this shift in theoretical and research direction is clarified by Trabasso. He notes that current work in cognitive psychology is preoccupied with the description of processes used for engaging in tasks rather than with how the processes required for engaging in them are learned. To remedy this, Trabasso calls for renewed attention to some of the questions of classical learning theory but within the new context of an enriched cognitive psychology. Resnick (Vol. 3) echoes the need in her summary discussion and develops a proposal for the kinds of questions a psychology of reading instruction would need to address and the methods it may require.

General Issues

The final chapters of each of these volumes are discussion chapters. In most of these, commentary is limited to issues raised in the chapters of the volume itself. However, four of the discussion chapters—those by Gordon and Resnick in Volume 2 and those by Carroll and Walton and by Resnick in Volume 3—present a more general set of reflections. These chapters, written after all the other chapters were submitted and discussed, are intended as integrative reviews highlighting particular issues in early reading instruction that were considered in the volumes as a whole. They do not attempt to respond chapter by chapter or point by point to the other contributions; instead, they use the issues raised in all three volumes as points of departure in considering broad concerns of research and practice in reading instruction.

Gordon's integrative chapter (Vol. 2) is concerned with the problem of reading instruction in the context of compensatory education programs. The chapter begins with a discussion of the concept of compensatory education itself—how the concept developed, the assumptions about the poor that surround it, and common conceptions of the children who receive compensatory education. Gordon suggests that these children have too often been grouped together under the label *disadvantaged* and characterized by their differences from the white, middle-class "norm," rather than being seen as individuals, with individual strengths and weaknesses. He proposes that it is these individual characteristics, and not group labels, that should be taken into account in the design of instruction for all populations. Against this background, Gordon discusses various chapters in the volumes with respect to their implications for compensatory reading programs.

Resnick's integrative chapter in Volume 2 represents an effort to distill from the many specific points of view presented in these volumes the major competing positions on the nature of reading and appropriate reading instruction. She identifies two major views of the nature of reading—reading as translation of print to sound and reading as an autonomous language process. These two positions, Resnick points out, lead to different prescriptions for reading instruction: Adherents of the reading-as-translation view prescribe early and systematic instruction on the alphabetic code; supporters of the reading-as-autonomous-process view prescribe early attention to functional and meaningful use of written language. After reviewing empirical research on instructional program effects, Resnick picks code-oriented instruction for the early years of reading, but cautions that this will not "solve" the reading problem. She goes on to suggest the kinds of research and development that are needed for more successful instruction in comprehension and the functional aspects of reading.

Carroll and Walton's chapter in Volume 3 reviews previous attempts at organizing knowledge about early reading, and discusses these volumes as part of this series of efforts to solve the reading problem. The chapter contains an extensive discussion of the positions and points of view expressed in the chapters of these volumes. This discussion is organized into two major sections: (1) conceptions of the nature of reading, and (2) how well early reading instruction as it is currently conducted reflects theory and knowledge about learning to read. The section on the nature of reading includes detailed analyses of particular points of view expressed in the various chapters of these volumes. It is thus an excellent guide to the often confusing and tangled arguments on topics such as the centrality of decoding, top-down versus bottom-up processing, direct versus mediated word access, and the role of language skills in becoming a good reader. The section on instruction includes a detailed discussion of beginning reading programs, which both comments on and extends the discussion of curriculum and pedagogy presented in various chapters. Throughout their integrative chapter, Carroll and Walton take definite positions on controversial instructional questions.

Finally, Resnick's chapter in Volume 3 addresses the questions of whether and how theory and basic research can contribute to practical pedagogy in reading. Resnick first considers some of the reasons that most basic research in reading has not been as helpful to practice as might be wished. She then proposes a variety of research questions and research methods that she believes would make future reading research both more useful in instructional design and better science in its own right. The result of such research, she suggests, would be a psychology of reading focused directly on instruction, a psychology centrally concerned with processes of acquisition and with the role of intervention (i.e., instruction) in these processes.

REFERENCES

Adams, M. J., & Collins, A. *A schema-theoretic view of reading* (Tech. Rep. No. 32). Urbana, Ill.: Center for the Study of Reading, 1977.

Buswell, G. T. An experimental study of eye–voice span in reading. *Supplementary Educational Monographs,* No. 17. Chicago: University of Chicago, 1920.

Cattell, J. M. The time it takes to see and name objects. *Mind,* 1886, *11,* 63–65.

Chall, J. S. *Learning to read: The great debate.* New York: McGraw-Hill, 1967.

Flesch, R. *Why Johnny can't read, and what you can do about it.* New York: Harper, 1955.

Fries, C. C. *Linguistics and reading.* New York: Holt, Rinehart & Winston, 1962.

Gibson, E. J., & Levin, H. *The psychology of reading.* Cambridge, Mass.: MIT Press, 1975.

Huey, E. B. *The psychology and pedagogy of reading.* New York: Macmillan, 1908. Republished by the MIT Press, Cambridge, Mass., 1968.

Mathews, M. *Teaching to read: Historically considered.* Chicago: University of Chicago Press, 1966.

Maugham, W. S. The verger. In *Cosmopolitans.* New York: Doubleday, Doran, 1937.

Resnick, D. P., & Resnick, L. B. The nature of literacy: An historical exploration. *Harvard Educational Review,* 1977, *47*(3), 370–385.

Riegel, K., & Freedle, R. Bilingualism. In D. Harrison & T. Trabasso (Eds.), *Black English: A seminar.* Hillsdale, N.J.: Lawrence Erlbaum Associates, 1976.

Rumelhart, D. E. Toward an interactive model of reading. In S. Dornic (Ed.), *Attention & performance VI.* Hillsdale, N.J.: Lawrence Erlbaum Associates, 1977.

LANGUAGE AND READING

1 Conflicting Approaches to Reading Research and Instruction

Frank Smith
Ontario Institute for Studies in Education

My theme is that there are two quite distinct ways of conceptualizing reading but that one of these perspectives tends to predominate when reading is considered from an experimental point of view. As a result, there is a critical bias in reading theory and research that has been extended to a bias in classroom practice—a bias that limits and possibly distorts the way many people think about reading and reading instruction. The greater part of this chapter is concerned with the cause, nature, and consequences of this bias, first in reading theory and then when theory is "translated" into practice. However, I conclude with a few general cautions about the application of theory to practice and some remarks about other issues that have tended to be of lesser concern in reading research but that may in fact be of major relevance to reading instruction.

OPPOSING THEORETICAL APPROACHES
TO READING

Although there are numerous theories of reading, they can in general be grouped into two distinct categories, depending on where the source and control of any particular reading act is presumed to lie. Many theories view reading as a process that begins with the print on the page and ends with some representation or interpretation inside the brain. I call such theories *outside-in theories*. The other class of theories perceives reading as a highly discriminative process that begins in the brain and ends with selective attention to only part of the printed text. I call such theories *inside-out theories*.

Outside-in theories are clearly dominant in both the research literature and instructional development. They are characterized by the notion that everything on a page of text is "processed" and that reading is primarily a hierarchical series of decisions—first letters are discriminated, then they are synthesized into words (usually, but not always, through "decoding" into a phonological or "underlying" level of spoken language), as a consequence of which comprehension takes place. It would be invidious to identify one or two of these theories, and I have neither the space nor the inclination to list them all. Examples proliferate in such recent compilations as Kavanagh and Mattingly (1972) and the final report of the U.S. Office of Education Targeted Research and Development Program in Reading (Davis, 1971). They also account for a large proportion of the studies reported in *Reading Research Quarterly* and predominate in most psychological and linguistic speculation about reading. Outside-in theories are frequently detectable from a distance by virtue of their elaborate flowcharts, with arrows leading from the "stimulus" of print through iconic storages, scanners, comparators, and decoders to destination boxes labeled "semantic store" or quite simply "meaning."

There is in fact no evidence that any reader pays attention to every letter— or in many circumstances, to every word—in any natural reading situation. Neither eye-movement studies nor analyses of oral reading indicate just how much or how little of the actual print readers "process" when they are reading meaningful text, although it is obvious that readers often identify words without attending to all the letters on the page, and that they can also make sense of text without identifying all the particular words in front of their eyes. Almost all the experimental work that has provided the conceptual basis for outside-in theories of reading has been done with tachistoscopic equipment and meaningless materials in unmotivated laboratory situations.

My main criticism of outside-in theories is not so much that they are wrong as that they are not representative. They provide reliable and replicable data about how individuals respond when confronted with atypical "identification" tasks in laboratory settings, but in fact they bear little resemblance to what takes place when individuals normally read street signs, telephone directories, labels, menus, newspaper reports, poetry, or anything else that is interesting or informative to them. More specifically, outside-in theories fail to account for intention (we usually read for a purpose), selectivity (we attend only to what we want and need to know), prediction (we are rarely bewildered or surprised by anything that we read), and comprehension (we are rarely aware of the enormous potential ambiguity, both syntactic and semantic, of the most common words and constructions of our language). It is invariably easier to read meaningful texts than nonsensical strings of words, just as letters in words are easier to identify than letters occurring randomly. In fact, we are normally aware of words only when meaning fails, and we attend to letters only when words are unfamiliar—the reverse of the outside-in view. Of course, the fact that readers are usually aware only of meaning does not logically entail that they are giving no attention to letters and words in the process, but the absence of direct or introspective evidence is hardly support for the outside-in point of view.

The selectivity that characterizes meaningful reading is not something that outside-in theories can cope with simply by appeal to specialized "filters" or by the introduction of additional arrows pointing upstream in the flowcharts and labeled "feedback" or "prediction." Nor can such theories assert that the reader looks for and processes "higher order invariances" or "largest meaningful units" without acknowledging that what determines the size of a unit is not the nature of the print on the page but the intention of the reader in the first place, an inside-out perspective.

The inside-out view begins with intention; it regards reading as a truly active, centrally motivated and centrally directed process in which readers hypothesize, or predict, among a certain range of meaningful likely alternatives and search and analyze among the featural information available in the print only to the extent necessary to resolve their remaining uncertainty. The inside-out view endeavors to account for the identification of words without the mediation of letter identification (readers search for features to decide among alternative word possibilities independently of a feature search to identify letters). It tries to explain why letters in words are easier to identify than letters in random sequences and why words in meaningful sequences are easier to identify than random words. In each case, a set of expectancies is established on the basis of prior knowledge, reducing the number of alternatives considered by readers. Readers look for the featural information that they need and ignore information that is irrelevant or redundant to their purposes. The inside-out perspective does not require recourse to spoken language for the comprehension of print. Meaning is directly accessible through print (as exemplified in the visible difference in meaning between *their* and *there*), and in fact it must be determined before the text can be read aloud in a comprehensible manner. Without prior comprehension, many words cannot even be allocated a grammatical function—for example, is *house* a noun or a verb?—let alone an appropriate pronunciation or intonation.

Inside-out theories are by no means adequate, of course. Indeed, when one considers the enormity of the attempt to understand how knowledge of the world is organized and integrated in the human brain, which is the beginning of the inside-out analysis of reading, then one comprehends why it has been asserted more than once that to understand reading would be the acme of a psychologist's achievement (Huey, 1908/1968; Neisser, 1967). But the acme of a psychologist's achievement is surely not a series of reaction time studies measuring how long it takes individuals to name letters and words. Gough

(1972) acknowledged the root of the problem when he characterized the end point of his outside-in theory of reading as "The Place Where Sentences Go When They are Understood," reached by a procedure that he left in the hands of a wizard in the head named Merlin. Such a magical approach cannot explain why readers remain unaware of letters or even words in the process of understanding sentences, nor why they are also unaware of potential ambiguities and even of the meaningful mistakes that all readers make from time to time. (These and other inside-out arguments are elaborated in Smith, 1971, 1973, and Smith and Holmes, 1971.) Normal reading seems to begin, proceed, and end in meaning, and the source of meaningfulness must be the prior knowledge in the reader's head. Nothing is comprehended if it does not reflect or elaborate on what the reader already knows.

It can rightly be objected that inside-out theories are vague. However, not enough is known about the way individual human knowledge is organized to provide a basis for more than cautious speculation (for examples and summaries see Anderson & Bower, 1973; Tulving & Donaldson, 1972). On the other hand, outside-in theories do not get very far in. Can "reading" really be studied if it stops short of comprehension?

Apart from the conceptual conundrums confronted by inside-out theories, they are also handicapped by the difficulty of designing "critical" experiments. Because of their scope and the inherent problem of exercising laboratory control in situations in which the major variable is something as unpredictable as an individual's prior knowledge and intentions, very few experimental paradigms for studying comprehension lend themselves to simple replication or quantitative analysis. Even the most compelling studies of language comprehension (such as Bransford & Franks, 1971) can be regarded only as illustrative. Most of the data relevant to inside-out theories of reading and language comprehension are based on anecdote, observation, or introspection, but so too are many of the studies on which today's powerful theories of spoken language acquisition are based.

Conversely, I think the dominance of outside-in theories in the research literature is entirely attributable to their conceptual simplicity and experimental tractability. It is far easier to design replicable experiments, conduct statistical analyses, and achieve reliable results when the concern is limited to reaction times to meaningless letters and words. When subjects succeed in imposing meaning on such tasks—by relating the stimuli to something they know beyond the constraints of the task—the well-ordered predictability of results breaks down. Meaning makes such tasks easier for subjects but harder for experimenters, thus the need in most outside-in studies of reading for the subject to be the most unrepresentative of all readers—an individual with no relevant prior knowledge or expectations about the task at hand.

Such essential nonsense in outside-in reading research mirrors the 100-year study of nonsense in experimental psychology's investigation of "verbal learning." Since the invention of the nonsense syllable, this investigation has been a constant battle between subjects striving to make sense of their tasks and experimenters trying to devise more effective nonsense, because it is only with nonsense that psychology's venerable "laws of learning" apply (Smith, 1975a, Chapter 5).

Preoccupation with the alphabetic nature of the particular written language with which they are usually concerned is a marked characteristic of outside-in theories. Reading is frequently seen as simply a matter of "decoding" these alphabetic symbols into sound by the application of spelling-to-sound correspondence rules, although the theoretical or empirical necessity for such decoding in normal reading (as opposed to laboratory studies of word recognition) is rarely explained. Many experimental situations leave no alternative to applying spelling-to-sound correspondences because the stimuli include sequences of letters that are either nonwords or only parts of words. Occasional specific justification for the assumption of decoding tends to argue for its necessity for learning to recognize unfamiliar words in the first place (which may be referred to as the *identification problem*) or for relieving an assumed memory burden of storing many thousands of unique configurations in the reader's sight vocabulary through some form of phonemic mediation (which may be termed the *recognition problem*).

Inside-out theories, on the other hand, tend to ignore or play down the relevance of decoding. They assert that the system of correspondences is extremely complex and of limited reliability for word identification, and that in normal reading situations there are alternative strategies (such as asking someone or using context) that are less time consuming, more efficient, and already well practiced in spoken language learning. For word recognition— the maintenance of a sight vocabulary of familiar words—decoding is regarded as completely unnecessary, since there is no known limit on human memory capacity. Readers of nonalphabetic scripts do not appear to have memory problems, and individuals seem to experience little difficulty in discriminating all the thousands of distinctive objects in their perceptual worlds without the need for mediating systems. Inside-out theories assert that the memory-load argument confuses recognition with reproduction, which is the writer's problem, not the reader's. In a general discussion of all these points (Smith, 1973), it has been argued that the alphabet may function primarily to assist the writer.

The inside-out approach sees as the primary overload problem the fact that the reader may be confronted by too many alternatives—letter combinations "decode" into too many alternative patterns of sound, and many common words have too many alternative meanings and even grammatical functions (e.g., *house, chair, table, empty, time, narrow, open, close*). Reducing the number of alternatives in advance by excluding unlikely instances accounts for the absence of awareness of potential ambiguity and also makes spelling-to-sound-correspondence rules effective in practice. This process of employing context and prior knowledge to eliminate alternatives in advance is sometimes termed *prediction* (Smith, 1975b) to avoid the educationally loaded term *guessing* by which inside-out theories have sometimes been characterized.

CONFLICTING APPROACHES TO READING INSTRUCTION

There are also outside-in approaches to reading instruction. Outside-in programs are founded on the general belief that children must first learn the alphabet and then the "sounds of letters" which can be combined to form words that they will recognize (it is hoped) as part of their spoken language. And that, from the outside-in point of view, just about accounts for learning to read. Typically, children who fail to learn to read by such treatment are given more of it.

One reason that outside-in instructional programs are so numerous and widespread in classrooms (and at reading conventions) is that they are a direct reflection of outside-in theories of reading. Outside-in theories "translate" naturally into outside-in instruction. But outside-in instructional programs are also prolific in their own right for the same reason that outside-in theories flourish—they are conceptually simple and lend themselves easily to measurement, manipulation, and control. With outside-in instruction there is little concern with comprehension, either in terms of content or in terms of why the child should be involved in the exercise in the first place. Comprehension of content is supposed to come about automatically if and when the child masters decoding skills, and it is in any case the child's responsibility. Comprehension by the child of the purpose of the drills and skills is disregarded; task achievement is everything. And not only are outside-in instructional methods frequently successful—within their own limited range of objectives—but they also have the great advantage of being able to demonstrate their success. Objectives can be set within the reach of any desired proportion of a particular population, and scores can be recorded to prove that criterion levels have indeed been achieved. By offering a convenient scale of scores, outside-in procedures will even "diagnose" which children are likely to be good students (i.e., will score high on similar tasks) and which children have learning disabilities.

The outside-in perspective is a boon to instructional program developers who need to decompose complex tasks into series of discrete and simple steps so that teaching can be standardized and made amenable to technology. To achieve this simplification, a few contemporary reading programs claim to teach only "subskills" of reading, relieving the teacher of anxiety about the total skill of which the subskills are a part. Because of their quantitative nature, outside-in procedures are generally adopted whenever someone wants to hold someone else accountable for progress or regression in literacy. Outside-in instruction is usually also the referent when there is concern for "getting back to basics."

Inside-out approaches to instruction, on the other hand, try to argue that children learn to read by reading, and that the teacher's role is to help children read (for a summary of these arguments see Smith, 1973). Such a perspective asserts that it is sense that enables children to learn to read, making use of inferred meaning and prior knowledge, just as the development of spoken language fluency is rooted in the sense children are able to bring to the learning situation (Macnamara, 1972; Nelson, 1974). According to the inside-out point of view, expecting children to "decode" letters into words is to expect them to learn words the hard way; it is familiarity with words that makes letter recognition (and phonics) easy. Similarly, the requirement that children should identify strings of words accurately in order to obtain meaning, or without recourse to meaning at all, is also to impose the most difficult task. Anything that does not make sense to children is regarded as a hindrance to their learning. Learning nonsense is not only harder; it is pointless.

The inside-out perspective appeals to the intuitions of many experienced teachers. Their own feelings—often only tentatively expressed because they fear they lack "scientific" validity—are that children learn by being immersed in meaningful written language, in situations that generate pleasure and assurance rather than bewilderment and apprehension. From such a perspective, the more structured outside-in approach may be seen as a systematic deprivation of important information. However, it must also be stated that other teachers are threatened by inside-out points of view, by their lack of structure, the responsibility they seem to throw on the teacher, and the fact that they are not amenable to simple packaging and measurement. They are not labor-saving. They are not explicit about what teachers should do, nor about how student progress would be measured.

Inside-out theories do not offer prescriptions for methodology. They are not directly translatable into practice (Smith & Goodman, 1971). Instead, they aim to inform teachers, to assist them in making their own diagnoses and decisions. Teachers who rely on outside-in instruction need advice, tests, or luck to make appropriate on-the-spot decisions. But the ultimate dilemma for such teachers is that they must still choose. They must select among programs, tests, and experts. And to make such choices they need information, an understanding of the nature of children and of reading. The inside-out perspective does not hold that reading teachers should ignore the tools of their trade, the methods and materials that are available, but it asserts that teachers should know how and when methods and materials are appropriate and when their use may make no sense at all. Inside-out theory can be practical but not by being strait-jacketed into programs.

"INTERACTIVE" APPROACHES TO READING

The relevance of prior knowledge and even of expectation in reading has, of course, not been completely overlooked by researchers. However, it is only in recent years that experimental studies have attempted to consider such central factors in a comprehensive and systematic way. Impetus for such studies has come from a perhaps unexpected source—the use of computers to simulate and test hypothesized processes of language and thought. A number of cognitive psychologists and psycholinguists have begun to move away from rather narrowly constrained speculations of how language-based knowledge might be represented in memory to a more elaborate study of reading.

To take just one example, Rumelhart (1977) has characterized reading as an "interactive process" involving a conjunction of "visually derived" and "expectation derived" information. Rumelhart and others have adopted computer terminology to refer to the flow of visually derived information (corresponding roughly to what I have been calling outside-in) as "bottom-up" and to the opposite flow of expectation derived information (my inside-out) as "top-down." Apart from some general background theorizing, however, the studies that have been so far reported have tended to get no farther in (or up) than word recognition and have once more typically allowed subjects little opportunity to demonstrate preferences and strategies they might exhibit in reading outside the laboratory. Visually derived information is still presented to readers for exhaustive analysis of one kind or another, rather than allowing them to sample it selectively for purposes of their own.

One reason that the interactive approach has in general been unable to break free of an outside-in bias in experimentation is that it has tended to lean on an extremely narrow conception of comprehension that characterizes computer-based models of language. Inspired largely by "case grammar" linguistic theories (e.g., Chafe, 1970; Fillmore, 1968), such models have been inclined to regard comprehension as a kind of abstract representation (generally in the form of a network of relations) of all the information contained within the structure of an "input sentence." For example, the "meaning" of a sentence such as *My sister is visiting us* would be represented by a logical argument of the form:

[RELATION: visit, SUBJECT: my sister, OBJECT: us]

Since comprehension is assumed to consist of the construction of such an abstract representation, the adequacy of the representation (and of the model) is tested by whether particular parts of the input sentence can be retrieved in response to questions. For example, comprehension of the preceding sentence would be demonstrated if the element *your sister* could be retrieved in response to the question *Who is visiting us?*.

However, such formulations are far from competent to handle the fact that comprehension of statements is rarely a matter of being able to regurgitate or even paraphrase what has just been said or read; instead, it depends largely on the receiver's purpose in attending to the statement in the first place. For example, as a response to the question *Could you put me up for a few days?* the statement *My sister is visiting us* means only one thing—No—and it would normally be comprehended in that way. Put more generally, speakers and writers do not normally produce statements in pointless context-free isolation, but with respect to an actual or assumed common interest on the part of both producer and receiver. The actual meaning to both parties is largely determined by factors extrinsic to the statement, namely, the situation in which it is uttered and the prior knowledge and mutual expectations of the two parties concerned. Comprehension is basically a matter of getting answers to questions implicitly asked by the recipient of a message (Smith, 1975b). The ability to paraphrase an utterance or to recall parts of it is no indication of comprehension at all. Yet parsing or paraphrasing are generally the most that computer models of comprehension aspire to achieve, and until further progress is made in the enormous enterprise of trying to represent human knowledge and intentionality in these models, it is unlikely that they will provide a basis for theories of reading that are representative of normal reading situations. Until interactive approaches break free of their dependence on outside-in experimentaion and enrich their theoretical foundation with respect to comprehension, expectation that they might have productive implications for classroom practice or instructional development would seem to be premature.

DIRECTIONS FOR FURTHER RESEARCH

For a start, it would be pointless to expect a critical experiment to determine whether outside-in or inside-out theories are correct. The data are rarely in contention, and the interpretation placed on them depends on one's theoretical proclivity. The issue is a pragmatic one, deciding which particular theories are the most useful for specific purposes—whether those purposes are predicting response latencies in letter or word recognition studies, providing an intuitively appealing model of reading, generating worthwhile practical consequences in classrooms, or stimulating productive research. Obviously, all theories of reading and of reading instruction require improvement and offer ample potential for research, but there is a particular need for more robust theories to stimulate research beyond the current rather tired experimental preoccupation with word identification and the seemingly endless and inconclusive comparisons of scraps of instructional technology. In particular, a better understanding is required of how and why children learn to read in the first place, and it is unlikely at present that such an understanding will come from rigorous experimentation under controlled laboratory conditions. There is a dearth of observational information capable of throwing light on the intellectual, emotional, and social needs that reading satisfies, or on why learning to read is often resisted. There is a need for more information about the manner in which children respond to print long before they receive any formal instruction and about the amount and nature of print in the world around them, analogous to the studies of development of spoken language in infants. Very few studies of reading development have been conducted that have not been contaminated by the effects of early instruction. Few studies have been concerned more with children's developing awareness of print than with their ability to cope with the demands and terminology of particular instructional methods.

Further pursuit of a universal method of teaching reading might appear pointless. A mass of existing research demonstrates that all methods of reading instruction achieve certain aims some of the time, although no method has been found to work all the time. Millions of children have learned to read with procedures and materials that are the same as those with which other children have failed. There is, in fact, no evidence that children who are motivated to learn to read experience difficulty in learning to read. And despite the millions of dollars spent on program development and testing by government agencies and commercial enterprises, there is not the slightest evidence that children who succeed in learning to read today do so with any more facility than those who learned with a hornbook and the family Bible.

More consideration must be given to the possibility that literacy problems will not be ameliorated by better descriptions of language or of cognitive processes. For example, a largely neglected theoretical issue that may play a considerable role in the apparent inadequacy of much of our reading instruction is the fact that language as it is normally encountered and employed outside the classroom has a variety of functions (Halliday, 1973). Children do not begin life by learning "language skills" as such; they are never engaged in a purely linguistic exercise. The language they first hear and use always has a function, and language and function are probably learned simultaneously. Children learn to talk while learning that language can be used to satisfy needs, express feelings, explore ideas, ask questions, obtain answers, assert oneself, manipulate others, and establish and maintain specific interpersonal relations. However, children may have acquired ability in one or two functions of language without being able to comprehend all its functions. Sometimes it may be thought that children lack language ability when they are merely unfamiliar with certain functions.

Language in school must often seem to children to have some very odd functions. Sometimes it is used without any obvious function at all, for example, when children are expected to attend to isolated words on chalkboards, meaningless sequences of words in books, and obscure exercises and drills. Schools may attempt to suppress entirely, both in teachers and in children, some functions of language that children find most important. There is very little theorizing and research on these issues, yet as far as literacy is concerned, they may have the most profound implications of all.

CONCLUDING COMMENTS

There are two other reasons why I feel caution should be exercised before acceding to the constant demand for theorists to be "practical" and for the translating of research into practice. The first is that the direct conversion of theoretical insights into practical terms—whether on the level of helpful hints to individual teachers or as full-blown instructional programs—tends to lead to egregious overgeneralization. What might be a good idea with a few children in a limited context becomes inflated into a foolproof system for teaching entire populations the whole time. Teachers who rely on experts rather than on their own accumulated wisdom and experience to solve day-to-day classroom problems become even more disappointed and disillusioned with the theorist or researcher when the desired improvement so rarely comes. More recognition should perhaps be given to the value of theories that assist teachers in making their own decisions.

My second concern is that the rush to be applied frequently confuses what a person is able to do as a consequence of being a reader with what is necessary in order to learn to read in the first place. A recent example was the effort to transmogrify large numbers of children into transformational grammarians when linguists discovered that transformational rules were a convenient way of characterizing part of their own language competence. Almost contemporaneously, many children were drilled in the identification of meaningless "distinctive features" as a preliminary to exposure to the alphabet, after theorists hypothesized that feature detection models might be a useful conceptual tool for examining letter and word recognition processes. Following recent theoretical interest in the roles of redundancy and prediction in reading, there have been attempts to develop programs for teaching children to become responsive to redundancy and to predict, although such abilities are integral parts of the natural capacity of all children to make sense of spoken language long before they get to school.

No theory of reading is likely to be of substantial utility in education unless it reminds teachers and researchers alike that the skill of reading remains largely a mystery because so much of it is embedded in the complex structures and functions of the brain. To discover why some children succeed and others fail we must understand more about what transpires in their heads as they strive to make sense of reading and reading instruction.

REFERENCES

Anderson, J. R., & Bower, G. H. *Human associative memory.* New York: WIley, 1973.

Bransford, J. D., & Franks, J. J. The abstraction of linguistic ideas. *Cognitive Psychology,* 1971, *2,* 331–350.

Chafe, W. L. *Meaning and the structure of language.* Chicago: University of Chicago Press, 1970.

Davis, F. B. (Ed.). *The literature of research in reading with emphasis on models* (USOE Final Rep.). Washington, D.C.: U.S. Government Printing Office, 1971. (ERIC Document Reproduction Service No. ED 059 023)

Fillmore, C. J. The case for case. In E. Bach & R. T. Harms (Eds.), *Universals in linguistic theory.* New York: Holt, Rinehart & Winston, 1968.

Gough, P. B. One second of reading. In J. F. Kavanagh & I. G. Mattingly (Eds.), *Language by ear and be eye: The relationships between speech and reading.* Cambridge, Mass.: MIT Press, 1972.

Halliday, M. A. K. *Explorations in the functions of language.* London: Arnold, 1973.

Huey, E.B. *The psychology and pedagogy of reading.* Cambridge, Mass.: MIT Press, 1968. (Originally published, 1908.)

Kavanagh, J. F., & Mattingly, I. G. (Eds.). *Language by ear and by eye: The relationships between speech and reading.* Cambridge, Mass.: MIT Press, 1972.

Macnamara, J. Cognitive basis of language learning in infants. *Psychological Review,* 1972, *79,* 1–13.

Nelson, K. Concept, word and sentence: Interrelations in acquisition and development. *Psychological Review,* 1974, *81,* 267–285.

Neisser, U. *Cognitive psychology.* New York: Appleton-Century-Crofts, 1967.

Rumelhart, D. E. Toward an interactive model of reading. In S. Dornic (Ed.), *Attention and performance VI.* Hillsdale, N.J.: Lawrence Erlbaum Associates, 1977.

Smith, F. *Understanding reading.* New York: Holt, Rinehart & Winston, 1971.

Smith, F. *Pscyholinguistics and reading.* New York: Holt, Rinehart & Winston, 1973.

Smith, F. *Comprehension and learning.* New York: Holt, Rinehart & Winston, 1975. (a)

Smith, F. The role of prediction in reading. *Elementary English,* 1975, *52,* 305–311. (b)

Smith, F., & Goodman, K. S. On the psycholinguistic method of teaching reading. *Elementary School Journal,* 1971, *71,* 177–181.

Smith, F., & Holmes, D. L. The independence of letter, word and meaning identification in reading. *Reading Research Quarterly,* 1971, *6,* 394–415.

Tulving, E., & Donaldson, W. (Eds.). *Organization and memory.* New York: Academic Press, 1972.

2 Approaching Reading Through Invented Spelling

Carol Chomsky
Harvard University

In a volume devoted to beginning reading, I would like to devote some time to beginning writing. There are accounts of children who began to write before they knew how to read, spelling words in their own invented spellings. Using their knowledge of letter names and in some cases letter sounds, these children were able to represent the sounds of words quite accurately and consistently (Bissex, 1976; Chomsky, 1971/1976, 1971, 1972; Read, 1971). The ability is interesting and worth exploring in some detail. Such work is now underway. In this chapter I suggest that the ability to write in this way, representing words according to the way they sound, precedes the ability to read among children more generally. I argue that from a developmental standpoint, children are ready to write before they are ready to read and that their introduction to the printed word should therefore be through writing rather than through reading. For maximum effectiveness, school instruction should begin with writing and progress to reading, as an outgrowth of abilities developed through experience with inventing one's own spellings.

INVENTED SPELLING

The evidence about children who write before they read has come largely from children who did so on their own, without specific instruction. Children between four and six who do not yet read but who know the letters of the alphabet and perhaps some of their sounds begin to compose words and messages on their own, inventing their own spellings as they go along. They may use letter sets or alphabet blocks, or they may print if they can form

43

letters. They represent words as they hear them, carrying out an impressive phonetic analysis as they work their way through the words. These invented spellings differ from standard spelling in many ways, of course. What is interesting is that they are highly systematic and, moreover, fairly uniform from child to child.

Characteristics of Spellings and Spellers

The nature of children's invented spellings has been described in some detail by Read (1975a); I mention just a few of the more striking features here. For example, long vowels are represented by the letter name that matches the sound: BOT boat, JMEZ jimmies, FEL feel, KAM came, TIGR tiger.[1] Short vowels are represented by the letter name that contains the closest sound: A [ey] for BAD bed, FALL fell; E [iy] for FES fish, FLEPR Flipper; I [ay] for GIT got, CLIK clock; O [ɔw] for OL all, WOTR water; U [yuw] for TUK took, LUKS looks. Typically L and R function syllabically with no vowel at all: GRL girl, FRN fern, KLR color. Nasals before consonants are standardly omitted: WOT won't, PLAT plant, BOPY bumpy, AGRE angry. Letters are sometimes used according to their full name: YL while, R are, THAQ thank you, NHR nature, PPL people.

What is most interesting is that different children invent very much the same system of spelling. Features that may appear to be idiosyncratic in one child's spelling turn out on inspection to be common to all the children. English contains some 40 sounds, but the alphabet provides only 26 symbols. The children all cope with this dilemma in much the same way, combining sounds into groups represented by a single letter. For example, the sounds [ey], [e], and [ae] are all written with the letter A, so that *bait, bet,* and *bat* are all spelled BAT. Other similar vowel combinations are made. Furthermore, the children fail to represent certain phonetic distinctions that they do have the alphabetic means to represent, such as certain forms of nasality and voicing. They write KAT for both *cat* and *can't,* and use S for the plural marker in both *caps* KAPS and *cabs* KABS. The significant thing is the systematic nature of the spellings and the uniformity from child to child. It would be an intellectual feat of some scope if the children merely produced an accurate phonetic transcription of their language. Apparently they do even better, classifying sounds into categories efficiently on the basis of perceived similarities. This is a fairly sophisticated form of linguistic abstraction.

Some samples of early messages are of interest: R U ɑF (*Are you deaf?*), EFUKANOPNKAZIWILGEVUAKANOPENR (If you can open cans I will give you a can opener) (5-year-old boy, Bissex, 1976), FES SOWEMEG EN

---

[1]Capital letters (e.g., BOT) represent children's spellings.

WOODR (*fish swimming in water*) (picture caption, 4-year-old boy, Read, 1975b). One boy of 5½, confined to his room as a punishment, sent paper airplanes downstairs with the following messages on them (Read, 1970):

DADE I DONT LIK THIS ROOM   WIN U GO UPSTERS
KEN I STA DAOON STERS
I AM CMIN DAOON STERS   YES
I WIL KOMM DAOON STERS

And a 6½-year-old girl produced this familiar plaint (Read, 1970):

MOMME I WOOD LIK YOU TOO GET UP BEKUS I WANT SMTHING FUNT DOO WAK OP MOMME (7 times) POLES (please; 4 times) I WONT SOMETHING FON TOO DOO WOT KAN I DOO THET IS FON

This appears to be a rather remarkable ability for children who do not yet read, and two questions come immediately to mind: What knowledge did the spellers have that enabled them to write, and what factors in their environment encouraged them to do so? With regard to knowledge, apparently all the spellers knew the letters of the alphabet and were aware of the sounds of words to the point of being able to segment words phonemically (see Liberman, 1973). They knew, for example, that in a word such as *table*, the first sound is a [tə], then comes an [ey], then a [bə], and finally an [əl]. They knew that letters can be used to represent sounds: for example, that [tə] can be represented by a letter that sounds like it, namely T. They were able to write their names, so they had the idea of a sequence of written letters.

As to environment, Read (1970) discussed the characteristics of the families of the spontaneous spellers who began to write at home. He reported that the main similarity among the families, beyond providing opportunities in a general atmosphere of freedom of expression, was their responsiveness to the child's interests and their acceptance and enjoyment of the results of the child's efforts. "All the early spellers had somehow come to believe that they could express themselves freely through spelling [p. 161]." The parents were tolerant and appreciative of their children's productions, and while they did not specifically encourage the children, neither did they inhibit them. Evidently the children were not expected to keep hands off—the parents did not transmit the attitude that spelling was arbitrary and had to be memorized. Read (1970) says that they simply "accepted and enjoyed what their children produced... reading what they had written, letting writing be an accepted form of communication, and hanging up stories in the home or office [p. 159]."

Spelling More Accessible Than Reading

The spelling activity may continue for months, or even up to a year, before the children move on to reading. In a number of ways the spelling appears to precede reading by its very nature. It is primarily a creative endeavor. The inventive spellers compose words according to the way they sound, figuring out for themselves what comes first, next, and so on. They do this for their own purposes as a means of self-expression. They appear to be more interested in the activity than in the product. In certain respects it is like drawing a picture. A child who draws a face, for example, is not trying to match a particular pattern or to reach a standard of correctness. In drawing, children work from their own perceptions, representing salient features. As time goes by they represent more detail, and perhaps the organization changes somewhat. One can detect the development from early productions to later ones. The spellings are much the same way. The children spell independently, making their own decisions. They have no preconceptions of how the word ought to be spelled or any expectation that there is a right or a wrong way to do it. They spell creatively, according to some combination of what they perceive and what they consider worthy of representation. They progress through several stages, their early productions differing in a number of respects from later ones. The development, as with drawing, can be traced.

The changes over time are interesting. One feature of many early spellings is the use of the letter H for the *ch* sound. The *ch* sound is in the name of the letter: *aitch*. Children who rely on a letter–name strategy (Beers, 1976) will quite logically choose H to spell the *ch* sound. It is no more surprising than choosing *eff* (F) to spell the *f* sound, or *ell* (L) to spell the *l* sound. This use of H for *ch* has been observed repeatedly in early invented spellings. For example, I MED A SBOYDR WEB ON A BRENH AND EFTR I WHT THE FILM AND I LOT AT KRAFIH (I made a spider web on a branch and after I watched the film and I looked at crayfish). Notice the spelling of *branch* and *watched*: BRENH, WHT. Above we noted the word NHR *nature*.

The letter H also serves to represent the sound *sh*. The child searching through the letter names to find a way to write *sh* will find the closest match in the name *aitch*. If pronounced very slowly, *aitch* does end in a *sh* sound. Notice KRAFI*H* above for *crayfish*. And in the following story by a 4½-year-old, there are two examples: YUTS A LADE YET FE*H*EG AD *H*E KOT FLEPR (Once a lady went fi*sh*ing and *sh*e caught Flipper). This story was accompanied by a picture of a woman fishing for dolphins, and HE was reported by the child as the word *she*. These "letter–name" spellings persist until the child learns the standard spelling for [č] and [š]. They are particularly early features and rarely appear beyond kindergarten age.

Another common early spelling feature is the use of CHR and JR (GR) for initial *tr* and *dr*. Words such as CHRAN train, CHRIBLS troubles, CHRAY tray, and JRIV drive, JRAGN dragon, JRAN drain, abound in the early spellings. Initial *tr* and *dr* are heard with a *ch* and *j* sound, not *t* or *d*. Since the children hear it this way, that is how they write it. One first grader wrote: I HAV A NUO CAR AND MI MOM DUSINT WNOU HOW TO *GRIV* IT (I have a new car and my mom doesn't know how to *dr*ive it). GR is not an error, but a correct choice, using the child's own perceptions and a letter–name strategy. This particular spelling tends to persist in children's writing well into first grade, where many children explicitly describe the first sound of *tree* as being more like a *ch* than a *t* (Read, 1975a).

Once the children get started, they can go on to write any message at all. For it is not that they know the spelling of certain words; instead, they possess the means to write any and all words. In this sense they are equipped to write much as are children who learn reading through an augmented alphabet such as the Initial Teaching Alphabet (ITA). Many children who have been trained in ITA are able to write freely, and this is sometimes considered an important benefit of the use of the alphabet. The creative spellers, however, are writing before they know how to read. Often they cannot read back what they have written, nor are they interested in doing so. For the time being they are concerned with production.

Another aspect of the spelling that makes it more accessible than reading is its direct relationship to the way words are pronounced. The task consists of translating from pronunciation to print. The alphabet lacks some symbols so that sounds must be classified together, but the classifications are made on a phonetic basis. If the children have sufficient metalinguistic awareness to permit the segmentation of words into phonemic components, and a knowledge of letter names or sounds, they can go ahead. Reading, on the other hand, is not simply the reverse of spelling, that is, translating from print to pronunciation. In English the relation of print to pronunciation is largely indirect, the spelling corresponding to a linguistic level considerably more abstract than pronunciation. Learning to read involves learning to relate spelling to this more abstract linguistic level. The child's task is thus a considerably more abstract and more difficult one in learning to read.

An additional factor in the greater accessibility of writing is that in writing the words and message are known, whereas in reading the words are not known ahead of time and must be identified. That is, the reader must recognize, from print, words chosen by someone else. This is an inherent difference between the two activities, regardless of the nature of the spelling system. Although much the same background information may be required in translating from pronunciation to print and from print to pronunciation, the need to identify the word, which reading involves, is a considerable extra step that is not required in learning to write.

Montessori (1964) commented as follows on this difference and the consequent greater accessibility of writing for children:

Experience has taught me to distinguish clearly between *writing and reading*, and has shown me that the two acts *are not absolutely contemporaneous.* Contrary to the usually accepted idea, writing *precedes reading* . . . . The child who *knows how to write*, when placed before a word which he must interpret by reading, is silent for a long time, and generally reads the component sounds with the same slowness with which he would have written them. But *the sense of the word* becomes evident only when it is pronounced clearly and with the phonetic accent. Now, in order to place the phonetic accent the child must recognise the word; that is, he must recognise the idea which the word represents. The intervention of a superior work of the intellect is necessary if he is to read [pp. 296–297].

Recognizing this difference, Montessori began reading instruction with word composition. She considered this order to be a natural one.

Writing Aids Learning to Read

The inventive spellers, during the months that they engage in their writing activities, are providing themselves with excellent and valuable practice in phonetics, word analysis and synthesis, and letter–sound correspondences. In addition, they are experiencing a sense of control over the printed word. There is an independence that is gained with print and a sense that print–sound relationships are something that one works out for oneself. This practice and this attitude serve them well when it comes time to read. The initiative and self-reliance developed through writing carry over into learning to read. The children expect to take an active role in learning to read, as they did with writing. In my opinion, this attitude is a crucial element in reading. Since the children are prepared to go ahead on their own, what they need is adequate input from the environment. They need to be exposed to large quantities of print.

The inventive spellers have not been limited to writing only, of course, over the months that they have been involved in spelling. Curiosity about reading grows, and the children find opportunities around them as they go about their day. Typically, spellers reach a point where they begin to ask about words in the environment. Either they try to pronounce them, reading them off phonetically in order to identify them, or they ask what they say. It is as if suddenly they begin to notice all the print in the world around them: street signs, newspaper headlines, billboards, cereal boxes, food labels. They try to read everything, already having a good foundation in translating from pronunciation to print. If help is provided when they ask for it, they make out wonderfully well. It is a very exciting time for them.

I think that what helps children most of all at this point is their heightened activity level. Learning to read, or at first to identify printed words, surely involves forming hypotheses about the relations (direct and indirect) of spelling to pronunciation, changing these hypotheses as new evidence is added, and eventually arriving at a system of interpretation that is in accord with the facts. This hypothesis construction is an active process, taking the child far beyond the "rules" that can be offered by the best of patterned, programmed, or linguistic approaches. The more the children are prepared to do for themselves the better off they are. Piaget (1972) has said, "Children should be able to do their own experimenting....In order for a child to understand something, he must construct it himself, he must re-invent it. Every time we teach a child something, we keep him from inventing it himself [p. 27]." This view applies quite well to learning to read. The printed word "belongs" to the spontaneous speller far more directly than to children who have experienced it only ready made. For once you have invented your own spelling system, dealing with the standard system comes easy. A considerable amount of the intellectual work has already been done.

The major need of inventive spellers who are beginning to read is to have someone to answer their questions and to correct their mistakes when necessary. Responding to "What does this word say?" becomes the primary form of instruction. And when they misread a word, they need to be corrected. When first learning to read, my son, an inventive speller, pronounced the name *Joan* as *Jane* in a book about cousin Joan. I told him no, the name was *Joan*. "Oh," he replied, "I see. The *a* is silent. I thought the *o* was silent." He had already been introduced to the idea of silent letters when asking about words like *ride* that he saw written and had pronounced with two syllables: ride-ee. This was not a bad way to account for the pronunciation of *Joan*.

Not long after this incident, he put this silent letter information to use again. He was playing one day with a music box that had the word *TURN* printed on the knob, with an arrow indicating the direction. He came running over to announce, "I figured it out! First I thought it said *toorn, toorn,* but then I saw that it says *turn*. The *u* is silent!"

This child, like most inventive spellers, had been using L and R syllabically in words like FRN fern, BRD bird, GRL girl, and used U according to its name, as in UNITD united. When it came time to figure out a word in reading, he assumed that the same conventions held. However, the strong assist from context plus the available silent letter idea permitted him to read the word *turn*. He used the same logic in dealing with the words *church, bird,* and *mermaid* that he encountered over the next weeks. He commented that "It's not *chuh-rch,* because the *u* is silent. It's *church*." And similarly, it's not *bih-rd* or *meh-rmaid* because again the vowels are silent.

These examples are indicative of the way in which inventive spellers begin to deal with conventional spelling. There is a recognition that the conventions are different and a willingness to undertake figuring it all out to one's own satisfaction.

Apparently, children are not confused by differences between what they write and what they read. Read (1970) commented that "there were no observations or reports of a child questioning the lack of correspondence between what he read and what he wrote [p. 184]." Whereas their own spellings were a form of phonetic transcription, standard spelling is not, and the children seemed to accept this distinction with no difficulty. In general as they learn to read, the spellers read standard spelling more easily than their own spellings.

It is interesting that spellers at first may treat writing and reading as distinct activities that they may separate quite effectively. The child above who spelled *turn* TRN and came to read *TURN* as the same word does not necessarily begin to spell it TURN in his own writing. It can be almost as if there is a writing mode and a reading mode that exist for the child, and he or she may operate in one mode at times without recourse or attention to the other. As they write, such children are concerned with representing the sounds of the words, using their productive systems actively and carefully. They attend to the sequence of sounds, choosing appropriate letters each step of the way. If they do check their results once the word or phrase is completed, they check it by starting again with pronunciation and making sure that they have chosen the requisite letters, syllable by syllable or sound by sound. They work from their pronunciation to the letters, not the other way around. That is, they do not read the product so much as review and check the production process.

I observed an example of this separation of writing from reading one day when I brought a young speller to visit a seminar on child language that I was teaching. He had agreed to come to class and write some words for my students. Jeremy was then 4½ years old, had been writing for some months, and had just recently begun to teach himself to read. He was quite cooperative about spelling words that the students asked for, using a plastic letter set spread out on the table in front of him. Among the words that the students requested was *pencils*. Jeremy spelled it PASLS, consistent with his other spellings and in accurate tradition: the letter A for the vowel [e], preconsonantal nasal [n] omitted, L used syllabically, and S for the plural [z]. Someone kept track of Jeremy's productions, copying each word onto paper as Jeremy composed it with the letters. Somewhat later in the session, it occurred to one of the students to ask Jeremy to read some of his own spellings. We reconstructed PASLS on the table and asked Jeremy what it said. [paezəlz], he answered confidently, to everyone's surprise. But indeed, that is the way one pronounces that sequence of letters if one is reading. Jeremy was operating with reading, which was a very different matter from writing. Still later in the session, we wrote PENCILS with the letters and asked Jeremy what it said. With no hesitation, he replied, "Pencils."

I think that this incident illustrates very well the fact that the inventive spellers may take a very different view of their two activities, writing and reading. This separation may persist for some time, until they eventually adopt standard spelling in their own writing.

With regard to the transition from invented spellings to standard spelling in their own writing, they make the replacement as they become more experienced with reading and are expected to abandon their earlier form of writing. Using standard spelling is a very different activity from inventing spellings, and the children that I have been able to observe have made the transition with no particular difficulty. Some children begin to use standard spelling in school and continue to use invented spellings at home. Others adopt standard spelling throughout. Some make the transition rapidly, apparently substituting the new principle rather easily. Others use a mixture of the two, using standard spelling when it is known and falling back on inventions when words are not known. Whatever the particular course of the transition, children seem to make it with no apparent difficulty or confusion.

Read (1970) stressed the lack of confusion or conflict between the child's spelling system and the standard forms. Children relinquished their private spelling systems and acquired standard spelling whenever demands were made on them to do so. None of them experienced any difficulty. He accounted for this ease of transition by a characterization of the invented spellings as constantly repeated inventions, never assuming the quality of a habit (Read, 1970):

> ...[Since] the transition [to standard spelling] was neither difficult nor necessarily slow, one conclusion seems justified: if "habit" refers to behavior that is acquired and altered by frequent repetition and constant correction, the early spellings were not habits. Some young spellers wrote hundreds of words before entering school; it seems inconceivable that each word could have required individual correction in the first grade without spelling becoming an issue between these children and their teachers and parents. The spontaneous beginning of the children's spelling also shows that it was not habit-formation, in the sense referred to. We can only believe that the children acquired... general notions of spelling that allowed them to spell virtually any word and that later altered quite readily, despite the fact that they had been applied many times [p. 189].

That the spellings did not become habitual seems borne out by the fact that they changed as the children matured. At each point the spellings were the products of a system of representation; as the system changed, so did the spellings. Acquiring standard spelling would appear to require replacing the principle of representation, not the individual spellings. Apparently the children were able to do this readily.

As I said earlier, children who have been writing for months are in a very favorable position when they undertake learning to read. They have at their command considerable phonetic information about English, practice in phonemic segmentation, and experience with alphabetic representation. These are some of the technical abilities that they need to get started. They have, in addition, an expectation of going ahead on their own. They are prepared to make sense of the print by figuring it out or by asking questions. They expect it to make sense, and their purpose is to derive a message from the print, not just to pronounce the words.

Spelling, Pronunciation, Phonology, and Word Identification

I think that an important advantage of these children's prior experience with writing is the lack of a dichotomy in their view of reading between pronouncing the words and understanding the meaning. At no point does sounding out the words become an activity of any relevance. Their approach from the start is "What does it say?" rather than "How is it pronounced?"

Children who are taught to read first are often taught to pronounce the sequence of letters and then to derive the meaning somewhat as an adjunct to the pronunciation. The view that converting from print to sound can somehow take place as an activity independent of or prior to word identification unfortunately often leads to a form of teaching in which children are taught to read English as if they did not already know the language. They are expected to react to print by converting to pronunciation, using methods appropriate to a foreigner who does not know English. Letter–sound correspondences and pronunciation rules form the substance of instruction. The assumption is that spelling corresponds directly to the pronounced form of words, and that whether one knows English or not, the activity of converting from spelling to sound is essentially the same.

English spelling, however, is a system designed for readers who know the language. Because it does not represent pronunciation directly, it cannot be read by applying a learned set of limited pronunciation rules. English spelling corresponds to a level of linguistic knowledge that is more abstract than pronunciation, and it is related to pronunciation by the phonological rules of the language. Speakers who know the language have these rules at their command as part of their tacit knowledge of the language.

The phonological rules supply much of what is necessary to convert the spelling to pronunciation. Correspondingly, the spelling omits a great deal of information about pronunciation that can be supplied by the phonological rules. Readers who attempt to pronounce English from its spelling without knowing the language will encounter a great deal of difficulty because they do not have recourse to the phonological rules.

The spelling to a large extent omits information that is predictable from the phonological rules. Stress placement, for example, is not indicated. The form *photograph* is written alike in phótograph, photógraph-y, and photográphic, although the stress is different in each case. The reader must supply this. Vowel reduction, a consequence of stress placement, is not indicated, but the reader who knows English will know to pronounce the italicized vowels above as the reduced vowel [ə], although they are written alike in the three forms. Certain voicing alternations are also not indicated where predictable, so that [s] and [z] are written alike, with the letter *s*, in the related forms *sign* [s] and *resign* [z]. Certain vowel alternations in related words are not indicated where predictable, so that *nature* and *natural* are written with the same vowel in the first syllable, although the pronunciation is [ey] in one case and [ae] in the other. *Child* and *children* are both written with *i*, although the pronunciation is [ay] in one case and [I] in the other. There are many examples of this sort. The point is that these examples are not exceptions but regular aspects of the orthography of English. The spelling, as I said earlier, is designed for a reader who knows the language.

Emphasis in beginning reading should be placed not on pronouncing the print but rather on determining which word or sentence is presented. Assigning a pronunciation follows such an identification. Identifying the word or sentence is the primary task. The spelling relates to pronunciation more by providing clues to it than by specifying it. There is a range of possible pronunciations, for example, for the letter *x*. It can be [ks], [gz], [kš], [eks], and [z], as in ta*x*, e*x*ample, an*x*ious, *x*-ray, and *X*erox. It cannot be [l] or [m] or [b]. Knowing the range of possible pronunciations helps in identifying the word. Once the word is recognized, the correct pronunciation follows automatically.

For the correct pronunciation to be assigned automatically from word identification, however, the reader must know the language. The pronunciation rules are part of the equipment of the native speaker. For example, consider the letter *x* more closely. It is [gz] in *example*, but [ks] in *exercise*. A foreigner who does not know English would have to learn a rule that says: Intervocalic *x* is voiced prestress and unvoiced poststress (mostly). Prestress examples are *exámple, exággerate, exáct, exám, exért, exíst, exúlt,* all [gz]; poststress examples are *éxercise, éxecute, éxodus, óxygen, áxis,* all [ks]. In some words there is dialectal variation, and exceptions result: *exíle, exít.*

The voicing of *x* is of concern to foreigners trying to read English aloud, because they lack the automatic voicing rule. Since the necessary information is not given in the spelling, they can pronounce *x* correctly only by working from explicit memorized rules. First they must use an explicit rule to assign stress to the proper syllable and then, on the basis of stress placement, apply the voicing rule correctly. Native speakers need not bother with such explicit rules. Stress placement and *x*-voicing rules are part of their phonological system. The rules operate automatically without conscious attention or explicit knowledge. Once the word is identified, the native speaker automatically knows where to place the stress and whether or not to voice the *x*.

This picture of reading describes the experienced reader. The question for the learner is: How does the nonreader proceed to identify a word, if not through the medium of its pronunciation? The learner's task is to develop the relations between spelling and the abstract linguistic level to which it corresponds. I think, quite seriously, that this is best accomplished not by learning rules but by repeated exposure to print with identification provided as, for example, in listening-while-reading activities. Extensive input of normal text that is understood is the raw material from which learners can derive the necessary connections and construct the relevant system to read on their own.

LEARNING TO READ THROUGH WRITING

It seems clear that, in order to learn to read, some background information is necessary, of the sort discussed here with regard to writing. It is also the case that once a person knows how to read, he or she has available quite extensive information about letter–sound correspondences and relationships, and spelling patterns. The person who knows how to read can determine, on reflection, all the pronunciations of *ough*, for example, or the 11 or more ways of writing the sound [š] reputed to exist in English. But this latter sort of information is the *result* of knowing how to read. It is not at all clear that memorizing such facts will be of any particular help in learning how. Although one ends up knowing such facts implicitly, explicit memorization of some specific number of them may be beside the point in learning to read. Instead, the process of learning how would seem to involve a good bit of hypothesis construction and testing, as in learning language in the first place. Children are well equipped to organize linguistic knowledge on the basis of rich and varied inputs, to seek regularities, and to construct tacit rule systems. What they need in reading, beyond the requisite background, is adequate input of understood text. When beginning to read on their own, they need to have their questions answered and their mistakes corrected when necessary. If this much help is forthcoming, they should be prepared to do the rest.

Developing Phonetic Abilities

How, then, do teachers begin if they wish to start with writing? Developing children's phonetic abilities and, of course, letter knowledge are the teacher's initial tasks.

By age five or earlier, many children's ability to analyze words phonetically will already be well developed. They can recognize words that begin with the same sound and words that rhyme. Those who cannot will need practice in this sort of analysis before they can be expected to spell (see Liberman, 1973).

It is surprising how much phonetic information is available to introspection at this age and how readily this knowledge can be raised to the level of awareness through word play, questioning, and talk about sounds. Easiest of all for the child is to recognize words that begin with the same sound, such as *toy, table, touch*. Once children can do this, they can become aware of what sound a word begins with—for example, that *table* begins with a [tə] sound. Awareness of rhyme, or knowing that *toy* and *boy* end alike, is also an early ability. Usually, sensitivity to rhyme precedes the ability to identify words that end alike only in their final sound, such as *dog* and *hug*. The syllable is easier to deal with than individual sounds at this stage. The most advanced ability is segmenting the entire word into its component sounds, that is, being able to figure out, on reflection, what sequence of separate sounds make up the word.

Practice in attending to sounds with guidance from a teacher who is aware of these separate abilities will be enormously helpful to the child, but in order to get started with spelling, only the simplest phonetic awareness is needed. Children who know that *man* begins with a [m] sound, for example, are ready. If they know letter names or sounds, they are prepared to find the letters that they need to spell their first word. Just the letters needed for the particular word are enough.

At first, children will sometimes use only the first letter to represent a word. *Man* will be written M; next, the final sound may be represented as well: MN; and finally, all the sounds of the word: MAN. Paul (1976) provided an excellent description of such beginnings in her kindergarten class in which she encouraged the children to spell inventively. One of the major benefits of the spelling, she reported, is the independence that children feel when they can write on their own without having to ask the teacher for help.

Much of the early writing looks unkempt until inexperienced fingers develop the control to make it more readable. But no matter. The message can usually be retrieved, and the children are deriving the satisfaction of self-expression. Most important, they are getting practice in figuring out their own spellings. For reading, this practice is the part of the job that matters at this stage, the part that requires thought. And this is the part that children are quite ready for in kindergarten and early in first grade. The mechanical handwriting skill can come later. Some children do better using plastic or wooden letters than attempting to write in their own handwriting. They find it easier, and there is no reason to discourage it. In time they will develop their handwriting to the point where they can use it, but for the time being the letter sets let them get their messages across. The letters provide a way of getting around the mechanics of writing so that the children can develop the *thought processes* that go into writing and eventually into reading.

In a first-grade classroom where children are encouraged to write freely, with attention to representing how words sound rather than standard spellings, an interesting attitude develops. There is a confidence that you can write anything you can say, because you have the principle of writing. It is not as if there are certain words that you know how to spell and others that you have to ask about. You can write anything, on your own. You learn to develop your own judgments and to trust them. Children who work from such a principle do so with initiative and self-reliance. They produce quantities of imaginative and creative writing, including diaries, letters, posters, illustrated stories, plays, and whole books. Most often artwork accompanies the writing. They also keep records and write reports. Accounts of science experiments, reports of trips, and research reports can be written in one's own spelling. The spontaneity and imaginativeness of the work are impressive. It is a creative outlet of the first order. (Some samples of children's work are presented in a subsequent section.)

Fostering Reading

When children are ready to begin reading, the teacher may wish to provide a structure to foster reading activity. There are a variety of ways to provide the inventive speller with reading exposure. To some extent, the children provide themselves with inputs from the environment, as mentioned earlier. The teacher, however, may wish to take a more directive role. For example, Florence Bailey of the Franklin School in Lexington, Massachusetts, starts her first graders off with writing and uses the following method for purposeful introduction of reading in standard spelling (see Chomsky, 1975).

The children write and illustrate books in their own spellings. These can be quite long at times and full of action and excitement. The children take their books home, but before they do so, Mrs. Bailey makes a copy in standard spelling. She copies the story onto cardboard sheets held together with large rings, in book form, and the child re-illustrates it. The child then reads it to the group at meeting time. The set of books grows through the year, and the collection of these child-written books forms a core of reading material for the whole class. The books are hung on a pegboard panel within easy reach, and the children read and reread them many times.

The role that these books play among the children is an excellent and an important one. One day when I was in the classroom Mrs. Bailey asked Christopher if he would read his latest book to me. He did so with some pride. When he was through, another child happened by and said, "Christopher, can I read your book now?" Christopher said yes, and she proceeded to read it aloud. When she hesitated over a word, Christopher provided the needed help. It was an activity entirely between the two children. She read the complete book, with Christopher's assistance as needed. They talked about the story, she asked him some questions, said she liked his book, and wandered off.

Another more formal way to provide the speller with exposure to print for reading purposes is to encourage the children to listen to stories and books read aloud while they follow along in the text. An easy way for the children to engage in this listening-while-reading activity is to use a tape recorder and listen quietly to a book, through earphones, at least once a day. Rereading a book in this way until it is well known is a particularly valuable activity. Children become "fluent" with a book that they perhaps cannot yet read independently. It provides them with a wealth of material from which to organize their reading knowledge. It also saves the children from constantly having to ask for help with words that they cannot figure out.

Examples of Children's Writings

A sample child-written book is presented below in standard spelling. Through first grade Christopher wrote a series of these books about a hedgehog, Moogye, who could transform himself (Superman style) into a superpowered hero, engaging mostly in crime-solving and rescue operations.

The Adventures of Moogye

Chapter 1.
The hedgehog was walking down the street, when suddenly a robbery at the corner! Quick into a nearby telephone booth, and it's Moogye!
Faster than a speeding comet! More powerful than all the superheroes put together! Able to leap right over Pluto in a single bound!
Phooey the robbers already got away. What's this! A seagull in the city.
Moogye flies to the sea to talk to the seagulls.

Chapter 2.   They Know Nothing
The seagulls know nothing. So Moogye waits, as the hedgehog.
Again the mysterious seagull comes! Again a robbery!

Chapter 3.   The Robbers are Captured
Moogye follows the seagull.
The seagull takes Moogye under water.
A sub under water. The seagull goes in! Moogye goes in!
They have a fight. Moogye wins! Moogye ties them up.

Part Two
A rocket is being launched. Everybody is there. 10-9-8-7-6-5-4-3-2-1-zero.
Up into space the rocket goes. What's this? The rocket's on fire.
Meanwhile, back at earth, street hedgehog is watching.
Quick! Into a nearby telephone booth, and it's Moogye!
Moogye speeds to the rocket.
Moogye blows the fire out!

The End

The children in Mrs. Bailey's room write scientific reports as well as fiction. George is a case in point. His willingness to write came slowly. He was involved with ships at the beginning of the school year. At first his teacher encouraged him to dictate his battleship stories: "This is a battleship. It can fight the Indians. It has radar and the Indians try to blow it up." He progressed to drawing pictures to go with his stories, and the pictures were accurately done. "It's a form of recording for George," said his teacher, "since drawing is a natural beginning for some children." Next came dictating mini-stories that were short enough for him to copy. These were simple things like "I made a submarine," but he began to get the practice of writing himself. Finally he was able to write a battleship story on his own (see Fig. 2.1):

WANTS THER WAS A SHIP   IT WAS A BATL SHIP
IT SELD THE SEVIN SESE   IT HAD RATRRE

(Once there was a ship. It was a battleship. It sailed the seven seas. It had radar)

George's dictation of the battleship story to his teacher took place in October. The self-composed story shown in Fig. 2.1 followed in a few weeks. By December his stories had lengthened, and he had moved on to planets and science reports:

THE WONDERS OF MERCURE
MERCURE THE SMALLIST PLANIT IN ARE SOLAR
SYSTEM. ON ONE SIDE IT'S STARCH AND ON THE
OTHER SIDE IT'S FROSIN. THE MOST FREQUINTN
WE THINK IS ON MERCURE IS VOLCANOSS.   GEORGE

George

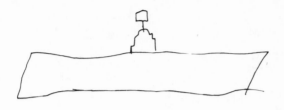

~~Wantsther~~ Wants ther Was a ship it was a Batl ship
it selo the sevin sese it HaD ratrre.

FIG. 2.1. Battleship story by a first-grade boy: Once there was a ship. It was a battleship. It sailed the seven seas. It had radar.

(Mercury[is]the smallest planet in our solar system. On one side it's stark and on the other side it's frozen. The most frequent thing we think is on Mercury is volcanoes.)

Figure 2.2 illustrates another planet report of George's:

> SATERN IS THE SECINT BIGIST PLANIT IN ARE SOLER
> SYSTM. THE SUN IS IT'S MUTHER STAR. SATERN HAS
> SUM CINDE OF HOT GAS RING'S. SATERN'S RINGS
> ARNT VERY THIC. SATERN IS A STERANJ PLANIT
> THE END   GEORGE

(Saturn is the second biggest planet in our solar system. The sun is its mother star. Saturn has some kind of hot gas rings. Saturn's rings aren't very thick. Saturn is a strange planet. The end. George)

And in January, he wrote the following elegant rocket piece under a careful drawing:

> THIS IS A ROCKIT. THE LOONER MOJRAI IS ON THE
> THERD DECK. IT'S A PEAS AV SIYINTIFIC EQUIPMENT.
> THE NEXT PEAS OF SIYINTIFIC EQUIPMENT IS THE
> CMAND MOJRAI.

(This is a rocket. The lunar module is on the third deck. It's a piece of scientific equipment. The next piece of scientific equipment is the command module.)

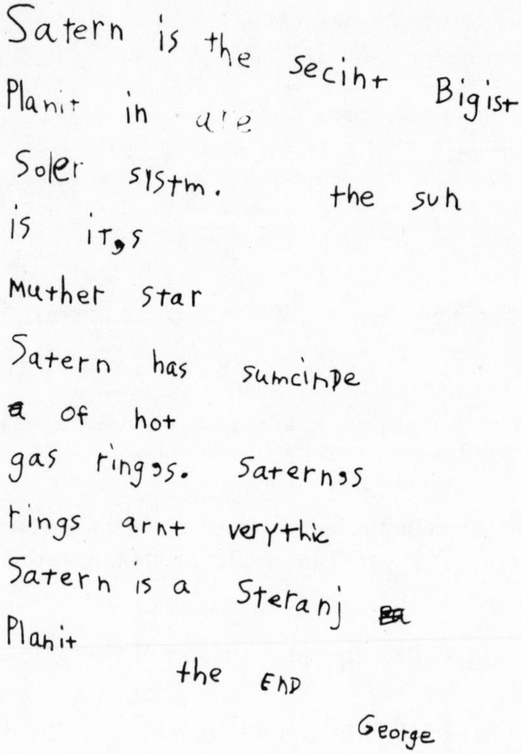

Satern is the seciht Bigist
Planit in are
Soler sistm.   the suh
is it,s
Muther star
Satern has sumcinpe
a of hot
gas ringos. Saternos
rings arnt verythic
Satern is a Steranj ~~a~~
Planit
          the END
                    George

FIG. 2.2.   Science report of a first grader: Saturn is the second biggest planet in our solar system. The sun is its mother star. Saturn has some kind of hot gas rings. Saturn's rings aren't very thick. Saturn is a strange planet.

George, not yet 7 years old, was writing science reports with very complex vocabulary. In a classroom where the do-it-yourself ethic holds top priority, creativity of this sort can flourish. Mrs. Bailey stresses that the teacher's belief in the value of the writing and its potential is most important. In her words, "Children need to feel that teachers do trust and believe in their sensible beginnings in writing. And teachers do need to believe that, with proper intervention and encouragement, this writing will develop and grow, as did George's."

Mrs. Bailey pointed out that children read what they themselves have written more easily than unfamiliar material. Whether it's in their original spellings or copied over in standard spelling, it's easier. In a way they are less fearful of reading their own writing than of undertaking a book, she says. "Someone *else* has written the book. While the pictures help and the story can be discussed in advance, still it is someone else's product. What they have written themselves is organically personal. Their own writing has virtue—it's sincere, genuine, and original. The children respect their stories and their own kind of thinking."

The language experience approach to reading is, of course, motivated by these same principles with regard to reading. However, the inventive spellers are expected to write first, independent of whether they can read back what they have written. The writing is a valued activity in itself and may be engaged in for months before the child moves on to reading.

After a class trip to a milk bottling plant, one girl wrote the following account:

THE MILK GOSE TO THE BOTLING PLAT WER THE MASHEENS PUT THE MILK INTO CARTENS AND THEN A TRUC CUMS AND TACS THE MILK THE MILK GOSE TO THE MARCET

When the children were asked to write about their wishes, one boy wrote:

IV I CUD WISH ENEASING (anything) IT WOD BE TO MC (make) EVEREBODE LIV FOREVR

At Christmas time, a number of diary entries reflected seasonal concerns (see Fig. 2.3):

IT WIL BI CRISMIS SOON BUT IF THE ENRGY CRISIS GES WRS WE MIT NOT HAF NO MOR CRISM LIS

MY SISTR MAD A KRISMIS RETH (wreath)   IT WUS A LITTLE RETH SATU CLOS (Santa Claus)

A snake book reported on boa constrictors, coral snakes, garter snakes, and cobras (see Fig. 2.4):

THE INDEAN BOA KINSTIRE IS THE LOGIST SNACK IN INDEA.
IT IS 39 FET.
THE CKOROL SNACK IS A CIEND OF RADOLER.
THE GARDINER SNACK YOU CAN ALLMOST ANY WAR.
THE SPITING KOEBERA IS WON OF THE SDOGIST SNACKS.
AND THE GIEINT CKOBERA IS THE SDROGIST!

(The Indian boa constrictor is the longest snake in India. It is 39 feet. The coral snake is a kind of rattler. The garter snake you can (find) almost

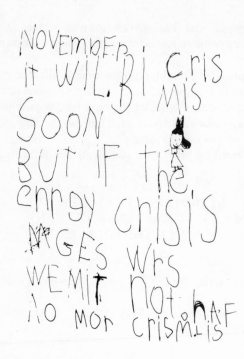

FIG. 2.3. Diary entry, first-grade girl: It will be Christmas soon but if the energy crisis gets worse we might not have no more Christmas lights.

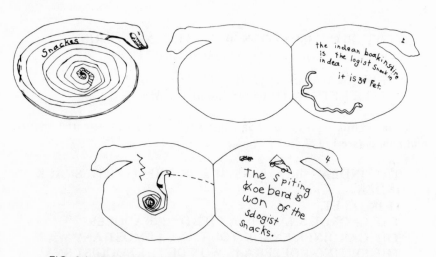

FIG. 2.4. Snake book, first-grade boy: The Indian boa constrictor is the longest snake in India. It is 39 feet. The coral snake is a kind of rattler. The garter snake you can (find) almost anywhere. The spitting cobra is one of the strongest snakes. And the giant cobra is the strongest!

anywhere. The spitting cobra is one of the strongest snakes. And the giant cobra is the strongest!)

And an illustrated story told of Brontosaurus coming home from school (see Fig. 2.5):

WUN DA BRUNTSRRS WUS CUMING HOM FRM SCOL WEN HIS BEST FRAES SUPT BY FR A CHAT   THE END

(One day Brontosaurus was coming home from school when his best friends stopped by for a chat.)

One group project to which the children were all asked to contribute was a monster book. They were told to imagine a monster, draw him, and write about what he looked like, what he ate, and how they would convince their mothers to let them bring the monster home. One girl wrote:

MI MONSTR FDS ON PEPOL AND I WD POSWAD MI MDR LC THIS
I WOD TOL HOR THET I WD BING THE MOSTR HOM

FIG. 2.5. Illustrated story, first-grade boy: One day Brontosaurus was coming home from school when his best friends stopped by for a chat. The end.

(My monster feeds on people. And I would persuade my mother like this. I would tell her that I would bring the monster home.)

And a boy wrote as follows, copied over in standard spelling:

My monster eats shakes, french fries, hot dogs, and hamburgers. He is 6 feet tall and 7 feet long, and weighs 600 pounds. His name is Crikasouris. How to con my mother to keep my monster. I'd beg and beg and beg and then I'd cry and then I'd sneak. I'd keep my monster in the woods, and he would live in a hole at the bottom of the Res, just beyond the first rope. I'd put on my suit and flippers and go down and play.

The children's writing is superb. A good bit of the reading that they do through the year is of each other's writings.

CONCLUSION

I have suggested that children be taught to read by beginning with writing. This reversal of the usual order of instruction allows children to practice with the more concrete activities of word composition before they undertake the relatively abstract task of reading. It provides the background information that they will need in a particularly active and functional way.

When such children move on to reading, they are prepared to take an active role in teaching themselves. They need exposure to print and someone to answer their questions and correct their mistakes when necessary. I suggest that the school conceive its role as one of providing the requisite background together with extensive reading exposure in an atmosphere of independence for the children. In effect, the children teach themselves to read, having received from instruction the basic tools needed to do the job. The primary function of the reading teacher becomes that of answering the questions.

REFERENCES

Bissex, G. *DO NAT DSTRB GNYS AT WRK: Invented spelling and beginning reading development.* Unpublished qualifying paper, Harvard Graduate School of Education, 1976.

Beers, J. *The development of spelling strategies in primary school children.* Unpublished manuscript, Oakland University, 1976.

Chomsky, C. Write first, read later. *Childhood Education,* 1971, *47,* 296–299.

Chomsky, C. Write now, read later. In C. Cazden (Ed.), *Language in early childhood education.* Washington, D.C.: National Association for the Education of Young Children, 1972.

Chomsky, C. How sister got into the grog. *Early Years,* 1975, *6,* 36–39.

Chomsky, C. Invented spelling in the open classroom. In W. von Raffler–Engel (Ed.), *Child language—1975*. Milford, Conn.: International Linguistics Association, 1976. (Originally published in *Word,* 1971, *27,* 499–518.)

Liberman, I. Y. Segmentation of the spoken word and reading acquisition. *Bulletin of the Orton Society,* 1973, *23,* 65–77.

Montessori, M. *The Montessori method.* New York: Schocken Books, 1964.

Paul, R. Invented spelling in kindergarten. *Young Children,* 1976, *31,* 195–200.

Piaget, J. Some aspects of operations. In M. Piers (Ed.), *Play and development.* New York: Norton, 1972.

Read, C. *Children's perceptions of the sounds of English: Phonology from three to six.* Unpublished doctoral dissertation, Harvard Graduate School of Education, 1970.

Read, C. Preschool children's knowledge of English phonology. *Harvard Educational Review,* 1971, *41,* 1–34.

Read, C. *Children's categorization of speech sounds in English* (Research Rep. No. 17). Urbana, Ill.: National Council of Teachers of English, 1975. (a)

Read, C. Lessons to be learned from the preschool orthographer. In E. H. Lenneberg & E. Lenneberg (Eds.), *Foundations of language development.* New York: Academic Press, 1975. (b)

3 Word Recognition: Theoretical Issues and Instructural Hints

Edward E. Smith
Glenn M. Kleiman
Stanford University

All the authors in this volume are concerned with reading, but there has been a division of labor. Our task is to focus on what psychologists know about the recognition of words and see what this suggests about the teaching of reading. Immediately, this task poses problems. For one, constraints of space make it impossible for us to provide an extensive summary of the experimental and theoretical literature on word recognition. So we are selective in our review of this literature, concentrating where possible on issues that may have some relevance to instructional concerns.

This brings us to our second problem. Because the research literature on word recognition is mainly concerned with adult skilled readers, how can we relate these findings to beginning readers? For example, suppose the adult literature tells us that skilled readers do not need to convert written words into speech in order to recognize them. Does it follow that children should be discouraged from using such conversions when learning to read? Not necessarily. Perhaps converting words to some sort of speech code is a necessary first step in the developmental path that culminates in fluent reading without conversion to speech. The problem, in a nutshell, is that although we may have some idea of what skilled reading looks like, we do not have the foggiest notion of how to get there. Without this requisite developmental knowledge, it is simply impossible to draw strong implications about reading instruction from the research on adult word perception. The best we can do under these circumstances is look at the adult literature for hints on what needs to be taught. After all, even though we do not know how to get to skilled reading, it has got to be a help to know where we are going. Some may think this an awfully precarious strategy, but may we remind you of Lyndon Johnson's finest line, "I'm the only president you've got." Let's see then what we can do with what we've got.

AN INFORMATION-PROCESSING APPROACH
TO READING

Metatheoretical Considerations

The research on adult word recognition is dominated by one approach called *information processing*. The general idea is that mental abilities such as reading can best be understood as an integrated composite of primitive mental operations. This approach is sometimes contrasted with the view that reading is a holistic activity that cannot be divided into component processes. This question of parts versus wholes comes up in reading instruction as well, and we are clearly on the side of the parts people. That is, we believe that training on individual component processes of reading is feasible and that at least some reading problems may be due to problems in a specific component process.

An information-processing analysis entails more than dividing a mental ability into component parts. This kind of analysis starts by likening mental processing to a computational system and then endeavors to spell out the exact sequence of computational mechanisms involved in executing a complex ability. It asks not only what components are involved but also how they are sequenced and integrated so as to produce the output (reading) of interest. This approach, therefore, differs in a fundamental way from the use of factor-analytic techniques to divide a mental ability into component processes. Factor-analytic techniques do not tell us how the component parts are sequenced and integrated; information-processing analyses attempt to do so.

The information-processing analogy with computational devices imposes some constraints on what can count as a component. The components that information processors are concerned with tend to be those that have wide applicability in a multitude of skills and that can be realized (at least in principle) on real machines. Two examples would be comparing two chunks of information to determine if they match or replacing one kind of symbol with another. Information-processing models abound with such primitive components, and numerous experiments have attempted to study these components in isolation.

The relevance of all this is that we think an information-processing analysis is the best one around for conceptualizing reading. Our main reason for thinking so stems from a consideration of causality. Take an example involving eye movements. Any analysis of reading into subskills might hit on brief eye fixations as a component of fluent reading. This discovery could lead educators to try to improve reading skills by training students to have brief eye fixations while reading. The folly of this stems from the lack of concern about the causal status of eye fixations in skilled reading. The duration of a fixation has long been known to be partly determined by how long it takes the reader to extract and interpret the input information (e.g., Tinker, 1958). Cutting down the time allowed for these processes is unlikely to help anyone who is slow on these processes to begin with. This does not mean that the study of eye movements is useless for analyzing reading; instead, eye movements must be studied within the context of an information-processing analysis (see Shebilske, 1975, for a nice example of such a study). Our next step, then, is an outline of an information-processing model of reading. Models of this type, when fully developed, should give us good ideas as to the tasks on which training will transfer to reading.

A Partial Model of Skilled Reading

There are numerous information-processing models of reading (see, e.g., Massaro, 1975), but none of these are perfectly suited for our purposes. We need a rather general model so that we can remain open on the critical substantive issues. Figure 3.1 illustrates such a proposal.

The model, derived from Kleiman (1975), is not intended as a complete description of reading. Instead, it consists of some of the component processes that must be included in any information-processing model of reading. We mention some of the missing components as we go along. What the model is supposed to do is: (1) provide a means of organizing some of what we know about skilled reading; (2) give us a way of raising critical questions about reading and make it possible to draw some distinctions among possible answers to these questions; and (3) force us to think about specific issues in word recognition in the context of reading as a whole. (In what follows, it is important to note that this is a model of skilled, that is, college-level, reading and that most of the empirical work we discuss used college students as subjects.)

The input to the model is written text. We know that the eyes make contact with the text in successive fixations. However, to keep things from getting too complex, we will ignore eye movements and fixation span. We will simply assume that the eyes are always in position to provide a visual pattern that serves as the input to the first stage in our model.

The first process involves getting a description of the input. In line with almost all recent work on this issue, we assume this description is in terms of distinctive features, although there must also be some mention of the structural relations between features (see, e.g., Reed, 1973). The exact nature of the features involved remains an open question. Clearly, some features will

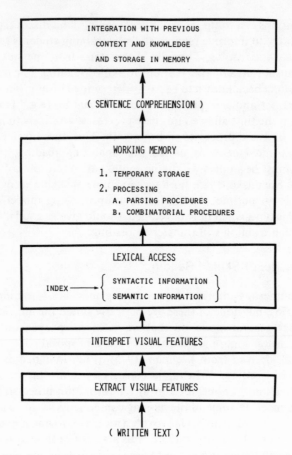

FIG. 3.1.   An information-processing model of skilled reading.

distinguish between letters, such as the horizontal line that discriminates *G* from *C*. Other features may pertain to letter groups or spelling patterns, such as the interletter spacing that distinguishes *th* from *sh*. Still other features may be characteristic of whole words, such as the length of a word or the pattern of ascending and descending letters within it. Although this issue of features is clearly of fundamental importance to reading, we have little new to say about it, and we do not pursue it further.

Next the reader must interpret the featural information. A featural description can be said to be interpreted when it has been matched or assigned to some stored category. That is, we think of the reader as having a set of preexistent categories corresponding to different letters, different spelling patterns, different syllables, and different words. Since several levels of categorization are possible, a crucial question arises: What is the usual level of interpretation for skilled readers—individual letters, spelling patterns, syllables, or words? Or, to use the terminology of Smith and Spoehr (1974), what is the functional unit of interpretation? This question seems potentially relevant to reading instruction, for problems in reading could be associated with inappropriate units of interpretation. (Later we treat this unit question and related issues at length.)

The next stage in our model is lexical access. The lexicon is like an internal dictionary that stores information about individual words and other units of meaning. Lexical access is simply the retrieval from memory of this information. As shown in Fig. 3.1, we divide each lexical entry into two parts, the lexical index and the lexical information. The index must be located for lexical access to occur, and consequently these indexes must be organized in some way so that the proper one can be located efficiently. (This is analogous to the words in a real dictionary being organized alphabetically.) The index leads to the lexical information, which consists of both syntactic and semantic information.

There are several critical questions that arise in relation to the lexical access stage. One is: What is the nature of semantic representations in the lexicon? This question is clearly relevant to listening as well as to reading, and consequently we do not dwell on this issue here. (See Clark and Clark, 1977, Chapters 11 to 13, and E. E. Smith, 1978, for recent reviews of this issue.)

Another important question is: What is the nature of lexical indexes and how are they organized? As our model now stands, this question is closely tied to the issue of the functional unit of interpretation. For example, if the lexicon is organized by the individual letters of each word (as in a real dictionary), then individual letters must be the output of the interpretation stage. If the lexicon is organized as a syllabary, then syllables must be the output of interpretation. However, we are open to the possibility that the output of the interpretation stage does not directly provide the input to the lexical access stage, but rather that it must undergo some transformation first. For example, it is possible that lexical indexes are specified in terms of the sounds of words rather than the orthography. This would require a conversion to a speech code before lexical access could occur, and therefore an additional stage would be needed in our model. We return to the nature of lexical indexes in a subsequent section.

Returning to Fig. 3.1, the reader is now at the stage of working memory, which includes all the processing mechanisms the reader needs to comprehend a sentence once he or she has the requisite syntactic and semantic information about individual words. But why do we call it working memory? Because we believe these comprehension procedures are carried out in a limited-capacity system that both performs computations and stores material on a temporary basis (see Baddeley & Hitch, 1974). Clearly, some sort of temporary storage is required. For example, in comprehending a sentence such as *The boy who has red hair and doesn't like school went fishing*, the reader must store the noun phrase *the boy* while processing the relative clause, and then hook up the stored noun phrase with the action described in the verb phrase *went fishing*.

As for the processes involved in this stage, there must be at least two different types. First, there are syntactically based parsing operations that divide a sentence into its grammatical constituents. We have in mind something like a standard phrase–structure analysis. These parsing operations are also useful in determining the function of each constituent, either a grammatical function such as subject and object or a more semantically based function such as agent and recipient. It is these parsing operations that allow the reader to comprehend the difference between *The dog bit the man* and *The man bit the dog*, as well as the similarity between *The dog bit the man* and *The man was bitten by the dog*. Second, there are semantically based processes that allow the reader to combine the meanings of individual words into larger meaning units such as clauses and sentences. These combinatorial procedures must be capable of selecting out particular meanings of words in the context of other words, as when we interpret the container to be something like a bottle in *The container held the drink* but something like a basket in *The container held the apples* (Anderson & Ortony, 1975). In any event, parsing and combinatorial processes together yield a representation of a clause or sentence—the output of the working memory stage.

The questions that arise about this stage form the core of most contemporary work in psycholinguistics. Thus, psycholinguists are concerned with the nature of: (1) parsing devices (e.g., strategies, as in Bever, 1970, or algorithms, as in Kaplan, 1973); (2) semantic combination rules (e.g., Katz & Fodor, 1963); and (3) the final representation of a sentence (e.g., Anderson & Bower, 1973; Clark & Clark, 1977; Norman & Rumelhart, 1975). Obviously, these questions are relevant to listening as well as to reading, and we again plead for a division of labor because we are primarily interested in the initial stages of the reading model. There is, however, one question about the working memory stage that is relevant to the initial stages: Can the result of this stage—a larger meaning unit—in some sense feed back to earlier stages of processing? That is, can the interpretation or lexical access of words be facilitated by semantic context? This is one of the most fascinating issues in current research, and we later spend some time considering it.

The final stage of the model integrates the semantic representation of a clause or sentence with the previous context and with other knowledge stored in long-term memory. Such integration is presumably the goal of most reading. Again, the issues involved are basic to all psycholinguistic skills (see, e.g., Kintsch & van Dijk, 1975; Rumelhart, 1975), and again we do not pursue them in this chapter.

Relevant Issues

In our discussion of the model, we noted three critical issues about word recognition that we intend to deal with at length. These are: (1) the units of interpretation; (2) the nature of lexical indexes; and (3) the possible influence of syntactic and semantic context on word recognition. The next three sections deal with these issues in turn.

Before turning to them, however, there is one more issue that must be confronted. Our model characterizes reading as a sequential progression through various stages of processing. The information starts as features, is converted to interpreted visual patterns, then to lexical indexes, next to syntactic and semantic representations of individual words, then to an integrated semantic representation, and finally becomes part of one's general stored knowledge. Such sequential processing is the way of most reading models, in fact of most information-processing models in general. But there is an alternative. What we have called stages can be thought of as various sources of information about the input, and some of these might operate simultaneously and interactively (as suggested by Norman & Bobrow, 1976). Consider an example. Suppose the reader initially extracts only a few features and forms a tentative interpretation on this basis. Then the reader attempts to access the lexicon by means of this tentative interpretation and simultaneously checks the input information further for features that would confirm the tentative interpretation. Now the stages of feature extraction, interpretation, and lexical access are all going on simultaneously. Furthermore, there is an interaction between the first two stages because the tentative outcome of interpretation is directing the future course of feature extraction. We could complicate this still further by also permitting lexical access and semantic representations to be tentative and to feedback to earlier stages. In this way, we would eventually arrive at a situation where all stages operate simultaneously and interactively.

This example essentially modifies the model in Fig. 3.1 by allowing information to flow from higher level stages to lower level ones. This is known as top-down processing, whereas information flow from lower to higher levels is called bottom-up processing. Using this terminology, the issue we are concerned with is whether reading consists entirely of bottom-up processes or whether top-down processes also play a role. This strikes us as one of the most important questions that one could raise about skilled reading (Don Norman has been raising it for years), but we do not think it can be given a global yes or no answer. Instead, for each stage or source of information one must ask whether specific higher level sources affect it. Only if the answer is "no" in each case (a most unlikely event) can the model in Fig. 3.1 remain unchanged. The top-down issue is considered further in the following sections.

UNITS OF INTERPRETATION
AND RELATED ISSUES

In the past decade there has probably been more experimental research on the perception of letter strings than on any other topic that relates to reading. A good amount of this research has dealt with the effects of structural factors (such as orthographic regularity and lexical status) on the perceptibility of letter strings. The major results that have emerged have substantially altered the way psychologists think about the interpretation stage of reading. These results indicate that certain structural factors, once thought to influence reading only at later stages, have their effect as early as the interpretation stage. In what follows we first present some of the findings of interest and then consider some theoretical explanations of the results. (The following literature review is quite selective; for fuller discussions see the recent reviews by Henderson, 1977, and Kreuger, 1975.)

Critical Findings

Some Background. The precursor of the recent research on structural factors is Reicher's (1969) rediscovery that an adult reader can perceive a word more accurately than an unstructured letter string. We call it a rediscovery because much the same thing had been demonstrated by Cattell (1886) more than eighty years earlier. Cattell found that when a letter string was presented tachistoscopically, subjects could accurately report more of the string when it formed a word than when it consisted of unrelated letters. Cattell, however, always required his subjects to report the entire item, making it possible that the word superiority effect was really due to memory or response factors. For example, words and unstructured letter strings may have been equal in their perceptibility, but subjects may have had a bias to report words in those cases where they did not extract sufficient information from the tachistoscopic presentation. To rule out such possibilities, some methodological refinements were needed, which is exactly what the Reicher study supplied.

In Reicher's paradigm (1969), a tachistoscopic presentation of a letter string—be it a word or a set of unrelated letters—was immediately followed by a two-alternative, forced-choice test of one of the letter positions. An illustration should be helpful. On one trial a subject might be presented the word *READ* followed by the alternatives *R* and *H* above and below the position of the first letter; the subject's task was to decide which of the two alternatives had occurred in the string. On another trial, a subject might be presented the unstructured string *RDAE*, again followed by the alternatives *R* and *H* above and below the position of the first letter; and again the subject would have to decide which of the two alternatives had been presented. This paradigm, called probe recognition, effectively eliminates any report bias favoring words, because when a word is presented both alternatives form words, and when a nonword is presented both alternatives form nonwords. With this more precise methodology, Reicher was able to reproduce Cattell's superiority of words, with the implication that words had an advantage over unstructured nonwords at a very early stage in reading. A host of subsequent studies using comparable paradigms have documented this basic effect. Reicher's study was thus important not only for the results it produced but also for the methodology it introduced. We do not dwell on methodology in what follows, but you may rest assured that any finding we present has been established (at least once) in a paradigm as pure as Reicher's probe-recognition task.

Finding that words are more perceptible than unstructured nonwords was the first step. The next was to ask what mediated this effect. Was it that words conform to English orthography whereas unstructured nonwords do not, or that words per se have some privileged status in the interpretation stage? Baron and Thurston (1973) and Manelis (1974) were among the first to explicitly raise these issues, and we now have some idea of the contributions of orthography and "wordness" in the perception of letter strings.

Orthographic Effects. Perhaps the best way to demonstrate that conformity to orthographic rules facilitates perception is to vary the orthographic regularity of nonwords and show that regular nonwords are better perceived than irregular ones. In this way, orthographic effects can be studied in isolation. For example, *BLOST* conforms perfectly to orthographic rules, *STOBL* less so, and *TSXBL* not at all. If orthographic regularity facilitates perception, then *BLOST* should be perceived the best of the three and *TSXBL* the worst.

Numerous experiments have used this strategy, and they consistently show that the perceptibility of a letter string increases with its orthographic regularity (e.g., Baron & Thurston, 1973; Gibson, Pick, Osser, & Hammond, 1962; Spoehr & Smith, 1975). Furthermore, at least some of these studies have shown that the structure effect was not mediated by the simple frequency with which letter groups appear (e.g., Spoehr & Smith, 1975), suggesting that the effect was due to the reader's knowledge of orthographic structure.

Wordness Effect. We now want to consider if any of Reicher's word-superiority effect was due to wordness per se. That is, are words more perceptible than nonwords that are equally structured? For example, is *BLAST* easier to perceive than *BLOST*? Several experiments have addressed this question, and the more recent ones leave no doubt that words have a perceptual advantage over comparable nonwords (Juola, Leavitt, & Choe, 1974; Kroll, 1974; Manelis, 1974; McClelland, 1976). So wordness joins orthographic regularity on the list of factors that can facilitate the perception of letter strings. That two distinct factors are involved has been shown by Kroll (1974), who demonstrated that some experimental variables (such as whether a block of trials contained items of the same structural type) affected the magnitude of the orthographic effect but left the wordness effect unchanged.[1]

The Word–Letter Effect.   In addition to a difference between words and nonwords, Reicher's (1969) report also contained another interesting result: Words were better perceived than were individual letters. This effect is of considerable importance to anyone interested in reading, for it argues strongly against a letter-by-letter approach [as Brewer (1972) pointed out in his criticism of Gough's (1972) controversial letter-by-letter model]. The word–letter effect has now been demonstrated in numerous sophisticated paradigms (Estes, 1975; Johnson, 1975; Johnston & McClelland, 1973; Wheeler, 1970), although there is still some uncertainty about the conditions needed to produce it (Johnston & McClelland, 1973; Mezrich, 1973).

We have classified the word–letter effect separately from the preceding factors because of our uncertainty about what causes it. It seems unlikely that the word–letter difference can be reduced to a wordness factor; *A* and *I* are words as well as letters, yet both can be better perceived when embedded in a word than when presented alone (Wheeler, 1970). It is possible that the effect is somehow due to orthographic structure, but this is difficult to determine without a complete list of orthographic rules.

Task Factors.   Thus far we have considered only structural or stimulus effects. It turns out, however, that all these effects may depend on the reader's trying to interpret letter strings at the level of letter groups and words. When readers are given a task that induces them to interpret letter strings at the level of features, all our structural effects simply disappear (Estes, 1975).

Let us illustrate this interaction of task and structure. Thompson and Massaro (1973) studied the word–letter effect in a paradigm in which the four words *APE, ARE, ADE,* and *ACE* and the four letters *P, R, D,* and *C* were repeated hundreds of times. Thus, the only thing that really varied was whether a *P, D, R,* or *C* occurred, alone or in a word, and subjects were aware of this. Under these circumstances, it seems likely that subjects restricted their interpretations to the features of the critical letters, and sure enough, there was no longer any difference between the perceptibility of words and letters.

---

[1]The fact that wordness facilitates perception suggests a further possibility. Perhaps the accessibility or frequency of a word also has an effect, such that more frequent words are more perceptible than less frequent ones. Recent studies, however, have yielded little support for this suggestion (see in particular Manelis, 1974; see also Theios & Muise, 1977).

In like manner, the difference between words and unstructured nonwords can also be eliminated (e.g., Bjork & Estes, 1973; Massaro, 1973).

We think that this set of studies has something important to say about the nature of skilled reading. Readers seem to have remarkable flexibility, even in some of the initial stages of the reading process. Specifically, readers seem capable of varying their level of interpretation so as to fit task demands. We also know from other sources that the later stages of reading are characterized by flexibility (e.g., Mistler–Lachman, 1972). In fact, the only stage of the reading process that does not seem to be very amenable to change is the first one, feature extraction (see, e.g., Shiffrin & Geisler, (1973). The general picture of a skilled reader that emerges is of one who can readily alter most of his or her processing to fit the situation.

Theoretical Explanations

Overview.   We know, then, that orthographic regularity and wordness can facilitate perception, that words are even more perceptible than their constituent letters, and that all three of these effects arise whenever the reader is operating at a level higher than that of letter analysis. The problem is how to account for these effects in the context of the general model we presented earlier.

There has been no shortage of explanations to account for some of the effects we described, but it is not our intention to review all proposed explanations. (For an attempt to do so, see Smith and Spoehr, 1974.) Instead, we focus on one class of explanations that seems to us quite promising. The type we have in mind assumes that the effects of interest are all due to the reader's interpreting letter strings in terms of multiletter units. Thus, whereas any letter string can always be interpreted in terms of single-letter units, structured nonwords can also be interpreted in terms of letter–group units, and words can further be interpreted in terms of word units. This idea derives from Frank Smith's (1971) conception of reading. However, we will have to go beyond Smith's theory, for his work was done before some of the findings of interest had been discovered. What we will do, therefore, is combine some of Smith's ideas with recent notions of LaBerge and Samuels (1974), Estes (1975), and Travers (1974) and sketch a detailed account of the interpretation stage. Our sketch should be treated as a kind of modal model for the class of current explanations that emphasize multiletter units of interpretation.

The Modal Model.   Figure 3.2 contains our account of the interpretation stage. It is an attempt to fill in some of the missing details in the interpretation stage of the general model we presented earlier. (To emphasize this, the feature extraction and lexical access stages are also indicated in the figure.)

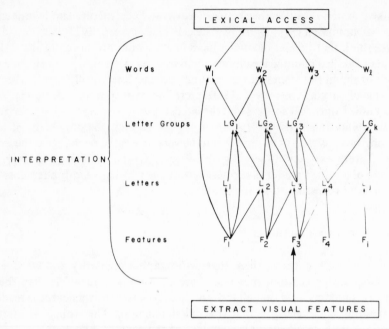

FIG. 3.2.   A multiunit model of the interpretation stage.

The modal model posits four distinct levels or units of interpretation, features (symbolized as F_i), letters (L_j), letter groups (LG_k), and words (W_1). Each unit has only one function: to detect the visual information that defines it. Let's take some examples. A possible feature unit might be defined by an upright line, and it would be activated whenever such a line was detected in the input. A possible letter unit could correspond to *B*, and it would be activated whenever all the feature units that define it are activated. A letter–group unit might be *BL*, and it would be triggered by either the feature units or the letter units that define it. Finally, a possible word unit could be *BLAST*, and it would be activated by its defining feature units, letter units, or letter–group units.

Notice that in the above examples, information may flow in one of two ways. First, information may move sequentially through the hierarchy of units, with feature units activating letter units, which in turn trigger letter–group units, which then activate word units. Thus, the activation of letter groups and words is mediated by the prior activation of letter units. Such mediated activation is found in the recent models of Estes (1975), LaBerge and Samuels (1974), and Massaro (1975). Second, information may flow directly between units that differ by more than one level. Thus, feature units may directly activate letter–group or word units, and similarly, letter units may directly trigger units corresponding to words. Here we have cases of nonmediated action, an idea borrowed from F. Smith (1971) that is also part of the LaBerge and Samuels (1974) model. Both types of information flow presumably go on concurrently, and whenever activation of some unit passes a critical level, that unit becomes a possible interpretation of the input or of part of the input.

There is one more critical assumption. Following Estes (1975), we assume that the actual task a subject is asked to perform (including the instructions) presets certain levels of units and that activation at these levels will ultimately determine the subject's responses in the task. A task in which the subject need only discriminate among a few alternative letters would presumably lead to presetting of the feature or letter level, whereas one that requires the subject to perceive many different structured patterns would supposedly lead to presetting the letter–group or word level.

This model appears to be consistent with all the findings we mentioned earlier. Let's start with the orthography effect. To keep things simple, just consider why a regular consonant cluster—initial TH—is more perceptible than an irregular one—initial HT—when the subject is preset to interpret letter strings at one of the higher levels. Our model offers two reasons for this difference, and both follow from the notion that TH is probably one of the reader's letter–group units. First, when the information flow is sequential or mediated, the activation will terminate at the TH unit for the regular consonant cluster but at the H and T units for the irregular cluster. Thus, information about the order of the two letters will be available for the regular cluster but not for the irregular one (Estes, 1975). Second, when information flows directly from features to letter groups, both features and letter units may activate TH, whereas only features can activate the H and T units that define HT. Thus, TH will be more perceptible than HT because the former has more sources of activation. (It should also be noted that the features that define letter groups such as TH may be redundant, and consequently fewer features may be needed to activate the TH unit than to trigger either the T or H unit.) These same two reasons will also account for more complex cases of the orthographic effect; all that must be assumed is that orthographically regular strings are more likely to contain letter groups that correspond to existent units than do irregular strings.

The wordness effect is explained in similar fashion. This effect would be due to the role of word units in the interpretation stage. The existence of such units means that any string that forms a word will have access to an additional interpretation unit than will a comparable nonword. Hence, the two reasons we just discussed can be invoked again, this time to explain the perceptual superiority of words over comparably structured nonwords. The same type of explanation also holds for the word-letter effect. In the word–letter effect word stimuli have access to letter–group and word units, as well as to letter units, whereas individual letter stimuli must suffice with only letter units.

Finally, because all our explanations depend on the activation of letter–group and word units, it follows that the effects in question should disappear when the subject is preset to respond at the feature level.

Issues.   In formulating the foregoing model we have been forced to take a stance on three major issues. Let us spell them out so that one can get an idea of what some alternative formulations might look like.

The first issue concerns the distinction between mediated and nonmediated processes in the interpretation of letter strings. In the modal model we allow both types of processes; the reader can either go through letters on the way to words or move directly from features to words. In making this assumption, we line up with LaBerge and Samuels (1974) and F. Smith (1971), who also permit nonmediated processing. However, other formulations are possible; both Estes (1975) and Massaro (1975) have proposed viable models that permit only mediated processing. Consider in particular the Estes formulation. It looks very much like the one in Fig. 3.2, except that information can flow only sequentially. The orthographic and word–letter effects arise because structured nonwords and words eventually gain access to multiletter units that supply positional information. Thus, this model holds that all the beneficial effects of structure on letter-string perception are due to the reader's gain in information about the order of letters and not to any gain in information about the identity of letters.

A second issue is one we mentioned earlier: top-down versus bottom-up processing. The modal model invokes only bottom-up processes, and this is true of most current models of word perception. However, it may well be possible to construct a model that uses top-down processes to account for the structural effects we are concerned with. Although few detailed accounts of this kind of model have been published, there are some leads in the literature. One of Wheeler's (1970) explanations of the word–letter effect involved a top-down process. When a word is presented, some of the features extracted may lead to a few tentative interpretations of the input. These can be used to access the lexicon and arrive at a set of lexical candidates, which in turn direct subsequent feature extraction so as to maximize discrimination among the lexical candidates. When a single letter is presented, no such top-down process can be used. Hence, single letters will not be perceived as well as words. A similar explanation could be devised for the wordness effect.

What is the likelihood that theorists will be able to model the interpretation stage without recourse to top-down processes? Very low, we think. For although we were able to get by without such processes in the modal model, we were concerned only with structural effects. When we turn to the effects of syntactic and semantic context in a later section of this chapter, we are forced to consider some top-down processes.

The last issue of interest is one we have not mentioned before. Our modal model, as do many others, assumes that the reader's orthographic knowledge is built into the units of interpretation rather than being in the actual use of rules. But things could be otherwise. For example, in Massaro's (1975) model, readers presumably make dynamic use of a set of orthographic rules to aid their interpretations. This issue of fixed units versus dynamic rules has been raised by Baron (1976) and Massaro (1975), and we think it an important one for theoretical and instructional approaches to reading.

One way to get some insights into this issue is to consider some related work. We are concerned with how skilled readers perceive familiar inputs; Chase and Simon (1973) have tackled an equivalent problem in chess. They asked what it is that a chess master knows that allows him or her to perceive a regular chess pattern better than an irregular one. Their research suggests that this ability is mediated by units corresponding to regular chess patterns rather than by the dynamic application of rules that generate permissible patterns. This theory raises the credibility of the unit approach to word perception. We get a different message, however, if we look at the research on speech perception. Consider the finding that adult speakers can perceive a string of words better if it follows the syntactic structure of English (e.g., Miller & Isard, 1963). No one has ever seriously suggested that such mastery depends on fixed units, because there are just too many units involved. Instead, mastery in this case presumably depends on the dynamic application of rules. What kinds of rules, however, is another matter. Many researchers now believe that the rules are really heuristic strategies and not algorithms (e.g., Bever, 1970; Clark & Clark, 1977, Chapter 5). It thus seems that there are successful precedents for taking either a unit or a rule approach to the use of orthographic structure in reading, although if one favors the latter it might prove profitable to look at heuristic strategies.

One final point about the matter of units versus rules: It may be that people use both units and rules, although some rely more on units whereas others depend more on rules. Baron and Strawson (1976) have proposed such an individual difference in reading strategy and have offered some nice experimental support for it. This kind of individual difference should be of interest to reading researchers because it carries with it the suggestion that there is more than one way to internalize the orthography.

LEXICAL INDEXES

Overview

In our general model, the interpretation and lexical access stages are closely interrelated, with the output from the former serving as the input to the latter. However, as mentioned earlier, it may be the case that the output of interpretation is not in the proper format to be used as an input to the lexicon; some sort of transformation may first be necessary. To determine whether such a transformation is necessary, we consider what is known about the nature of lexical indexes. Two possibilities are considered. One is that lexical indexes are represented in some sort of speech code. This would require the addition of a speech-recoding stage between interpretation and lexical access. The second possibility is that lexical indexes are represented in an orthographic code. If this is the case, the output of interpretation can directly provide the input to lexical access.

Before looking at the experimental evidence, we would like to be certain that there is no confusion on one important point. The view that speech recoding is unnecessary for lexical access does not imply that it is also unnecessary for later stages in the reading process. For example, it may be essential to recode words to speech prior to the working memory stage because the temporary store needed during this stage might hold more speech symbols than orthographic ones (Kleiman, 1975). Because we are focusing on the early stages of the reading process, we do not consider the evidence in regard to this possibility. Instead, we consider only evidence from experimental tasks that we believe tap the lexical access stage, that is, those studies that require subjects to retrieve information about individual words.

Critical Findings

There is more relevant literature than can be reviewed here, so we are selective. (For a more detailed review, see Kleiman, 1975.) There is a set of studies that has been interpreted as showing that speech recoding occurs before lexical access in skilled reading. In one such study, Rubenstein, Lewis, and Rubenstein (1971) found that when subjects are asked to decide if a visually presented string of letters forms a word (a lexical decision task), reaction time is affected by the phonemic properties of the letter string. For instance, nonwords that would be pronounced like English words (e.g., *brume*) take longer to reject than other pronounceable nonwords. Rubenstein et al. interpreted this finding as showing that speech recoding occurs before lexical access. Meyer, Schvaneveldt, and Ruddy (1974a) came to the same conclusion on the basis of experiments showing that reaction time to decide that two strings of visually presented letters both form words is affected by the phonemic similarity of the words, even when orthographic similarity is controlled. For example, subjects could decide about two phonemically similar words (e.g., *bribe-tribe*) faster than two phonemically dissimilar words (e.g., *couch-touch*).

We do not find these experiments convincing. Often there is a crucial problem in that the manipulated phonemic variables may be confounded with orthographic variables (Gibson, Schurcliff, & Yonas, 1970; Meyer & Ruddy, 1973). Also, some of these studies may have biased subjects toward using a recoding strategy. [See Kleinman (1975) for further discussion of why these experiments are not convincing.] We do not doubt that skilled readers can recode written words to their spoken equivalents and will do so under certain circumstances. The more interesting question is whether they are capable of lexical access without recoding. In the next few paragraphs we describe several studies that convince us that lexical access without recoding is feasible. It is interesting to notice that the studies supporting recoding generally use tasks that subjects can do without retrieving the meanings of the words, whereas those that show that recoding is not necessary use tasks requiring the use of word meanings.

Baron (1973) reported two experiments of interest. In one he timed subjects while they decided whether short written phrases made sense. The crucial comparison was between two types of phrases that did not make sense when read: those that would have made sense if pronounced (e.g., *peace of pie, my knew car*), and those that would not (e.g., *pie pod, our no car*). If subjects recoded to speech before deciding whether the phrase made sense, they should take longer on the *peace of pie* phrases because they would have to check the spelling in addition to the sound. The results showed, however, there was no difference in the time needed to decide about the two types of phrases, although there was a significant difference in error rates. In his second experiment, Baron asked subjects to decide if the written phrases would sound sensible if pronounced. Here the crucial comparison was between two types of phrases that sounded sensible: those that were also sensible when read (e.g., *peace treaty*) and those that were not (e.g., *peace of pie*). If recoding to speech always occurs before the decision, the time to decide about these two types of phrases should be equal. In fact, phrases like *peace of pie* took longer to decide on. Therefore, it seems that recoding to speech is not necessary.

Kleiman (1975) has also shown that college readers can retrieve information about individual words without speech recoding. Subjects were timed while they made three different decisions about pairs of visually presented words. For some pairs, subjects decided whether the two words were spelled alike after the first letter. The words never sounded alike (e.g., *lemon* and *demon* are spelled alike), so that subjects had to make this decision on the basis of visual information. For other pairs, subjects decided whether the two words rhymed. In both the rhyming and nonrhyming pairs, the words were spelled alike (e.g., *blame–flame* vs. *lemon–demon*), thereby forcing subjects to recode to speech before making their decisions. For the remaining pairs, subjects decided whether the words were synonyms. Because this task requires information about the meaning of individual words, it was assumed to tap the processes of lexical access. Each subject performed the spelling, rhyming, and synonymy decisions both with and without a concurrent interference task. This task consisted of repeating digits that were presented rapidly, and it was designed to disrupt recoding to speech. The measure of interest was the effect of this interference task on the three decisions. Because the spelling decision does not require recoding, it should not show a large interference effect. Because the rhyming decision required recoding, it should show a large interference effect. What about the synonymy decision? If recoding is required, this decision should show a large interference effect, comparable to that on the rhyming decision. If the synonymy decision does not require recoding, it should show a small interference effect, comparable to that on the spelling decision. The results clearly support this second prediction—both the spelling and synonymy decisions show a small interference effect, whereas the rhyming decision shows a much larger one.

The issue we have been discussing bears some relationship to the classic debate on the phonics method versus the sight method in teaching reading. However, we doubt that any implications for teaching can be drawn directly from our conclusion that speech recoding is not necessary before lexical access in skilled reading. It seems quite possible that although skilled readers may not use recoding, teaching a recoding strategy could be a good beginning. One reason implications cannot be drawn directly from studies of skilled reading to methods of teaching reading is that the child's lexicon might be organized differently from that of the adult's. Chomsky (1970) suggested that the child's lexicon is organized phonetically and that with development it is reorganized to code the similarities in meanings of related words. For example, *courage* and *courageous* may be totally separate lexical entries for the child, but both may be derived from a single lexical entry for the adult. Chomsky's proposal is very speculative at this point, so we do not wish to push it too far. However, the possibility of fundamental differences between children's and adults' linguistic knowledge must be considered before drawing implications for instructional procedures from studies of skilled readers.

CONTEXT EFFECTS IN THE INITIAL PROCESSES OF READING

So far our discussion of the processes involved in reading has been almost entirely bottom-up. In this section we look more closely at the need to include top-down processing in our model of reading. More specifically, we consider the effects of preceding syntactic and semantic context on word perception, where these effects seem to arise because of a top-down process. The psychological literature contains quite a few demonstrations of such context effects. Some of these (e.g., Goodman, 1969; Kolers, 1970) show that certain types of errors common in oral reading can be accounted for only if previous context is considered. This is true even with oral reading in the first grade (Weber, 1970). Other studies have demonstrated that the size of the perceptual span or effective visual field depends partly on characteristics of the preceding context (Marcel, 1974). However, our model of reading does not address either oral reading or the perceptual span. We once again plead a division of labor and limit our discussion to the effects of context on the extraction, interpretation, and lexical access stages.

Let us first look at two representative experiments that demonstrate a facilitating effect of context on processing individual words. One of these is by Morton (1964), who measured the threshold to recognize a word presented alone and compared it to the threshold for the same word presented after a context. His results showed that context reduces recognition threshold, and the amount the threshold is reduced depends on how highly expected the word is when the context is given. For example, the context *The cup was placed on the* --- reduces the thes\hold for *table* a great deal because *table* is highly expected. The same context also reduces the threshold for *saucer*, but not as much because *saucer* is not as highly expected. Notice that this reduction is of the mean threshold for sets of subjects, so that it is possible that the effect is specific to the one most expected word but that this word differs for different subjects.

The second experiment is by Meyer, Schvaneveldt, and Ruddy (1974b), who measured reaction time while subjects determined if strings of letters formed words. Each trial consisted of two successive decisions, with the second letter string presented immediately after the first decision. We need only consider the cases in which both strings of letters formed words. Meyer et al. varied the semantic relationship between the two words so that for some trials they were highly related (e.g., *bread–butter, doctor–nurse*), whereas for others they were unrelated (*bread–nurse, doctor–butter*). The finding of interest is that reaction time for the second word is less when it is semantically related to the first than when it is not. That is, context of a semantically related word facilitates the decision.

Both of these studies show a context effect on the early stages of the reading process, and other studies document the consistency of this effect (e.g., Meyer & Schvaneveldt, 1971; Tulving & Gold, 1963; Tulving, Mandler, & Baumal, 1964). The issue is how to account for these results. There is some agreement on the broad outlines of an explanation. A preceding context, such as *The cup was placed on the* _____, somehow activates the meaning(s) of the possible next word, and this activated meaning then provides another source of information to be used during the recognition of the next word. A glance at Fig. 3.1 will show that we are now talking about information from the higher stages combining with information from the lower stages. This is top-down processing par excellence, and it seems to be a useful starting point for thinking about the context effect.

Beyond this outline, there is little agreement on how context works. Roughly, there are two types of theories of the context effect, corresponding to what researchers have called passive and active models. The passive models are probably the better developed, and these include the theories of Collins and Loftus (1975), Morton (1969), and Schvaneveldt and Meyer (1973). Let's take the Schvaneveldt and Meyer formulation as an example of this class. Consider first the case in which only two words are involved, with one being the context word and the other the test word. When the context word is recognized, its lexical representation will be activated, and this activation then spreads to the lexical representations of related words. If the test word is one of these, it will be partially activated and so require less processing at the lower levels. Hence, the beneficial effect of context on early processing. In the more interesting case in which the context involves an entire phrase, the phrase would now become the source of activation, and this activation would presumably spread to all words semantically related to the phrase as a whole.

In contrast, active models (e.g., Norman & Bobrow, 1976) assume that context plays a more selective role. In active models context supposedly sets up some specific lexical or semantic expectancies that then selectively guide processing at the lower levels. For example, the expectancy of a particular lexical item might lead to a selective examination of features that would tend to confirm it. This is quite similar to the top–down interpretations we have mentioned earlier.

One essential difference between passive and active models thus concerns the range of words whose perception can be facilitated by a particular context. For passive models this range includes all words semantically related to the context, whereas for active models this range is restricted to a few specific expectancies. Another difference between the two types of models concerns the interaction between contextual and perceptual information. In a passive model, both sources of information simply feed into a common point (say, the lexical representation of a word), and in no way does the contextual information directly affect the quality or quantity of perceptual information. That is why it is called *passive*. In an active model, the context can actually determine what perceptual information the reader should look for.

What does all this have to do with reading instruction? Unfortunately, at the present time, very little. We do not see any possibility of instructional hints being derived from the work that is currently available, chiefly because so little experimental work has been done. We have included this section because we expect a great deal of attention to be directed to the effects of context in the next few years. More detailed information on how skilled readers use context should then provide hints as to what we should try to teach children about the use of context in reading words.

SUMMARY

We began by arguing for an information-processing approach to reading. We then proposed a general information-processing model for adult, skilled reading that includes the stages of feature extraction, interpretation, lexical access, working memory, and integration. Of these stages, we focused on interpretation and lexical access and discussed some of the issues that have arisen in the study of these stages, namely, units of interpretation, speech recoding and lexical indexes, and context effects. In the course of our discussion, we were able to fill in some of the details about the mechanisms underlying these stages, but of course much remains to be done.

Throughout the chapter, we noted areas of research that had potential implications for instruction. These included units of interpretation, the use of orthographic units versus orthographic rules, and the involvement of speech recoding in lexical access. However, we could do little in the way of drawing any firm instructional implications because we lacked the developmental findings that could bridge the gap between knowledge about adult reading and the requirements of an instructional program. Such developmental research must become a high-priority item for those who desire to link theory to practice.

ACKNOWLEDGMENTS

This research was supported by the U.S. Public Health Service Grant MH-19705. Glenn M. Kleiman is now at the University of Illinois at Urbana–Champaign.

REFERENCES

Anderson, J. R., & Bower, G. H. *Human associative memory.* Washington, D.C.: Winston, 1973.

Anderson, R. C., & Ortony, A. On putting apples into bottles: A problem of polysemy. *Cognitive Psychology,* 1975, *7,* 167–180.

Baddeley, A. D., & Hitch, G. Working memory. In G. H. Bower (Ed.), *The psychology of learning and motivation* (Vol. 8). New York: Academic Press, 1974.

Baron, J. Phonemic stage not necessary for reading. *Quarterly Journal of Experimental Psychology,* 1973, *25,* 241–246.

Baron J., & Strawson C. Use of orthographic and word-specific knowledge in reading words aloud. *Journal of Experimental Psychology: Human Perception and Performance,* 1976, *2,* 386–393.

Baron, J., & Thurston, I. An analysis of the word-superiority effect. *Cognitive Psychology,* 1973, *4,* 207–228.

Bever, T. G. The cognitive basis for linguistic structure. In J. R. Hayes (Ed.), *Cognition and the development of language.* New York: Wiley, 1970.

Bjork, E. L., & Estes, W. K. Letter identification in relation to linguistic context and masking conditions. *Memory & Cognition,* 1973, *1,* 217–223.

Brewer, W. F. Is reading a leter-by-letter process? In J. F. Kavanagh & I. G. Mattingly (Eds.), *Language by ear and by eye: The relationships between speech and reading.* Cambridge, Mass.: MIT Press, 1972.

Cattell, J. M. The time taken up by cerebral operations. *Mind,* 1886, *11,* 220–242.

Chase, W. G., & Simon, H. A. Perception in chess. *Cognitive Psychology,* 1973, *4,* 55–81.

Chomsky, C. Reading, writing and phonology. *Harvard Educational Review,* 1970, *40,* 287–309.

Clark, H. H., & Clark, E. V. *Psychology and language: An introduction to psycholinguistics.* New York: Harcourt Brace Jovanovich, 1977.

Collins, A. M., & Loftus, E. F. A spreading-activation theory of semantic processing. *Psychological Review,* 1975, *82,* 407–428.

Estes, W. K. Memory, perception, and decision in letter identification. In R. L. Solso (Ed.), *Information processing and cognition: The Loyola symposium.* Hillsdale, N.J.: Lawrence Erlbaum Associates, 1975.

Gibson, E. J., Pick, A., Osser, H., & Hammond, M. The role of grapheme-phoneme-correspondence in the perception of words. *American Journal of Psychology,* 1962, *75,* 554–570.

Gibson, E. J., Shurcliff, A., & Yonas, A. Utilization of spelling patterns of deaf and hearing subjects. In H. Levin & R. P. Williams (Eds.), *Basic studies on reading.* New York: Basic Books, 1970.

Goodman, K. S. Analysis of oral reading: Applied psycholinguistics. *Reading Research Quarterly,* 1969, *5,* 9–30.

Gough, P. B. One second of reading. In J. F. Kavanagh & I. G. Mattingly (Eds.), *Language by ear and eye: The relationships between speech and reading.* Cambridge, Mass.: MIT Press, 1972.

Henderson, L. Word recognition. In N.S. Sutherland (Ed.), *Tutorial essays in experimental psychology.* Hillsdale, N.J.: Lawrence Erlbaum Associates, 1977.

Johnson, N. F. On the function of letters in word identification: Some data and a preliminary model. *Journal of Verbal Learning and Verbal Behavior,* 1975, *14,* 17–29.

Johnston, J. C., & McClelland, J. L. Visual factors in word perception. *Perception and Psychophysics,* 1973, *14,* 365–370.

Juola, J. F., Leavitt, D. D., & Choe, C. S. Letter identification in word, nonword, and single letter displays. *Bulletin of the Psychonomic Society,* 1974, *4,* 278–280.

Kaplan, R. A general syntactic processor. In R. Rustin (Ed.), *Natural language processing.* Englewood Cliffs, N.J.: Prentice-Hall, 1973.

Katz, J. J., & Fodor, J. A. The structure of a semantic theory. *Language,* 1963, *39,* 170–210.

Kintsch, W., & van Dijk, T. A. Recalling and summarizing stories. *Language,* 1975, *40,* 98–116.

Kleiman, G. M. Speech recoding in reading. *Journal of Verbal Learning and Verbal Behavior,* 1975, *14,* 323–339.

Kolers, P. A. Three stages of reading. In H. Levin & J. P. Williams (Eds.), *Basic studies in reading.* New York: Basic Books, 1970.

Kreuger, L. E. Familiarity effects in visual information processing. *Psychological Bulletin,* 1975, *82,* 949–974.

Kroll, J. *Familiarity and expectancy in the perception of words and letter arrays.* Unpublished manuscript, Brandeis University, 1974.

LaBerge, D., & Samuels, S. J. Toward a theory of automatic information processing in reading. *Cognitive Psychology,* 1974, *6,* 293–323.

McClelland, J. L. Preliminary letter identification in the perception of words and nonwords. *Journal of Experimental Psychology: Human Perception and Performance,* 1976, *2,* 80–91.

Manelis, L. The effect of meaningfulness in tachistoscopic word perception. *Perception and Psychophysics,* 1974, *16,* 182–192.

Marcel, T. The effective visual field and the use of context in fast and slow readers of two ages. *British Journal of Psychology,* 1974, *65,* 479–492.

Masarro, D. W. Perception of letters, words, and nonwords. *Journal of Experimental Psychology,* 1973, *100,* 349–353.

Massaro, D. W. Primary and secondary recognition in reading. In D. W. Massaro (Ed.), *Understanding language: An information-processing analysis of speech perception, reading, and psycholinguistics.* New York: Academic Press, 1975.

Meyer, D. E., & Ruddy, M. G. *Lexical-memory retrieval based on graphemic and phonemic representation of printed words.* Paper presented at the meeting of the Psychonomic Society, St. Louis, November, 1973.

Meyer, D. E., & Schvaneveldt, R. W. Facilitation in recognizing pairs of words: Evidence of a dependence between retrieval operations. *Journal of Experimental Psychology,* 1971, *90,* 227–234.

Meyer, D. E., Schvaneveldt, R. W., & Ruddy, M. G. Functions of graphemic and phonemic codes in visual word-recognition. *Memory & Cognition,* 1974, *2,* 309–321. (a)

Meyer, D. E., Schvaneveldt, R. W., & Ruddy, M. G. Loci of contextual effects on visual word-recognition. In P. M. Rabbit & S. Dornic (Eds.), *Attention and performance* (Vol. V). New York: Academic Press, 1974. (b)

Mezrich, J. J. The word superiority effect in brief visual displays: Elimination by vocalization. *Perception and Psychophysics,* 1973, *13,* 45–48.

Miller, G. A., & Isard, S. Some perceptual consequences of linguistic rules. *Journal of Verbal Learning and Verbal Behavior,* 1963, *2,* 217–228.

Mistler–Lachman, J. Levels of comprehension in processing of normal and ambiguous sentences. *Journal of Verbal Learning and Verbal Behavior,* 1972, *11,* 614–623.

Morton, J. The effects of context on the visual duration threshold for words. *British Journal of Psychology,* 1964, *55,* 165–180.

Morton, J. Interaction of information in word recognition. *Psychological Review,* 1969, *76,* 165–178.

Norman, D. A., & Bobrow, D. G. On the role of active memory processes in perception and cognition. In C. N. Cofer (Ed.), *The structure of human memory.* San Francisco: Freeman, 1976.

Norman, D. A.,& Rumelhart, D. E. *Explorations in cognition.* San Francisco: Freeman, 1975.

Reed, S. K. *Psychological processes in pattern recognition.* New York: Academic Press, 1973.

Reicher, G. M. Perceptual recognition as a function of meaningfulness of stimulus material. *Journal of Experimental Psychology,* 1969, *81,* 274–280.

Rubenstein, H., Lewis, S. S., & Rubenstein, M. A. Evidence for phonemic recoding in visual word recognition. *Journal of Verbal Learning and Verbal Behavior,* 1971, *10,* 647–657.

Rumelhart, D. Notes on a schema for stories. In D. Bobrow & A. M. Collins (Eds.), *Representations and understanding: Studies in cognitive science.* New York: Academic Press, 1975.

Schvaneveldt, R. W., & Meyer, D. E. Retrieval and comparison processes in semantic memory. In S. Kornblum (Ed.), *Attention and Performance* (Vol. IV). New York: Academic Press, 1973.

Shebilske, W. Reading eye movements from an information-processing point of view. In D. W. Massaro (Ed.), *Understanding language: An information processing analysis of speech perception, reading, and psycholinguistics.* New York: Academic Press, 1975.

Shiffrin, R. M., & Geisler, W. A. Visual recognition in a theory of information processing. In R. L. Solso (Ed.), *Contemporary issues in cognitive psychology: The Loyola symposium.* Washington D. C.: Winston, 1973.

Smith, E. E. Theories of semantic memory. In W. K. Estes (Ed.), *Handbook of learning and cognitive processes* (Vol. 5). Hillsdale, N.J.: Lawrence Erlbaum Associates, 1978.

Smith, E. E., & Spoehr, K. T. The perception of printed English: A theoretical perspective. In B. H. Kantowitz (Ed.), *Human information processing: Tutorials in performance and cognition.* Hillsdale, N.J.: Lawrence Erlbaum Associates, 1974.

Smith, F. *Understanding reading.* New York: Holt, Rinehart & Winston, 1971.

Spoehr, K. T. & Smith, E. E. The role of orthographic and phonotactic rules in perceiving letter patterns. *Journal of Experimental Psychology: Human Performance and Perception,* 1975, *1,* 21–34.

Theios, J., & Muise, J. G. The word identification process in reading. In N. J. Castellan, Jr., D. B. Pisoni, & G. Potts, (Eds.), *Cognitive theory* (Vol. 2). Hillsdale, N.J.: Lawrence Erlbaum Associates, 1977.

Thompson, M. C., & Massaro, D. W. Visual information and redundancy in reading. *Journal of Experimental Psychology,* 1973, *98,* 49–54.

Tinker, M. A. Recent studies of eye movements in reading. *Psychological Bulletin,* 1958, *55,* 215–231.

Travers, J. R. Personal communication, August, 1974.

Tulving, E., & Gold, C. Stimulus information and contextual information as determinants of tachistoscopic recognition of words. *Journal of Experimental Psychology,* 1963, *66,* 319–327.

Tulving, E., Mandler, G., & Baumal, R.   Interaction of two sources of information in tachistoscopic word recognition. *Canadian Journal of Psychology,* 1964, *18,* 62–71.

Weber, R. First graders' use of grammatical context in reading. In H. Levin & J. P. Williams (Eds.), *Basic studies on reading.* New York: Basic Books, 1970.

Wheeler, D. D. Processes in word recognition. *Cognitive Psychology,* 1970, *1,* 59–85.

4 What Do Children Learn When They Learn to Read?

James F. Juola
Margaret Schadler
Robert Chabot
Mark McCaughey
John Wait
University of Kansas

Learning to read involves the acquisition of a few skills specific to reading and the use of many other abilities that are common to a variety of cognitive processes. Previously acquired linguistic and conceptual knowledge relevant for understanding oral language and interpreting visual experience is also necessary for reading. Learning to read largely involves the learning of a new language code that is based primarily on spatial relations rather than on the temporal relations of the speech code. Most children in the primary grades possess the necessary perceptual, linguistic, and conceptual abilities to process some written language. Much of beginning reading instruction is therefore directed toward activities unique to processing the visual code. Beginning students of reading must be taught the left-to-right ordering of the letters and words in the text and their sometimes arbitrary relationships to spoken language. Thus, the teaching of reading is focused mainly on the acquisition of basic visual recognition and decoding skills. The teaching of decoding often involves drills on specific letter–sound correspondences, but teaching methods can differ in the amount of emphasis placed on more general relationships between English orthography and phonology.

The emphasis on the relationship between oral and written language is evident in most, if not all, beginning reading programs. Training in phonics or decoding to sounds has been a fundamental part of reading instruction for decades (Chall, 1967 and Vol. 1, this series: Huey, 1908/1968). This is the case despite the fact that decoding is only one method of recognizing words.

91

Research has indicated that phonemic encoding plays a relatively minor role in rapid word identification and skilled reading (Henderson, 1977; Kleiman, 1975; Massaro, 1975). For the beginning reader, however, phonics has traditionally been taught in order to enable children to decode any unfamiliar printed word into a recognizable approximation of its pronunciation. Yet many common English words are blatant exceptions to letter–sound correspondence rules, making the need for some sight–word recognition inevitable.

A secondary goal, or at least a result, of phonics training is to provide the beginning reader with some knowledge of the regularities of English orthography. Just as English phonology restricts the combinations of phonemes that can follow one another in words, orthographic rules constrain graphemic constructions. Phonics drills that relate regularly occurring graphemic and phonemic groupings presumably call attention to these regularities and thereby help the beginning reader to become familiar with them as general linguistic rules. Knowledge of English orthography could therefore come to faciliate word recognition, regardless of whether phonemic encoding is used as a route to comprehension in skilled reading (Venezky & Massaro, this volume).

It is obvious that at least some words are recognized by both skilled and beginning readers while they are reading a passage of text. Rapid word identification is an effective subskill of reading in that it can free attentional demands from decoding to accessing lexical and semantic information about words stored in memory. In fact, when word recognition becomes an automatic process (LaBerge & Samuels, 1974; Perfetti & Lesgold, Vol. 1, this series), it might be unnecessary during reading to divert attention from the processing of meaning to the recognition of individual letters and words. Thus, we might expect word recognition skills to be related to reading ability. This is apparently true for beginning readers, as some research has shown high correlations between word recognition skills and other measures of reading ability. For skilled readers, such as the average college student, word recognition has become automatic or at least rapid enough that such correlations between single-word-processing skills and reading abilities are low (Perfetti & Lesgold, Vol. 1, this series).

The issue that we wish to raise concerns the way rapid word recognition skills develop as children learn to read. That is, does phonics training or other experience with written English foster the development and use of orthographic rules to infer word structure based on preliminary and partial visual analyses? Or are common words and other familiar morphemic units recognized as "wholes" in the same way that single letters are? These are, of course, questions that concern purely perceptual aspects of reading. By limiting our discussion to the way single words are recognized, we must obviously ignore many other cognitive and linguistic processes that intervene between glimpses of text and comprehension of written language. Furthermore, whether individual letters or whole words are identified as elements of perceptual categories in memory probably depends on the level of information being sought by the reader. Nevertheless, if rapid word recognition is the only important skill unique to reading (as Venezky and Massaro claim), then the study of the development of this skill is important for our understanding of beginning reading. By identifying what adults recognize when they are presented with visual displays containing words, we can discover what to try to teach children to look for in text. And we might also learn about what they see despite our attempts at instruction.

THEORIES OF WORD RECOGNITION

Most theories of word recognition begin with a sometimes vague set of elementary features as the initial central representations of visual experience. That is, brightness contours and other information such as the presence of lines, edges, and corners are detected by cells in the visual cortex of the brain. Featural information is briefly held in memory until the input from succeeding eye fixations replaces it. This registration of information is assumed to be precategorical in the sense that its quality is largely independent of the type of display presented, be it a word, a random letter string, or any other combination of features with a similar contour density. Information in preperceptual storage (Massaro, 1975) is then synthesized or categorized with respect to a set of relevant perceptual categories in memory. It is the nature of this categorization process that serves to differentiate among theories of word recognition.

Most adults and first-grade children can easily name a letter when it is visually presented alone and in a familiar form. The assumption is that internal categories exist for the letters that are defined in terms of sets of critical features. These categories allow auditory and visual translations of the letter codes if the assignments for visual shapes to certain sounds have been learned. Thus, a visually presented word can be quickly converted to a string of letter names of their phonemic codes by a literate adult. This conversion is an obligatory route to word recognition in some theories, whereas others characterize word recognition as a process similar to letter recognition. That is, when a word is viewed, the features in preperceptual storage could be used to recognize individual letters until the word itself is uniquely determined. Alternatively, units larger than single letters could be recognized directly from their visual features, and word recognition could be a holistic process or one based on recognizing component letter clusters as units. This distinction is clearly illustrated in Neisser's (1967) description of the competing theoretical outlooks as being based on inference or on unitization (see also

Henderson, 1977; Juola, Taylor, & Choe, 1977; Smith & Haviland, 1972; Smith & Spoehr, 1974).

Inference theories (e.g., Massaro, 1975) base word perception on the prior recognition of one or more letters. Not all letters need to be identified before the word can be recognized, however. The identification of any letter in an English word limits the possible alternatives for what its neighbors can be. Thus, the identification of a few letters can lead to word recognition by facilitating or eliminating the need for subsequent letter identification. In this way it is clear that word recognition could be accomplished by processing fewer visual features than would be necessary if each letter had to be identified independently. Inferential processes could also operate in decoding. The identification of a few letter sounds could be used to generate the entire phonemic code of the word, on at least a recognizable approximation to its normal sound pattern.

Unitization theories (e.g., F. Smith, 1971), on the other hand, do not maintain that word recognition is necessarily based on the prior identification of letters or speech sounds. Rather, as the visual features and their respective locations are processed, competing word alternatives are eliminated. In this process, some letters in the word might be identified incidentally, but they do not contribute to word recognition unless the word is not recognizable as a sight-word unit. Hypothesized perceptual units have included letters, words, and familiar letter clusters such as spelling patterns that could all be recognized directly from their visual features (Juola, Taylor, & Choe, 1977; Taylor, Miller, & Juola, 1977).

Distinctions between inference and unitization theories are often difficult to make in practice, however. For example, words can sometimes be identified under impoverished visual conditions that would preclude identification of any individual letter (Huey, 1908/1968). This result is often used as evidence that words are perceived as wholes, without depending on prior letter identification processes. However, even if no letter is seen clearly enough to be recognized, the available information might be sufficient to limit the possible alternatives to only a few at each position. The limitations on the letter alternatives could be used in conjunction with knowledge of orthographic structure to identify the word. There are other complications in trying to decide between the theories. For example, advocates of the unitization view often claim that word perception can be based either on letters or on higher-order units depending on what the subject's expectancy or processing strategy is. Thus, a letter-by-letter model could be supported by the data from a given experiment involving word displays if the task can be performed more efficiently by using a letter recognition strategy than by first identifying the overall pattern and then checking to determine what its component letters are (Bjork & Estes, 1973; Estes, 1975; Estes, Bjork, & Skaar, 1974: Massaro, 1973; Thompson & Massaro, 1973, Exp. II). On the other hand, if the task encourages recognizing the entire display, it might appear to be the case that letters are actually seen better when presented in a familiar (word) context than when presented in an unfamiliar string of letters (Juola, Choe, & Leavitt, 1974).

In the next section we review some studies of the perception of words and other letter strings that have been used in the past to support one or another of the theoretical positions. Although we do not think that the time has come for a final dispensation with regard to the inference versus unitization issue, we do feel that a model based exclusively on letter identification and orthographic knowledge is inadequate to explain rapid word identification and skilled reading. It remains to be determined if either inference or unitization theories can provide an adequate description of developmental changes in children's word recognition processes as they learn to read.

THE WORD SUPERIORITY EFFECT

There are many experimental tasks that show advantages for common words over letter strings that are not familiar, orthographically regular, or meaningful in any way. Some of these tasks confound perceptual, memory, and response processes, thereby concealing the source of word advantages (see Henderson, 1977; Smith & Spoehr, 1974). It is now generally accepted, however, that Reicher's (1969) procedure eliminated enough of the artifactual causes of word superiority effects to allow the conclusion that a word-advantage exists in perceptual recognition processes. Reicher specified two letter alternatives either immediately before or soon after a brief visual display that contained one of the letters. The display types consisted of four-letter words, anagrams of the words, or single letters only. The subjects were more accurate in picking the correct letter alternative when it was included in a word display than when it was included in a nonsense string of letters or presented alone. (Our discussion of the word superiority effect will henceforth be limited to comparisons between the perception of words and the perception of meaningless letter strings.)

Reicher's results appear to support the unitization theory since, when words were displayed, each of the two letter alternatives formed a common word when included in the appropriate display position. The effects of orthographic redundancy should thus have been controlled for and eliminated as a possible cause of the word advantage over nonwords. However, Massaro (1975) has argued that redundancy can still play a role in the Reicher task if the subjects attempt to synthesize a word from letter and featural information before the two response alternatives are considered. In this case partial information about the critical letter could be used to assist the synthesis of the actually presented word on word trials, thus ensuring a correct response. On nonword trials, however, this attempted synthesis would fail or arrive at a word that was not actually presented. In most cases the subject would then be left with two alternatives between which to choose, and neither might match any letter that had been identified. Because of the greater potential for failure in the synthesis process on nonword trials, the probability of a correct response would be less than when words were presented.

Recognition experiments similar to Reicher's (1969) have been used to demonstrate that letters are more readily perceptible when they are included in orthographically regular and pronounceable pseudowords than when they are part of an irregular string (Aderman & Smith, 1971; Baron & Thurston, 1973). One can understand how pseudowords could be more perceptible than irregular nonwords from either an inference or a unitization point of view. Pseudowords could be processed more efficiently because their regular orthographic structure facilitates letter identification. However, pseudowords contain letter clusters that are familiar components of common words, and these units might be recognized directly from their visual features. In either case, the use of redundancy could operate at the featural level, basing identification of the entire display on fewer features than those necessary to identify all the component letters if they were to be considered separately.

We have reported the results of several experiments designed to test inference and unitization hypotheses in a task similar to Reicher's. In one study (Juola, Leavitt, & Choe, 1974) the displays included common words and orthographically regular pseudowords. Letter alternatives were specified either in advance or after the display, as in Reicher's study. In both conditions, letters were shown to be more perceptible in words than in pseudowords. Although the pseudoword–nonword difference discussed earlier is consistent with either an inference or unitization theory, an additional perceptual advantage for words is consistent only with the unitization view, under the assumption that the pseudowords have in fact been equated with the words in terms of orthographic structure. In the absence of any agreed upon and general set of rules for determining the degree of orthographic regularity in letter strings, this last assumption cannot be validated (Venezky & Massaro, Vol. 1, this series).

It should be noted that there are experiments similar to Reicher's that fail to show word superiority effects. These studies have typically involved practice with a fixed and small set of letter alternatives as well as, sometimes, specific knowledge about the relative position of the critical letter in the display (Bjork & Estes, 1973; Estes et al., 1974; Massaro, 1973; Thompson & Massaro, 1973). We argue that this variant of the Reicher procedure disrupts the typical strategy of attempting to recognize the display before considering the response alternatives. Instead, practice with a specific set of letter alternatives encourages a letter-processing strategy that results in the disuse of orthographic information of perceptual units larger than single letters. For these reasons, we have called experiments using a fixed set of target letters for a series of displays detection tasks to distinguish them from recognition tasks of the Reicher type. Consistent with this dichotomy, Juola, Choe, and Leavitt (1974) demonstrated that the visual similarity between two target letters has no effect on recognition performance, but greater similarity produces poorer performance in detection (see also Thompson & Massaro, 1973).

This discussion of the word superiority effect has been limited to a consideration of data and theories relevant to perceptual recognition tasks. There are a number of other experimental procedures that have also been used to demonstrate advantages for words in perception, and some of these might prove to be more practical in experimental work with children. For instance, a task involving search for a given letter in a display containing several letters can be performed by children who have not yet learned the names of the letters. The use of this type of search task also allows for the study of the perceptual processes involved in recognizing the display information and subsequent comparison processes operating between the target letter and the encoded display information after it has been recognized. Finally, this task eliminates many of the motivational problems that can arise for subjects (especially children) who are continually confronted with brief displays that are difficult to identify.

In the remainder of this chapter we discuss some earlier results from visual search tasks that have been designed to study developmental processes related to reading ability. We then consider the data from a study of visual search recently completed in our laboratory. The results are relevant to the issues of how children learn to recognize words rapidly and how they come to process words in memory after the words have been recognized.

VISUAL SEARCH

Visual search tasks are of two general types: One involves large displays or long lists of items that must be searched using several eye fixations (e.g., Neisser, 1963), and the other involves the presentation of a small amount of information to central vision such that it can be processed during a single eye fixation (e.g., Atkinson, Holmgren, & Juola, 1969). Krueger (1970a, 1970b) has shown that a single target letter can be found faster in both kinds of search tasks if words rather than unpronounceable nonwords are used. Krueger concluded from his research that familiar and highly redundant words are encoded more rapidly than are irregular nonwords but that subsequent comparison processes are largely the same for the two types of displays. We tested the generality of this conclusion by presenting visual displays containing from three to five letters that were either common words or orthographically regular and pronounceable pseudowords (Gilford & Juola,

1976). A different target letter was specified on each trial. It was included in the display on half the trials (positive response required), and it was absent on the other half (negative response required). In this task errors were relatively infrequent, and the relevant data are response latencies. Consistent with earlier findings (Atkinson et al., 1969), response times increased linearly with the number of display letters. The slopes of the best-fitting linear equations were equivalent for positive and negative trials, and they were also equal for word and pseudoword displays. However, the overall response time was about 40 msec faster for words than for pseudowords.

To interpret these results it is first necessary to develop a model for visual search involving the information available in foveal vision. We assume that when a single target letter is presented, it is held in memory as a visual code. [It is possible, as Townsend and Roos (1973) have argued, that the target letter is held in either an auditory or a visual form in preparation for subsequent processes that can be based on either type of code. We argue, however, that this type of search task is based on visual codes, and we will support our argument with data that are discussed later.] When the visual display is presented, it is encoded into a form compatible with the target item. The target letter is then exhaustively compared with each of the items in the display before a decision to make a positive or negative response is made. The interpretation that the comparison process is exhaustive is consistent with the result that response times increase at the same rate for positive and negative trials. A search that terminated with the finding of the target on positive trials would produce a function that increased half as rapidly across the display size as that for negative trials (Sternberg, 1966). The interpretation of the overall word–pseudoword difference would be that words are encoded more rapidly than are pseudowords, perhaps by being recognized more often as single units. Once encoding is complete, however, the quality of the encoded letter string is equivalent for words and pseudowords. This conclusion is based on the finding of equivalent slopes of the functions relating mean response times to number of display letters for words and pseudowords. According to the model, these slopes are estimates of the letter comparison times, and their equivalence for words and pseudowords indicates that the comparison process is the same for both types of displays.

The model can be summarized by representing the processes that occur between display onset and response output as a series of independent stages (see Sternberg, 1975). These processes include display encoding, letter comparison, response decision, and response execution. The overall mean response time is assumed to be equal to the sum of the mean execution times for each of the stages. Note that we are assuming that the comparison stage is the only one affected by the number of display letters. Although we could assume that the encoding process takes longer when a larger number of letters is present in the display, we then would have expected different results. Any process that changes as a function of display size should result in changes in the slope of the function relating response time to the number of display letters. If words tend to be perceived as units and pseudowords as several spelling patterns or individual letters, and if encoding time depends on the number of units being recognized, then the slope should have been less for words than for pseudoword displays. This was not the case in the Gilford and Juola data, and our assumption that encoding time is a constant for from one to about five unrelated letters presented foveally is supported by other arguments (Massaro, 1975; Shiffrin & Gardner, 1972).

In the next section we describe the results of a visual search experiment that was designed to answer several questions. First, the model described above was to be tested using word, pseudoword, and nonword displays. By sampling a wide range of materials that vary in their structural similarity to words as well as in their familiarity, we can more adequately test the inference and unitization theories of word perception. We can also more closely assess whether recognition or visual scanning processes are affected by these variables. Second, these methods were extended to the study of visual search in children at different ages and levels of reading instruction. This procedure allowed us to determine the effects of learning to read on perceptual encoding and letter comparison processes. The aim is to gain more evidence for the way words are perceived and the way changes that accompany learning to read affect visual processing capabilities and strategies.

A DEVELOPMENTAL STUDY OF VISUAL SEARCH

There are several published studies of visual search performance in children. For example, Krueger, Keen, and Rublevich (1974) compared letter search performance in college students and fourth-grade children using displays of six-letter words, pseudowords, and nonwords. Although the adults were about twice as fast overall as the children, both groups showed about the same advantage for words over pseudowords (about 3%) and for words over nonwords (about 9%). Krueger et al., also found that children with better reading skills tended to search faster but that reading ability was not related to the relative differences among words, pseudowords, and nonwords. In a similar study, Katz and Wicklund (1972) presented single-letter targets and visual displays of one, two, or four unrelated letters to second- and sixth-grade children. They reported that the overall search time and the increase in search time across display size were both greater for second-grade than for sixth-grade children. They reported no effects of reading ability on search performance and concluded, as Perfetti and Lesgold (Vol. 1, this series) have for adults subjects, that reading ability is related only to visual information-processing skills that exceed the span of apprehension.

Our research was designed to extend these results by covarying display size and display regularity within subjects. This procedure should allow us to localize the processing stage or stages affected by differences among words, pseudowords, and nonwords. We also recognized the necessity to investigate word-processing skills in younger children in order to study the changes that occur in word perception as children learn to read. Finally, we wanted to examine more closely the relationship between reading ability and visual search performance.

Our experiment was carried out using identical sets of materials and procedures for groups of college students, fourth-grade, second-grade, and kindergarten children. Each group contained 20 individual subjects who were run in two or three separate sessions. The task sequence consisted of a 1.5 sec presentation of a single target letter, followed by a visual masking field for .5 sec, which was followed by a 3-, 4-, or 5- letter display. The display contained the target letter on half the trials. The subjects indicated whether the target was present or absent in the display by pressing either of two response buttons. Both speed and accuracy of responses were emphasized in the instructions. All subjects were run for 270 trials involving one trial for each of 90 words, 90 pseudowords, and 90 nonwords. See Juola, Schadler, and Chabot, and McCaughey (in press) for a more complete description of the stimulus materials and procedures involved.

The stimuli were selected from Kučera and Francis (1967) such that (1) all words were among the most frequently occurring words in English (averaging about 275 occurrences per million words); (2) mean frequency was approximately equated across 3-, 4-, and 5-letter words; (3) all words contained one syllable; and (4) no letters were repeated within any word. The pseudowords and nonwords were formed by making pronounceable and unpronounceable anagrams of the words, although for about 11% of the stimuli a single letter in the word had to be changed in order to form an acceptable pseudoword or nonword anagram. The orthographic regularity and pronounceability of the pseudowords was affirmed by five independent judges, and necessary changes were made. The judges also certified the general unpronounceability of the irregular nonwords.

The stimuli were typed in lowercase letters and photoenlarged so that they could be seen clearly and in about their normal reading size when presented in a tachistoscope. (A 5-letter word subtended a horizontal visual angle of about 1.5°.) The assignments of target letters to the stimuli were made for two different stimulus sets such that each display was used equally often on positive and negative trials within each group of subjects, and on positive trials the target letter appeared about equally often in each serial position of the display. The college student subjects were volunteers who participated in the experiment for course credit in an introductory psychology course at the University of Kansas. The children were recruited from local public schools.

At the end of two or three experimental sessions the children were tested with the oral reading section of the Wide Range Achievement Test (WRAT) and were paid $3.00 for their participation.

The results are presented in two parts: The first is concerned with the overall visual search data, and the second is concerned with the effects of display type. Figure 4.1 presents mean response times for positive and negative responses separately for each group of subjects. Both overall search time and the mean search time per display letter (as measured by the slopes of the best-fitting lines) decrease with age. Furthermore, there is an apparent shift in processing strategy from kindergarten subjects to older subjects. Whereas the slopes of the functions for positive and negative responses are about equal for adults (being about 25 msec per letter and 28 msec per letter, respectively), the slope for positive responses for kindergarten children (172 msec per letter) is about half the slope for negative responses (331 msec per letter). The two-to-one ratio of slopes for negative and positive responses is what would be expected if a self-terminating search process were used. In this case, on the average positive trial only about half of the display letters would

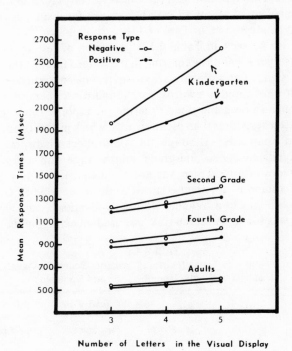

FIG. 4.1. Mean response times for positive and negative responses plotted as functions of the number of display letters for kindergarten, second-grade, fourth-grade, and college students.

need to be scanned before the target would be found and the process terminated. The relatively slow search rate of kindergarten subjects is also consistent with a search strategy based on auditory codes. That is, it is possible that the kindergarten subjects successively named each display letter and made a positive response as soon as this name matched that of the target letter. The results for children in the second and fourth grades were more consistent with the adult data. For these subjects, the comparison process can be more adequately described as a rapid, exhaustive scan of the target lettter against all the display letters before a response is made.

The data in Fig. 4.1 combine mean response times for words, pseudowords, and nonwords. The effects of display type did not interact with the number of display letters. That is, the results replicated and extended our earlier findings (Gilford & Juola, 1976) indicating that the search process is the same for words, pseudowords, and nonwords. We conclude that this search process is based on a visual image of the display that does not vary in quality for the various types of letter strings. There were significant differences among the overall response times for the three display types, but these effects did not interact with response type nor with the number of display letters. Therefore, the data were collapsed across all variables except for display type and age, and these results are shown in Table 4.1.

Again, as can be seen in Table 4.1, the pattern of results obtained for kindergarten subjects was different from that obtained for the other groups of subjects. No significant differences among the mean response times for words, pseudowords, and nonwords were found for kindergarten children. All other groups showed the same ordering of response times with words resulting in faster responses than pseudowords, which in turn produced faster response than nonwords. Although the main effect of display type was statistically significant for second-grade, fourth-grade, and college subjects, the word–pseudoword difference was not significant within any group.

These results stand in apparent contrast to those reported by Gilford and Juola (1976) in which a reliable 40-msec advantage for words over pseudowords was found. A search task was used involving similar materials

TABLE 4.1
Mean Response Times (in msec) for Letter Search in Visual
Displays of Words, Pseudowords, and Nonwords

	Display Type		
	Words	Pseudowords	Nonwords
College students	543	553	568
Fourth-grade students	933	945	967
Second-grade students	1,258	1,266	1,301
Kindergarten students	2,128	2,112	2,104

and procedures with two exceptions: (1) The displays were 50% smaller than those used in the present study. The smaller displays were somewhat more difficult to see, and if individual letters had been presented, they would have been recognizable only by subjects with normal or better acuity. (2) Only words and pseudowords were presented; thus, words occurred on 50% of the trials versus 33% in the present study. Either or both of these factors could have reduced the magnitude of the word advantage in the data reported in Table 4.1 by lessening the subjects' reliance on a whole-word-processing strategy (see also Aderman & Smith, 1971; Juola, Taylor, & Choe, 1977; Manelis, 1974).

The mean error rates across all conditions decreased with age, from 9.9% for kindergarten children to 5.7%, 3.3%, and 2.6% for second-grade, fourth-grade, and college students, respectively. Although the error percentages showed a slight increase as the number of display letters increased, the type of display (word, pseudoword, or nonword) had no significant effect on the error rate. These results allow the response time data to be interpreted directly, without attempting to account for speed–accuracy tradeoffs within any group of subjects.

Finally, there were no consistent relationships between reading ability as measured by the WRAT and any of the results reported here. A few reliable correlations were found between reading level and overall response time, scanning rate, and word–pseudoword–nonword differences, but the pattern of results was inconsistent across grade levels. Unless we can find another measure of reading skill that leads to a reliable pattern of results, we will be forced to agree with Krueger et al., (1974) and Katz and Wicklund (1972) that word-processing skills, as measured in letter search tasks, are not closely related to reading ability.

SUMMARY AND CONCLUSIONS

The fact that words are more readily perceptible than are strings of unrelated letters has been demonstrated in many experiments (see reviews by Henderson, 1977; Huey, 1908/1968; Juola, Taylor, & Choe, 1977; Smith & Spoehr, 1974). Word superiority effects in perception have been interpreted within two theoretical frameworks. One theory assumes that letters are the primary units of recognition and that with inferences based on orthographic knowledge, word and wordlike letter strings are recognized more efficiently than strings that violate rules of English orthography. A second theory assumes that frequently occurring letter clusters, such as spelling patterns and common words, are learned as perceptual units through reading experience. These higher order units are then capable of being recognized directly from their primitive visual features, without necessitating prior letter identification. Although several recent experiments have been specifically designed to settle the inference versus unitization issue (e.g., Juola, Choe & Leavitt, 1974; Smith & Haviland, 1972; Thompson & Massaro, 1973), it is unlikely that we will be able to eliminate one or the other of these theories given our present methods. A major difficulty lies in developing a measure of regularity for orthographic structure along which both words and pseudowords can be scaled. In the absence of an adequate measure, advantages of words over pseudowords in perception experiments can be accounted for by either theory.

With these theoretical problems in mind, we decided to study the development of word superiority effects by using a letter search task. Finding a given target letter in a visual display containing several letters is a task that can be performed by children who have not yet learned to read. By examining search performance in children in several primary grades, we hoped to learn about changes in visual information-processing capabilities that accompany learning to read. If word superiority effects in perception develop as a result of learning orthographic rules or of internalizing spelling patterns and larger units, then teaching methods could be designed to facilitate the acquisition and use of perceptual strategies typically employed by children in recognizing words.

Our results have shown that children at least as young as those in the second grade can use their knowledge about English words to speed visual search performance. That is, decisions about whether a given target letter is present in a 3- to 5-letter display were made more rapidly for words and orthographically regular pseudowords than for irregular nonwords. The advantage for words and pseudowords over nonwords appears to be localized in recognition processes, since search rates did not differ for the three types of displays. The lack of a significant difference between performance for words and pseudowords seems to indicate that either inference based on knowledge of English orthography or the use of spelling patterns as perceptual units is the key to the word identification process.

Our results have also shown that major changes in visual search performance accompany learning to read during the first years in which the skill is acquired. In contrast to the second-grade and older subject groups, whose search data are more similar than different, the kindergarten children show an entirely different pattern of results. First, their search rates were much slower than those for older children and adults and could conceivably have been based on auditory encodings of the letters rather than on visual codes. Second, the search process for kindergarten children terminated with the finding of a match with the target letter, whereas subjects in all other groups were apparently more likely to use an exhaustive scanning process. Finally, the kindergarten subjects showed no differences between word, pseudoword, and nonword displays, indicating that all the displays were processed in an identical letter-by-letter fashion. In contrast, second- and fourth-grade children and adults showed similar effects for displays with regular spelling patterns versus those that were irregular. That is, all subjects except for those in the kindergarten group responded more rapidly when words or pseudowords were presented than when nonwords were displayed. We conclude that these differences between kindergartgen children and those in the second grade and beyond are not due as much to maturation and general learning experience as to specific skills acquired during reading and reading instruction.

The lack of any correlation between reading level and visual search performance is somewhat surprising to us, despite the equivocal evidence presented earlier (Katz & Wicklund, 1972; Krueger *et al.,* 1974; Perfetti & Lesgold, Vol. 1 this series). We are not ready to give up on this issue, however, because major changes in visual search performance appear to occur quite rapidly; Our data show no effects of orthographic regularity in kindergarten children, yet the complete pattern of results observable in the adult data was also obtained for second-grade children. We believe that a closer investigation of the relationship btween reading ability and visual search performance should be made at the first-grade level, when changes in visual scanning strategies and the use of redundancy in English words should first occur. This approach should be fruitful in using visual search tasks to measure changes in perceptual processes that parallel developments in reading ability.

Finally, we are in general agreement with Venezky and Massaro's (Vol. 1 this series) discussion of the role of orthographic regularity in word recognition. The benefit of phonics training apparently extends beyond just the development of decoding skills. Researchers from Huey (1908/1968) to Kleiman (1975) have argued that as reading skills increase, reliance on phonemic encoding plays a lesser role in word recognition and that the process becomes more dependent on purely visual codes. This is not to deny that phonics training is important as an aid in decoding when visual recognition fails. We also recognize the fact that phonemic or more general auditory codes are important in reading in order to retain and comprehend the information gained from several eye fixations (as Huey and Kleiman have also claimed). Nevertheless, the route to rapid word identification and skilled reading depends on the development of visual processing skills that make use of orthographic regularities or the direct recognition of frequently occurring letter clusters and words. If this is the major skill unique to reading that is to be learned, then perhaps phonics training should specifically include emphasis on the regularities in English orthography. The materials normally used to teach decoding could then be designed to facilitate acquisition of rapid word recognition skills that are important in reading for comprehension.

ACKNOWLEDGMENTS

Research for this chapter was supported in part by National Science Foundation Grant BMS74-12801 to the first author, Biomedical Sciences Grant RR-07037 to the University of Kansas, and a grant from the general research fund of the University of Kansas. We thank Robb Gilford, Lisee Erickson, and Timothy Miller for their assistance, as well as John Stewart, principal of Riverside School, and Paul Dickens, principal of Cordley School, and the teachers, parents, and children of Lawrence Public Schools who enabled the research reported here to be carried out.

REFERENCES

Aderman, D., & Smith E. E. Expectancy as a determinant of functional units in perceptual recognition. *Cognitive Psychology,* 1971, *2,* 117–129.

Atkinson, R. C., Holmgren, J. E., & Juola, J. F. Processing time as influenced by the number of elements in a visual display. *Perception and Psychophysics,* 1969, *6,* 321–326.

Baron, J., & Thurston, I. An analysis of the word superiority effect. *Cognitive Psychology* 1973, *4,* 207–228.

Bjork, E. L., & Estes, W. K. Letter identification in relation to linguistic context and masking conditions. *Memory & Cognition,* 1973, *1,* 217–223.

Chall, J. S. *Learning to read: The great debate.* New York: McGraw-Hill, 1967.

Estes, W. K. Memory, perception, and decision in letter identification. In R. L. Solso (Ed.), *Information processing and cognition: The Loyola Symposium.* Hillsdale, N.J.: Lawrence Erlbaum Associates, 1975.

Estes, W. K., Bjork, E. L., & Skaar, E. Detection of single letters and letters in words with changing vs. unchanging mask characters. *Bulletin of the Psychonomic Society,* 1974, *3,* 201–203.

Gilford, R. M., & Juola, J. F. Familiarity effects on memory search and visual search. *Bulletin of the Psychonomic Society,* 1976, *7,* 142–144.

Henderson, L. Word recognition. In N. S. Sutherland (Ed.), *Tutorial essays in psychology* (Vol. 1). Hillsdale, N.J.: Lawrence Erlbaum Associates, 1977.

Huey, E. B. *The psychology and pedagogy of reading.* Cambridge, Mass.: MIT Press, 1968. (Originally published, 1908).

Juola, J. F., Choe, C. S., & Leavitt, D. D. *A reanalysis of the word superiority effect.* Paper presented at the meeting of the Psychonomic Society, Boston, November 1974.

Juola, J. F., Leavitt, D. D., & Choe, C. S. Letter identification in word, nonword, and single letter displays. *Bulletin of the Psychonomic Society,* 1974, *4,* 278–280.

Juola, J. F., Schadler, M., Chabot, R. J., & McCaughey, M. The development of visual information skills related to reading. *Journal of Experimental Child Psychology,* in press.

Juola, J. F., Taylor, G. A., & Choe, C. S. Perceptual processes in reading and word recognition. In K. S. Fu & A. B. Whinston (Eds.), *Pattern recognition: Theory and application.* Alphen aan den Rijn, The Netherlands: Sijthoff & Noordhoff, 1977.

Katz, L., & Wicklund, D. A. Letter scanning rate for good and poor readers in grades two and six. *Journal of Educational Psychology,* 1972, *63,* 363–367.

Kleiman, G. M. Speech recoding in reading. *Journal of Verbal Learning and Verbal Behavior,* 1975, *14,* 323–339.

Krueger, L. E. Search time in a redundant visual display. *Journal of Experimental Psychology,* 1970, *83,* 391–399.(a)

Krueger, L. E. Visual comparison in a redundant display. *Cognitive Psychology,* 1970, *1,* 341–357.(b)

Krueger, L. E., Keen, R. H., & Rublevich, B. Letter search through words and nonwords by adults and fourth-grade children. *Journal of Experimental Psychology,* 1974, *102,* 845–849.

Kučera, H., & Francis, W. N. *Computational analysis of present-day American English.* Providence, R. I.: Brown University Press, 1967.

LaBerge, D., & Samuels, S. J. Toward a theory of automatic information processing in reading. *Cognitive Psychology,* 1974, *6,* 293–323.

Manelis, L. The effect of meaningfulness in tachistoscopic word recognition. *Perception and Psychophysics,* 1974, *16,* 182–192.

Massaro, D. W. Perception of letters, words, and nonwords. *Journal of Experimental Psychology,* 1973, *100,* 349–353,

Massaro, D. W. *Understanding language.* New York: Academic Press, 1975.

Neisser, U. Decision-time without reaction-time: Experiments in visual scanning. *American Journal of Psychology,* 1963, *76,* 376–385.

Neisser, U. *Cognitive Psychology.* Englewood Cliffs, N.J.: Prentice-Hall, 1967.

Reicher, G. M. Perceptual recognition as a function of meaningfulness of stimulus material. *Journal of Experimental Psychology,* 1969, *81,* 275–280.

Shiffrin, R. M., & Gardner, G. T. Visual processing capacity and attentional control. *Journal of Experimental Psychology,* 1972, *93,* 72–82.

Smith, E. E., & Haviland, S. E. Why words are perceived more accurately than nonwords: Inference vs. unitization. *Journal of Experimental Psychology,* 1972, *92,* 59–64.

Smith, E. E., & Spoehr, K. T. The perception of printed English: A theoretical perspective. In B. H. Kantowitz (Ed.), *Human information processing: Tutorials in performance and cognition.* Hillsdale, N.J.: Lawrence Erlbaum Associates, 1974.

Smith, F. *Understanding reading.* New York: Holt, Rinehart & Winston, 1971.

Sternberg, S. High-speed scanning in human memory. *Science,* 1966, *153,* 652–654,

Sternberg, S. Memory scanning: New findings and current controversies. *Quarterly Journal of Experimental Psychology,* 1975, *27,* 1–32.

Taylor, G. A., Miller, T. J., & Juola, J. F. Isolating visual units in the perception of words and nonwords. *Perception and Psychophysics,* 1977, *21,* 377–386.

Thompson, M. C., & Massaro, D. W. Visual information and redundancy in reading. *Journal of Experimental Psychology,* 1973, *98,* 49–54.

Townsend, J. T., & Roos, R. N. Search reaction time for single targets in multiletter stimuli with brief visual displays. *Memory & Cognition,* 1973, *1,* 319–332.

5

Speech, the Alphabet, and Teaching to Read

Isabelle Y. Liberman
Donald Shankweiler
*University of Connecticut
and Haskins Laboratories*

In the research we have done on reading acquisition, we have been governed by the assumption that reading is somehow parasitic on speech (Liberman, 1971, 1973; Shankweiler & Liberman, 1972). We have been led to this assumption by certain observations that seem obvious. First, speech is unquestionably the primary language system, naturally and universally acquired without direct instruction. Reading, being secondarily derived from speech, is relatively unnatural, far from universally learned, and must be taught. Second, an alphabetic writing system is a more or less phonetic representation of the spoken language; it is not a separate symbol system that is keyed directly to meaning. And finally, speech appears to be an essential foundation for the acquisition of reading. Children who are blocked in the acquisition of speech, such as the congenitally deaf, do not readily learn to read, even though they have access to the printed word through the visual channel.

In an effort to explore the implications of the dependence of reading on speech, we have, in our studies of young children, investigated three related aspects of the problem: linguistic awareness of phoneme segmentation, phonetic coding in short-term memory, and the phonetic pattern of reading errors.

To learn to read, children must map the written word to the spoken word. It has seemed plain to us that to do this, they must have some recognition of the phonetic structure of their spoken language (Liberman, 1971). We know from speech research that phonetic structure is complexly encoded in the speech signal (Liberman, Cooper, Shankweiler, & Studdert-Kennedy, 1967). The consequence is that there is no obvious acoustic criterion that marks the phonemic segments. We were thus led to ask whether the development of the awareness of these segments might be difficult for the child. Accordingly, we have investigated the child's development of phoneme segmentation ability and the relation of this ability to reading (Liberman, 1973; Liberman, Shankweiler, Fischer, & Carter, 1974).

The role of the phonetic representation in speech perception is to hold information about shorter segments (say, words) in short-term memory until the meaning of longer segments (say, sentences) can be extracted. That led us to wonder if the phonetic representation derived from optical information might not serve the same purpose in reading. Therefore, we have investigated the use of phonetic coding in reading and, particularly, the differences in this ability between good and poor readers (Liberman, Shankweiler, Liberman, Fowler, & Fischer, 1977; Shankweiler & Liberman, 1976).

Finally, guided by what we hope is common sense, we have supposed that by noting the particular errors that beginning readers make and by analyzing them appropriately, we might gain some insight into the processes underlying reading acquisition and at the same time test our hypotheses about linguistic factors in beginning reading (Fowler, Liberman, & Shankweiler, 1977).

In this chapter we review our findings in these three areas of investigation, emphasizing recent work, and suggest some of the ways in which these findings can be applied in reading instruction. We conclude with some observations about the possible contribution of the orthographic complexity of English to the problems of the beginning reader.

LINGUISTIC AWARENESS AND THE ALPHABET

In languages that are written alphabetically, the unit characters—letters—are keyed to the phonological structure of speech. We are aware that the mapping from written symbols to phonemes is more nearly one to one in other alphabetic languages, such as Finnish and Serbo-Croatian, than in English. The many departures from one-to-one mapping make English difficult to spell and probably more difficult to learn to read than is the case in languages whose alphabetic writing systems have a simpler structure. We defer matters concerning the role of the orthography in the acquisition of reading until later sections of this chapter. For the present it is sufficient to underscore the fact that English spelling, in common with other orthographies that employ an alphabet, is, for all its peculiarities, in essence a cipher on the phonemes of the language.

The child's fundamental task in learning to read is to construct a link between the arbitrary signs of print and speech. We have pointed out (Liberman et al., 1977) that there are different ways in which the child might do this. Words written by an alphabet can be read as though they were logograms, and many children undoubtedly begin reading in this way, apprehending the word shapes holistically rather than analyzing them as letter strings. However, the reader who employs a nonanalytic strategy of this sort cannot benefit from a unique advantage of alphabetic writing. We refer to the fact that the alphabet enables its users to generate a word's pronunciation from its spelling. Thus, users can recognize in print a word they have never before seen written down, and they can (at least to a rough approximation) pronounce a word they have never before either heard or read. These powerful advantages are open only to a user who knows how the alphabet works, that is to say, one who can approach the reading task analytically.

Let us first outline briefly what is involved in reading analytically. First, readers must realize that speech can be segmented into phonemes, and they must know how many phonemes the words in their vocabulary contain and the order in which they occur. Second, they must know that the letter symbols represent phonemes, not syllables or some other unit of speech.

In our earlier writings (Liberman, 1971; Shankweiler & Liberman, 1972, 1976; Liberman *et al.,* 1977) we have considered what it means for a child to know that speech can be segmented into phonemes. It does not mean simply that the child is able to discriminate word pairs that are minimally different. Every normal child of school age can do that. However, a child may be able perfectly well to discriminate between pairs of spoken words such as *bet* and *best* and to recognize each as a distinct word in his or her vocabulary without being aware that *bet* contains three phonemes and *best* contains four. Such a child, as we have said elsewhere, has only a tacit awareness of phoneme segmentation. This is sufficient, of course, for comprehension of the spoken message. Writing and reading, on the other hand, demand an additional capacity to analyze words as strings of phonemes. Mattingly (1972) and others have called this capacity *linguistic awareness.*

We have suggested that an understanding of the acoustic structure of speech can help to explain why the ability to analyze syllables as strings of phonemes is rather difficult to attain (Liberman, 1971). We suspect that in part the difficulty has to do with the fact that the phonemes are not represented in the acoustic signal in discrete bundles but rather are merged— "encoded"—into the structure of the syllable (as suggested by Liberman *et al.,* 1967). The word *dig,* for example, has three phonetic segments but only one acoustic segment. This merging of phonemes in the sound stream complicates the process of becoming actively aware of the phonemic level of speech for the would be reader. We do not mean to imply that the young child has difficulty differentiating word pairs, such as *bad* and *bat,* that differ in only one phoneme. On the contrary, there is reason to believe that most children hear these differences as accurately as adults (Read, 1971). As we have said, the problem is not to teach the child to discriminate minimally different word pairs but rather to bring the child to realize that each of these words contains three segments and that they are alike in the first two and differ in the third.

Elsewhere (Liberman *et al.,* 1977) we have dwelt on another important consequence of the encoded nature of phonemes that must contribute to the difficulty of learning to read analytically. Because the syllable, and not the phoneme, is the minimal unit of articulation, it is impossible to read by sounding out the letters one by one. On the contrary, it is necessary to discover how many of the letter segments must be taken simultaneously into account in order to arrive at the correct phonetic rendition of each syllable. Thus, we have stressed that to read analytically is not to read letter by letter, even in languages in which the letter-to-sound mapping is more direct than in English.

We have argued that effective use of an alphabet requires a degree of active awareness of phonological structure that goes beyond the tacit level of comprehension adequate for speaking and listening. As we have seen, it is one thing to understand and to speak one's language and quite another thing to have an analytic understanding of the language's internal structure. We have noted (Liberman, 1973) that the late appearance of the alphabet in the history of writing may be an indication that it is rather difficult to become aware of the phonological underpinnings of speech. If the obscurity of phoneme segmentation is a psychological fact about speech that indeed is related to the late appearance of alphabets on the world scene, then it is reasonable to suppose that the child might find phonemic segmentation difficult, and there might be in the development of the child an order of difficulty of segmentation from word to syllable to phoneme that parallels the historical development of writing systems.

Development of the Awareness
of Speech Segments in the Young Child

We tested that supposition directly in a recent experiment. The point was to determine how well children in nursery school, kindergarten, and first grade (4-, 5-, and 6-year-olds) can identify the number of phonetic segments in spoken utterances and how this compares with their ability to deal similarly with syllables (Liberman et al., 1974). The procedure was in the form of a game that required the child to indicate, by tapping a wooden dowel on the table, the number (from one to three) of segments (phonemes in the case of one group, syllables in the other) in a list of test utterances.

At age four, none of the children could segment by phoneme, whereas nearly half could segment by syllable. Ability to carry out phoneme segmentation successfully did not appear until age five, and then it was demonstrated by less than a fifth of the children. In contrast, almost half of the children at that age could segment syllabically. Even at age six, only 70%

succeeded in phoneme segmentation whereas 90% were successful in the syllable task.

Segmentation Ability and Reading Skill

The difficulty of phoneme segmentation has been remarked by a number of investigators besides ourselves (Calfee, Chapman, & Venezky, 1972; Elkonin, 1973; Gibson & Levin, 1975; Gleitman & Rozin, 1973; Rosner & Simon, 1971; Rozin & Gleitman, 1977; Savin, 1972). Their observations, as do ours, also imply a connection between the awareness of phoneme segmentation and early reading acquisition.

We explored this question in a preliminary way by measuring the reading achievement of the children who had taken part in our experiment on phoneme segmentation the year before. Testing our first graders at the beginning of their second school year, we found that half the children in the lowest third of the class in reading achievement had failed the segmentation task the previous June; on the other hand, there were no failures in phoneme segmentation among children who scored in the top third of the class in reading ability (Liberman, et al., 1977). Rosner (1975) has also found that the partial phoneme segmentation required by his elision task is also a significant predictor of reading achievement.

Three new studies by our research group now confirm these results. Despite widely varying school populations and diverse procedures, each of these studies shows a high and significant correlation between phoneme segmentation and early reading ability.

Helfgott (1976) recently completed a study of the segmentation and blending skills of kindergarten children in a white, middle-class suburban school in Connecticut. In connection with this study, she looked at the usefulness of several different skills as predictors of first-grade reading achievement in the following year. Using an adaptation of the Elkonin procedure (1973) for the assessment of phoneme segmentation, she found that the best predictor was the ability to segment spoken consonant–vowel–consonant (CVC) words into their three constituent phonemes. The correlation of this ability with reading achievement on the word recognition subtest of the Wide Range Achievement Test (WRAT) (Jastak, Bijou, & Jastak, 1965) was substantial ($r = .75$).

In an investigation of the phonological awareness and reading acquisition of first graders in an integrated city school in Rhode Island, Zifcak (1977) demonstrated a highly significant relationship between ability to segment phonemes on the Liberman tapping task (Liberman et al., 1974) and reading success as measured by the Gallistel–Ellis Test of Coding Skills (Gallistel & Ellis, 1974) and by the WRAT.

Treiman (1976) examined first and second graders in an inner city school with a largely black population in New Haven. She used a task requiring the placement of the correct number of tokens (rather than dowel tapping) to indicate the number of the constituent phonemes. Her stimuli were not words, but two- and three-segment syllables in which the incidence of eight vowels, four stops, and four fricatives was carefully equated. She added the much needed control of ascertaining the counting ability of the subjects. In addition to the WRAT, she included an experimenter-devised reading test that allowed for a more analytic assessment of early reading skills. Once again, in spite of these many variations, the relationship between segmenting ability and reading success was highly significant.

These investigations of the relation between segmentation abilities and reading proficiency suggest that the ability to analyze speech phonemically is indeed relevant to success or failure in learning to read. The results so far lend encouragement to our hypothesis that segmentation abilities are cognitive prerequisites for reading. We turn now to consider another aspect of language development that may bear on reading acquisition.

THE ROLE OF THE PHONETIC REPRESENTATION

At this point we should explain in general terms how we view the role of a phonetic representation. It is characteristic of the perception of language, as Liberman, Mattingly, and Turvey (1972) have noted, that the perceiver remembers the gist of what was said and not the exact sentences, word for word, that the speaker uttered. That is, the speaker's original message is recalled in the form of a paraphrase. However, the praphrase depends on the operation of a highly temporary memory system that contains a literal record of a small portion of the message as the hearer receives it. When we perceive a stretch of running speech, we rely on a working memory span of a few words that are held in phonological form. This can be demonstrated informally by abruptly interrupting a spoken communication. Typically the listener can, on demand, repeat word for word the last few words or the last sentence that was uttered. One of the aspects of this short-term memory representation, then, is that it retains the most recent portion of the utterance in exact phonological form.

In speech, the primary function of this literal, limited-capacity, and highly temporary memory representation is, in Liberman et al.'s (1972) view, to permit comprehension of the message. To comprehend what was said, we need to hold information about shorter segments (in our example, words) in memory until the meaning of the longer segments (here, sentences) can be grasped. But does reading necessarily require the same kind of memory representation as speech? If reading is rightly conceived of as an alternative means of perception of language, then we may expect it to share many processes in common with the perception of speech. Reading involves interpretation of symbols that stand as surrogates for speech segments. Thus, the reader's task, as we conceive it, is literally to convert print to speech, whether overtly or (more usually in the case of the experienced reader) into some covert form. Although we do not rule out the possibility that read words can be held temporarily in some visual form, it seems reasonable to suppose that in reading, no less than in perception of speech by ear, the perceiver makes use of a phonetic representation in order to comprehend the message.

In the case of an alphabetic language, there is an additional reason for supposing that the reader derives a phonetic representation from print. The fundamental characteristic of alphabetic writing systems is that the letter symbols are a cipher on the phonemes of the language. Thus, a reader who uses the alphabet analytically (in the sense of our earlier discussion) necessarily derives a phonetic representation. It is certainly the case that readers must recode the written script phonetically if they are to decode a word that they have never seen before. But do they need to recode phonetically words and phrases that they have read many times? Do they in these cases continue to construct a phonetic representation, or do they, as some believe, bypass the phonetic level and go directly from visual shape to meaning?

It seems plausible to us that phonetic recoding might occur even with frequently read materials and may persist in experienced, skilled readers precisely, as we have intimated above, because a phonetic representation plays a functional role in comprehension. Elsewhere (Liberman et al., 1977; Shankweiler & Liberman, 1976) we have speculated that the perceiver needs a phonetic base in order to index the mental lexicon and to reconstruct those prosodic cues so essential to comprehension of spoken language that are not directly represented in print.

Apart from our speculations on the role of a phonetic representation in reading, there is much experimental evidence that phonetic recoding does typically occur in a variety of situations in which perceivers are confronted with visually presented linguistic material that they have to recall later. Most of the relevant experiments take the following form: Lists of letters or alphabetically written words are presented to be read and remembered. Confusions in short-term memory are based not on visual similarity but on phonetic similarity to the presented material. Conrad (1972) has noted that even nonlinguistic stimuli may be recoded into phonetic form and stored in that form in short-term memory. It was found, in this connection, that in recall of pictures of common objects, the confusions of children aged 6 and over were clearly based on the phonetic forms of the names of the objects rather than on their visual or semantic characteristics.

All these experiments are relevant to the assumption that even skilled readers might recode phonetically in order to gain an advantage in short-term memory and to use the primary language processes they already have available. In saying this, we do not imply that the only way to obtain meaning from script is through the intermediary of a phonetic representation. Our intent, instead, is to question the assumption (see Bever & Bower, 1966) that a direct mapping strategy that bypasses the phonetic level would always be the preferred mode of the mature reader. Such an assumption is unwarranted in our view because it overlooks the large bulk of evidence that suggests that the organization of short-term memory is phonetic.

Phonetic Coding in Good and Poor Readers

As we have seen, a significant characteristic of poor readers is their difficulty in identifying the phoneme, the unit most directly represented by the alphabet. In view of the short-term memory requirements of the reading task and evidence for the involvement of phonetic coding in short-term memory, we might expect to find that those beginning readers who are progressing well and those who are doing poorly might be further distinguished by the degree to which they rely on phonetic coding.

To explore the hypothesis that good and poor readers differ in the degree to which they use phonetic coding in short-term memory, we have carried out three sets of experiments with second graders. In two of the experiments we used a procedure similar to one devised by Conrad (1972) for adult subjects in which the subject's performance is compared on recall of phonetically confusable (rhyming) and nonconfusable (nonrhyming) letters. In the first of these experiments (Liberman et al., 1977) the stimuli were strings of five uppercase consonants, half rhyming (drawn from the set BCDGPTVZ) and half nonrhyming (drawn from the set HKLQRSWY), presented tachisto-scopically in a 3-sec exposure. Recall was tested under two conditions—immediately after presentation and after a 15-sec delay. In the second experiment (Shankweiler & Liberman, 1976) the same procedure was followed except that the letters were presented aurally on tape. Since auditory presentation requires successive input, a parallel condition using visual serial presentation was added in this experiment.

No matter whether the presentation was visual or auditory, simultaneous or successive, the results were virtually identical. Though the superior readers were better at recall on the nonconfusable items than were the poor readers, their advantage was virtually eliminated when the stimulus items were phonetically confusable; and though the effect was particularly marked in the delay condition, phonetic similarity always produced a greater penalizing impact on the superior readers than on the poor ones. And it made practically no difference whether the items to be recalled were presented to the eye or to the ear.

These first two experiments strongly suggested that the difference between good and poor readers in phonetic coding turns on their ability to use a phonetic representation, whatever the source, and not merely on their ability to recode from script. However, two major criticisms might be leveled at both experiments. First, because the stimuli used were strings of unrelated consonants, the generalizability of the results to more realistic reading situations could be in question. Second, because the procedures did not control for the effects of rehearsal, the differences between the two reading groups might be accounted for by different rehearsal strategies.

A third experiment (Mark, Shankweiler, & Liberman, 1977) using an adaptation of the Hyde and Jenkins (1969) memory paradigm, addressed itself to both criticisms. The subjects were given a list of 28 words to read aloud, followed by a second, or recognition, list containing all the original words and 28 new words, or foils. Half the foils were phonetically confusable with (but visually dissimilar from) a given word on the original list. The remaining 14 foils had no rhyming counterpart on the list. The subjects were required simply to respond *yes* or *no* as to whether a given word on the recognition list had appeared on the original list. Once again, though the stimuli were words, not strings of letters, and though rehearsal could not have been involved, the good readers were much more strongly penalized by the confusable items than were the poor readers.

We regard these as interesting results. It is a relatively easy matter to demonstrate that good readers do better than poor readers on a variety of language-dependent tasks. In these three experiments, however, we have been able to show that it is possible to penalize good readers by making it disadvantageous for them to use a phonetic coding strategy. Therefore, it now seems reasonable to conclude with some confidence that good readers are more likely than poor readers to use a phonetic coding strategy effectively.

THE ANALYSIS OF READING ERRORS

One aim of our early research efforts (Shankweiler & Liberman, 1972) was to determine whether the errors made by beginning readers, when they attempt to read words and syllables, pattern consistently and if so, whether an analysis of their pattern of errors might provide insights into the problems of reading acquisition. Accordingly, we carried out a phonetic analysis of reading errors in a number of experiments with beginning and disabled readers. A consistent pattern emerged from this analysis: errors on the final consonant of a CVC syllable were roughly double those on the initial consonant, while errors on the medial vowel exceeded those on consonants in both initial and final positions. It seemed apparent from these experiments that the error frequency varied systematically with the position of the target phoneme in the syllable.

We considered that this distribution of errors in the syllable could be interpreted as reflecting the child's lack of understanding of the phonological segmentation of his or her spoken language. If children have not yet developed an ability to analyze the phonetic structure of their speech, they might be expected to show just this pattern of error—success with the initial segment, which can be extracted without further analysis of the internal structure of the syllable, and comparatively poor performance beyond that point. Such children, who know some letter-to-sound correspondences and know that they must scan in a left-to-right direction, might simply be searching their lexicons for a word, any word, beginning with a phoneme that matches the initial letter. By this reasoning, if they were presented with the word *big,* they might, in context, give a response like *beautiful* or, out of context, *butterfly.* Neither response could occur if they were searching their lexicons, as they should, for a word that has three phoneme segments corresponding to the letter segments in the printed word. If, however, they are unaware that words in their lexicons have a phonetic structure, or if they have difficulty in determining what that structure is, their errors would increase after the initial segment. As to the relatively high incidence of their errors on vowels, it could, in these early experiments, have been simply attributed to the imbedded position of the letter representing the vowel in the CVC syllable of the stimulus list.

Though the pattern of consonant and vowel errors obtained in this early work was suggestive, certain controls were needed before we could accept its reliability. The purpose of a new series of experiments (Fowler et al., 1977) was to confirm this pattern and, by the addition of various controls, to test its generality. Second, third, and fourth graders were the subjects in the new experiments. They were asked to read items from two lists of words,[1] one in which the incidence and location of the consonant phonemes were controlled, and the second in which these conditions were taken into account for the vowels.[2]

Differences in Consonant and Vowel Error Patterns

In this new set of more fully controlled experiments, we found the same pattern of consonant errors as previously obtained. Though the absolute number of errors decreased as the grade level of the child increased, the consonants in final position continued to produce approximately twice the number of errors as those in initial position. We were able to conclude that the

---

[1]A third list, used to study the error pattern in relation to the orthographic complexity of the vowels, was presented at the same time. Those results are described in detail in another paper (Fowler, Shankweiler, & Liberman, 1979).

[2]Ideally, it would have been desirable to provide both the consonant and vowel controls within one list. Contingencies relating to reading and vocabulary levels made this impossible to achieve.

consonant error pattern did indeed represent a true position effect and could, with some confidence, be attributed to the difficulties of phonological segmentation. In contrast to the findings on consonant misreading, errors on vowels showed no effect of position. When the vowels were placed in initial, medial, and final position, the errors did not vary systematically in frequency according to their location. Moreover, vowels continued to elicit a greater number of errors, regardless of their location in the syllable. Thus, the high error rate for vowels in the earlier experiment could no longer be explained by the medial position of the vowel and could not be related primarily to the difficulties of phonological segmentation.

The possibility that consonant and vowel errors might have different causes was supported by the results of a further analysis that took account not of the location of the errors in the syllable but of the phonetic nature of the substitutions. In that analysis, it was found that consonant errors were systematically related to the target phoneme in the word, differing from it most often in only one of the three distinctive features of consonants (voicing, place of articulation, and manner of articulation). The proportion of consonant errors sharing two features with the target phoneme was remarkably stable across the grades: 60% of second-grade errors, 61% of third-grade errors, and 62% of fourth-grade errors. The results suggested, therefore, that phonetically motivated substitutions contribute substantially to the consonant error pattern, both at the very early stages of reading acquisition and beyond. Vowel errors, in contrast, were not systematically related to the phonetic features of the presented vowel (tenseness, tongue advancement, tongue height, and diphthongization); indeed, the feature distribution of the vowel errors was essentially random at every grade level. Thus, the concept of featural similarity, so successful in rationalizing the substitutions among the consonants, does not enable us to understand the vowel errors.

The contrasting results obtained for consonants and vowels are indeed striking. The opposition of these phonetic classes was revealed, as we have seen, by both approaches to error analysis: the first, in which we investigated misreadings in relation to their location in the syllable, and the second, in which we considered the phonetic characteristics of the substitutions. As to the consonants, their position in the syllable accounted for the frequency of their occurrence while the phonetic features of the target phoneme largely determined the nature of the substitution. With the vowels, on the other hand, neither of these relationships obtained. Factors other than these must, therefore, be considered to account for the vowel error pattern. One factor that suggests itself immediately is the variability of vowel orthography. Whereas the rules relating spelling to phonetic segment are relatively straightforward for consonants, they are quite complex for English vowels. Work in progress appears to single out the complexity of the orthography as a contributing factor in the vowel error pattern, though it was not so for the consonants.

The Error Pattern and Nonvisual Factors in Reading

These differences in error pattern lend credibility to the position taken by us and other investigators (Liberman, Shankweiler, Orlando, Harris, & Bell–Berti, 1971; Vellutino, Pruzek, Steger, & Meshoulam, 1973; Vellutino, Steger, & Kandel, 1972) that visual perceptual factors are not sufficient to account for the difficulties of the beginning reader. It is hard to see how deficits in scanning, eye movements, and/or the discrimination of the optical form of letters can explain the differences we have found in consonant and vowel error patterns. Taken as optical shapes, the set of letters representing consonants is not marked in any distinctive way from the set representing vowels. The differences in error pattern between consonants and vowels, therefore, cannot be related to a classification based on visual characteristics.

In contrast, consonants and vowels do form distinctive categories in the language and have different functional roles in communication that might well lead to correspondingly different error patterns. Considered from the standpoint of their contribution to the phonological message, consonants carry the heavier information load. (A demonstration of this fact can be easily made: One needs only to compare the information obtainable in a sentence from which all the vowels have been deleted with one in which the consonants have been similarly treated.) The vowels, on the other hand, are the nucleus of the syllable structure and as such are the carriers of prosodic features. They are more subject than consonants to phonetic variation across individuals and dialect groups and are more subject to phonetic drift of time. As we suggested in an earlier paper (Shankweiler & Liberman, 1972), the relatively greater variability of vowels than of consonants may even account in part for the different ways these segments are represented in the orthography, particularly the larger variations in vowel spellings.

Additional evidence that language-related rather than visual factors may be critical in early reading acquisition comes from a series of studies we have begun with good and poor second-grade readers. In this recent research, we are investigating coding in short-term memory, not the error pattern in reading. However, the results of one of the experiments are nonetheless directly relevant here. The paradigm used was an adaptation of Kimura's (1963) test of memory for recurring figures. In this test, a series of stimuli is presented consecutively, and the subject simply has to report *yes* or *no* as to whether the stimulus has already been seen in the series. There are 4 recurring stimuli, which are exposed once in each set of 10 cards, randomly interspersed with 6 nonrecurring stimuli. Eight sets (of 10 cards each) make up a total of 80 cards in the test. The first set of 10 cards constitutes the presentation trials; the following 7 sets are the recognition trials. This same procedure was carried out with three different sets of 80 stimuli—nonsense designs, photographed faces, and nonsense syllables. The results speak for themselves. The poor readers were slightly better than the good readers in memory for nonsense designs but not significantly so. There was also no difference between the two groups of readers in face recognition. The good readers were better than the poor readers only in the nonsense syllables test, and there the difference was highly significant. Thus, despite identical procedures, neither nonlinguistic visual task differentiated between the good and poor readers, whereas the language-based visual task did. We would reason that in the nonsense syllable task, though not in the others, the good readers had a clear advantage: They could recode the information phonetically and thus hold it more efficiently in short-term memory.

At all events, perhaps the most general implication of these findings and those we have obtained in the error analysis is that they again underscore the importance of nonvisual cognitive processes in reading—specifically those relating to language, such as awareness of phonological segmentation, phonetic recoding, and knowledge of the orthography.

IMPLICATIONS FOR INSTRUCTION

It has become fashionable to say that very little is known about how to teach reading and that the teacher makes a greater difference than the method. We agree that the teachers' flexibility and wisdom in adapting existing curricula to meet individual differences, as well as their ability to recognize the necessity for doing so, will always be important variables in the success of any instruction procedure. However, we also maintain that the little we do know about reading is often not reflected in reading curricula. If it were, even the less creative teacher might be more successful and the proportion of children resistant to reading instruction might be decreased.

To take a very basic example, consider what we know about our writing system—namely, that it is alphabetic and not ideographic. From this it would seem to follow that instructional procedures should inform children early on that the printed word is a model of the component phonemes and their particular succession in the spoken word. Conversely, it would follow that the instruction should not, as it often does, mislead children into assuming that the printed word is an ideographic symbol, a notion that will have to be corrected later and, apparently for some children, with great difficulty. Procedures that initiate children into the mystique of reading by drawing their attention to the visual configuration ("remember this shape; it has a tail") and its associated meaning ("the one with the tail means monkey") without alerting them to the relevance of the sound structure of the word may lead them into a blind alley. Their ability to memorize the shapes and associated meanings of a handful of words may lull them and their parents into the comforting belief that they can read, but it may leave them stranded at that stage, functional illiterates with no keys to unlock new words.

Teaching a child how to use an alphabetic system to fullest advantage is complicated by the difficulty young children have in explicitly understanding the phonemic structure of their speech. As we have said, phonemic analysis is hard because of the encodedness of spoken speech into units of syllabic size; syllabic segmentation is demonstrably much easier. However, it need not follow that the phonemic level of analysis should be bypassed at the beginning in favor of the syllable or the word. Instead, perhaps the child can be given a better preparation for phoneme segmentation before reading instruction begins. With that preparation, certain elements of both the so-called phonic and syllabic methods can be introduced later to good effect.

How to Prepare the Child for Phonemic Analysis

The groundwork for this difficult level of analysis begins at home before the child is old enough to go to school. A proper foundation laid at this point can continue to be built upon in the prereading stages of kindergarten and at each succeeding stage of reading acquisition.

Word Play in Early Childhood.   Games in early childhood that draw children's attention to the phonemic content of their spoken language and that give them extended practice in "playing" with words may provide a foundation for future segmentation ability. Examples of such word play would include the learning of nursery rhymes and the introduction of rhyming games that use both real words and nonsense syllables. The value of rhyming activity is that it varies the phonemic content while making few semantic or syntactic demands on the child.

Prereading Techniques.   When the child reaches kindergarten, prereading techniques would stress the phonemic structure of the spoken word before the written letters are introduced. "Listening games" that require the child to identify the initial, medial, and final phonemes in spoken words are in common use and need not be described here. Our only complaint about them is that they are not emphasized sufficiently in prereading training and that in actual practice they often stop with the initial consonant. Teacher-devised methods that might help the child to hear sounds in words are limited only by the creativity of the teacher. One teacher (Marian Howard, 1974) reports that she began prereading instruction for her kindergarteners at the Horace Mann School in New York by first teaching them to listen for the five short vowel sounds in words. Among the games she describes is one that seems particularly useful. In the first stage of the game, the teacher says a given vowel sound once, twice, or three times and asks the class in each case to raise as many fingers as sounds they have heard. After the children can do this correctly with all the short vowel sounds, she adds a consonant to the vowel, thus producing VC syllables ("am," "it," "op," etc.). She intersperses these syllables with single phonemes of the previous lesson and again asks for finger raising. She then progresses to CV syllables, then to CVC, CCVC, and so on, varying vowels and consonants at each stage as needed. She reports that after instituting this "auditory program" in the fall, she could begin teaching reading by Christmas and that 90% of her kindergarteners were decoding print by April (the date of her report to us).

Several auditory training programs that emphasize the analysis of syllables into phonemes (rather than the discrimination of nonspeech sounds) have been available commercially for some time (see, e.g., Lindamood & Lindamood, 1969), but none to our knowledge has as many worthwhile features as that outlined by the Soviet psychologist, Elkonin (1973). In the procedure described by Elkonin, children are presented with a line drawing of an object, animal, and so on, the name of which is in their active vocabulary. Below the picture is a rectangle divided into sections equivalent to the number of phonemes in the pictured word. The children are taught to say the word slowly, putting a counter into the appropriate section of the diagram as they pronounce the word. After this "game" has been played with many different pictured words and the children can do the task successfully without the diagram, the idea of vowel and consonant sounds is introduced. At this time, the color of the counter is differentiated for the two phonetic classes—say, pink for the vowels, white for consonants. The children are first taught the difference between them with one vowel sound, being asked to put down a pink counter whenever they hear that sound. Not until the children can do this with the five short vowel sounds is the graphic form corresponding to the sound introduced.

The Soviet procedure has many pedagogical virtues. First, the line drawing keeps the whole word in front of the children throughout the process of analysis so that they do not have to rely on auditory memory to retain the word being studied. Second, the diagram provides the children with a linear visual-spatial structure to which they can relate the auditory-temporal sequence of the spoken word, thus reinforcing the key idea of the successive segmentation of the phonemic components of the word. Third, the sections of the diagram call the children's attention to the actual number of segments in the word, so that they do not resort to uninformed guessing. Fourth, the combination of drawing, diagram, and counters provides concrete materials that help to objectify the abstract ideas being represented. Fifth, the procedure affords the children an active part to play throughout. Finally, the color coding of the counters leads the children to appreciate the difference between vowels and consonants early in their schooling.

The actual content of the Elkonin procedure can, of course, be varied to fit the needs of the particular child or group of children, thus permitting its use not only for kindergarteners but also as a remedial technique for older children. For example, the teachers can select for analysis syllables that contain whatever phonemes in whatever sequence they deem appropriate.

Three general rules might be suggested for the selection of syllables to be segmented. First, for this early training period, the noise portion of a fricative such as /s/ or the nasal murmur of /n/ or /m/ would be the consonants of choice for the prevocalic position in the syllables to be analyzed. These have the advantage that, unlike other consonants (particularly the stops), they can be produced in isolation. They can thus be used to acquaint the child with the general idea of word analysis without undue interference from coarticulation. Second, because two-segment analysis is easier than three-segment analysis (Helfgott, 1976), training in segmentation might start with two-phoneme syllables. Finally, pilot data (Treiman, 1976) suggest that VC syllables are easier to analyze than CV syllables and that both are (as we have said) easier than CVC syllables. Therefore, a VC to CV to CVC succession in segmentation training would probably be most efficacious.

Another approach to training in phonological analysis, the elision technique outlined by Rosner (1975) in his auditory skills program, places a somewhat greater conceptual burden on the child, but it could profitably be used in conjunction with the Soviet procedure. It is always useful to offer a variety of different methods for attaining the same goals—with the proviso that the emphasis in the auditory training should be on the analysis of the sounds of speech. Training in nonspeech sounds, which are processed quite differently, cannot be expected to have the same effect (Liberman, 1971).

Once the child has been taught, by whatever method, to segment spoken syllables into their phonemic components, the graphic representations of the phonemes can be introduced. The Elkonin technique of adding the letter form to the blank counters might be adopted for teaching the graphic representation of the short vowels and one or two consonants. Thereafter, it would probably be preferable to shift to a more direct procedure for teaching the letters and their phonemic equivalents. This is the stage at which the child progresses from the prereading phase to reading instruction proper.

Basic Procedures for Initial Reading Instruction

We believe that the primary emphasis in teaching to read in an alphabetic system should be on mapping the components of the printed word to those of the spoken word. This analytic conversion from print to speech is best accomplished, in our view, by a method that presents reading, phonics, spelling, and handwriting in coordination with one another so that the instruction in each of these skills reinforces and illuminates the others. The integration of these four aspects of alphabetic communication serves to inform the child that they are indeed different facets of the same process and not separate, unrelated skills.

The First Step: Letter Names and Sounds. We would begin by reading instruction, as many so-called phonics programs do, by teaching the child to associate the shape of the letter with its name and the sound it makes. We have come to agree with Mathews (1966) in his appraisal of this crucial first step: "... no matter how a child is taught to read, he comes sooner or later to the strait gate and the narrow way: he has to learn letters and the sounds for which they stand. There is no evidence whatever that he will ultimately do this better from at first not doing it at all" [p. 208].

The simplest and most efficient way of teaching the sound–symbol correspondences is by the direct teaching of paired associates. Children should not be expected to abstract the correspondences for themselves by a discovery method. Though some can do so, too many fail. Useful materials for teaching the alphabet are alphabet cards that include not only the upper and lower case form of the letter but also the mnemonic of a pictured key word beginning with the sound of the letter (Slingerland, 1971). On presentation of the card, the children are trained to recite the name of the letter, its keyword, and its sound (ā *apple,* ă). As the children learn each vowel, its symbol should be listed in a vertical column on the blackboard and reviewed each day. After the children have learned the five short vowels in this way, a few consonant symbols are introduced. Teaching of the remaining consonants by the same procedure can be continued in tandem with the next step. Meanwhile, the children are taught to write these same letters that they have learned to identify, not as an unrelated series of letters presented in a separate "writing lesson."

Conversion from Speech to Print. The next step in most reading programs that emphasize phonics would probably be "blending." Because letter-to-sound correspondences have been learned in isolation, the traditional phonics method requires that these be combined or blended to form words. There the methods run afoul of the fact about speech that we have emphasized earlier: The spoken word is not a merging of a string of consecutive sounds. In speech, information about the three segments of the word *cat* is encoded into a single sound, the syllable. Therefore, no matter how fast the consecutive phonemes are spoken, "kuh-ă-tuh" merged together consecutively will produce only the nonsense trisyllable "kuhatuh" and not the monosyllabic word *cat* (see Liberman et al., 1967, and Liberman, 1971,for extended discussions of this point).

How can we get around the problem of the fusion of phonemes by coarticulation? Though she also uses the more traditional blending method, Slingerland (1971) described another technique that solves this problem fairly well. In effect, it is a spelling procedure that goes from speech to print and builds on skills that have been learned in the prereading program. Instead of demanding of the child the impossible task of blending "huh-ǎ-mm" to produce *ham,* the teacher first slowly says, *ham,* emphasizing the medial vowel. The child repeats the word, listens for the vowel sound, selects its letter card (color-coded as a vowel) from a wall pocket chart, and places it in a lower tier of the pocket chart. The teacher then repeats the whole word and asks the child for the initial sound in the word. The child selects the appropriate letter card, identifies it, and places it, at the teacher's direction, in front of the vowel ("Where does it go? Before the *a,* because it's the first sound we hear"). The teacher then draws his or her finger along the two letters that the child has placed in the lower tier and says, "Now we have made 'ha.' Let's listen to our word again. Our word is 'ham' (drawing out the sounds). What is the last sound we hear in 'ham'? That's right, it's 'mm.' Find the letter that makes the 'mm' sound. Where do we put the*m?* At the end of the word, because it's the last sound we hear." The lesson continues with the child reading aloud the whole word that has just been constructed and ends with the child writing the word, either on the blackboard or at his or her desk, and reading it back after writing it. This procedure makes concrete for the child a key fact about writing that is difficult to explain in the abstract, namely, that the temporal succession of the overlapping and nondiscrete speech segments (the phonemes) is represented spatially by a left-to-right linear succession of discrete characters (the letters).

A question that arises about this particular lesson is whether it might not confuse children who have sequencing problems because it requires them to start word analysis with the medial vowel sound and then to shift backward to the initial consonant sound. The answer is that in actual practice it does not seem to cause confusion. Typically, most children have sequencing problems in early reading acquisition only because they do not understand the sound structure of the word and its relation to the written word. This spelling procedure has been preceded by much practice in listening for the components of spoken syllables. By building on a foundation of knowledge of the sound structure of the word, this spelling procedure simply clarifies the relationship of the spoken word to print.

Thus far, then, the child has learned the letters and their sounds in isolation and has been taught, without using questionable blending methods, how to convert speech to sequences of letters, that is, how to analyze the spoken word and to construct its written model. But he or she still needs to be taught how to go from print to speech.

Conversion from Print to Speech.   The next step is probably the most critical one because it should prepare the child to make the conversion from any printed word to speech, which is what early reading acquisition is all about. We are indebted to two teachers, Nancy Chapel and Cynthia Conway (1976), formerly learning disability specialists in the Greenwich, Connecticut public schools, for a sequence of lessons that has been highly successful at this stage of reading training. Their procedures can be best characterized as a modification of the "linguistic" method of minimal contrasts, in which the unit under study is the syllable. The goal of their procedures is to make the conversion from printed syllables to speech more nearly automatic by circumventing the letter-by-letter sounding out and blending of the phonics method. The difference between their procedures and other syllabic methods is in the added structure built into the procedure, which elucidates the internal construction of the syllable for the child.

In the Chapel–Conway lessons, the short vowels are listed on the blackboard in a vertical column and reviewed, just as they had been during the alphabet drills. At this time, however, a dash is added after each letter (a__, e__, i__, o__, u__). The children are taught that the short vowel is always followed by a consonant and that the dash represents a missing consonant that will be filled in later. The children are then taught the game of adding a letter in front of the short vowel and pronouncing the resultant combination (mă__, mĕ__, mĭ__, mŏ__, mŭ__). The prevocalic consonant is then varied (să__, sĕ__, sĭ__, sŏ__, sŭ__, etc.). Meanwhile, the children are encouraged to think of words beginning with those syllables and are taught to fill in the missing final consonants in those words (ma*n*, me*t*, mo*p*, etc.). The lessons continue with the addition of consonant blends to the front of the vowel (smă__, smĕ__, smĭ__, etc.).

When the short-vowel, closed syllable has been mastered, the idea of the long vowel is introduced, again with a structured model (a__e). It is pointed out that the missing letter in the model is now followed by an *e*, which is silent but marks the long vowel. Games of word construction with this model are then added. In the last stage, the children learn that when these consonant–vowel combinations appear alone without the added consonant (the dash representing the missing letter is now erased), the vowel is long and matches the letter name.

The children now have at their command a number of the major elements needed for decoding phonetically regular words. They can read closed syllables much more readily than they would if they had to depend on three-step (C–V–C) analysis and blending. At worst, since they know CV syllables, they will have to resort only to a two-step blending (CV–C), which has been found to be easier (Helfgott, 1976). The basic contrast between the short and long vowels has been clarified, as has that between closed and open syllables. Both of these understandings will be of importance to the children in learning to read polysyllabic words and words with more complex vowel orthography.

In conclusion, we must emphasize that we do not pretend to have developed a reading curriculum. What we have offered here are simply the outlines of a few basic procedures for initial reading instruction that seem to follow logically from what is known about the reading process and that have proved successful in informal tests by teachers in the field. We would expect that the use of these and other procedures that relate print to speech will work more rapidly to achieve "reading for meaning," with fewer casualties than could be accomplished by a program that stresses meaning at the outset.

A POSTSCRIPT ON THE CONTRIBUTION
OF ORTHOGRAPHY TO READING PROBLEMS

As we noted earlier, one source of difficulty in reading English is the nature of the orthography and the complex ways in which it represents the language. It is clear, however, that the complexities of the English orthography cannot be the sole explanation of reading difficulties, because some children continue to have problems even when the spelling of the words used in their instruction is phonetically regular and maps the sound directly (Savin, 1972). Nonetheless, we think it useful to look at early reading acquisition in an alphabetic writing system where the complications of orthography are minimized. Serbo-Croatian, the chief language of Yugoslavia, is such a case. The Serbo-Croatian writing system was devised on the principle of one letter shape for each phonemic unit in the language ("Write as you speak and read as it is written!' was the working motto of F. S. Karaćić, who introduced the new orthography).

However, before we can consider the consequences of the regularity of Serbo-Croatian orthography, we must take note of another characteristic of that writing system, namely, that for reasons of politics and religion, two alphabets—one Cyrillic and the other Roman—were developed. Though they both represent the language quite directly, these two alphabets bear a complex relation to each other.[3] While some letters in the two alphabets share both the same shape and the same phonetic value, others are the same in shape but have different phonetic values. In still other instances, different letter shapes are used to represent the same phonetic units. Despite all those possibilities for confusion and interference, one of us was assured in a recent

---

[3]Because Serbo-Croatian has two distinct alphabets for the same language, but with various overlaps in letter shapes and their correspondence, questions arise about how these ambiguous letter shapes are interpreted and where in the processing sequence the assignment to one alphabet or the other is made. Michael Turvey of the Haskins Laboratories, in collaboration with George Lukatela of the Department of Electrical Engineering at Belgrade University, has begun a series of cross-language studies to investigate these interesting questions (Turvey, 1976).

visit to Belgrade schools that the double alphabet presents no problem: All the children learn the forms and letter-to-sound correspondences of both alphabets by the end of the second grade.[4] The children are taught one alphabet for the first year and a half and then master the other by the end of the second year. This should certainly give pause to those who would espouse visual-perceptual and simple memory deficits as causal factors in early reading disability—that is, if their faith had not already been somewhat shaken by the ability of Japanese first graders (and, recently, even kindergarteners) to learn the shapes and sound correspondences of two different sets of some 49 kana symbols (Makita, 1968).

As to the consequences for reading acquisition of the simple orthography of the Serbo-Croatian writing system, that is harder to evaluate. In the first place, children in Yugoslavia enter school at age seven, thus affording them an extra year of development before they must face the reading task. Second, no data are available on the actual incidence of reading disability. It would appear, however, that some children do have reading problems, because the schools have developed extensive programs of prevention and remediation. One school we visited in Belgrade, for example, had a thorough preschool screening procedure. In the spring before school entrance, all the children are individually examined for intelligence, handedness, speech and motor development, sociocultural background, and emotional adjustment. Those with special problems are identified and given additional diagnostic testing and assistance as needed. Another facet of the built-in preventive program in the primary grades of this school is team teaching. Teachers of each grade exchange classes at frequent intervals throughout the school year and hold regular consultations with one another on how best to teach all their problem children. If they decide that additional special remediation in reading is indicated, they refer the children to therapists who advise the teachers and work directly with the children.

It is interesting to note that the basic training of these therapists is in phonetics and speech pathology. We should suppose that the educators require that background in their therapists because they assume a close relation between speech and reading. In any event, the therapy certainly

---

[4]We are grateful to Djordje Kostić, director of the Institute of Experimental Phonetics and Speech Pathology, for providing us with illuminating insights into the Serbo-Croatian language. Special thanks are due to Spasenija Vladisavljević of the Institute for arranging the school visits and serving as interpreter, guide, and informant throughout our discussions with teachers and school administrators. We are also particularly indebted to Ljubica Taipi, director of Branko Radicević school in Novi Beograd, for her generous cooperation in permitting us to talk freely with her staff, and to Ljubica Budimirović, vice-director, for her informative review of their educational programs. Numerous staff members there and in other schools in Belgrade also deserve grateful acknowlededment, but space does not permit mentioning them all by name.

reflects that particular bias, just as ours does. For example, heavy emphasis is placed in both developmental and remedial instruction on prereading drill, and exercises in the analysis of the spoken word. Moreover, once the alphabetic letters are introduced, the procedures are again quite similar in general approach to those we have outlined here. That is, the instruction is directed toward clarifying for the child the relationship between the spoken word and its written counterpart.

The importance that Yugoslavian instructors attach to relating print and speech was made clear to us by Professor Spasenja Vladisavljević of the Institute for Experimental Phonetics and Speech Pathology at Belgrade University, who is in charge of the training and supervision of the therapists. She illustrated her point by describing a typical first-grade reading lesson that follows much practice in listening for sounds in words. The teacher pronounces the sound of the initial consonant of the CVC word to be read (always a nasal or fricative in the early lessons) and writes its letter on the blackboard with a line following it. As the teacher draws out the spoken word for varying periods of time, he or she shortens or lengthens the line following the letter (s_____, s__, s_____). This exercise is repeated with the vowel (ă_____, ă_____, ă__). Then both sounds are spoken and the interval between them is varied and represented accordingly (s_____, ă_____, s__ă_____, să____). The consonant in final position is then added (să_____t), and the word is spoken as a whole (sat). Finally, the word is written without the lines and read aloud. In subsequent lessons, the children are taught to read and write other words by the same procedures. When they have mastered a word, they write it in their notebooks and perhaps use it in a written sentence, which they also read aloud. Thus, reading, writing, and spelling exercises are always coordinated, as we have also proposed.

In summary, it must be said that despite the regularity of the Serbo-Croatian orthography, some children—we do not know how many— apparently do encounter difficulties in early reading acquisition. What proportion of these ultimately become fully literate we also do not know. We have no hard data on either of these questions, though we are told that in the end the children do well and reading disability is not a problem. At all events, cross-national assessments of reading achievement are difficult to evaluate. In this particular case, one does not know how much weight should be given to the regularity of the orthography and how much to the special characteristics of the reading instruction. The answer to this question must await further research.

ACKNOWLEDGMENT

We are indebted to our colleague, Robert Verbrugge, for a critical reading of the manuscript.

REFERENCES

Bever, T. G., & Bower, T. G. How to read without listening. In *Project literacy reports, No. 6.* Ithaca, N.Y.: Cornell University Press, 1966. (ERIC Document Reproduction Service No. ED 010 312)

Calfee, R., Chapman, R., & Venezky, R. How a child needs to think to learn to read. In L. W. Gregg (Ed.), *Cognition in learning and memory.* New York: Wiley, 1972.

Chapel, N., & Conway, C. Personal communication, May, 1976.

Conrad, R. Speech and reading. In J. F. Kavanagh & I. G. Mattingly (Eds.), *Language by ear and by eye: The relationships between speech and reading.* Cambridge, Mass.: MIT Press, 1972.

Elkonin, D. B. U.S.S.R. In J. Downing (Ed.), *Comparative reading.* New York: Macmillan, 1973.

Fowler, C. A., Liberman, I. Y., & Shankweiler, D. On interpreting the error pattern in beginning reading. *Language & Speech,* 1977, *20,* 162–173.

Fowler, C. A., Shankweiler, D., & Liberman, I. Y. Apprehending spelling patterns for vowels: A developmental study. *Haskins Laboratories Status Report on Speech Research,* 1979, SR-57, 231–240, and *Language and Speech,* 1979, *22.*

Gallistel, E., & Ellis, K. *Gallistel-Ellis test of coding skills.* Hamden, Conn.: Montage Press, 1974.

Gibson, E. J., & Levin, H. *The psychology of reading.* Cambridge, Mass.: MIT Press, 1975.

Gleitman, L. R., & Rozin, P. Teaching reading by use of a syllabary. *Reading Research Quarterly,* 1973, *8,* 447–483.

Helfgott, J. Phonemic segmentation and blending skills of kindergarten children: Implications for beginning reading acquisition. *Contemporary Educational Psychology,* 1976, *1,* 157–169.

Howard, M. Personal communication, April, 1974.

Hyde, T. S., & Jenkins, J. J. Differential effects of incidental tasks on the organization of recall of a test of highly associated words. *Journal of Experimental Psychology,* 1969, *82,* 472–481.

Jastak, J., Bijou, S. W., & Jastak, S. R. *Wide range achievement test.* Wilmington, Del.: Guidance Associates, 1965.

Kimura, D. Right temporal-lobe damage. *Archives of Neurology,* 1963, *8,* 264–271.

Liberman, A. M., Cooper, F. S., Shankweiler, D., & Studdert-Kennedy, M. Perception of the speech code. *Psychological Review,* 1967, *74,* 431–461.

Liberman, A. M., Mattingly, I. G., & Turvey, M. T. Language codes and memory codes. In A. W. Melton & E. Martin (Eds.), *Coding processes in human memory.* Washington, D.C.: Winston, 1972.

Liberman, I. Y. Basic research in speech and lateralization of language: Some implications for reading disability. *Bulletin of the Orton Society,* 1971, *21,* 71–87.

Liberman, I. Y. Segmentation of the spoken word and reading acquisition. *Bulletin of the Orton Society,* 1973, *23,* 65–77.

Liberman, I. Y., Shankweiler, D., Fischer, F. W., & Carter, B. Explicit syllable and phoneme segmentation in the young child. *Journal of Experimental Child Psychology,* 1974, *18,* 201–212.

Liberman, I. Y., Shankweiler, D., Liberman, A. M., Fowler, C., & Fischer, F. W. Phonetic segmentation and recoding in the beginning reader. In A. S. Reber & D. Scarborough (Eds.), *Towards a psychology of reading: Proceedings of the CUNY conference.* Hillsdale, N.J.: Lawrence Erlbaum Associates, 1977.

Liberman, I. Y., Shankweiler, D., Orlando, C., Harris, K. S., & Bell-Berti, F. Letter confusions and reversals of sequence in the beginning reader: Implications for Orton's theory of developmental dyslexia. *Cortex,* 1971, *7,* 127–142.

Lindamood, C. H., & Lindamood, P. C. *Auditory discrimination in depth.* Boston: Teaching Resources, 1969.

Makita, K. The rarity of reading disability in Japanese children. *American Journal of Orthopsychiatry,* 1968, *38,* 599–614.

Mark, L. S., Shankweiler, D., & Liberman, I. Y. Phonetic recoding and reading difficulty in beginning readers. *Memory and Cognition,* 1977, *5,* 623–629.

Mathews, M. *Teaching to read historically considered.* Chicago: University of Chicago Press, 1966.

Mattingly, I. G. Reading, the linguistic process, and linguistic awareness. In J. F. Kavanagh & I. G. Mattingly (Eds.), *Language by ear and by eye: The relationships between speech and reading.* Cambridge, Mass.: MIT Press, 1972.

Read, C. Pre-school children's knowledge of English phonology. *Harvard Educational Review,* 1971, *41,* 1–34.

Rosner, J. *Helping children overcome learning disabilities.* New York: Walker, 1975.

Rosner, J., & Simon, D. P. The auditory analysis test: An initial report. *Journal of Learning Disabilities,* 1971, *4,* 384–392.

Rozin, P., & Gleitman, L. R. The structure and acquisition of reading. In A. S. Reber & D. Scarborough (Eds.), *Toward a psychology of reading: Proceedings of the CUNY conference.* Hillsdale, N.J.: Lawrence Erlbaum Associates, 1977.

Savin, H. B. What the child knows about speech when he starts to learn to read. In J. F. Kavanagh & I. G. Mattingly (Eds.), *Language by ear and by eye: The relationships between speech and reading.* Cambridge, Mass.: MIT Press, 1972.

Shankweiler, D., & Liberman, I. Y. Misreading: A search for causes. In J. Kavanagh & I. G. Mattingly (Eds.), *Language by ear and by eye: The relationships between speech and reading.* Cambridge, Mass.: MIT Press, 1972.

Shankweiler, D., & Liberman, I. Y. Exploring the relations between reading and speech. In R. M. Knights & D. J. Bakker (Eds.), *Neuropsychology of learning disorders: Theoretical approaches.* Baltimore: University Park Press, 1976.

Slingerland, B. H. *A multi-sensory approach to language arts for specific language disability children: A guide for primary teachers.* Cambridge, Mass.: Educators Publishing Service, 1971.

Treiman, R. A. *Children's ability to segment speech into syllables and phonemes as related to their reading ability.* Unpublished manuscript, Yale University, 1976.

Turvey, M. Personal communication, February, 1976.

Vellutino, F. R., Pruzek, R. M., Steger, J. A., & Meshoulam, U. Immediate visual recall in poor and normal readers as a function of orthographic-linguistic familiarity. *Cortex,* 1973, *9,* 368–384.

Vellutino, F. R., Steger, J. A., & Kandel, G. Reading disability: An investigation of the perceptual deficit hypothesis. *Cortex,* 1972, *8,* 106–118.

Zifcak, M. *Phonological awareness and reading acquisition in first grade children.* Unpublished doctoral dissertation, University of Connecticut, 1977.

II INSTRUCTION

6 Teaching Hard-to-Teach Children to Read: A Rationale for Compensatory Education

Jerome Rosner
University of Houston

One emphasis of these volumes is early reading and compensatory education. I am taking this to heart as I offer my remarks. I interpret the word *compensatory* in a literal sense—providing special assistance that will make up for, or offset, one's inability to perform "normally" in a given situation.

Society has developed many compensatory devices, particularly for persons with physical and sensory deficits. There are eyeglasses and hearing aids, crutches and wheelchairs, ramps in lieu of stairs, and special handrails in toilets. All of these, and many more are accepted by the general public. No one insists that children with hearing losses throw away their hearing aids and "listen harder." No one makes analogous demands on children with muscular dystrophy who cannot walk more than a step or two without assistance. In these cases, we assure the persons requiring the compensatory devices that there is nothing offensive about needing special assistance, that what really matters is that with the assistance they can perform in ways that more closely approximate the norm.

I concur with that position and insist that it is a proper one for us to take in education. Lots of children do not perform satisfactorily in school. Why? For many reasons, I suppose, but for the present, most of these reasons are best ignored by educators because: (a) educators can rarely, if ever, do anything about the "cause"; and (b) focusing on the cause tends to distract educators from their legitimate professional mission—teaching children. Whatever the reasons are, the point is that most children who require compensatory education really do require it. That is, they require "special" accommodation—special instructional conditions. To search for ways that will elicit from these children the kind of independent learning behaviors one sees in

135

satisfactory school performers is, in many instances, to waste resources and invite continued failure. This is especially true with children past preschool age. In other words, it does little good to try to teach them to do what we have seen adequate performers do on their own, such as induce the phonetic values of letters when given appropriate examples. Instead, we have to accept certain children's need for compensatory education and provide it.

My comments reflect a viewpoint that is based on certain well-established facts:

1. Children display a variety of individual differences.
2. Some of these differences appear to be relatively unchangeable, at least in the short term.
3. Some of these differences have major impact on how readily a child profits from standard reading instruction—on how teachable he or she is.

In light of these facts, I use the construct of *relative teachability* throughout my comments. This is meant to be more than a semantic exercise wherein the phrase *how teachable* substitutes for *how intelligent*. The two may mean the same thing, but the one—*how teachable*—tends to impose the responsibility for children's learning on those assigned to do the teaching, whereas the other—*how intelligent*—blames the children for their lack of progress in the classroom. Said differently, the former implies that virtually all children are teachable, although more effort, more ingenuity, more adaptations may be required for some than for others. The latter implies that classroom procedures and outcomes are fixed and predictable, that the instruction should be the same for all and will simply be less effective with the less intelligent children, no matter what. Extending that construct, I propose certain assumptions:

1. At least some of the traits that determine a child's relative teachability can be identified, described, and measured in fairly precise terms.
2. Standard instruction comprises a finite number of separate components. These can be characterized in fairly precise terms and modified in controllable ways.
3. Given that the foregoing two assumptions are correct, it is possible to match student's traits with instruction in such a way as to effect a "best fit," to optimize instructional outcomes. This can be accomplished by: (a) changing the students, helping them to acquire those traits that will make them more teachable (this is often relatively effective with young, preprimary-grade children); and/or (b) changing the instructional conditions so as to accommodate optimally the children's unique traits.

Relative Teachability

Some children are exceptionally "easy to teach" (ETT). Given exposure to information that presents a set of salient characteristics (e.g., relevant similarities and differences), they are quick to recognize those characteristics, even when they are not highlighted. ETT children are better-than-average inventors of heuristic systems that they use, evaluate the outcomes of, and modify accordingly. They are better organizers of information; hence, they display better memories. They are able to learn, to make satisfactory progress in the classroom, regardless of the instructional approach that is used. As such, they are reinforced in the classroom and at home, practice what they learn in various settings, become even better organizers of information, and so on.

Another group of children—most, in fact—are of average teachability. They are not so adept at inducing concepts from minimal information, but they do not require the explication of everything they have to learn. Given a certain amount of appropriately designed direction, they can invent—discover—the rest. Given a certain amount of appropriate drill and practice, they memorize adequately. Although they are not as adaptable as ETT children, they are sufficiently so to be able to make satisfactory classroom progress with a variety of instructional approaches.

Other children are "hard to teach" (HTT). They require a good deal of explicit instruction. They are not so adept at analyzing information according to its salient attributes. Hence, they are not so adept at organizing that information according to various classification schemes, nor are they good memorizers or good inducers of general concepts. They must be precisely directed to what it is they are to attend to. This, in turn, must be organized in a way that makes it highly apparent and readily memorable, and even then the HTT child requires extended drill and practice in order to retain specific information.

Stated in fewer words, ETT children tend to achieve satisfactorily regardless of instructional approach, although there is little doubt but that some approaches are more interesting, more appealing, than others. HTT children, on the other hand, reflect instructional conditions, approximating satisfactory classroom achievement only when the instruction is specifically designed to accommodate their unique characteristics.

If these principles are accepted, it becomes necessary to define the relevant components of instruction, that is, those student traits that must be accommodated when a "best fit" is sought and the instructional conditions that are amenable to modification for providing that best fit.

THE COMPONENTS OF INSTRUCTION:
THE STUDENT AND THE
INSTRUCTIONAL CONDITIONS

The assumptions already presented assert that standard instruction comprises a finite number of components that can be defined in fairly precise terms and that the same can be done with relevant student characteristics (Cooley & Lohnes, 1976). Clearly, this could yield a lengthy list if one were to succumb to hairsplittling. For this discussion, I suggest that instruction be conceived of as comprising only three major components: program, teacher, and physical environment.

The trick, then, is finding the best organization among the three components and the best interaction between those three and the student. Given a good fit, the student should learn—indeed, that is the best criterion for determining whether the fit is a good one. (Learning, in this instance, is defined as the acquisition of skills and knowledge that were not present prior to the interaction between the student and the instruction.) Before attempting to determine how to construct the best fit among these components, one must examine and define them separately. As I do this, I address particularly the needs of the HTT child. By definition, the others require less individual concern. They are at least adequately teachable under a variety of conditions; hence the fit need not be so precisely designed.

The Student

What student charactistics are particularly important in terms of affecting learning outcomes? Obviously, a child's physical state is crucial. The child who is drastically undernourished, the child whose vision or hearing is less than adequate, the child who cannot sit upright for extended periods of time because of some physical disability—those children will not profit optimally from standard instruction. For my purposes, however, these characteristics are not of direct concern. When they exist, they should of course be identified and taken care of, to whatever extent possible, by the proper health-care professionals. The primary interventions should come not from the educational system but rather from the outside agents who are prepared to provide proper professional care. Education's responsibility commences after the outside professionals have done all they can; further discussion of the educator's role in these situations is beyond the scope of this chapter.

Motivation is another important variable, one that strongly affects a child's classroom performance. However, it is not useful to address the question of motivation out of context, that is, without also discussing the environment in which the desired behavior is to be elicited and the tasks that are to be engaged in. For the present, I ignore the topic and assume that every child can be motivated so long as we are clever enough to provide the kinds of conditions that will generate that motivation: for example, conditions that make it possible for the child to learn and to progress at some satisfactory rate, conditions that emanate from effectively matching instruction to the child's unique characteristics.

There are, I believe, two basic differences among children that we should worry about: namely, certain of the basic aptitudes and the amount of information that they have acquired to date—their knowledge base. These characteristics have strong effects on learning, and we can do something about them in terms of improving them and/or accommodating them in the classroom by making appropriate modifications in instruction.

Basic Aptitudes.   This category could include a long list of abilities. However, only two general abilities are discussed, two that have been shown to be exceptionally important in school learning (Bond & Tinker, 1967; Gibson & Levin, 1975; Rosner, 1972, 1975): (a) the child's ability to identify the salient structural attributes of a concrete spatial array and then to map the interrelationships among those attributes (visual-analysis skills): and (b) the child's ability to identify the salient phonological attributes of a verbal acoustical array and then to map the interrelationships among those attributes (auditory-analysis skills). Said differently, visual-analysis skills are those abilities that enable us to perceive a spatial array as being made up of a finite collection of separate parts that fit together in a specific way; auditory-analysis skills are those abilities that enable us to perceive spoken language as being made up of a finite collection of separate sounds that fit together (sequence) in a precise way.

It has been well documented that children acquire these analytical skills as they mature; in fact, the acquisition of these skills is often noted as a milestone for plotting development. Six-year-olds, for example, are expected to display better visual and auditory skills than are 4-year-olds. Six-year-olds are expected to be able to copy geometric designs as complex as triangles or divided rectangles, whereas 4-year-olds have probably just acquired the capacity to copy squares (Ilg & Ames, 1964). Six-year-olds are typically able to analyze spoken words into their phonemes, demonstrating this capacity by responding accurately to the request to say the portion of a word that remains after deleting a phoneme. Four-year-olds cannot ordinarily do this; at best, their unit of analysis in attending to spoken language is a semantic one—for example, the syllable in a two-syllable compound word (Rosner & Simon, 1971).

There is strong evidence to support the argument that until a certain level of competency is attained in these skills, children will not profit optimally from standard primary-grade instruction in reading or arithmetic; they will not be able to perceive the underlying coding systems, to induce those critical concepts from minimal information. Instead, since they will not recognize that letters and numerals serve to "code" the salient attributes of spoken words and spatial arrays respectively, they will be forced into trying to memorize printed words and number facts as separate bits of information—an approach that has finite limitations, given the capacity of normal short-term and working memory.

It appears further that these skills are, at least to some degree, subject specific. Visual-analysis skills tend to relate most directly to arithmetic and reading and listening comprehension, auditory skills to the primary-grade aspect of reading commonly identified as "decoding" (Rosner, 1973). It follows, therefore, that a child who displays substandard visual- and/or auditory-analysis skills is likely to experience learning difficulties if standard instruction is employed.

Knowledge Base.   In addition to the two basic aptitudes, certain facts must be available to the student. ("Facts" differ from "aptitudes" in this context in that aptitudes are ordinarily acquired as a normal outcome of growth and development, whereas facts are acquired as the outcome of specific learning experiences and would not be known if they had not been taught in one way or another.) For example, if a child is to learn to read, he or she must come to the task with a great deal of factual information. In order to be a reader—to be able to obtain meaningful information from orthographic symbols—the child must be able to map language onto those symbols with ease—fluently. This implies a fair degree of familiarity with those symbols; they must be in the child's knowledge base. If the child cannot accurately identify certain letters without first identifying some of their salient attributes, the extra step in the process will have a remarkable disruptive effect on his or her reading. In addition, the child must be familiar with the spoken version of the words that are to be read; they must be in the child's knowledge base. If the child is not familiar with the spoken words, learning to read them will be extremely difficult. There are many other relevant examples that could be given, but these two should be sufficient to illustrate the point.

The interrelationship between these two variables, basic aptitudes and knowledge base, is strong and evident. A child with highly competent basic aptitudes who lacks a sufficient knowledge base—because of having recently immigrated from Poland, say, and therefore being totally unfamiliar with the letters—will be forced to attend to minute attributes of the printed letters. This will slow down reading to the point where extracting meaningful information is impossible, even if the spoken forms of the words to be read are already known.

If the premise is accepted that the two student variables of concern are the child's basic aptitudes and the child's entering knowledge base, then the necessity of exercising one or both of the two options already mentioned can be perceived—change the child and/or modify instruction to accommodate the child. The first option, change the child, implies that something can be done about teaching children more efficient basic aptitudes and expanding their knowledge bases. This does appear to be possible, at least to some extent. That children's knowledge can be increased is obvious; the trick is to do it before they enter the classroom and start to fail. Although it is not so blatantly obvious, it is also true that many children respond favorably to programs that are appropriately designed to teach them better visual-and auditory-analysis skills and that the effects of this training can be observed in their school performance (Rosner, 1972). Again, the trick is to intervene early, before the child starts to fall behind in classroom programs.

I now turn to examining the three components of standard instruction, paying special attention to ways in which one or more of these components can be modified to accommodate effectively a child's unique needs, especially when that child is HTT. (Someday, of course, the implications of "best fit" with the ETT child should be examined; that ETT children do not present learning problems is no reason for them to be ignored. But for the moment, this aspect of the topic is set aside.) The three components of standard instruction, identified earlier, are the program, the teacher, and the physical environment.

The Program

This is the component that has been given the most attention in these volumes—indeed, in nearly every publication pertaining to reading instruction. Perhaps this is justified; perhaps, instead, it is more the case that since it is the component that is best defined, it is the one that is examined most often. (This is a little like the old joke about the village idiot who explains that he is looking for a lost coin under a streetlight rather than at the place where he dropped the coin—some remote, darker place—because "there is more light here.") There are many different reading programs available today, and these can be described and compared in a variety of ways. (*Reading program,* as I use the phrase in these remarks, refers to the instructional materials—their objectives, scope, and sequence.) In attempting to devise a system where the program can be optimally articulated with other instructional components and with the unique characteristics of the student, it seems reasonable to suggest that reading programs should be examined in terms of:

1. The extent to which the basic concepts of phoneme/grapheme relationships are made explicit; that is, the extent to which phonemic principles are introduced overtly and precisely instead of being implied. Some reading programs lean heavily on explicating the relationships between letters and sounds; these are usually identified as "phonics" programs. Others tend to be biased in the opposite direction, claiming that emphasizing letter–sound correspondences will interfere with the ultimate goal of reading—extracting meaningful information from printed texts. Most of the currently popular basal programs follow this rationale and introduce a number of "sight words" in the beginning lessons.

2. The extent to which appropriate "chunks"—larger units of analysis, specific strings of letters in addition to just individual ones—are taught explicitly. It seems obvious that it is not possible to get beyond the primary level of reading if one is limited to reading letter by letter, sound by sound. The competent reader must deal with larger units, letter clusters that represent units of blended sounds. Yet this skill of reading larger units is not taught directly in most reading programs.

3. The extent to which drill and practice materials are made available and interesting. Some children—especially, by definition, ETT children—do not require much drill and practice. They memorize easily, simply because they are such good organizers. Hence, they do their drill and practice outside the classroom; they tend to read more, because they know how to read. Other children—the HTT, by definition—are not good memorizers. Obviously, since they are not good analyzers, they cannot be very good classifiers; hence, they cannot be good organizers; hence, they cannot be good memorizers. The units they attend to are small. Their processes are too primitive to deal with larger units in a differentiated fashion. This places serious limitations on their reading speed and comprehension. As a result, they do not practice very much; they cannot read very well, if indeed at all. Thus, they require a lot more drill and practice of the proper type.

Suppose we speculate on how two sets of children—one ETT, the other HTT—respond to a standard linguistic reading program where a good number of "phonically regular" sight words are introduced early; where phonics principles are not taught in a structured, precise way but are strongly hinted. The ETT children would probably memorize—learn to recognize on sight—a limited number of words such as *fat* and *sat*. Once this was accomplished, they would (because they have competent analysis skills) recognize that these two words are in some ways the same and in other ways different. then they are taught another word, *fit* for example. Again, ETT children would quickly note how this new word compares visually and acoustically with *fat* and *sat*. Having done this, they would not have to be taught or need to memorize the word *sit*. They would read it on their own and explain that it "has to say *sit,* what else could it say?" The system, from the ETT child's knowledgeable view, is obvious.

Over time, these children add more words to their storehouse of memorized knowledge (knowledge base), thereby acquiring an even better ability to figure out unfamiliar words. Not surprisingly, these children like to read; they read voluntarily, for pleasure. After all, they can read! Thus, the circumstances are circular. ETT children figure out the system, because they: (a) can analyze the visual and acoustical construction of words into salient separate parts; (b) quickly recognize where these constructions are the same and where they differ; (c) make better "educated guesses" when a word is encountered that is not as regular in spelling as it might be; and (d) are inclined to read, at least in part, because it is something of which the adults around them enthusiastically approve. Reading makes them even better at analyzing words, printed and spoken, and at methodically comparing them, thereby enabling them to make better educated guesses, and so on.

There is more to learning to read than this, of course. ETT children usually have a fair number of words in their speaking vocabulary (knowledge base) before they enter school; you cannot make an educated guess unless you are educated, unless you know the words. And ETT children read enough that their reading becomes fluent—where most words become familiar and are recognized on sight, and only a few have to be sounded out. This point is crucial. Words that contain more than a few letters cannot be sounded out very well. It takes too much time; by the time readers get to the letters at the end of a moderately long word, they tend to forget the sounds at the beginning of the word. Furthermore, in many words in our language, sounding out will not work, because the letters have more than a single sound representation. The more time spent on sounding out words, the less time available to think about, to comprehend, the meaning that the words convey.

Good readers sound out very few words; they recognize most of them on sight. But they did not originally learn them all through memorization, even though they ultimately do memorize them. At first, they probably did sound out a good number of those words, but it was done often enough that the words became completely familiar. They stopped paying attention to the separate letters and sounds and dealt with the whole word as a unit, rarely having to resort to sounding-out strategies. And in those cases where the whole word was not a familiar unit, then a least part of the word was.

This last point is important. All learning depends on adding new knowledge to knowledge already acquired, as in a nesting process where the new knowledge encompasses the old rather than simply attaching to it. Rarely are we asked to learn something that is entirely novel. There are always some components that are already familiar. Thus, by recognizing those familiar components, we reduce the learning task—there is not all that much that is new. And in those instances where there is a lot of new information to acquire, we know that the task will be more difficult and require more time.

Unfortunately, HTT children do not respond as just described. By definition, these children do not readily perceive salient similarities and differences, because they are not adept analyzers of visual and/or acoustical arrays. As a result, they resort to attempting to memorize all the words they are asked to learn to read; and worse yet, they do not invent heuristic strategies for facilitating memorization.

Such children require forthright instruction in letter–sound correspondences. It is foolhardy to assume that they will discover this concept within a reasonable length of time, before motivation is utterly extinguished. In addition to straightforward phonics instruction, these children must also be shown how very small words fit into larger words and be given sufficient drill, so that they begin to perceive those smaller words—letter clusters—as single units of analysis rather than as collections of separate letters with each letter representing a separate sound. Having been shown, they are likely to apply the concept and display this in improved reading skills (Rosner, Cass, & DiCostanzo, 1976).

Teacher

What teacher traits are pertinent in terms of accommodating at student's unique characteristics? I propose the following:

1. The extent to which the teacher is acquainted with the subject being taught; specifically, the degree to which the teacher is familiar with the basic concepts of reading. It may come as a surprise to some, but it is indeed shocking how many teachers enter their profession totally unaware of the relevant dimensions of teaching reading, of the principles that underlie the various reading programs they will encounter in schools. It is even more shocking how many teachers continue to be unaware of these things, even after they have taught for more than a few years.

2. The extent to which the teacher is willing (and able) to be pedantic, to be precise and repetitive—this in contrast to being the kind of teacher who thrives only in an instructional environment where "discovery learning" is the desired outcome. (HTT children are not good discoverers. If they were, they would not be HTT; they would not need compensatory education.)

3. The extent to which the teacher can perform in a structured, relatively nondynamic environment. Some teachers are exceedingly comfortable in such a setting—in a classroom where the desks are arranged in orderly rows, where the children are conditioned to raise their hands before speaking, and so on. Some are not; they have been influenced by "modern" notions to the degree that they perceive such environments as punitive, "repressive," or in

general, negative. Yet in my experience, HTT children seem to require such settings, at least during that portion of the school day when reading is taught.

4. The extent to which the teacher can cope with a slowly rising, small-increment learning curve. HTT children can be taught (that is the underlying assumption of my remarks, of course), but they learn more slowly. Some teachers can cope with this, some cannot; they lack the clinical confidence, the experience, to know that an approach will "work" if they will only persevere.

Physical Environment

What are the important physical variables of an instructional environment in terms of accommodating the individual needs of HTT children?

1. The extent of physical structure available. Many schools in recent years have been built as "open space" facilities; walls between classrooms have been eliminated. This has created buildings that often are attractive, novel looking, even exciting, but not necessarily what the HTT child needs. If the child requires more explicit instruction and more drill and practice than do most, then the open space and its accompanying noise and other distractions are not desirable.

2. The extent to which the students make decisions regarding the organization of their school day. Certain classroom management schemes are designed to allow the children to determine which classroom activities they wish to engage in and when to do so. Children with competent analytical skills, children who are adept at analyzing and organizing concrete spatial arrays, are likely also to be adept at organizing time. In contrast, children who are not competent at sorting and ordering the structural components of a spatial array are likely to encounter similar confusion when faced with the task of organizing something less concrete, such as the time available in a school day. HTT children are not apt to be good organizers of time. Hence, they are likely to be better off in an environment where scheduling is relatively rigid—predictable —and done by someone else.

3. The extent to which class makeup is homogeneous in terms of ability in the subject being taught. This, I recognize, is a controversial issue. There are those who argue that homogeneous grouping is the catalyst for "self-fulfilling prophecies." In one sense, of course, this argument can be supported in that all of the children in a "slow" group tend to be perceived that way by their teachers. On the other hand, there is less sense in placing children who require the kind of structure just described with children who make at least satisfactory progress under less precisely organized circumstances. How can a teacher be induced to teach explicitly to a handful of HTT children when the others in the classroom do not require that? What is the teacher to do with those other children? And what is the teacher to do with the HTT children

during those times when the instruction is being aimed at their more competent classmates? Surely the impact on self-image—recognition of their inferior abilities—is as destructive as are the negative effects of homogeneous grouping.

Homogeneous grouping need not lead to self-fulfilling prophecies, nor need it be maintained for the entire school day. Why cannot children be grouped one way—homogeneously—for reading instruction and another—heterogeneously—for other classes? And secondly, is it not reasonable to argue that given a classroom teacher who displays the traits necessary to succeed with HHT children, given an appropriately accommodating reading instruction program, given a physical setting that is suitable for these children, learning will occur—that the children will make progress and may, in fact, ultimately be able to be blended in with their ETT classmates?

4. The extent to which there is an appropriate student–teacher ratio. As noted, HTT children require more careful instruction and more teacher attention, because they are not so adept at self-instruction; hence, the teacher must spend more time with each student; hence, the teacher will not be able to manage effectively as many students as will the teacher whose class comprises ETT children. Thus, student–teacher ratio must be kept as low as possible. Again, this need not be for the entire school day or for the duration of the child's school career. It should be provided for as long as, and in those subjects where, the child requires it. It is nonsensical to insist that this is not reasonable, that student–teacher ratio must be the same across classrooms. It simply will not work: It will only perpetuate what is now going on—continued failure of those children who can least afford to fail.

5. The extent to which the length of instructional sessions is appropriate. Some children, the ETT, can sustain interest in certain tasks for days on end. Obviously, this is at least in part due to the fact that they can make sufficient progress in whatever they are doing to keep it interesting. HTT children, in contrast, must deal with smaller increments of instructional material and usually must be drilled on it. Thus, they are not as likely to retain enthusiasm for the task beyond a limited period of time. This should be accommodated. There should not be fixed time periods of instruction. If 10 minutes at a particular task is the child's limit, that is what should be accommodated, with the teacher constantly being attentive to signals that indicate when the child is able to sustain interest for longer periods of time. And this will occur as the child starts to make progress.

6. The extent to which teachers are reinforced by school administrators, parents, and others. Teachers are people too. They must complete their workday with a feeling that they have demonstrated professional competence. If they do not end the day with that sense, they will probably do one of two things: (a) quit their job; or (b) develop a rationale for explaining why their students are not progressing, a rationale that excuses them and fixes

the blame on some outside factor—most often, the students themselves, their "abilities," lack of motivation, socioeconomic factors, and so on. Clearly, the first option is not exercised very often. Teachers do not work just for money, but it is not a trivial consideration. Hence, since they enjoy earning a salary, they are not apt to quit so quickly, especially in this era in which alternative teaching situations are not readily available. Thus, they are most often apt to accept the second option, and once it is accepted, there is very little likelihood that the children in their classrooms will change their patterns of behavior.

It is essential therefore that school administrators provide adequate and appropriate reinforcement that goes beyond salary. The teacher must be assured that HTT children may not make great strides each day but that they will progress so long as they are being provided with what they need in terms of instructional conditions. The teacher must know that lack of progress on Monday does not predict no progress the other days of the week, that professional gratification may be delayed but that it will be available if they persevere. (In truth, of course, this may not be so in every instance, but the mental attitudes must be sustained.)

CONCLUSION

I want to end with an admission: I have oversimplified. I know I have ignored many factors that strongly influence how well children do in school. But I do not acknowledge that because of this oversimplificiation, what I propose in this chapter will not work. On the contrary, I argue that unless we oversimplify, unless we recognize that we cannot possibly take into consideration *all* the factors that affect how well a child learns to read, unless we therefore focus on those factors that we can identify and are able to control, many children will continue to do poorly in school, and schools will continue to fix blame on the children—fail them—when in fact it is the school's failure.

Schools exist so that children may be taught. Some children require more teaching than do others; they require teaching that recognizes their deficits and provides appropriate compensatory accommodations. The purpose of this chapter is to propose an organized approach for determining what these accommodations should be.

REFERENCES

Bond, G. L., & Tinker, M. A. *Reading Difficulties: Their diagnosis and correction.* New York: Appleton-Century-Crofts, 1967.

Cooley, W. W., & Lohnes, P. R. *Evaluation research in education.* New York: Halstead Press, 1976.

Gibson, E., & Levin, H. *The psychology of reading.* Cambridge, Mass.: MIT Press, 1975.

Ilg, F., & Ames, L. B. *School readiness.* New York: Harper & Row, 1964.

Rosner, J. *The development and validation of an individualized perceptual skills curriculum* (Publication No. 1972/7). Pittsburgh: University of Pittsburgh, Learning Research and Development Center, 1972. (ERIC Document Reproduction Service No. ED 062731)

Rosner, J. Language arts and arithmetic achievement, and specifically related perceptual skills. *American Educational Research Journal,* 1973, *10,* 59–68.

Rosner, J. *Helping children overcome learning difficulties.* New York: Walker, 1975.

Rosner, J., Cass, J., & DiCostanzo, J. *Adapting reading instruction to accommodate variance in student's structural analysis skills.* Unpublished manuscript, University of Pittsburgh, Learning Research and Development Center, 1976.

Rosner, J., & Simon, D. The auditory analysis test: An initial report. *Journal of Learning Disabilities,* 1971, *4,* 384–392.

7
Theoretical Research and Instructional Change: A Case Study

Marie M. Clay
University of Auckland New Zealand

What happens when the results of a research program in beginning reading are translated into classroom practice through the processes of publication, in-service training, and workshop or study-group activities? What influence can research findings have on instruction? This chapter treats separately an evolving theory of reading development and field communication aspects of the question, using a long-term project in New Zealand as a case study. The research questions were posed in 1962, and several projects were reported in academic journals by 1971. In 1972 texts were published, and an intensive program of talks, workshops, and reporting for teachers was undertaken. For the purposes of this chapter, this exercise in communication ended in 1976 with the release of an innovative in-service program purporting to bring some of the research insights to classroom teachers.

ORIGINS OF THE RESEARCH QUESTIONS

From my teaching and clinical experience and an academic training in developmental psychology, I posed this question: Can we see the process of learning to read going wrong within a few months after school entry? There was little New Zealand research on reading at any level and none on the first year to answer the question. A review of overseas literature suggested three approaches to reducing reading failure: (1) predict reading failures from certain characteristics of children prior to or at school entry and give them special instruction; (2) continually revise the instruction in beginning reading; (3) use a diagnostic-remedial approach with the children who have been allowed to progress at their own rates for more than two years before remedial help is offered.

From the literature I concluded (1) that predictions of success or failure prior to entry to programs were only moderately successful, with correlation coefficients of the order of .4 to .5; (2) that the new reading methods and materials did not seem to alter significantly the percentages of children failing; and (3) that the success rates of children in remedial programs were also low.

Perhaps most unsettling of all was my personal experience. I had taught two remedial pupils who, after a few months of instruction, made sudden and spectacular gains in reading amounting to three years of reading age. My theories of reading processes did not explain these successes, and these positive instances sent me searching for a better model than the Schonell–Gates–Monroe–Durrell type of reading theory that I had studied. It was probably this search for explanation in these particular cases that drew me toward an information-processing framework because I knew my own instructional behaviors in my remedial program: I could record, count, and interpret the changed behaviors, but there were some unknowns between these. What precisely had the children done with the instruction that had wrought such effective changes in their behavior?

A pilot study answered my major question. It was possible to record objectively the behavior of children who were establishing a success or failure pattern in the first year of instruction. Rather more exciting, however, was a recording of self-correction behaviors, an unlooked-for explanatory variable, by which children could teach themselves, irrespective of the program they were in. (This crucial theoretical variable is discussed later in the chapter.) My understanding of error behavior also changed in that year, 1962, because the high-progress readers made the most errors.

As the pilot study seemed to be probing new territory, I began to tighten up the research design. I planned (1) to start at school entry on the child's fifth birthday (in New Zealand, children enter school on their fifth birthday, which may be any day of the school year); (2) to make weekly observations, an intensive longitudinal method; (3) to administer a test battery within 2 weeks of the child's reaching ages 5.0, 5.6, and 6.0, providing a tight control over age variability; (4) to record observable behaviors in an individual reading situation and attempt to obtain a total record; and (5) to adopt deliberately and obstinately an atheoretical, no-hypotheses, stance to data collection.

Somewhere in these design decisions lay the seeds of productivity for any instructional changes I would be able to recommend:

1. A detailed description of what happened to Auckland children in their first year of instruction could lead directly to ideas for classroom improvements.

2. The year-long study would allow time for the child to adjust to school, for variability in the child's performance to be recorded, and for experimentation with the program by the teacher. There would be time for the instruction to show effects and for trends to become apparent. Implications from this longitudinal approach could differ markedly from those that emerge from one-point-of-time cross-sectional studies or from before-and-after studies of educational treatment.

3. The search would be directed toward behaviors that would detect early failure rather than toward methods of stimulating high-progress readers. All children entering school would be used, and the failures would be seen against the backdrop of the succeeding children. High- and low-progress readers would be compared to locate discriminating variables. Although this procedure could lead to suggestions that would raise the mean level of progress by narrowing the distribution of the lower 50% of readers, it was unlikely to address more general problems of instructional approach.

4. Some theoretical integration of the findings with reviewed theory and research might be possible because the data base would be sound. The theory building would have internal validity only for urban New Zealand. The research would have no external validity for other programs or other cultures.

Between the end of the pilot study and the beginning of the main study in 1963, a major curriculum revision occurred. With the free distribution of a new series of reading books, the centralized Department of Education ousted the word-learning method of the past 10 years and placed New Zealand reading outside the bounds of methods promulgated in the reading literature. In response to the requrests of teachers' committees, the Department of Education had in 1950 officially discarded letter–sound approaches as being central to reading. Now, the teachers' recommendations were to reject a sight–vocabulary approach, and the new curriculum supported this change. In the new program, children would read many interesting short books in a new graded series. Teachers would introduce new concepts and language and the plot of the short story to a reading group, and within 1 or 2 weeks, children would have completed the book. The approach has been called "a book experience approach." It is analogous to language experience methods, but the stories are introduced to the children rather than elicited from them. Comprehension would have the highest value. Teaching points would arise as the child read, and prior teaching of sounds or of words on lists would seldom occur. Not all the vocabulary of the early books would need to be learned—only the high-frequency words (Clay, 1976; Simpson, 1962). This major shift in teaching method may have produced sufficient uncertainty at the classroom level to create a receptiveness to new ideas in the 1970s.

Muttering to myself about the grim effects of practicing errors and with blind trust that my carefully designed procedures for studying reading in the context of the old instructional program would be equally effective in the new program, I began my recording in the first week of the new style of instruction. (The timing was fortuitous: The Department of Education had not replied to my inquiry about the timing of the introduction of the new program.) It was not so difficult to adopt an atheoretical position in this situation. The schools I selected were those where I was personally welcome, although the socioeconomic range of the students was similar to that of the city as a whole. I approached schools with great respect for their sensitivity, aware that the intrusion of my research needs called for their cooperation, and more alert than the staff themselves to the exposure of poor teaching that could result from my record keeping. I became a friend of the schools and of the children, but I felt the cold suspicion of the department in the background. That is where the research program began in 1963.

FINDINGS AND THEORY

First Year Progress

Every child who entered each of 6 schools in Term 1, 1963, was included in the descriptive study. By 1966 there was a report plotting the progress from their fifth to sixth birthdays of 100 urban white children in the instructional program (Clay, 1966b). What the children did, what progress occurred, the grouping and regrouping, and the confusions and retardations were recorded.

The Use of Syntax.   An analysis of 8,000 substitution errors made by the 100 children showed a high incidence (72%) of syntactic equivalence between error substitutions and the textual stimulus (Clay, 1968). The children's first guesses at the points of uncertainty in their reading tended to be dominated by their control over the syntax of their language. In several parts of the world, researchers were arriving at the same insights at the same time. The oral language habits of the linguistically average child provide a source of relatively stable responses that give the child some success in predicting what words are likely to occur in a text and in detecting reading errors.

The Use of Visual Cues.   The error analysis showed that the use of visual perceptual cues for encoding and verifying was slow to emerge and was for a long time unreliable and unstable. In this program of instruction, cues from situation or story and from spoken language were supplemented slowly by cues from letter knowledge, word knowledge, letter–sound associations, and syllabic awareness. Seen in perspective, the child's oral language skills make an excellent starting point because they provide a set of well-established stable responses. However, visual perception must proceed toward a fine knowledge of letters within words, and some children maximize the importance of oral language and fail to attend to visual cues. Adequate learning must proceed in the direction of more receptiveness to visual perceptual cues, which must eventually dominate the process. They did not do so in the first year. The average 6-year-old could identify only half of the letter symbols of the upper- and lower-case alphabets, although within the local definition, he or she was reading.

Self-Correction. In the error analysis, account was taken of the spontaneous correction of errors, which presumably stems from the awareness, however vague, that there is not always a neat fit between the spoken and printed words. Readers may become conscious of the difference between what they have said and one of the several messages of the text for several reasons:

1. The response may not make sense—in the sentence, in the story or with the pictures. This creates cognitive dissonance. For example, a child may read, "Dad, let me paint you," for *Dad, let me paint too,* and exclaim, "Hey! You can't paint YOU!

2. The response may make sense, but something in the print may be incongruous with the response given. This creates perceptual dissonance. For example, the child may read, "Mother said," for *Mother asked* and then protest, "It hasn't got the same letters as *said*" (visual cues), or "But it starts with an *a!*" (letter–sound awareness).

3. Berlyne (1960) suggested that a dissonant relation can also exist between cognitive elements and an overt action that the subject has already executed or is contemplating. This type of dissonance might be expected in early reading behavior. Movement across a line, and the finger pointing that supports it, are action sequences involved in the beginning reading process. Another action sequence consists of the speech impulses emitted as the child invents or reads a text. Somehow the word unit must be isolated from the flow of speech and matched to a word pattern located in the text in a sequential coordination of visual locating and speech impulses.

Dissonance may arise from action sequences, from spatial cues, from semantic, syntactic, or morphophonemic cues, or from visual perceptual cues. The child, aware that "something is wrong," may search for a response that resolves the dissonance (Clay, 1969).

An Information-Processing View.

From the foregoing and other analyses the interpretation was made that efficient information-processing strategies are developed by children who make good progress in learning to read. That such strategies can be developed by young children at a stage of intuitive, rather than logical, thinking may be explained in terms of Neisser's (1963) concept of multiple processing, which he considers appropriate for dealing with novel, irregular stimuli (also see Clay, 1969). The first steps toward such multiple-processing strategies are taken very early in the reading program as children begin to choose between alternative responses. Gradually, their choices become more and more constrained by the visual and linguistic features of the texts.

These arguments were included in Goodacre's *Methods—A Reading List and Glossary of Terms* (1971), and they have been made by Weber (1968, 1970), K. S., Goodman (1969), Y., Goodman, (1970), and Nurss (1969). In 1972 Goodacre drew extensively from my work (Clay, 1966a, 1969) in her publication *Hearing Children Read* (1972), comparing the results with those of Biemiller (1970), Burke and Goodman (1970), and Christenson (1969). The theory that was emerging in my research was convergent with that in other reported research.

The Third Year of Instruction

Children in their third year of instruction were also studied (Williams & Clay, 1973). The average age of the children was 7.9 years. A record was made of all observable behavior as the children read five graded passages: words correct and words incorrect, pausing, omitting or inserting or substituting words, ignoring punctuation, self-correction and repetition, attacking words, whispering, lip movement, finger pointing, and appeals for help and refusals. The techniques derived in the study of beginning readers proved equally appropriate for the older children. This, in itself, was interesting.

Word Solving.   From the error analyses it was possible to conclude that the children used their knowledge of the English language as a guide to the choice of the types of words that could occur. They used meaning cues, and they used letter–sound relationships in association with other cues, without audible analysis of words. Most errors had a high degree of agreement with the syntax, meaning, and visual cues of the text word.

In studying the first year of learning to read, it had been found that visual cues played less of a role than did syntactic and semantic cues in the errors the children made. At the third-year level, visual cues played a role for children at all levels of progress—high, average, or low. Visual cues contributed to 85% to 91% of the errors at this level, despite the slow progress in this area during the first year. Reversal of letter order was rare.

Children did not overtly use analytic strategies. The audible analysis of words into sounds, (sl–a–sh–d) or syllables (sur–faced) was found for only 5.5% of successful attack, although teachers had been stressing analysis in word study lessons for two years. A further 6% of responses involved a delay that might have been due to covert analysis, making 11% of successful solving. On the other hand, almost half of the word solving was achieved by self-correction. An error was made, but the child solved the problem at a second or third attempt without prompting, help, or audible analysis. If the error sentence was sensible and acceptable English, there was less likelihood of the error being corrected. The importance of this kind of word solving is emphasized by the high rates at which it occurred.

Confirming Checks.   The easy flow of reading is interrupted when children repeat a word that they have already read correctly. This kind of nonfluency occurred almost as often as self-correction, in nearly 40% of all successful attacks. Why? One can only guess. Perhaps the child was unsure of the word or its relation to other words. He or she may have expected something different. It may have sounded wrong. It may have looked wrong. Each assumption implies that the child who read correctly and repeated the same word was checking something. There must be a cognitive component in this. The child seeks to understand what has been read. It is not enough merely to emit a response.

A Self-Improving system.   From this error-detecting, correcting, and confirming behavior children learn how to search, how to use cues, and how to check on their responses (given that no counterproductive teacher behavior occurs). Self-correction emerges in the beginning reading stage, has some continuing advantage in the third year of instruction, has been reported for fluent readers in their fifth year of instruction, and can be observed in adults who are asked to read aloud from a difficult text. When a correct reading response is found, it fits all the sources of cues like the last piece in a jigsaw puzzle. This can be positively reinforcing. Successful decoding creates its own positive feedback. It readily produces positive feedback from the teacher or listener in the one-to-one oral reading setting. A capacity independently to convert a difficulty into an opportunity to master some new features of print or some new operation should make the system self-improving.

The Units or Chunks.   Juncture, pitch, and stress were studied in this third year. The behavior of the best readers suggested the hypothesis that they were processing cues at the intersentence, sentence, phrase, and word level, whereas the poor readers worked at best on the two- or three-word phrase level and more usually at the word, syllable, and letter level. It seems likely that these suprasegmental variables indicate something about the organization of the response repertoire of the reader (Clay & Imlach, 1971).

At points of difficulty poor readers depended too much on the letters of the word. One could guess that, not having several sources of cues to converge on a correct response, they do not have an adequate signal to tell them when they are right or wrong and so their reading behavior does not become self-improving. In spite of its lack of success, this unprofitable behavior did not disappear. What adjustments are normally made for slow reading groups in school? Remedial programs tend to focus children on exercises that draw attention to the elements of words, word attack, and sounding out. It is assumed that this is the means by which people do read, the way children learn to read, and the way failing children need to relearn to read. None of these assumptions is necessarily true. Could we be directing poor readers' attention away from the behaviors that would bring about the most rapid improvement in their reading? Identification of letters and words is important but not sufficient.

A challenge emerges here. Reading materials that are controlled and purport to offer the child one new difficulty at a time are based on one kind of learning theory. Perhaps materials that are rich in language cues allow for dissonance and permit the cross-checking and self-correction strategies that construct and support a self-improving system.

After Three Years of Instruction

A word recognition task was given annually to the same children, recording their responses to words written in normal, reversed, and inverted form. Beginning readers seemed to be less disturbed over reading word cards upside-down than were older readers. Did poorer readers read letters and words without apparent heed to the position that they occupy in space?

The children who were followed for the first year of their schooling were retested at 6, 7, and 8 years of age (Clay, 1970c). The word lists used the 48 most frequently used words in the first-year reading books, allocated systematically to 3 lists. Statistical tests supported the assumption that the three lists could be considered to be of equivalent difficulty, and treatments were rotated across the three lists to minimize any effects that changed orientation might have on the difficulty level of the lists. The words, printed on four-by-one-inch cards, were presented singly in decreasing order of frequency and without timing. The treatment order was normal orientation, then reversed orientation, and last, inverted orientation. The children were encouraged to try, but no prompting or verbal reinforcement was given after the practice item.

The differences were in favor of normal orientation for good-progress readers. In the reversed and inverted orientation conditions, children who were normally competent readers stumbled, paused for long periods, offered no response as if nonplussed, squinted at the words, backed away from the print, and tried to apply some strategy for unraveling the words that were easily read in normal orientation. The cues that good readers commonly used to identify words and discriminate one response from another appeared to be seriously disrupted by changed orientation, particularly in the reversed condition. In contrast, and perhaps remarkably, very little of this concern was shown by poor readers.

Visual Scanning.   The trends were related to successful reading progress and active processing of information rather than to mere exposure to print. Directional cues were obviously involved. Reversed orientation was at first the most difficult, but inverted orientation became the most difficult as reading improved, which suggests a two-stage learning sequence of the visual scanning. The first stage, having a left-to-right, horizontal directional component, would be in conflict with reversed presentation of word stimuli. At a second stage, with a subschema to scan and categorize individual letters, inverted presentation could interfere with performance. If the lower-case alphabet is written in reversed orientation, only 5 letters can change their identity, that is, can be categorized as another known letter (*b, d, p, q, g*). However, if the alphabet is written in inverted presentation, 15 letters can readily be identified as other letters (*b, d, f, g, h, k, m, n, p, q, r, t, u, v, w*), give or take some variations that allow *h* and *k* to approximate *y* when inverted.

Attentional expectations, perceptual scanning, or search-and-check strategies have some explanatory relation to the results. It is reasonable to suggest that strategies change throughout the three-year period. Indeed, some hierarchical ordering of skills seem to be implied. In the organization of early reading behavior, directional behavior and the perceptual analysis of symbols are important, but the preceding argument would imply an earlier attention to directional behavior and a later attention to letter identity. One cannot assume, however, that the low-progress children were following the same track as the high-progress groups one or two years later. It is likely that qualitative differences exist between children who interweave perceptual, cognitive, and motor learning into coherent functioning within a year and children who learn these responses more slowly with much error and confusion.

This study comes close to the metatheoretical issues of my initial question. Does behavior become organized in different ways? If so, can different types of organization be characterized as self-improving and others as self-limiting? Reading instruction regularly produces its failures. We blame the programs, the educational system, the material resources, or the children, but almost never do we attribute the result to the sequence of instruction itself creating in the particular child a set of behaviors that are self-limiting rather than self-extending.

Related Research

Other studies that have rounded out our understanding have reported on the linguistic structures of the texts, motor behaviors (McQueen, 1975), predicting reading progress from behavior observation data (rather than from test data), error analysis of 13-year-olds' reading (Watson & Clay, 1975), early writing behavior, and sentence repetition skills (Clay, 1971; Clay, Gill, Glynn, McNaughton, & Salmon, 1976). In a special class for retarded children, reading behaviors (such as self-correction) were reinforced in a behavior modification program, with spectacular gains recorded (Glynn & McNaughton, 1975). This was a challenging use of two seemingly incompatible theories—information-processing and behavior modification.

A research follow-up to my first project was funded by the Maori Education Foundation in 1968 to record the progress of Samoan and Maori urban children in their first two years at school (Clay, 1976). Because most Auckland schools are multiracial, any classroom application of my ideas would need research evidence from ethnic groups. The results did not modify the basic theoretical schema: The ethnic differences found could be explained within the general theory.

Implications of Theory and Research for Possible Change

I have been watching children succeed and fail in a quality teaching program for 14 years. I have been searching for ways in which the learning needs of individual children can be detected and understood by busy teachers of class groups. An outcome of the research program is that the reading process can be described as a complex set of hierarchically organized behaviors acquired over 3 to 4 years of graduated instruction and practice. The challenge for young immature learners is how to acquire the functional system of interrelated behaviors and how to elaborate them as more difficult and more varied written English language styles are encountered. The learners must achieve this without knowing what lies ahead of them. The teacher must teach for this without knowing the characteristics of a particular learner's system of behaviors. The reading behaviors may be seen as the observable outcomes of the ways in which the learners process the information they selectively attend to. Teachers can observe the behaviors, but their naive or tutored theories of reading account for the way they plan to develop these behaviors in their program.

After the descriptive research, the need for and possibility of change in theory and in practice were apparent in some areas:

1. *Early confusions.* The first study underlined the importance of the first year of instruction, and vivid illustrations were provided of children becoming confused, establishing faulty habits, and failing to make successful progressions.

2. *Matters of organization.* The first study also showed up matters related to school organization, such as teachers with large classes and no time

for observation, children with five teachers in their first year, and failures to transmit appropriate information from teacher to teacher after a change of class or school or after the long vacation.

3. *Techniques for observing.* The study provided techniques for monitoring day-to-day progress on classroom tasks and current reading books (rather than tests), the results of which were reliably and validly related to test results (Clay, 1972a). These are referred to as "running records" and resemble the Goodman (1969) miscue analysis techniques.

4. *A diagnostic net.* The study produced a set of survey checks that could be applied at the end of the first year of instruction to catch, in a diagnostic net, those children who were seriously confused or very slow starters. (For example, checks on the child's control of appropriate directional behavior and on his or her concepts about print.) This is a set of checks on reading items known and on reading strategies employed; it is not an attempt to predict reading progress from nonreading behaviors. It should lead easily to program changes (Clay, 1972a).

5. *Interrelating of cues.* Records that traced children's transformations of their preschool behaviors into early reading behaviors showed that directional behavior, language cues (from syntax and meaning), and visual cues (especially from first letters) were early aids to correct responding. They also showed that the high-progress child readily coordinated all three sources of cues, using efficient cross-checking or confirming strategies. It is this interrelating of cues that low-progress children find difficult.

6. *A self-improving system.* Self-correction and confirming checks were a signal that the children were cross-relating cues from more than one source, that they were attempting to achieve a match. It was a good sign, if present, even if labored and frequent, because it directed children's attention to the printed message, providing them with an opportunity to learn at the point where they had made an error. The children who did not self-correct were depending on less adequate strategies of memory, fragmented cues, decoding, and external reinforcement.

7. *A behavior system.* In the first two years of instruction children learn how to teach themselves to read. They learn the aspects of print to which they must attend (e.g., letters ordered within words), the aspects of oral language that can be related to print (e.g., sound segments within words), the kinds of strategies that maintain fluency (e.g., anticipation of what could follow), the kinds of strategies that explore detail (e.g., discrimination between words that differ by one letter), the kinds of strategies that increase understanding (e.g., phrasing and using intersentence relationships), and the kinds of strategies that detect and correct error (e.g., cross-relating language and visual cues). They also learn how to relate new information to what they have already learned. In the process of learning how to learn, they master a reading vocabulary of familiar words, the set of letters used to record language, and the sound equivalents of common spelling patterns and of single letters. The

first two years of instruction appear to be critical for learning to read because this is the formation stage of an efficient or inefficient behavior system (Clay, 1972b).

8. *When the child fails.*   We begin the production of our reading failures by allowing some children to build inefficient systems of functioning that keep them crippled in this process throughout their school careers. As older readers, they are difficult to help because they are habituated in their inefficiency. In the terms of the computer age, they have been poorly programmed. Some of them have developed inefficient responses for finding, using, or checking information as they read (Clay, 1972a, 1972b).

TOWARD INSTRUCTIONAL CHANGE

Have any of these ideas or findings influenced instructional change in New Zealand during the 1962–1976 period? The research program began under the suspicion of the central Department of Education, who did not reply to my initial approach although permission to work in schools was granted locally. Important factors operating through this period were the following: (1) there has been no financial support for instructional change research; (2) the traditional change processes lie in grassroots consultations between teachers and curriculum development officers of the Department of Education; (3) publishers play a minimal role because free publications come from the Department; (4) the quality of teaching is good due to effective transmission of skills in the field by experienced teachers rather than to explicit preparation at a teachers' college or study of the literature on reading; (5) the educational operation is on a small scale; and (6) the centralized authority promulgates guidelines, and their school inspectors in the field expect, encourage, and promote teacher innovation. During this period the International Reading Association (IRA) grew rapidly in New Zealand, but it was not an effective force until the 1970s.

In that context, I considered reporting to people at one or more of the following levels (later references to levels refer to this ordering):

1. International seminars with researchers
2. Academics and research people
3. Trainers and advisers of teachers
4. Organizers of classroom teachers
5. Classroom teachers
6. Parents

If I reported only to international researchers, there would be several steps in the communication chain, if it worked, and the ideas might never reach the classroom. Conversely, reports for teachers would be unlikely to draw the critical appraisal from research people that was needed for theory construction. One could communicate with each of the groups directly in a program of talks, or remotely by writing, or indirectly by working with the next higher level and hoping for transmission downward.

Contacts with Level 1 (international researchers) have been minimal: three IRA conferences (1968, 1970, 1975) and personal consultations with some reading researchers. Some articles on theoretical aspects of the work were published in psychological journals, which persons concerned with reading are not likely to see. For instructional change in New Zealand, I was interested in Levels 3, 4, and 5, teachers' college lecturers, reading advisers, administrators, and class teachers. Acceptance or rejection of the ideas by these people would be on the basis of the practical value of the ideas. Local ideas are commonly displaced by new ideas from abroad.

First Contacts and Organization Changes

During 1965-1967, I spoke to three groups of organizers in Auckland—the (elementary) Principals' Association (Clay, 1967) and two groups of those persons in charge of junior classes. I stressed the need to organize so that teachers could set time aside for sensitive observation of what children were doing and map the progressions over time that occurred in their own schools. This is essential in any informal, nonprescriptive, or individualized program. I think this approach helped to remove any threat of criticism at this point, and an anticipation of usable results was created. Some new modes of organization have been tried, and small classes for new entrants are considered necessary.

Publication

I had a clear division in my publication program: research reports would be submitted to recognized journals, and communication would go out to teachers through their own periodicals and through books. The ideas in each of these lines of communication were the same; it was only the manner of communicating the information that was different. The strict constraints journal editors place on authors as to the manner in which reports should be made enable the academic specialist to quickly review the research reported and make a decision that it is worth attending to or not. However, these formal reports would be difficult for teachers to read, if they ever discovered them, and, in particular, they would find it difficult to derive implications and program suggestions from them.

The first report of the study was published in an educators' journal (Clay, 1966b) reaching Levels 2 and 3. In 1970, an article in the simplest language appeared in a freely distributed good quality publication by the Department of Education, but it was edited first by a senior official, an indication of continuing departmental suspicion. My ideas do not occur in departmental reports or publications published before my books became available in 1972. A teachers' guide to reading by the Department of Education (1971) shows little evidence of the influence of my work. There is a 10-year lag here from the research pilot study to extensive influence in the school system.

I was approached by a New Zealand publisher to write a book. This presented me with some problems. I had been trying to find out what children were doing, how they read, what were the strengths and weaknesses of their behaviors given the program under which they were being taught. It was not my desire to write a methods book for teachers as to what they should do in reading, although my research certainly had implications for instructional change. The request was that I should write a book for preservice training for teachers (which is not a university concern), because teachers in New Zealand were reported to do very little professional reading. I tried to write a text aimed at changing some traditional ideas about the reading process in the first year of learning to read. For example, I wrote (Clay, 1972b):

> Reading behavior concerns all the things teachers have always thought it did— word knowledge, meaning, story sense, word study skills. It also includes directional behavior, letter identities, pronounceable clusters, grammatical sense, fluent processing of items of knowledge
> - to anticipate what can occur in meaning and in language
> - to search for cues
> - to self-correct
> - to form intuitive rules that take the child beyond what he already knows.
>
> The good reader manipulates a network of language, spatial and visual perception cues, and categorizes these efficiently, searching for dissonant relations and best-fit solutions. Familiar responses which become habitual, require less and less processing and allow attention to reach out towards new information that was not previously noticed [p. 148].

Possibly the text would help teachers to be sensitive observers of the children in their classes. It would explicitly document for new and inexperienced teachers what sensitive experienced teachers already knew. Above all, it had to be written in a way that would communicate to teachers (Levels 4 and 5), and this meant that it could not be an academic book. The sales to teachers rather than students have surprised the publisher; only one of seven teachers' colleges had adopted the book as a text, but all of them use class sets in in-service training (Letter to the Editor, 1976).

A separate and linked publication (Clay, 1972a) described the techniques that had been devised for observation of reading behavior. Weighing the time demands on teachers, the adjustments children must make to school, and the evidence of early failure, I recommended that each child's progress should be checked on his or her sixth birthday. With staggered entry to school, this was a feasible proposition. The diagnostic survey was written for teachers who were not psychometricians. It gave some guidance as to which children the teacher should select for assessment and described how to measure the accuracy with which they read their texts, noting self-correction, directional movement, error types, letter identification confusions, concepts about print, and writing vocabulary skills. (These materials became available in 1972.)

By 1973, my books had been reviewed without the usual rejection of the academic, but with the patronizing assurance that Dr. Clay had been a teacher. Comments from reviewers pointed up the problems of communicating to Levels 2 through 5 with these books (Beardsley, 1973; Doake, 1973; Freyberg, 1973). Depending on the reviewer's level of interest, different aspects of the publications were valued.

Workshops on Observation

My contacts in 1965-1970 were mostly through teacher-created groups, because the Department of Education remained mistrustful until about 1970. By working directly with teachers who were eager for information, I avoided the departmental defenses and the translation process. I was in direct communication with the practitioners, which undoubtedly influenced my messages, traveling throughout the country conducting workshops in the technology of observation for IRA groups.

In a 2-hour workshop, which was usually the limit of my availability, I adopted two deliberate strategies to break through preconceptions about reading and particularly about testing. Classroom experience and years working with children does not imply anything about accurate observational skills. In fact, it probably implies a naive theory that prevents accurate observation. In Step 1, I asked for volunteers to read aloud to the group, and I gave the readers a smudgy carbon, a badly-printed stencil, a Churchill speech in Initial Teaching Alphabet, some specialized scientific prose, and a newspaper text upside-down. The participants could observe under these conditions the same strategies in the reading process of their peers that children show—self-correction, sound analysis, backtracking, syllabic attack, context guessing, and so on. When they accepted that anyone's reading behavior at times involves these strategies, they were ready to observe them in children. However, teachers who assume that they know what children are doing are not always sensitive listeners. Step 2 in the workshop made the participants listen for "reading behaviors" in child readers without the support of text. Guided thus, they were ready to move into taking observation records of children's reading, following a text as they listened and recorded. I was training sensitive observers to use techniques that began as research procedures for data collection.

The most productive application of my research has been these procedures for observing children. This is an atheoretical contribution because it provides a technology that does not serve to test hypotheses. These techniques can be used at all ages. In a pilot study of four different programs in Scotland in 1972–1973, it was found that the techniques translate outside of the New Zealand culture and the New Zealand reading program. In the new Early Reading Inservice program (mentioned later), this recording skill is represented as a necessity if every teacher is to become a sensitive observer, and two of my articles (Clay, 1970a, 1970b), originally written for a teachers' journal, were issued to the teachers being trained in the recording skills.

A 1-Year Study Group

During 1973 I met monthly with a special group of interested professionals. The district psychologist assigned each of his six interns to six participating schools. The senior teacher of junior classes ran a program of early detection based on my books, assisted by interpretation from the trainee psychologist. We met monthly with the reading advisers as a group under the chairmanship of a teacher, and I was consulted to amplify or clarify my writing. From the minutes of the meetings (Nalder, 1972–1973) the following points can be made to illustrate how the teachers' questions changed during the year:

1. *Orienting to the new approach* (November 1972): "Most queries were concerned with administration and the need to conform to the instructions. Is flexibility to be allowed and if so, to what extent? [p. 1]." This quotation presents the conflict between the accepted standardized test procedures and the concept of sensitive observation.

2. *Clarifying administration details and interpretation points* (March 1973): "Several forms for recording the different tests were discussed. . . . A working party on record forms was set up [p. 3]." Group members were now concerned with efficiency in administration and reporting back to class teachers.

"Guidelines: Points of clarification noted so far should be recorded [p. 3]." These referred to conceptual points in my books that were not understood by the group. It may have been a matter of poor communication; it may have been the inevitable process of shifting one's concepts to take in a new way of looking at things. The application of the techniques was to send the teachers to the text for explanations of the behaviors observed.

3. *Extension of insights within and beyond the trial schools* (August 1973): "Topics discussed were (a) assessment before six years of age and (b)

assessment of writing behavior [p. 1]." Group members were confident with the reading techniques as recommended. They were exploring extensions of these insights and advising teachers in other schools.

4. *Monitoring leads to understanding* (October 1973): "The importance of class teachers (rather than supervisors) doing their own monitoring was stressed [p. 2]." The group seemed to consider that the techniques were valuable for understanding something but what was to be understood was not verbalized.

5. *Back to techniques* (Final report). The group wrote *Supplementary Notes for Administering Dr. Clay's Diagnostic Survey* and stated that the objective of the meetings was merely "to develop practical knowledge of the techniques and survey procedures." (Early Reading Evaluation Project, 1973).

Perhaps the teachers who talked about procedures and materials were shifting their understanding without articulating the theoretical assumptions on which they based their new kinds of judgments. That would be an optimistic interpretation of what occurred. Although these teachers became a resource group for introducing the research ideas to others, the ease with which they generated creative ideas that differed markedly from mine and did not check them against the theory was disconcerting.

An In-Service Training Proposal

At the end of 1972 an action research program in an Auckland school was set up "to co-ordinate current knowledge about early reading, early detection and the prevention of failure in relation to different ethnic, cultural and social groups" (Holdaway & Penton, 1973, p. 1). A new interest in research by the Department of Education probably stemmed from the social issue of ethnic educational problems. A proposal was made to plan a prototype multimedia in-service resource to reeducate most, if not all, infant-school teachers in an area in, say, 12 months (Department of Education, 1976). A team consisting of an inspector, a reading adviser, and a teachers' college lecturer was formed to develop an in-service training program ambitiously directed to massive retraining of teachers of first- and second-year children. The initial proposal stated: "Continuous monitoring of early behavior of individual children in the earliest stages of reading, combined with sensitive, rapid feedback to classroom programs is perhaps the most important single innovation required. We now possess the instruments to set up such a monitoring system" (Holdaway & Penton, 1973, p. 13). The Department of Education program was released in 1976, and 250 teachers began the course.

Tully (1976), the *Auckland Star*'s education reporter wrote:

Project ERIC was set up in 1971 to find the best ways to prevent failure during the early years of schooling, particularly in multi-cultural classrooms and among groups of children who had shown themselves to be at a disadvantage on entering school.

The first step was to document knowledge in this field in Auckland, where considerable experience had been gained in inner-city schools and through the research of Marie Clay, now head of education at Auckland University. Overseas material was also evaluated.

There followed trials of materials, and methods in teaching reading.

About 18 months ago work began on planning and developing an in-service course to enable the reeducation of most infant teachers in the Auckland district within one to two years.

The development team of an inspector of schools, a senior lecturer at Auckland Teachers' College, and a reading adviser have been assisted by an advisory committee of 18 that includes teachers, psychologists, and specialist advisers, and 12 resource teachers.

And in the journal of the elementary teachers' union (*ERIC Is Afraid*, 1976) similar comments appeared:

The audio-visual course is designed to stimulate professional thinking and development and crucial features of its structure are the follow-up activities by teachers in their own classrooms between each unit, and the discussion with other teachers from the same school who are also currently taking the units.

Eventually the course will be available to all teachers. It will be re-located term-by-term until all Auckland teachers have had convenient access to it. Then it will move to rural centres within the Auckland education district. Arrangements are being made for further copies of the course to be duplicated and made available throughout New Zealand. The course offered in Term 1 will be reviewed in the light of comments from participating teachers.

The independent evaluation of the first intake (paid for by the Department of Education) is being conducted by a teacher who is presenting the evaluation for his master's thesis at the University of Auckland under a supervisor who has not been involved in the research program. There has been a move from an attitude of cold suspicion on the part of the Department of Education to one of cooperation and professional trust.

THE EARLY READING IN-SERVICE COURSE
(ERIC) AND THEORETICAL RESEARCH

Referring back to the implications of theory and research outlined earlier, four points are covered in some measure by the ERIC program: (1) It calls teachers' attention to areas of confusion for children in their early attempts to read. (2) It provides a first-class, carefully sequenced training in monitoring reading behavior. (3) The last three units cover the diagnostic or early detection survey after the first year of instruction, adding recommendations for intensified teaching effort to overcome difficulties. (4) Concerning the interrelating of cues, the points are made in the following way: Meaning arises from syntax, semantics, and intonation; directional conventions are arbitrary and must be taught; children should be able to predict on the basis of context, sentence structure, and letter detail; and as children begin to read, they should be encouraged to confirm or correct their own responses by use of meaning, sentence structure, and letter detail.

Areas of omission are the implications of the notions of a self-improving system, an efficient behavior system, and why children develop inefficient behavior systems. There is little application of such concepts in the ERIC program.

Another problem occurs when what is known is used for extrapolation. One unit in the ERIC program begins with a tape of one of my original research children reading a Seuss book and infers from her 5-year-old skill what the preschool learning of high-progress children from and about books must be. Most of this is an extrapolation, the validity of which might be contested by a researcher.

Out in the Culture

In 1975 we established an adult literacy service, and it is necessary to use the newspapers to call for volunteer tutors. An April call drew the following headlines in the *Auckland Star* (*Schools Too Late*, 1976): "Schools Too Late with Remedial Work" and "City Illiterates Total Thousands." I was delighted to see the quiet tone of the second subeditorial in the same edition:

> There is cause for continuing concern in the reminder given by the Workers' Educational Association that thousands of young Aucklanders have left school without the ability to read and write well enough to serve them in their adult life.
>
> The situation is not new. Yet although much more is known about causes and remedies than in earlier years, the problem persists.
>
> It makes sense to concentrate what special resources and assistance are available in the early years of schooling, so that children do not lag further and further behind as they are socially promoted up the school.

If I did not know how ephemeral the newspaper's views on education were, I might dare to hope that they had become informed about the importance of the early years of schooling. What these stories probably show is that the reporters are in communication with the advisers in the field who are adopting this focus. That network is a satisfactory communication system.

APPRAISAL—RESEARCH AND PRACTICE

Public and professional attention is now being directed to the early years of instruction. Book sales, the newspaper report, and the ERIC program support this conclusion. Organizational shifts are relatively easy to recommend and achieve. They can be very necessary to establish the framework and support system within which instructional change can occur.

Communication is the problem of the researchers. They can write their ideas and have the concepts translated down through the hierarchy of experts, losing integrity at each translation point. Or they can communicate directly at each level and still be met with selective attention to relevant evidence on the part of the practitioner.

All participants in reading instruction have assumptions about what the reading process is. I have been able to stand outside the in-service course and look with interest at which ideas have been built into it. There are areas about which I do not have information. These are the areas in which the New Zealand teachers make intuitive judgments on the basis of their experience in the field, and from these they generate program ideas. I think the researcher has to look at such teacher-generated ideas very carefully. On the one hand, they can be inspirational if they stem from careful observation, and they are sometimes the jumping-off points for new questions in research. At other times, one may feel that they are unwarranted extrapolations that could probably be disproved, but one doesn't have the information from research on hand to offer any evidence to the contrary. The 1963 reading program that had been generated from the grass roots was very successful, and I have great respect for the potential of New Zealand's particular brand of teacher-consultation for generating valuable new insights. However, my best guesses as a theorist do not always coincide with the guesses of those who are active in the field. I am usually not prepared to take the methodological leaps that they take; I wish to evaluate and reject if necessary.

The researcher questions, accepts ideas on the basis of evidence, and rejects or reserves judgment when there is no evidence. The practitioner revises programs and procedures, reuses old resources, and fills the gaps in proven practices with (1) best guesses from accumulated experience, (2) new ideas prettily packaged or extensively proclaimed, or (3) favored untested hypotheses. Thus the practitioner must bridge the knowledge gaps and act, whereas the researcher thinks of how the ideas could be evaluated.

In a process as complex as reading, different professionals (and also parents and reporters) make assumptions that are not verbalized and that are not understood in interprofessional dialogue. These are two potential sources of error in teachers' assumptions in the nonprescriptive program about the reading process. First, they are likely to mentally pool or average a vast amount of evidence in order to arrive at a program decision. Second, they may do this on the basis of superficial observations. Teachers are less likely to make gross averaging judgments about children's needs when they work closely with individual children and/or if they use techniques for sensitive observation. Under these circumstances, the teacher is likely to bridge gaps in the exposition of theory or method with more insightful assumptions and fewer naive or superficial ones. The techniques of my research program may lead to field-hypotheses of better quality.

Perhaps we can arrive at a metatheoretical concept of instructional change. Any theorizing we do about learning to read has to account for the important fact that well-trained teachers teach at least 70% to 80% of children to read under a variety of theories, programs, or sequences of instruction. Since the formal aspects of direct instruction can differ markedly, I can draw only two conclusions: Children supplement the program with their own efforts, and teachers adapt to individuality more than any program descriptions imply. If teachers under any instruction program are sensitive observers of the children's progress, then they are in a position to notice more and more of the behaviors that confirm a valid theory, and/or they are able to reject notions that do not fit with their careful observations. At the same time, their questions and their creative solutions will be subjected to feedback from the continued monitoring. Taking observation records may, like self-correction in early reading, provide teachers with a basis for their self-improving theory of instruction.

A current trend in New Zealand is to move away from prescribed reading texts toward maximum use of real books as a basis for the program. The technology of monitoring becomes useful for controlling task difficulty. Under such a program, self-correction behavior becomes the key indicator that progress is satisfactory, and running records provide the technology for the teacher to observe progress on any selection of materials. So the shift from basic texts could become a possibility with a minimum of risk because monitoring techniques are available. The generic nature of the technological procedures provides this insurance.

A theme of discussion and consultation recurs in this account of instructional change. Talks, workshops, consultations with study groups, dialogue between different types of professionals—these activities seem to have been as important as the research and publication programs for achieving instructional change. In the evaluation study of the in-service training program by a teacher for a master of arts thesis, we have the academic objectivity evaluation function being applied to the program which arose, in a major sense, out of the earlier program of the university. This seems to be an appropriate role for the university to adopt.

Disjunction may be inherent in the respective roles of researcher and practitioner. Perhaps a continuing dialogue between experts with diverse roles, in a rolling revision of both theory and practice, cannot be avoided. It provides a system of checks and balances on the excesses and perceptual problems of each specialist. If theory has any overriding status in this interchange, this ought to stem from its generic nature. Instructional questions and decisions between equally attractive practical alternatives may be given direction by some priorities or ordering stated in theory.

Finally, there is for me frustration in the thought that I have not communicated more of the theoretical concepts. That is a task for the future. If teachers are to generate individual programs to meet particular needs, and if the matter of strategies for processing information is critical for some learners, then this must be written down in a way that enables teachers to go easily from behavior signals, through theoretical constructs, to program. By offering teachers the means to sensitive observation of children's reading behavior, I hope I have not merely opened a Pandora's box of creative teaching gimmicks, unchecked by reference to theory.

REFERENCES

Beardsley, M. Review of *Reading: The patterning of complex behavior* by M. M. Clay. *Education,* 1973, *7,* 31.

Berlyne, D. E. *Conflict, arousal and curiosity.* New York: McGraw-Hill, 1960.

Biemiller, A. The development of the use of graphic and contextual information as children learn to read. *Reading Research Quarterly,* 1970, *5,* 75–96.

Burke, C., & Goodman, K. S. When a child reads—a psycholinguistic analysis. *Elementary English,* 1970, *47,* 121–129.

Christenson, A. Oral reading errors of intermediate grade children at their independent, instructional, and frustrational levels. In J. A. Figurel (Ed.), *Reading and realism.* Newark, Del.: International Reading Association, 1969.

Clay, M. M. *Emergent reading behavior.* Unpublished doctoral dissertation, University of Auckland, 1966. (a)

Clay, M. M. The reading behavior of five year old children: A research report. *New Zealand Journal of Educational Studies,* 1966, *2,* 11–31, (b)

Clay, M. M. A challenge to some educational concepts form recent research on Auckland school entrants. *Extension Course Lecture.* Auckland, New Zealand: Headmasters' Association, 1967.

Clay, M. M. A syntactic analysis of reading errors. *Journal of Verbal Learning and Verbal Behavior,* 1968, *7,* 434–438.

Clay, M. M. Reading errors and self-correction behavior. *British Journal of Educational Psychology,* 1969, *30,* 47–56.

Clay, M. M. The early detection of reading difficulties. *Education,* 1970, *19,* 26–31. (a)

Clay, M. M. Early reading behavior: A guide to sensitive observation. *Education,* 1970, *19*(1), 14–20. (b)

Clay, M. M. An increasing effect of disorientation on the discrimination of print: A developmental study. *Journal of Experimental Child Psychology,* 1970, *9,* 297–306. (c)

Clay, M. M. Sentence repetition: Elicited imitation of a controlled set of syntactic structures by four language groups. *Monographs of the Society for Research in Child Development,* 1971, *36*(3).

Clay, M. M. *The early detection of reading difficulties: A diagnostic survey.* New York: International Publications, 1972. (a)

Clay, M. M. *Reading: The patterning of complex behavior.* New York: International Publications, 1972. (b)

Clay, M. M. Early childhood and cultural diversity. *Reading Teacher,* 1976, *29,* 333–342.

Clay, M. M., & Imlach, R. Juncture, pitch and stress as reading behavior variables. *Journal of Verbal Learning and Verbal Behavior,* 1971, *10,* 133–139.

Clay, M. M., Gill, W. M., Glynn, E. L., McNaughton, A. H., & Salmon, K. W. *Record of oral language.* Wellington, New Zealand: New Zealand Education Institute, 1976.

Department of Education. *Reading in the infant classes (Pts. 1 & 2).* Wellington, New Zealand: Department of Education, 1971.

Department of Education. *Early reading in-service course (Units 1–12).* Wellington, New Zealand: Department of Education, 1976.

Doake, D. Review of *Reading: The patterning of complex behavior* by M. M. Clay. *Journal of the New Zealand Teachers' Colleges Association,* 1973, *21,* 13–14.

Early Reading Evaluation Project. *Supplementary notes for administering Dr. Clay's diagnostic survey.* Unpublished manuscript, Auckland, New Zealand, 1973.

ERIC is afraid of teachers and young readers. *National Education,* February 1976, pp. 35–36.

Freyberg, P. S. Review of *Reading: The patterning of complex behavior* by M. M. Clay. *New Zealand Journal of Educational Studies,* 1973, *8,* 81–82.

Goodacre, E. J. *Methods—A reading list and glossary of terms.* Reading, England: Centre for Teaching Reading, 1971.

Goodacre, E. J. *Hearing children read.* Reading, England: Centre for Teaching of Reading, 1972.

Goodman, K. S. Analysis of oral reading miscues: Applied psycholinguistics. *Reading Research Quarterly,* 1969, *5,* 9–30.

Goodman, Y. M. Using children's reading miscues for new teaching strategies. *Reading Teacher,* 1970, *23,* 455–459.

Glynn, E. L., & McNaughton, S. S. Trust your own observations: Criterion referenced assessment of reading progress. *The Slow-Learning Child* (University of Queensland), 1975, *22,* 91–108.

Holdaway, D., & Penton, J. *Proposal for the early reading in-service program.* Unpublished report, Auckland, New Zealand, Department of Education, 1973.

Letter to the editor and replies from six teachers' colleges. *Education,* 1976, *4,* 31–32.

McQueen, P. J. *Motor responses associated with beginning reading.* Unpublished master's thesis, University of Auckland, 1975.

Nalder, S. *Minutes of the early reading evaluation project meetings.* Unpublished minutes, Auckland, New Zealand, Department of Education, 1972–1973.

Neisser, U. The multiplicity of thought. *British Journal of Psychology,* 1963, *54,* 1–14.

Nurss, J. Oral reading errors and reading comprehension. *Reading Teacher,* 1969, *22,* 523–527.

Schools too late with remedial work. *Auckland Star,* April 1976.

Simpson, M. M. *Suggestions for teaching reading in infant classes.* Wellington, New Zealand: Department of Education, 1962.

Tully, J. Early reading in-service course. *Auckland Star,* February 1976.

Watson, S., & Clay, M. M. Oral reading strategies of third form students. *New Zealand Journal of Educational Studies,* 1975, *10,* 43–50.

Weber, R. The study of oral reading errors: A survey of the literature. *Reading Research Quarterly,* 1968, *4,* 96–119.

Weber, R. A linguistic analysis of first-grade reading errors. *Reading Research Quarterly,* 1970, *5,* 427–451.

Williams, B., & Clay, M. M. The reading behavior of children in standard one. *Education,* 1973, *22,* 13–17.

8

How the Researcher Can Help the Reading Teacher With Classroom Assessment

Robert C. Calfee
Stanford University

Priscilla A. Drum
University of California at Santa Barbara

To many educators, tests seem an unavoidable nuisance. Although they are useful to some people for certain purposes, increasingly their usefulness and appropriateness are questioned. A rising chorus asks whether tests really provide fair and useful measures of educational progress, and colleagues caution against overuse of tests to no good purpose (e.g., Levine, 1976; Venezky, 1974a). However, tests are one of the few "scientific" elements in educational research and practice, and they can serve a vital role by providing information for effective and efficient instruction. For instance, there are definite limits to what lecturers can hope to achieve, because they obtain relatively little substantive information from the members of their audiences. Instead, they must rely on eye contact, on signs of attentiveness, and on questions from the listeners, which may indicate interest but cannot measure it. At the other end of the continuum, individualized instruction builds on the continual exchange of information between teacher and student; the instructional program is continuously realigned to the student's needs and strengths (e.g., Atkinson & Paulson, 1972). Frequent, precise, and appropriate assessment is critical to this process. But testing of this sort must be designed to fit the instructional needs of the teacher.

The testing tradition, following the lead of Alfred Binet, has focused attention on the selection and sorting of individuals. One can find occasional comment on "teacher-made" tests in books on educational testing. But even here the criteria are those applied to tests for selection and sorting. That other needs exist is reflected in the plethora of terms—*criterion-referenced, domain-referenced, behavioral objectives, diagnostic*—all of which purport to do something other than the conventional testing approach.[1] There is little evidence that the "new" tests do a job different from that done by the old ones; it is also worth noting that tests with different labels look similar. Researchers can provide a service to teachers by looking systematically at the needs for assessment in the classroom and by analyzing the theoretical and empirical issues in this area. The goal of the present chapter is to suggest to researchers some specific issues that warrant attention; a companion paper has been prepared to look at these issues from the teacher's perspective (Calfee, Drum, & Arnold, 1978).

AN OVERVIEW AND TWO CONCLUSIONS

How can assessment be tailored to fit the needs of the classroom? To answer this question, we need to consider three other questions: (a) Assessment for what; what are our goals? (b) How to assess; what methods should we use? (c) Is assessment doing its job; what are acceptable criteria? We consider in turn each question as it relates to reading, but first, two major conclusions:

1. Teachers need to learn more about the process of assessment in order to assess for instructional purposes.
2. Classroom assessment ought to aim toward the precise and efficient measurement of specific component skills for short-term decisions.

The bulk of this chapter buttresses and illustrates these two generalizations, but some preliminary comments will set the stage. Much research on reading assessment aims toward goals quite different from those that are foremost for the classroom teacher. The goal of conventional achievement test construction (and of the research that centers around such test construction) is the measurement of reliable and substantial individual differences based on stable scores for each student that place the student at some point below, at, or above the average for some larger population. The aim is an instrument for making major, long-term decisions about students, teachers, and programs (Carver, 1974). However, the teacher needs information of a much more immediate character. How well can the student read now? What specific reading instructions should be given next? Is the instruction successful? To

---

[1]Domain-referenced testing probably comes closest in spirit to the conceptualization that seems most useful to us. Theory and practice remain to be established for domain-referenced tests, although some interesting beginnings exist (Hively, 1974, especially chapters by Millman, Miller, and Nitko; Knapp, 1968). A related though separable issue is the matching of assessment instruments to the goals and substance of the instructional program, a point we view as important though not the focus of our paper (cf. Walker & Shaffarzick, 1974; Zigler & Trickett, 1978).

the question, "What does the research literature on assessment have to say to classroom teachers about their instructional needs?" the answer appears to be: "Not much!"

To our knowledge, no existing assessment system handles the range of assessment tasks encountered by the reading teacher. Most commercial tests provide little evidence useful for instruction and are too expensive in time and effort for the teacher's needs. It is not that commercial tests are faulty; instead, they are designed for purposes other than immediate instructional decisions. Moreover, the researcher cannot focus attention solely on the characteristics of the assessment system if the goal is the proper assessment of students in the multifaceted happenings of the classroom. The researcher must plan investigations where variation in the characteristics of the assessment system is only one set of factors. The design must also call for variation in the teacher's background and training, in the makeup of the class, and in the nature of the instructional program. Designs that are this comprehensive require more thought than has been typical of educational research, but they are technically feasible (Calfee, 1975a).

In fact, one can argue that research on classroom assessment should not center on test construction at all, but instead on teacher training. We hope that public and private contractors will improve the kinds of assessment systems available to the teacher. But we suspect that the key to adequate assessment for instructional decision making in the classroom is the classroom teacher who knows how to select with care from what is available for other purposes and who can modify and simplify these materials with an eye to practical application. If so, the chief task of those who would improve assessment of reading for purposes of instruction lies, not in psychometrics, but in improving teaching. This does not mean that all the psychometric problems have been solved; to the contrary. It simply means that psychometrics may not be at stage center.

GOALS OF ASSESSMENT

What are alternative goals in assessment? First, certain goals aim toward long-term prediction. This is true in evaluation of the individual (Cronbach & Gleser, 1965) for job placement, for school admission, for a grade or achievement mark of some sort. It is true when assessment serves for evaluation of a program. The administrator has to decide whether a curriculum is effective, whether a special program is better than the regular program, whether extra money is making a difference. Diagnosis also falls in this category. Diagnosis is for special cases, like physical anomalies. A person who cannot see well has trouble learning to read. If a person cannot hear very well, there may be trouble in school tasks, including reading. These are special cases and may require a clinical specialist.

Other goals aim toward short-term decisions. Assessment can serve for instructional decision making by the classroom teacher. The instructor has to stay current on what each student knows if instruction is to be precisely directed toward specific needs. *Individualization* is the usual label for this concept. Each student is assessed as to present skills, abilities, and knowledge, so the student can be helped to move toward some reasonable goal.

Tasks other than individualization also require the classroom teacher to apply skills in assessment:

1. It is the beginning of the school year. The teacher is new to the school and wants to supplement information in the "cum" folder with other evidence.

2. A new student arrives in class at midyear, and there is little information available on how well he can read.

3. The teacher plans to introduce a new topic (e.g., how to handle polysyllabic words) and needs to know which students already know something about the topic and which ones are totally unprepared.

Assessment for short-term instructional decisions applies to many other situations: (a) optimizing instructional sequences; (b) measuring immediate response to instruction; (c) regrouping for specialized instruction; and (d) selecting and allocating resurces (who needs the aide's time, the tutor's time, the terminal's time?).

PRESENT METHODS OF ASSESSMENT
IN EDUCATION

Psychometrically "sound" tests in use today include normative and criterion-referenced tests; these two types of tests differ little in content, although they are designed for different applications (Green, 1976). A norm-referenced test shows how the student's score or the class's score compares with the other students or classes who provided the standards for the test. A criterion-referenced test provides a score for a student or a class based on a number of items mastered (answered correctly) compared with some absolute standard. Neither type of score tells the teacher what a student knows or does not know; direction for further instruction is not indicated. Both types of tests are standardized; an exact procedure for administration is called for, with little room for clinical probing. Most tests are group-administered and use a multiple-choice format to facilitate machine scoring. The content resembles "goulash"; although a subtest structure is often imposed on the test items, the high intertest correlations belie the different names assigned to subtests.

It can also be said of these tests that they are reliable, that the student's relative standing is stable over time, and that they are highly predictive of one another (Bloom, 1964). They are time-consuming to administer; they are generally not suitable for repeated administration—two or three times a year at most. They yield a single type of measure (percentage correct or some transformation thereof).

Such tests have been developed to meet certain implicit and explicit criteria. It therefore makes sense to consider the standards and criteria that apply to the construction, administration, and interpretation of a test.

CRITERIA FOR EVALUATING TESTS

We want to examine briefly several criteria for evaluating tests: reliability, validity, appropriateness, independence, discriminability, cost, and repeatability. The first two are usually discussed in texts on testing; the others generally are not (e.g., Anastasi, 1968; Cronbach, 1970; Farr & Tuinman, 1972). Each criterion has several facets to it.

Reliability

In general, reliability refers to the degree to which a measurement is consistent. We can consider the consistency in performance when a person is tested with one form of a test and then retested with a slightly varied form. Several things have changed. The exact form and content of the test have changed. The student has probably changed, either having learned something, having forgotten something, or having a headache that wasn't present when taking the first test. All these sources of variability tend to reduce the reliability in test–retest situations.

Test developers tend to emphasize within-test reliability. There are a variety of ways of thinking about this form of consistency (Cronbach, 1970, Chapter 6). For instance, suppose you randomly divide the items in two and correlate the two subscores. Repeat this operation for all possible split-half divisions of the test, and then compute the average correlation between the half-scores (Cronbach, 1951). This provides a measure of the extent to which each item contributes consistently to the total test score. One way to obtain "perfect" intratest reliability is to use a test in which the student either fails all items or passes all items. Test developers, to the degree that they strive for intratest reliability, are under pressure to eliminate test items that yield divergent patterns of performance from one student to the next. The items that remain seem likely to measure general performance characteristics rather than performances that reflect specific instructional outcomes. So if you want a perfectly reliable test, ask the same question 20 times. A student either knows the answer or does not. This would be absurd, of course, but it is the "ideal" toward which reliability aims.

Maximizing intratest reliability is important when the test score is used to make a major decision, but it may be counterproductive for instructional decision making. Teachers need to know more than the student's general ability. Individualization requires knowledge of diverse patterns of performance on specific tasks for different students. For the teacher, a "reliable" assessment instrument is more properly defined as one that accurately and consistently indicates the specific patterns of instruction that best fit the student's needs and capabilities. We examine this matter in more detail later in this chapter.

Validity

As with reliability, the concept of validity assumes many guises. Face validity means that the test looks as if it measures what it claims to be measuring. Construct validity means that if several tests seem to measure the same thing, there must be something there to be measured. Predictive validity means that there is a correlation between a test and a criterion of performance (usually another test).

To possess adequate validity for most educational purposes, a test usually has to satisfy all of these criteria. For instance, one can predict reading achievement reasonably well from mathematics test scores, but teachers and parents would question the face validity—it would be unseemly to measure reading performance with a test containing arithmetic "word problems." The researcher could provide a service by exploring the issue of instructional validity—a test is valid when it points to an instructional treatment that improves the student's performance on a specified task. From this point of view, aptitude–treatment interaction research aims to validate various aptitude tests (Cronbach & Snow, 1977; Walker & Schaffarzick, 1974).

Appropriateness

Appropriateness is introduced here as a fuzzy concept covering several related matters. In part, it has to do with whether a test is linked to the goals of an instructional program with sufficient directness and breadth. Researchers learn the meaning of this concept when public school teachers ask why no one tests what they teach. This complaint is fair and deserves the attention of evaluators.

Appropriateness is disregarded in the common practice of assigning a student to a particular level of a test according to age or nominal grade placement rather than actual performance level. The experience of the Chicago schools when they selected achievement tests to be appropriate to the students' actual reading level and the resulting drop of 1.8 years in certain school scores is instructive in this connection (Banas, 1975). Asking a high school student who reads at the first- or second-grade level to take an advanced level of the Metropolitan Achievement Tests is a mistake; whatever the score, it is unlikely to reveal the student's actual skill in reading. The advanced test is for those reading at grade six or above. Students reading at a lower level are likely to guess randomly at the answers, and this performance is likely to lead to a grade level score that is higher than their actual reading ability.

Finally, lack of appropriateness seems to distinguish many conventional academic achievement tests from the alternatives represented in the National Assessment of Educational Progress (NAEP). The goal of the NAEP was to cover the range of reading tasks that a literate person might confront at school, at work, at play, and in the other aspects of life in our society. The typical comprehension test is simply not appropriate to cover the broad array of "themes" that seemed important to the NAEP staff (Mellon, 1975): (1) understanding words and word relationships (literal comprehension of isolated words, phrases, and sentences); (2) understanding graphic materials (comprehension of the linguistic components of drawings, signs, labels, charts, maps, graphs, and forms); (3) understanding written directions (comprehension of directions and the ability to carry them out); (4) understanding reference materials (comprehension and knowledge of indices, dictionaries, alphabetizing, and TV listing formats); (5) gleaning significant facts from passages (comprehension and, to a limited extent, recall of literal content in the context of a larger reading passage); (6) understanding main ideas and organization (ability to abstract the main ideas and organizational features of a passage); (7) drawing inferences (ability to reach a conclusion not explicitly stated in the passage, in most instances relying only on information given but in a few cases on information not presented in the passage); (8) critically reading (ability to recognize the author's purpose and to understand figurative language and literary devices).

It is also the point of the research of Sticht and his colleagues (Sticht, 1975; Sticht, Caylor, Kern, & Fox, 1971) that the assessment of a person's reading ability (and the selection of reading materials) should be appropriate to the task demands—don't make life unnecessarily difficult by asking hard, tricky questions when easy, plain ones will do.

Independence

To be most useful, the several scores from an assessment battery should provide the teacher with distinct pieces of information. When all the subtest scores are highly intercorrelated, the teacher receives little guidance about specific courses of action. As Thorndike (1973) pointed out, even a modest degree of correlation between two scores ($r \geq .6$) makes it difficult to make differential diagnoses, given that the scores are normally distributed. The magnitude of this problem for certain commercial tests has been discussed by Calfee and Venezky (1969), and possible remedies have been suggested (Calfee, 1977). One desirable condition is that each test be "clean," that is, that steps be taken to ensure that the test measures the desired skill and none other. We describe later a second approach built on factorial test design in which systematic variation in the materials and conditions of testing allows the tester to discover the circumstances under which a student can and cannot perform a task.[2]

Discriminability

It takes more expertise and attention to monitor an ammeter and make decisions about an automobile's electrical system than to notice simply whether the generator light is on or off. The situation is similar in testing: When the scores on a test take the form of a normal distribution, then fine gradations in performance matter a lot and interpretation is more difficult. It is much easier to interpret performance when it is either clearly at the mastery level or altogether faulty, with no "in-between" scores. Careful specification of the task is required, but the benefits for instructional decision making can be considerable (Calfee, 1977).

Cost

Tests cost money, and they cost time. The time costs may be overlooked by teachers, even when they are the ones who pay. For instance, in one school, teachers spent three days testing the third- and fourth-grade students' reading skills. The scores were then used for the sole purpose of sorting students into three reading groups: high, medium, and low. Obtaining a 10-minute oral reading sample from each student would probably have done the sorting job as well or better and at much less cost. When a major decision is to be made, substantial cost is justified; when continuous short-term decisions are required, low cost is essential.

Repeatability

The time and cost required by many tests make repeated administration impractical. Besides this, the psychometric concern with reactivation of the

---

[2]McCullough (1957) has presented evidence for independence of comprehension processes in the form of low to moderate correlations between elementary students' responses to comprehension questions about details, main idea, sequence, and creative reading. Unfortunately, the number of items was small, and test reliabilities were not reported. Thus, the modest size of the correlations is not strong evidence of independence, although the data are suggestive.

performance on the first test in retesting leads to advice against repeated administrations of the same form. It is rare to find more than two forms of most commercial tests. For evaluation of a program or an individual, assessment once or twice a year is sufficient. But the teacher who wants evidence on the effectiveness of yesterday's instruction needs an "off-the-shelf" test that comes in many forms and can be used as often as necessary.

A CLOSER LOOK AT RELIABILITY

If any concept is central to research on assessment, reliability certainly seems to be the candidate. As already noted, in its simplest form reliability means that a measure is consistent and reproducible. Suppose that when a carpenter used a ruler to measure the length of a board, each "inch" on the ruler acted somewhat differently during the measurement process. Then the results of the measurement would vary depending on which particular ruler was used and the length of what was being measured, among other things. This is manifestly undesirable. By analogy, the designer of a test for the measurement of academic outcomes seeks to build a test from a set of items that act together consistently to measure the skill of knowledge of interest. Indices of intratest reliability such as split-half reliability, the point-biserial coefficient, alpha, or the KR-20 reveal the extent to which performance on each item in a test contributes in a consistent fashion to the total score.

Another way of thinking about reliability builds on the analysis of variance procedure (Cronbach, 1970, p. 158ff.). For instance, consider the scores for six students shown in Table. 8.1. These records show a fair amount of consistency. Students may do well or poorly, but each item contributes consistently to the total score. Item 4 is harder than the other items, and the students who do most poorly always do poorly on this item. Similarly, Item 1 is relatively easy and consistently so for the students who do best.

TABLE 8.1
Example of Student–Item Matrix with Consistent Items
(0 = correct, 1 = error)

Students	Items				Student Total Score
	1	2	3	4	
A	1	1	1	1	4
B	0	1	1	1	3
C	0	1	1	1	3
D	0	0	0	1	1
E	0	0	0	1	1
F	0	0	0	0	0
Item totals	1	3	3	5	

TABLE 8.2

Analysis of Variance of Student–Item Matrix, Estimation
of Variance Components, and Calculation of Reliability

1. Analysis of variance summary table

Source	df	MS	EMS
Students	5	.600	$\sigma_{SI}^2 + \sigma_S^2$
Items	3	.433	$\sigma_{SI}^2 + \sigma_I^2$
SI	15	.113	σ_{SI}^2

2. Estimation of variance components

$\sigma_S^2 = MS(S) - MS(SI) = .487$

$\sigma_{SI}^2 = MS(SI) = .113$

3. Reliability of contribution of each item to individual
differences in student's total score

$$\alpha = \frac{\sigma_S^2}{\sigma_S^2 + \sigma_{SI}^2} = \frac{.487}{.487 + .113} = .81$$

The magnitude of the consistency can be determined through the standard
analysis of variance (Refer to Cronbach, 1970, p. 159, for details of the
procedure). The total variance in the scores can be partitioned to yield three
variance estimates. The expected value of each variance estimate allows one
to compute the variance component for each source, as shown in the analysis
of variance summary table in Table 8.2. Thus, the variance of the students'
"true" scores is estimated to be $\sigma_S^2 = .487$; the variance in the student–item
interactions, σ_{SI}^2, is estimated to be .113. The student total-score variance is a
measure of individual differences in the total scores. The student–item
interaction is a measure of inconsistencies in the way different students react
to different items. In this example, the idiosyncratic variation in items is
relatively slight compared with total score variance. As an index of the
consistency of the contribution of individual items to the total score,
Cronbach (1951) proposed the ratio of true score to observed score variances
(also cf. Winer, 1971, pp. 283–287). This is equivalent to the ratio between
total score variance and overall variance (total score variance plus
idiosyncratic student–item variance):

$$\alpha = \frac{\sigma_S^2}{\sigma_S^2 + \sigma_{SI}^2}.$$

The principle here is quite simple—to take seriously the student's total score
as an index of individual difference, variation in the set of "true" scores should
account for a fairly large proportion of the overall variance in the observed
scores, which can be shown to be the sum of σ_S^2 and σ_{SI}^2. As can be seen at the
bottom of the table, the Cronbach alpha for these data, $\alpha = .81$, is quite high
given the small amount of data.

As an example of an inconsistent set of items, consider the student–item matrix in Table 8.3. The variation in the total scores of individual students is exactly the same as in Table 8.1, but the items are less consistent. Items 1 and 2 are passed by some of the students whose total scores show many errors; the same items are failed by some of the students whose total scores show many successes. These idiosyncratic reactions of particular students to particular items in an unpredictable and inconsistent manner are referred to as subject–item interactions. The estimate of student–item variance is indeed higher for this matrix, $MS(SI) = .200$, and the reliability is .67, or 17% less than the results in Table 8.2.

What are the characteristics of a test with a high reliability coefficient? First, there must be individual differences of substantial magnitude in overall performance. This is another way of saying that σ_S^2 must be relatively large. Second, idiosyncratic reactions to particular items by individual students must be small; put otherwise, σ_{SI}^2 must be relatively small. Items that do not fall into line are relatively easy to detect, and the dependability of the student's total score is markedly improved by eliminating those items that do not fall into line. For instance, if Items 1 and 2 in Table 8.3 are eliminated from the test, the test becomes perfectly reliable.

Suppose, however, that the purpose of the test is not to generate a single total score but to detect patterns of strengths and weaknesses, which might be more useful for prescribing instruction. The conventional approach of emphasizing total-score reliability can lead to the elimination of items that provide essential information about such patterns. However, extensions of the same basic procedure for determining reliability can be used to evaluate the dependability of those patterns that do exist in the data. These extensions build on the landmark work of Cronbach and his colleagues on generalizability theory for psychological assessment (Cronbach, 1951; Cronbach, Gleser, Nanda, & Rajaratnam, 1972; Cronbach, Rajaratnam, &

TABLE 8.3
Example of Student–Item Matrix with Items Less
Consistent than those in Table 8.1

Students	Items 1	2	3	4	Student Total Score
A	1	1	1	1	4
B	0	1	1	1	3
C	1	0	1	1	3
D	1	0	0	0	1
E	0	1	0	0	1
F	0	0	0	0	0
Item totals	3	3	3	3	

Gleser, 1963; for a different perspective on a similar problem, see Calfee, 1976; Calfee & Elman, 1977).

The key to the evaluation of patterns of individual differences is to think about the reliability of the patterns rather than the reliability of the total test score or a particular subtest score. The analysis of variance technique provides the methodology to support this thinking, which is why we introduced it earlier. The concepts are introduced with the aid of a specific example, the student–item matrix in Table 8.4. Suppose a teacher has developed an 8-item test and has collected scores from 20 students. You, the researcher, are given the data and asked to determine the reliability of the test to ensure that the instrument meets customary standards. At first glance, the test will appear relatively unreliable. However, paying closer attention to the structure of the data—a process much like peeling an onion—uncovers a great deal of reliable information. The analysis of variance provides a systematic accounting of the information, and at each stage of analysis reliability coefficients of increasing specificity are determined.

TABLE 8.4
Student-Item Matrix with Items Grouped According to Test Factor T

				Items					Student Total Score	Subtest Totals	
Students	1	2	3	4	5	6	7	8		Items 1–4	Items 5–8
1	1	1	0	1	0	0	0	0	3	3	0
2	0	1	0	0	1	1	1	1	5	1	4
3	1	0	0	0	0	0	0	0	1	1	0
4	1	1	1	1	0	1	1	1	7	4	3
5	1	1	1	1	0	0	0	1	5	4	1
6	1	0	0	0	1	1	1	1	5	1	4
7	1	1	1	1	1	1	1	1	8	4	4
8	1	0	0	0	0	0	0	0	1	1	0
9	0	0	0	0	1	0	1	1	3	0	3
10	1	1	1	1	0	0	1	0	5	4	1
11	1	1	0	1	1	1	1	1	7	3	4
12	1	1	1	1	1	0	1	1	7	4	3
13	0	0	0	0	0	0	0	0	0	0	0
14	0	0	1	0	1	1	1	1	5	1	4
15	1	1	1	0	0	0	0	0	3	3	0
16	1	1	1	1	0	1	0	0	5	4	1
17	1	1	0	1	1	1	1	1	7	3	4
18	0	0	0	0	0	0	0	1	1	0	1
19	0	0	0	0	0	0	1	0	1	0	1
20	0	0	0	0	0	1	1	1	3	0	3
Item totals	13	11	8	9	8	9	12	12			

TABLE 8.5
Analysis of Variance of Original Student–Item Matrix,
Estimation of Variance Components, and
Computation of Overall Reliability

1. Analysis of variance

Source	df	MS
Student	19	.749
Item	7	.196
SI	133	.183

2. Estimation of variance components

$$\sigma_S^2 = MS(S) - MS(SI) = .566$$
$$\sigma_{SI}^2 = .183$$

3. Reliability of item contribution to total score

$$\alpha = \frac{.566}{.566 + .183} = .756$$

Casual examination of the matrix in Table 8.4 shows that although there are substantial individual differences in the total scores, there is also considerable idiosyncratic variation in the reaction of particular students to particular items. The situation is not too bad, as can be seen from the analysis in Table 8.5. The reliability measured by α is of a respectable magnitude by some standards, although a bit on the low side.

The test designer then remarks that the test actually comprises items from two distinct categories, and the designer is curious about whether the two subtests reveal the differences in performance they were designed to measure. In Table 8.4 the items can be arranged according to a subtest structure. Looking at the first four and last four items for each student reveals more consistent patterns within each subtest than appear when the test is examined as a whole. Each student tends to succeed or to fail on all the items within a subtest; there is only modest deviation from the all-or-none pattern. This suggests that the performance patterns are more reliable than the overall measure in Table 8.5 suggests.

Table 8.6 shows the determination of reliabilities for this situation. The analysis of variance now includes the test factor as a source of variance, along with the student–test interaction. Two reliability indices can be computed in answer to two questions. First, how consistent is the contribution of the subtest score to the total score? The answer is, only slightly so, $\alpha = .162$. (The subtest is the "item" in this analysis.) A glance at the data shows that some students have a high score on T_1, some a low score; some have a high score on T_2, some a low score; and all combinations of high and low on each subtest are represented. In other words, there are substantial student–subtest interactions. Second, how consistent is the contribution of each item within a subtest to the difference between the student's subtest scores? The consistency here shows up in this reliability coefficient, $\alpha = .836$.

TABLE 8.6
Analysis of Variance, Estimation of Variance Components, and
Calculation of Reliability Indices for Total and Subtest Scores

1. Analysis of variance

Source	df	MS	EMS
Students	19	.749	$\sigma^2_{SI(T)} + \sigma^2_{ST} + \sigma^2_S$
Tests	1	.0	$\sigma^2_{SI(T)} + \sigma^2_{ST} + \sigma^2_{I(T)} + \Sigma^2_T$
ST	19	.645	$\sigma^2_{SI(T)} + \sigma^2_{ST}$
Items (T)	6	.229	$\sigma^2_{SI(T)} + \sigma^2_{I(T)}$
SI(T)	114	.106	$\sigma^2_{SI(T)}$

2. Reliability of subtest contribution to total score

$$\sigma^2_S = MS(S) - MS(ST) = .104$$
$$\sigma^2_{ST} = MS(SI(T)) = .539$$
$$\alpha = \frac{.104}{.104 + .539} = .162$$

3. Reliability of item-within-subtest contribution to subtest scores

$$\sigma^2_{ST} = .539 \quad \sigma^2_{SI(T)} = .106$$
$$\alpha = \frac{.539}{.539 + .106} = .836$$

Note. σ^2 is a random effect; Σ^2 is a fixed effect in the analysis of variance model.

The increase in the last mentioned reliability coefficient compared with the total-test coefficient in Table 8.5 seems modest, only about 10%. But there is a substantial gain in our understanding of the test structure, we can see that individuals differ considerably in the subtest patterns, whereas the total test score is not reliable compared with variations in subtest–student interactions.

What does the preceding analysis of reliabilities tell the test designer in this particular instance? The overall reliability of the total test score (Table 8.5) is moderate but not spectacular. From this analysis alone, the test designer might be advised to throw away some of the items that contribute least consistently to the overall test score. That would be a mistake, however, because these same items contribute most consistently to the subtest patterns. The subtest analysis (Table 8.6) reveals that the subtests themselves contribute inconsistently to the total test score, but the items within each subtest yield fairly consistent patterns of individual differences in the subtest scores. These patterns are readily visible to the naked eye. To be sure, we created the data set, and so we knew what the underlying structure really was. But there is an important moral: It behooves the test designer to think seriously about the dimensions of the test when it is being designed and analyzed (Calfee, 1976).

We have illustrated how the reseacher can help the teacher in the conduct of classroom assessment, using one of the oldest tools of the educational psychologist's trade—the analysis of test reliability. More is needed than the examination of reliability of a total score. The tools exist today for the investigation of the reliability of structural patterns, and it is these that are likely to be of service to the classroom teacher. Incidentally, the payoff from structural analysis increases with the complexity of the structure. The test in the foregoing example had the simplest possible structure—two subtests. As the number of independent dimensions of pattern increases and as the number of student groups for which these are useful dimensions increases, it becomes more important that the researcher turn away from simple "omnibus" reliability to the more precise investigation of structural reliabilities.

THE INSTRUCTIONAL VALIDITY OF
SIMPLE DECISIONS

After reliability, the second cornerstone of test theory is validity. We want to consider here some ideas about the validity of decisions based on test results where a major consideration is the simplicity of the decision. A decision in this context is a prediction, based on the evidence, the student is likely to succeed if the situation remains as it is, or the student is likely to fail unless something out of the ordinary is attempted. One could also inquire whether the test points with accuracy toward a specific instructional treatment, but we do not deal with that issue here.

The usual approach to prediction in educational settings is the venerable Pearson correlation coefficient. It assumes that two normally distributed covariates share some common variance in the form of a linear relation. This solution is elegant, and most teachers learn something about correlation during their preservice training.

The technique is straightforward. If we know: (a) a student's score on the predictor test, A; (b) the mean and variance of A; (c) the correlation between A and the criterion or to-be-predicted test, B; and (d) the mean and variance of B—then we can readily compute an estimate of the student's probable performance on B, along with confidence bounds on the estimate if the distribution of scores is normal.

Teachers seldom make use of the procedure just described. They are not comfortable with statistics; they have neither the time, the information, nor the computational formula. Thus, knowing that .70 is the correlation between a child's score on a readiness test at the beginning of kindergarten and in a first-grade reading achievement test is little help to typical classroom teachers, no matter how dedicated they might be. Of even less help are predictive relations established by more sophisticated techniques such as stepwise multiple regression, discriminant analysis, factor anaysis, and the like.

In our research we explored some alternative approaches to prediction based on all-or-none tests, with interesting consequences.[3] The general technique is most conveniently presented by a concrete example. A kindergartner's knowledge of the names of the letters of the alphabet is known to be predictive of subsequent performance on reading achievement tests (see, e.g., Gibson & Levin, 1975; Venezky, 1975). The reasons for this relation are complex and undoubtedly have more to do with home environment, general ability, amount of time spent watching "Sesame Street," and so on than with specific training on letter names. Alphabet knowledge is an indicator, not a cause, of reading success or failure.

The technique works as follows: Early in the school year, ask a group of kindergartners to name each letter of the alphabet; this yields the predictor score. What shall we predict? Suppose we measure reading achievement of these children 2 years later when they complete the first grade. Divide the students into two groups—those who read at or above grade level and those who are below grade level. The former group has "succeeded" by conventional standards. The children in the latter group are below an acceptable level of performance and might have profited from additional instruction during kindergarten and first grade. In any event, we have a simple metric to be predicted—success or failure.

Now for the validation. How well can the kindergarten teacher sort children, using their knowledge of letter names, into those who will probably succeed and those who probably will need additional help? What is the decision rule for sorting? How complicated does it have to be? How accurate will it be?

We have some data on these questions. Kindergarten children were tested in 1970 on their ability to name each of the 26 uppercase English letters (Calfee, 1977). Two years later, at the end of first grade, they took the Cooperative Primary Reading Test (Educational Testing Service, 1970). We obtained complete records for 144 children from the original sample of 276. There is a marked relation between alphabet knowledge and reading achievement in this group of students; the correlation is .50.

More interesting than the correlation is the frequency distribution of alphabet scores shown in Fig. 8.1. First, the distribution for the entire sample

---

[3]Holland (1975) has given thought to desirable characteristics of tests for instructional decision making and presents some interesting indices: (a) What proportion of the instructional time is used by testing versus teaching? (b) Does the test provide useful information for sorting students into instructional groups? If the test results say "assign all students to instruction A," the test has served no useful role for making a decision. (c) Does the test promote valid decisions? Does the student who passes the test succeed without instruction, and contrariwise? Holland's methods of analysis are fairly crude, but it seems to us that the questions are right. His conclusions about the usefulness of several instructional systems are generally disappointing and seem to us to be based on too little data and too limited an analysis.

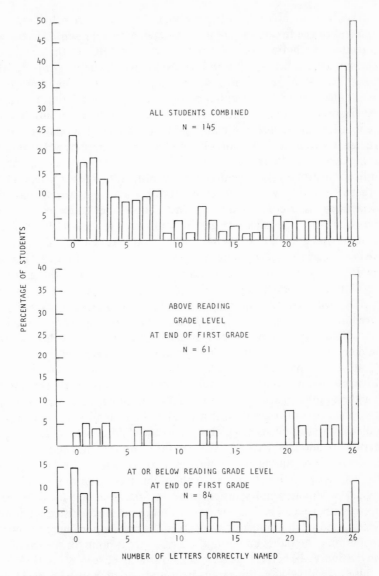

FIG. 8.1. Frequency distribution of kindergarten alphabet scores for total sample, for students above, and for students below grade level in reading achievement at end of first grade. (From "Assessment of Independent Reading Skills: Basic Research and Practical Applications" by R. C. Calfee. In A. S. Reber & D. Scarborough (Eds.), *Toward a Psychology of Reading: The Proceedings of the CUNY Conference.* Hillsdale, N.J.: Lawrence Erlbaum Associates, 1977. Copyright 1977 by Lawrence Erlbaum Associates, Reprinted by permission.)

is markedly bimodal (top panel). Second, children who are below grade level at the end of the first grade are disproportionately represented at the lower end of the distribution (they did not know their ABCs at the beginning of kindergarten), whereas the children who were above grade level are disproportionately represented at the upper end (they did known their ABCs). The correlation describes accurately the linear relation between the two variables, but it reveals neither the bimodality of the distributions nor the potential for simple decision making inherent in that bimodality.

In particular, suppose we sort children into two groups by a "cut-point" on the alphabet knowledge distribution; we might classify as "in need of additional instruction" all children who identified 10 or fewer letters. Then 12 of the 61 children who were at or above grade level would have been misclassified as needing additional instruction (they knew more than 10 letters when they entered kindergarten but met the grade level criterion at the end of the first grade); 28 of the 84 children who were below grade level would have been misclassified as not needing additional instruction (they knew more than 10 letters on entry to first grade but failed to meet the grade level criterion). This means that by placing a cut-point at 10 or fewer letters correctly identified, 12 of the total 144 students, or 8%, would be misclassified as needing instruction when they would end up doing all right without it; and 28 out of 144, or 19%, would be misclassified as not needing instruction but would end up below criterion. The total misclassification rate would thus be 27% at this cut-point.

Figure 8.2 shows what happens as the cut-point is moved from the lowest to the highest alphabet score for this set of data. If the cut-point is at the extreme left of the abscissa, then even if a child cannot identify a single letter, no supplementary instruction is given. All of the children who fail to reach the criterion are misclassified under this condition; none of the children who meet the criterion are misclassified, since by definition they need no additional help. As the cut-point is moved to the right, more and more students are assigned to supplementary instruction. At first, most are from the below-criterion subgroup. There is a wide flat spot in the misclassification function reflecting the small number of students in the middle portion of the bimodal distribution of alphabet knowledge scores. At a cut-point (or critical value) of 10 in the figure, the percentages just mentioned can be seen; 8% of the students are falsely classified as needing more help, and 19% of those who need help are not so classified, for a cumulative misclassification rate of 27% (the sum of the previous two percentages). Eventually, at the far right side of the abscissa, all students receive supplementary instruction, even those who know all the letter names. This means that all the above-criterion students are, by definition, misclassified.

Let us emphasize two features of this procedure. First, it is simple. We can say to the teacher: "Give the child a test. If the child makes more than X

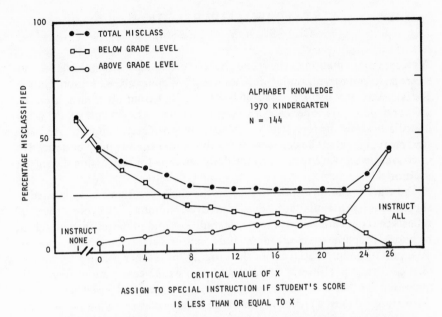

FIG. 8.2. Cut-point results based on kindergarten alphabet scores and first-grade reading achievement. (From "Assessment of Independent Reading Skills: Basic Research and Practical Applications" by R. C. Calfee. In A. S. Reber & D. Scarborough (Eds.), *Toward a Psychology of Reading: The Proceedings of the CUNY Conference*. Hillsdale, N.J.: Lawrence Erlbaum Associates, 1977. Copyright 1977 by Lawrence Erlbaum Associates. Reprinted by permission.)

successes, everything is probably (this can be made more precise) going to be all right. If the child makes X successes or less, then there is probably going to be trouble and you had better think about what might be done to prevent failure." There are no complicated statistics. Second, it is robustly accurate. The total misclassification rate in Fig. 8.2 drops to a low of 25% and stays at that level over a broad range of cut-points. (Incidentally, Feshbach, Adelman, & Fuller, 1973, using a predictive test battery or teacher judgment or both, found that the misclassification rate from their multivariate measures and procedures ranged around 25% for a sample of almost 600 students.)

It should be stressed that the present analysis of alphabet knowledge scores and reading achievement implies nothing about what is the most appropriate action for a child in need. This test is clearly not precise enough to call for a specific treatment. Instead, it probably is a general indicator of a variety of abilities and skills, and the instructional response can be only a general one.

STANDARDS FOR PRACTICAL
CLASSROOM ASSESSMENT

A cursory examination of the research literature reveals the emphasis on tests suitable to long-term, major decisions (e.g., Weintraub, Robinson, Smith, Pleasas, & Rowls, 1974, pp. 460–464; Weintraub, Robinson, Smith, & Roser, 1973, pp. 429–447). The teacher's need for in-class assessment, on the other hand, is best met by tests that are speedy, precise, clearly "appropriate," and flexibly repeatable. The concepts of reliability and validity must be defined in unconventional ways to serve in the design of tests for instructional decision making.

The teacher cannot expect to find on-the-shelf tests that are well suited to short-term instructional decisions. Moreover, training in "test construction" reflects the conventional psychometric tradition, and so the teacher is likely to be poorly prepared to select, adapt, and create useful instruments; it is not our intention to go into detail about the program of teacher training that might alleviate this gap. However, we suspect that it would center about an analytic approach to "what is being taught"; we have referred elsewhere to the distinction between a "jello" model of the mind in contrast with the "works in a drawer" model—the former being more Gestalt-like, the latter more analytic and information processing in character (Calfee & Floyd, 1973). Although the literature on teaching effectiveness should be approached with caution, one can find consistent signs to support the notion that the analytically minded teacher is more effective in promoting academic growth (Potter, 1975; Rosenshine & Furst, 1971). Another instance comes from the work of Evertson and Brophy (1973): "The teacher who is well organized, who monitors the class regularly and nips potentially serious problems in the bud, and who has well established routines for handling everyday procedural matters tends to be more successful in producing learning gains [p. 11]." This sounds to us like a description of a highly analytic teacher.

Next, we want to highlight three desirable characteristics of tests intended for short-term instructional decisions:

1. The individual test needs to be "clean" in the sense that demands on the student extraneous to the skill being measured are kept to a minimum. The results from a clean test are much easier to interpret than those from a test where many factors enter in an uncontrolled fashion.

2. Rather than being rigorously standardized, the testing system should permit clinical probing. Such variations in the testing procedure need not be random. We have proposed factorial test designs as a method for systematic exploration of the student's ability to handle a task.

3. Tests for instructional decision making require more attention to breadth than precision (Cronbach, 1970, refers to these as "band-width" and

"fidelity," respectively). Achieving this goal requires attention to efficiency in the testing procedure and especially in the choice of where to begin testing for a student.

Each of these issues—clean tests, factorial test design, and efficient entry testing—is a complex matter. We cannot do more than emphasize a few of the main points.

Clean Tests

A clean test is one in which a single, well-defined component is examined (Calfee, 1977; Calfee, Chapman, & Venezky, 1972). The test begins as simply as possible; ideally, no student should make a mistake under the simplest conditions. This shows that the student understands the nature of the test and can handle the general test-taking requirements. Then the difficulty of the test is increased systematically. As errors occur, they indicate the nature of the student's problem. Developing a clean test often requires working backwards, asking the question, "What must the student know to be able to succeed in this task?" In answer to the question, "What does a failure mean?" the teacher must make a guess. Based on the guess, the teacher decides how to simplify the test. If the guess was correct and the student is now successful, the problem has been isolated. If the student still makes mistakes, the guessing–testing process is pursued further.

The major barriers to a clean test are often the general test requirements. To do well on a test, the student must understand what is expected and must feel encouraged and motivated to do well. Listening carefully and following instructions are important for success, and some students are better at these general skills than are others. Individual or small-group testing makes it easier for the teacher to be sure that all students know what they are to do and makes it more likely that performance will reflect specific rather than general skills. The clinical tester receives the training needed to gain understanding; the classroom teacher may not have had any such training but can be aided by guidelines for determining readiness for a test and by suggestions about how to promote readiness.

Factorial Tests

Complementing the notion of a clean test is the idea of factorial test structure. The clean test approach aims toward constancy in all dimensions of the test except one; the factorial approach aims toward systematic variation in several dimensions of the test. Because the concept is new, we illustrate in Fig. 8.3 how a factorial structure provides a framework for the instructor to think about in testing reading comprehension. One dimension is the nature of the

TASK		MATERIALS			
		Familiar Topic		Unfamiliar Topic	
Reading Mode	Question Mode	Easy Vocabulary	Difficult Vocabulary	Easy Vocabulary	Difficult Vocabulary
Read Aloud	Oral/ Literal				
	Recognition/ Literal				
	Recognition/ Interpreta- tive				
	Production/ Essay				
Read Silently No Time Pressure	Oral/ Literal				
	Recognition/ Literal				
	Recognition/ Interpreta- tive				
	Production/ Essay				
Read Silently Time Pressure	Oral/ Literal				
	Recognition/ Literal				
	Recognition/ Interpreta- tive				
	Production Essay				

FIG. 8.3.   A factorial structure for reading assessment.

task: oral reading, silent reading with no time pressure, and silent reading with time pressure. As students become competent, they should be able to perform equally well under all these conditions. A second dimension is the "question mode." How should the teacher request information from students after they have finished reading? Perhaps the simplest approach is to ask direct, literal questions; these can be quite specific, or they may allow for a more general response to the passage. A recognition test is slightly more difficult, because the students have to read the question and the alternatives, but at least the answers are provided. Production and essay tasks demand even more from students. To summarize a story requires some sophistication, and failure can be traced to any of several possibilities. If performance has been measured under simpler conditions, most of these possibilities can be evaluated. Variation in materials is the third major dimension. It makes quite a difference whether students are reading a familiar or an unfamiliar topic; difficulty level of vocabulary also makes a difference.

Envision each student's performance in the multidimensional space of Fig. 8.3. The task of the instructor is to locate the student in this space in the sense that the instructor knows whether the student can perform accurately and quickly in each cell. In fact, one might conceive of testing that aims to trace through the three-dimensional space a line that represents the boundary between where the student can perform adequately and where there is trouble. Lord's (1974) discussion of "tailored" testing provides a rationale for the unidimensional situation; the multidimensional case, to the best of our knowledge, remains to be developed.

Entry Level Assessment

We agree fully with Guszak's (1972) characterization of the good diagnostic reading teacher as someone "capable of making a sequence of relatively simple determinations of a pupil's reading achievement level, his achievement potential, and his prominent skills needs [p. 22]." To accomplish this task with any precision, especially when the individual differences within the class are substantial, the teacher must make quick and accurate determinations of the student's level of performance. Starting an assessment in the right "neighborhood" is essential if time is to be used wisely.

Where the teacher has continuing day-to-day knowledge of the student, choosing the proper "entry point" for assessment may be fairly easy. But what about the new student? The new subject matter? The first day of class? Developing instruments to meet this need seems to us an interesting challenge, and so we report our experiences. We have little evidence on the reliability of these procedures, although they spring from a well-established statistical framework (Wald, 1947; Cronbach & Gleser, 1965).

Here is a systematic but flexible technique for rapidly classifying students whose level of decoding, vocabulary, and comprehension is unknown and may range anywhere from first to eighth grade (Calfee & Hoover, 1974). Choose a few lists of words arranged by difficulty level, and say to the student, "Here are some word lists I would like you to read. Which list, A, B, C, D, or E, do you think you can read?" As soon as the student has pointed to a list, the teacher has some useful information: If the student's self-assessment agrees with subsequent performance, then a realistic assessment has been made; if performance is two or three levels below the estimate, the student at least has a good self-concept. The teacher then asks the student to read the list. If the student has trouble with several words, the teacher selects an easier list. If every word is pronounced quickly and correctly, the teacher asks the student to read a harder list. The student will reach the limit within a few minutes. A similar procedure is used to assess the level of understanding of word meanings and of paragraph comprehension.

We have used a test built around this model for research activities and are pleased with the rich return from what is generally less than a 30-minute test session. But the point to be stressed here is the value of this test for purposes of determining entry level to other tests (and to instruction, of course). Precise assessment of a student's skills and knowledge, if it is also to be efficient and not time-consuming, requires a quick screening to determine relative standing in different component areas of reading.

CATEGORIES OF READING SKILLS

Reading includes several areas of knowledge and skill, and any analytic effort to assess reading must attempt a "first cut" of the collection into reasonably digestible pieces. We have suggested elsewhere (Calfee & Drum, in press) this list: decoding, vocabulary, grammar, transliteral comprehension, and inferential comprehension.

Decoding is the translation from print to sound. It is not clear at what point during the acquisition of reading the student can best develop this skill. Neither is it clear how decoding skills serve the advanced reader. But a good deal of data supports the proposition that the reader of English who cannot look at new sets of words and decode them with fluency is likely to have trouble acquiring mastery of other reading skills. We must look at program differences in developing decoding skills and at student attainments at different ages, for certain facts seem clear:

1. Not all reading programs do a good job of training students to decode. Certain approaches are noticeably less effective in promoting the acquisition of decoding skills (Barr, 1974; Chall, 1967).
2. Not all students learn decoding skills in the elementary grades. At the end of the fifth grade, many children still evidence lack of skill in handling basic decoding skills (McDonald & Elias, 1975).
3. Substantial correlations are found between decoding skill and school performance up through college (Venezky, 1974b).[4]

---

[4]Laboratory research from several sources demonstrates the important relation between fluent skilled decoding and comprehension (Cromer, 1970, following the reanalysis in Calfee, Arnold, & Drum, 1976; Perfetti & Hogaboam, 1975a, 1975b). To be sure, the training studies needed to establish causality remain to be done. It is far from clear that teaching decoding skills in regular classrooms receives the emphasis that some reports suggest. For instance, in questioning

Reading teachers realize that *vocabulary development* is vitally important to success on academic tasks. Austin and Morrison (1963) reported that more than 75% of the teachers in their sample spent "considerable" or "moderate" time in vocabulary development. Rubin, Trismen, Wilder, and Yates (1973) reported comparable findings in their survey of teachers in compensatory reading programs. Unfortunately, it is far from clear that the instructional emphasis is accompanied by assessment sufficient to show not only whether the student "knows" a word but also at what level and with what degree of fluency.

The student needs to be able to define words, to appreciate synonyms, and to recognize common usage of a word. The dictionary definition is a start. But few words have a single meaning, and common words have many meanings. Furthermore, even if the student were to internalize the dictionary, society and individuals keep devising novel and idiosyncratic meanings.

Some may find it quaint to include *grammar* as part of the reading process, but it probably has as much place as comprehension skills. In both instances, understanding requires the transfer of skills from oral language to a new context and the expansion and elaboration of those skills to meet the peculiar demands of the written language (Olson, 1975). An important distinction also exists between style and substance. Style refers to following the proper convention: producing all the past and plural markers, using proper word order, and the like. If the student is going to speak or write English "properly," then the conventions must be known and used in the proper context. There are also substantive matters in grammar. Sometimes meaning is disambiguated only when the plural marker, the past marker, or some other morphological ending is noted. If a particular word order has one meaning and a different word order conveys a different meaning, a substantive difference in grammar is apparent. "Bill told Jane to snitch the ice cream" has a meaning different from that of "Bill was told by Jane to snitch the ice cream." The answer to "Who will be punished for snitching the ice cream?" depends on recognizing this difference. Many children come to school with adequate knowledge of English syntax; others may need some help. It is the task of instructional assessment to distinguish one group from the other.

Comprehension is a complicated matter; it can be virtually synonymous with thinking. Trying to analyze the process of comprehension is an

---

teachers whose classrooms included some kind of compensatory reading program, it was found that less than one in five teachers of sixth-grade students made any extensive use of phonics curriculum programs (Rubin et al., 1973). More than 95% of the teachers at all grade levels said that comprehension was a major goal. Another piece of information from this study bears on the relative emphasis on decoding skills: In second grade, 75% of the teachers report that each child reads aloud to an adult once a week or more often. By fourth grade, only 63% of the teachers report this much oral reading, and by sixth grade the figure is 57%.

interesting challenge. We propose here two broad categories of comprehension tasks—transliteral and inferential. Transliteral comprehension requires students to have meanings for the words, recognize word order, and have either direct or analogical experience with the content, so they can extract and remember information conveyed directly by the passage—information fairly close to the surface. Some questions can be answered by using matching techniques, some by prior experience without reading the passage, and some require an understanding of key terms. Useful assessment procedures sort out the strategies used by students to answer various types of questions.

There is a kind of comprehension that requires a broader and deeper analysis of the textual information. For instance, consider this "comprehension" question:

"Most of the women in the United States are_____.
(a) plumbers, (b) citizens, (c) redheads, or (d) waitresses."

With no passage to read, how does the student select the right answer? The task is only modestly related to reading, although it comes from an actual comprehension test. The student unfamiliar with our culture might think that "redheads" was right; "waitresses" makes sense if many of the women in the student's experience have been waitresses. An advocate of the women's liberation movement might choose "plumbers." The "correct" answer to the question actually seems stilted and perhaps absurd. The student must rely on knowledge and experience that goes beyond the question and looks at the demands of the task. Good readers bring to bear on the topic what they know, what they learn from the passage, and what they can figure out about the tester's reasoning and intentions. The teacher needs to know which of these is behind the "poor" students' failures.

The teacher who wishes to "measure comprehension" should be prepared to cover the full range of the student's skills; these include not only finding facts and making simple inferences but also solving the problem of when to do one or the other. Moreover, making inferences is not only a logical process. Many comprehension questions require a process of inference that is more analogical than logical. This requirement seems altogether reasonable, because life experiences are often based more on metaphor than on logic. We make comparison with experience and fill in the missing parts of an event by analogy rather than by Aristotelian inference.

The reason for the separation of reading into components like those listed is straightforward: Methods of assessment and selection of instructional treatment are distinctive for each component. If such is not the case, then the division into components is a useless exercise. The methodology for evaluating the hypothesis that these are independent components—and such a hypothesis is inherent in the listing of the components, we believe—is also straightforward (Calfee, in press), although only a smattering of research exists currently. We realize that our "shopping list" is not the same as others might propose; indeed, with more thought and evidence, we would want to change it. But we see little point to continued argument about the "fundamental components" in skilled reading and the acquisition of reading. Let researchers move on to propose the systematic, comprehensive, and generalizable research designs necessary to decide which of the many process models are viable. Such research will have theoretical and practical payoff. In the meantime, we might put a moratorium on models with more than 7 ± 2 information-processing stages; these tend to overload the capacity of the reader to understand the model.

Task Requirements in Assessment

In examining these categories of reading skills, we also need to analyze the task requriements for successful performance on a particular test within a given category. Some task requirements are specific to a given area, but others cut across all areas. For instance, the same basic situation may be presented to the readers so that they recognize the correct answer from a set of alternatives or must produce the correct answer from memory. A person may perform well on one form of the task and not on the other. As Kintsch (1978, Chap. 5) noted, different performances under the two task formats permit the researcher (or tester) to infer underlying processes. Recognition of previously studied information suggests the information has been stored adequately; recall suggests that it was stored in a retrievable format.

To find what a person "really" knows, the teacher must devise various ways to tap that knowledge. As noted earlier, it is relatively easy to show that the student cannot remember it under certain conditions. The most direct way to assess a person's knowledge is to ask a direct question. If there is no answer, then a second more probing question can follow. "Do you think it's this?" Maybe the probe will trip the memory key so the student responds with the correct answer.

Speed and accuracy comprise another important task dimension. Speed is not always "good," but often it is. Automaticity in basic skills can be especially critical (LaBerge & Samuels, 1974). For example, a few years ago we worked with some researchers who were developing a reading series for kindergartners. They had devised an algorithm for teaching children to decode. First the students learned a few letter–sound correspondences; then they moved their fingers from one letter to another to blend the sounds: "b"; "b-a, ba"; "ba-t, bat." Within a short time, the kindergartners could decode a fairly substantial set of words. Some students were much faster than others, of course. Some could look at the word and say "bat," and others were still saying "b-a-t, bat." Then they were asked to read sentences for the first time. The task changed from decoding one word at a time at a relatively easy pace to decoding a whole string of words. Furthermore, the children were expected to answer questions when they finished the sentence. A few seemed to become "instantly dyslexic" at this juncture in the program. In our opinion, this resulted from differences in speed of decoding. Speed of reading single words was not important per se. But it took so long for some students to translate the sentence word by word that by the time they reached the end of the sentence, they had forgotten the beginning. Since the decoding strategy did not work, these students began to guess from initial letters, or they looked at the pictures, searching for meaning with little regard for the print—strategies typical of poor readers.

What is the import of the speed–accuracy distinction for the classroom teacher? Formerly, teachers were encouraged to test for both speed and power. Today, in the era of behavioral objectives and mastery learning, the distinction is largely overlooked. The student who is correct on 80% of the items on a multiple-choice test has "mastered" the objective without regard to how quickly and easily the task was performed and without regard to performance under different conditions and different demands (e.g., Block, 1974). If the objective is fundamental to the learning of another task, the student may come to grief unless fluent with the first objective. In this connection, some evidence has been cited in support of the relative independence of speed of reading and accuracy of comprehension (Gates, 1921; Singer, 1970). Unfortunately, our reading of the evidence leaves us far from convinced about the actual degree of separability of these two measures.

Another point can be mentioned only in passing. Assessment is often most meaningful when carried out in a training context (Calfee, Cullenbine, dePorcel, & Royston, 1971). Short-term training may serve to clarify the task demands for the student. The teacher can note questions and comments by the students as they perform the task. In California, at least one major assessment project includes a pretest that the teacher is encouraged to give to students until they are thoroughly familiar with how to take the test. Certain commercial tests (e.g., Stanford Achievement Test Battery) also include short practice tests to familiarize the students with the format and type of content they can expect to encounter. This seems a most sensible practice. More generally, the teacher's assessment should aim to measure the student's response to the ongoing instructional program.

Assessment of Transfer

Educators must aim to teach for transfer. Teaching students everything they need to know is impossible. Acquiring knowledge that is transferable generally requires that the student understand principles as well as basic facts.

Transfer sometimes happens automatically, but it is often advisable to teach the principle and then to check or assess whether the principle has actually been acquired. Giving many examples of a principle allows students to have experience with a variety of instances to which the principle applies. This procedure means that the teacher must be continually checking not only what students have learned but also whether the students have attained the principles.

How does one assess the extent of transfer? By changing certain features of the situation from those that existed during training and seeing whether performance remains stable. By choosing novel instances of a general principle that is not part of training and seeing whether the student can apply the principle. By asking the student to state the principle and to supply novel instances exemplifying the principle.

Silberman (1967) demonstrated the importance of assessment of transfer in the evaluation of a beginning reading program. Teaching students to read a list of words by rote is fairly easy; it may be dull for the teacher and student, but it can be done. However, when Silberman tested for transfer using a variation of the Esper (1925) paradigm, in which one portion of a set of associations is learned and transfer is measured by testing other portions of the system, he found that the students had learned what they were taught, nothing more. Using the transfer measure as the standard for a good training program, Silberman proceeded to modify the training program until it worked, until the students learned not only what the were taught but also the principles that allowed them to apply the knowledge in new situations.

Silberman tested transfer through the Esper paradigm. This is only one of several paradigms developed by experimental psychologists to measure "what is learned" in a deeper sense than simple rote associations (Calfee, 1975b, pp. 393–398; pp. 423–429; Calfee, 1975c; Martinson, 1978). The advantage of these paradigms is that they provide precise information about what elements of original learning have and have not transferred to a new situation. This precision is in contrast to the vague measures that are all too often used as an index of "transfer" in reading research; the criterion measure is performance on the California Achievement Test, and the transfer measure is performance on a Metropolitan Achievement Test. Whether one observes transfer or not, the exact meaning of the results is uncertain.

SUMMARY

What can the researcher do to help the reading teacher with the task of classroom assessment? In our opinion, this is an area of need that has scarcely been touched. To be sure, many of the new movements in testing appear to have the goal of improving classroom assessment. But the new tests seem quite like the old ones in appearance and application. The teacher is told not to measure the student's performance against the norms of grade level equivalent or percentile rank. Instead, the teacher is told to use a criterion— the student must pass 80% of the items on a multiple-choice test. But are the items really appropriate? What is the relevant domain for generalization. To what degree does the multiple-choice task relate to other tasks? Why 80%? Why not 50% or 100%? How reliable are the data for a particular decision? How valid is the decision? These are not esoteric questions. They are at the core of the issue of whether it is worth the teacher's and student's time and effort to carry out the assessment.

Conventional norm-referenced tests build on a substantial and well-developed theoretical base. With suitable modification, the same principles can serve in the development of tests for in-class use. The empirical procedures for certifying the adequacy of conventional tests is also well established. Little more is needed for certifying in-class tests, save for the linking of these tests to the instructional base. The norm-referenced test is curriculum free. The in-class test has to prove its usefulness for making effective and efficient instructional decisions and for assessing the direct and indirect results of instruction flowing from such decisions.

Carrying out research within this framework poses special challenges to the behavioral scientist. It requires continuous assessment while the student is engaged in instruction. Computer-assisted instruction solves some problems of control over instruction, and for certain purposes this may be desirable. But most students learn to read in classrooms with a teacher, and it is in this context that we think the greatest payoff will be found. The costs are substantial; the investigator must be welcome in the classroom to the point of establishing a collaborative relation with the teacher (see White, this volume). The instructional materials and the instructional activities of the teacher must be monitored and in some instances brought under control. We believe that the payoff can also be considerable: increased knowledge about the cognitive processes that mediate the acquisition of reading skill and the development of practical assessment tools for more effective teaching of reading.

ACKNOWLEDGMENTS

Preparation of this paper was supported in part by a grant from the Carnegie Corporation. Many of the ideas are reported in a slightly less technical form in "What Research Can Tell the Reading Teacher about Assessment," by R. C. Calfee, P. A. Drum, and R. D. Arnold, to appear in S. J. Samuels (Ed.), *What Research Has to Say to the Teacher of Reading,* an IRA publication. The assistance of Elizabeth Orem, Dorothy Piontkowski, Barbara Tanner, and Barbara Tingey is gratefully acknowledged. A special debt is owed Kathryn Hoover Calfee for her practical counsel about the classroom.

REFERENCES

Anastasi, A. *Psychological testing.* New York: Macmillan, 1968.

Atkinson, R. C., & Paulson, J. A. An approach to the psychology of instruction. *Psychological Bulletin,* 1972, *78,* 49–61.

Austin, M. C., & Morrison, C. *The first R: The Harvard report on reading in elementary schools.* New York: Macmillan, 1963.

Banas, C. New testing method cited for drop in reading scores at public schools. *Chicago Tribune,* December 4, 1975, pp. 1; 23.

Barr, R. The effect of instruction on pupil reading strategies. *Reading Research Quarterly,* 1974, *10,* 555–582.

Block, J. H. *Schools, society and mastery learning.* New York: Holt, Rinehart & Winston, 1974.

Bloom, B. S. *Stability and change in human characteristics.* New York: Wiley, 1964.

Calfee, R. C. *The design of experiments and the design of curriculum.* Paper presented at Stanford Evaluation Consortium, Stanford University, March 1975. (a)

Calfee, R. C. *Human experimental psychology.* New York: Holt, 1975. (b)

Calfee, R. C. Memory and cognitive skills in reading acquisition. In D. Duane & M. Rawson (Eds.), *Reading, perception and language.* Baltimore, Md.: York press, 1975. (c)

Calfee, R. C. Sources of dependency in cognitive processes. In D. Klahr (Ed.), *Cognition and instruction.* Hillsdale, N.J.: Lawrence Erlbaum Associates, 1976.

Calfee, R. C. Assessment of independent reading skills: Basic research and practical applications. In A. S. Reber & D. Scarborough (Eds.), *Toward a psychology of reading: The proceedings of the CUNY conference.* Hillsdale, N.J.: Lawrence Erlbaum Associates, 1977.

Calfee, R. C., Arnold, R. D., & Drum, P. A. Review of *The psychology of reading* by E. J. Gibson & H. Levin. *Proceedings of the National Academy of Education,* 1976, *3,* 1–80.

Calfee, R. C., Chapman, R. S., & Venezky, R. L. How a child needs to think to learn to read. In L. W. Gregg (Ed.), *Cognition in learning and memory.* New York: Wiley, 1972.

Calfee, R. C., Cullenbine, R. S., dePorcel, A., & Royston, A. B. *Further explorations of perceptual and cognitive skills related to reading acquisition.* Paper presented at the meeting of the American Psychological Association, Washington, D.C., September 1971.

Calfee, R. C., Drum, P. A., & Arnold, R. D. What research can tell the teacher about assessment. In S. J. Samuels (Ed.), *What research has to say to the teacher of reading.* Newark, Del.: International Reading Association, 1978.

Calfee, R. C., & Elman, A. The application of mathematical learning theories in educational settings: Possibilities and limitations. In H. Spada & W. Kempf (Eds.), *Structural models of thinking and learning.* Bern, Switzerland: Hans Huber, 1977.

Calfee, R. C., & Floyd J. The independence of cognitive processes: Implications for curriculum research. In K. Frey & M. Lang (Eds.), *Cognitive processes and science instruction.* Bern Switzerland: Hans Huber, 1973.

Calfee, R. C., & Hedges, L. E. Independent process analyses of aptitude treatment interactions. In R. E. Snow, P-A. Federico, and W. E. Montague (Eds.), *Aptitude, learning and instruction: Cognitive process analyses.* Hillsdale, N.J.: Lawrence Erlbaum Associates, in preparation.

Calfee, R. C., & Hoover K. A. *Interactive reading assessment system.* Unpublished mimeographed manuscript, Stanford University, 1974.

Calfee, R. C., & Venezky, R. L. Component skills in beginning reading. In K. S. Goodman & J. T. Fleming (Eds.), *Psycholinguistics and the teaching of reading.* Newark, Del.: International Reading Association, 1969.

Carver, R. P. Two dimensions of tests: Psychometric and edumetric. *American Psychologist,* 1974, *29,* 512–518.

Chall, J. S. *Learning to read: The great debate.* New York: McGraw-Hill, 1967.

Cromer, W. The difference model: A new explanation for some reading difficulties. *Journal of Educational Psychology,* 1970, *61,* 471–483.

Cronbach, L. J. Coefficient alpha and the internal structure of tests. *Psychometrika,* 1951, *16,* 297–334.

Cronbach, L. J. *Essentials of psychoogical testing* (3rd ed.). New York: Harper & Row, 1970.

Cronbach, L. J. & Gleser, G. C. *Psychological tests and personnel decisions* (2nd ed.). Chicago: University of Illinois Press, 1965.

Cronbach, L. J., Gleser, G. C., Nanda, H., & Rajaratnam, J. *The dependability of behavioral measurements: Theory of generalizability for scores and profiles.* New York: Wiley, 1972.

Cronbach, L. J., Rajaratnam, J., & Gleser, G. C. Theory of generalizability: A liberalization of reliability theory. *British Journal of Statistical Psychology,* 1963, *16,* 137–163.

Cronbach, L. J., & Snow, R. E. *Attitudes and instructional methods.* New York: Irvington, 1977.

Educational Testing Service. *Cooperative primary reading test.* Princeton, N..J.: Educational Testing Service, 1970.

Esper, E. A. A technique for the experimental investigation of associative interference in artificial linguistic material. *Language Monograph,* 1925, *1,* 1–47.

Evertson, C. M., & Brophy, J. E. *High-interference behavioral ratings as correlates of teaching effectiveness.* Austin, Tex.: University of Texas, Research and Development Center for Teacher Education, 1973. (ERIC Document Reproduction Service No. ED 078 042)

Farr, R., Tuinman, J. J. The dependent variable: Measurement issues in reading research. *Reading Research Quarterly,* 1972, *7,* 413–429.

Feshbach, S., Adelman, H., & Fuller, W W. *Early identification of children with high risk of reading failure.* Paper presented at the meeting of the American Educational Research Association, New Orleans, February 1973. (ERIC Document Reproduction Service No. ED 082 139)

Gates, A. I. An experimental and statistical study of reading and reading tests. *Journal of Educational Psychology,* 1921, *12,* 303–314,

Gibson, E. J., & Levin, H. *The psychology of reading.* Cambridge, Mass.: M.I.T. Press, 1975.

Green, D. B. *The nature and use of criterion-referenced and norm-referenced achievement tests.* Burlingame, Calif.: Special report by the Association of California School Administrators, Vol. 4, No. 3, 1976.

Guszak, F. J. *Diagnostic reading instruction in the elementary school.* New York: Harper & Row, 1972.

Hively, W. (Ed.). *Domain-referenced testing.* Englewood Cliffs, N.J.: Educational Technology Publications, 1974.

Holland, J. G. *Variables in adaptive decisions in individual instruction.* Pittsburgh, Pa.: University of Pittsburgh, Learning Research and Development Center, 1975. (Publication No. 1975/10; ERIC Document Reproduction Service No. ED 110 442)

Kintsch, W. *Learning, memory and conceptual processes* (2nd ed.). New York: Wiley, 1978.

Knapp, T. R. An application of balanced incomplete block designs to the estimation of test norms. *Educational and Psychological Measurements,* 1968, *28,* 265–272.

LaBerge, D., & Samuels, S. J. Toward a theory of automatic information processing in reading. *Cognitive Psychology,* 1974, *6,* 293–332.

Levine, M. The academic achievement test: Its historical context and social functions. *American Psychologist,* 1976, *31,* 228–238.

Lord, F. M. Individualized testing and item characteristic curve theory. In D. H. Krantz, R. C. Atkinson, R. D. Luce, & P. Suppes (Eds.), *Contemporary developments in mathematical psychology. Vol. II: Measurement, psychophysics and neural information processing.* San Francisco: Freeman, 1974.

Martinson, L. *The acquisition of decoding skills in beginning readers.* Unpublished doctoral dissertation, Stanford University, 1978.

McCullough, C. M. Responses of elementary school children to common types of reading comprehension questions. *Journal of Educational Research,* 1957, *51,* 65–70.

McDonald, F. J., & Elias, P. *Beginning teacher evaluation study: Phase 2 final report* (Vol. 1, Chap. 10). Princeton, N.J.: Educational Testing Service, 1975.

Mellon, J. C. *National assessment and the teaching of English.* Urbana, Ill.: National Council of Teachers of English, 1975.

Olson, D. R. A review of *Toward a literate society* by J. B. Carroll & J. Chall (Eds.). *Proceedings of the National Academy of Education,* 1975, *2,* 109–178.

Perfetti, C. A., & Hogaboam, T. *The effects of words experience on decoding speeds of skilled and unskilled readers.* Paper presented at the meeting of the Psychonomics Society, Denver, Colorado, November 1975. (a)

Perfetti, C. A., & Hogaboam, T. The relationship between single word decoding and reading comprehension skill. *Journal of Educational Psychology,* 1975, *67,* 461–469. (b)

Potter, D. A critical review of the literature: Teacher performance and pupil growth. In F. J. McDonald & P. Elias (Eds.), *Beginning teacher evaluation study: Phase 2 report.* Princeton, N.J.: Educational Testing Service, 1975.

Rosenshine, B., & Furst, N. Research in teacher performance criteria. In B. O. Smith (Ed.), *Research in teacher education: A symposium.* Englewood Cliffs, N.J.: Prentice-Hall, 1971.

Rubin, D., Trismen, D. A., Wilder, G., & Yates, A. *A descriptive and analytic study of compensatory reading programs: Phase 1 report.* Princeton, N.J.: Educational Testing Service, 1973.

Silberman, H. F. Experimental analysis of a beginning reading skill. In J. P. DeCecco (Ed.), *The psychology of language, thought, and instruction.* New York: Holt, Rinehart & Winston, 1967. (Also in *Progammed Instruction,* 1964, *3,* 4–8.)

Singer, H. Research that should have made a difference. *Elementary English,* 1970, *47,* 27–34.

Sticht, T. G. (Ed.). *Reading for working: A functional literacy anthology.* Alexandria, Va.: Human Resources Research Organization, 1975.

Sticht, T. G., Caylor, J. S., Kern, R. P., & Fox, L. C. Project REALISTIC: Determination of adult functional literacy skill levels. *Reading Research Quarterly,* 1971, *7,* 424–465.

Thorndike, R. L. Dilemmas in diagnosis. In W. H. MacGinitie (Ed.), *Assessment problems in reading.* Newark, Del.: International Reading Association, 1973.

Venezky, R. L. *Testing in reading: Assessment and instructional decision-making.* Urbana, Ill.: National Council of Teachers of English, 1974. (a)

Venezky, R. L. Theoretical and experimental bases for teaching reading. In T. Sebeok (Ed.), *Current trends in linguistics* (Vol. 12). The Hague, Netherlands: Mouton, 1974. (b)

Venezky, R. L. The curious role of letter names in reading instruction. *Visible Language,* 1975, *9,* 7–23.

Wald, A. *Sequential analysis.* New York: Wiley, 1947.

Walker, D. F., & Schaffarzick, J. Comparing curricula. *Review of Educational Research,* 1974, *74,* 83–111.

Weintraub, S., Robinson, H. M., Smith, H. K., Pleasas, G. S., & Rowls, M. Summary of investigations relating to reading July 1, 1973, to June 30, 1974. *Reading Research Quarterly,* 1974, *10,* 247–513.

Weintraub, S., Robinson, H. M., Smith, H. K., & Roser, N. Summary of investigations relating to reading July 1, 1972 to June 30, 1973. *Reading Research Quarterly,* 1973, *9,* 247–513.

Winter, B. J. *Statistical principles in experimental design* (2nd ed.). New York: McGraw-Hill, 1971.

Zigler, E., & Trickett, P. K. IQ, social competence, and evaluation of early childhood intervention programs. *American Psychologist,* 1978, *33,* 789–797.

9 Process Deficits in Learning Disabled Children and Implications for Reading

Doris J. Johnson
Northwestern University

In recent years considerable attention has been given to children who underachieve in our schools. Special services, teacher preparation programs, legislation and research studies have been initiated in order to provide for children with unique needs. The problems are highly complex, because underachievement may result from a variety of causes including sensory impairments, mental retardation, emotional disorders, lack of stimulation, and specific learning disabilities. Thus, it is frequently necessary to have comprehensive diagnostic services to determine why a child is not learning. The ultimate goal of these services is to develop an educational plan designed to meet the child's cognitive and affective needs.

Although it is clear that some children have multiple problems, the focus of this chapter is on children who are classified as having a learning disability. The term *learning disabilties* in this discussion is used as defined by the National Advisory Committee on Handicapped Children (1968) in the Education of the Handicapped Act:

> Children with specific learning disabilities exhibit a disorder in one or more of the basic psychological processes involved in understanding or in using written or spoken language. These may be manifested in disorders of listening, thinking, talking, reading, writing, spelling or arithmetic. They include conditions which have been referred to as perceptual handicaps, brain injury, minimal brain dysfunction, dyslexia, developmental aphasia, etc. They do not include learning problems which are due primarily to visual, hearing or motor handicaps, to mental retardation, emotional disturbance or to environmental disadvantage [Part G, P. L. 91–230].

Although there are many persistent questions and problems related to the definition, most special educators recognize that there are children who have difficulty learning even though they have good mental ability and motivation. They also recognize that the population of children with learning disabilities is heterogeneous. Some have problems understanding or using spoken language; others speak well but cannot read; still others have no problems reading, but they are unable to express ideas in writing. Because of the variability in the complexity of the symbol systems that children are expected to learn, and because of the variability within the group, the age of identification varies. Some youngsters, particularly those with language disorders, may be identified during the preschool years, whereas others may not encounter difficulty until third or fourth grade when they are expected to acquire more abstract vocabulary or write lengthy compositions.

Many, but not all, children with learning disabilities encounter difficulty learning to read. Because reading requires complex auditory, visual, linguistic, and cognitive skills, it is apparent that children who have one or more deficits in processing information are apt to have problems at some point while they are learning to read. However, the nature of their problems varies. Those who have strong visual memory abilities but poor auditory analysis skills may do fairly well if they are first introduced to a whole-word, sight approach to reading. They may have problems, however, when asked to rhyme or to generalize from a known word to an unknown word. Likewise, children with comprehension problems may do quite well on auditory–visual association tasks but be unable to interpret what they read.

At the present time extensive research remains to be done. No firm conclusions can be drawn with regard to either the prediction of reading failure or the most effective forms of instruction for various children. We need comprehensive, longitudinal studies of both efficient and inefficient readers to determine which combination of skills are necessary for various aspects of reading, including decoding and comprehension. It is doubtful that simple correlational studies can provide all the relevant information. Cluster analyses may be necessary to determine which combinations of strengths and weaknesses are found among good and poor readers. It is my impression that we need to investigate children's deficits in relation to their strengths, or their low abilities in relation to their strengths. Certain children with minor processing deficits may compensate for problems if they have strengths in other areas. For example, some with poor phonemic discrimination may actually improve when reading (the printed word) is introduced. They have good visual skills that permit them to detect differences they do not perceive auditorily.

Research on children with specific learning disabilities is emerging, but it is difficult to analyze and compare the findings of the studies, because the populations and procedures are not always well defined. Intelligence is not always considered, and when it is, the measures used to assess mental ability vary greatly. Thus, the composition of the groups may be quite different. Studies that include children on the basis of average nonverbal intelligence may yield results quite different from those in which auditory verbal measures are used as the selection criterion.

Another reason for variability of results is the nature of the experimental tasks. For example, on tests of auditory discrimination, the cognitive requirements for comparing two words ("Do these sound the same or different? *Cub–Cup*") are quite different from those in which the child is asked to point to a picture ("Point to *cup–cub*"). Moreover, some tests use nonmeaningful stimuli such as nonsense syllables, whereas others use real words. Thus, to compare results, one must know very specifically what the children were asked to do and how they were asked to respond.

Nomenclature also varies. For example, the term *perception* is used in many different ways, varying from simple, low level responses to relatively high levels of cognition.

Still another factor are the parameters of reading that were measured in various correlational studies. It is important to know whether certain auditory processes were correlated with oral reading or silent reading, with reading of single words or words in context, and with comprehension of facts or comprehension of the general significance of the content.

Given these problems, it is difficult to draw firm conclusions regarding the relationships between specific deficits in perception, memory, or other cognitive processes and the reading problems of learning disabled children. Nevertheless, I discuss some of the disturbances, particularly those in the auditory system, that seem to interfere with the acquisition of reading skills. (Some of these problems persist through the adolescent and young adult years; hence, special attention should be provided in the early grades.) My orientation is one that views the child as an "information processor," as one who has multiple modalities for input and output of information and the potential for a variety of complex integrative networks. Thus, in beginning an investigation of children, it is important to know which systems for input are intact and which may be less efficient, which modes of response are available, and which types of information the children are able to process, especially verbal and nonverbal.

FRAMES OF REFERENCE FOR CHILD STUDY

Several theoretical frames of reference serve as the basis for our evaluation of learning disabled children. The first pertains to the broad categories of "input, integration, and output." The diagnostic educator is concerned with whether children have a disturbance at the level of input, integration, or output—

whether they have difficulty receiving and assimilating the information they receive or whether they are unable to retrieve and express that which they know. Generally, children who have difficulty understanding also have limited expression. That is, a disorder of input limits the output. Thus, children who fail to comprehend spoken words cannot be expected to express more than they receive. Similarly, children with a reading disorder cannot be expected to use written language, even though they may be able to copy words. In contrast, there are children who have adequate receptive capacities but cannot encode their ideas into oral or written form. For example, children with a word-retrieval problem may comprehend language but be unable to spontaneously recall words they wish to use. Similarly, those with severe auditory-motor integration disorders or apraxia may be unable to speak, although they can comprehend or read silently. Thus, it is necessary to do as complete a "systems analysis" as possible to determine which channels are efficient for decoding and encoding various types of information.

A second frame of reference pertains to the semiautonomous systems concept of Hebb (1963). He proposed that the brain is made up of semi-independent systems and that at times, a given system such as the auditory or the visual system functions semi-independently of others. At times, one system functions in a supplementary way with another; and at times, all systems function interrelatedly. This concept has many implications for diagnosis and education (Johnson & Myklebust, 1967). Each psychosensory system is appraised as it functions semiautonomously, in coordination with another system, and as all the systems function simultaneously. In our evaluations at the Learning Disabilities Center, we try to ascertain whether a child can perceive, remember, and interpret what he or she hears, sees, or feels. We also explore the ways in which the systems work together. This being the case, we have suggested that three types of learning must be evaluated: (a) intrasensory—that is, learning requiring only one system such as audition or vision; (b) intersensory—learning requiring two or more but not all systems; and (c) integrative—learning requiring all the systems to function as a unit. The major purpose is to determine which learning "circuits" are operative or inoperative. A second purpose is to determine how the child should be taught, that is, to clarify which combination of inputs will facilitate learning.

In our research, diagnosis, and remediation, we have observed that some children are overloaded by multisensory inputs. They become confused if they are required to assimilate information through more than one system at a time. The information being received through a given sensory channel impedes integration of that being received through another. The concept of overloading has considerable relevance for instruction. If a multisensory or VAKT (visual, auditory, kinesthetic, and tactile) approach is used inappropriately, learning actually may be impeded. On the other hand, some children with learning disabilities cannot profit from intrasensory stimulation; they need input from more than one modality to help them perceive or retain information. This often is apparent among children with severe auditory disorders. When given an intrasensory auditory task, they may fail to perceive unless visual stimuli such as objects, pictures, or printed words are placed before them. Other children may not profit from intrasensory visual information. Thus, they may have difficulty with certain programmed readers.

The goal of instruction is to "balance the input stimulation" according to the child's pattern of strengths and weaknesses. Typically, it is necessary to use a series of diagnostic teaching probes to determine which combination of inputs is more effective. To illustrate this, consider the following options or strategies that might be used for auditory perceptual training. First, one might explore intrasensory stimulation. That is, the child is asked to close his or her eyes and listen for pairs of words or pheonemes that are similar (e.g., "bat–back"). We find that some children improve with this approach, because they cannot look and listen easily; they seem overloaded with multiple stimulation. On one occasion a 6-year-old boy could not take a hearing test wtih his eyes open. He closed his eyes and raised his hand each time he heard a sound. If children are distractible, it may be advantageous to reduce visual input in order to enhance learning.

A second option uses visual movement cues. In this instance, the child is asked to watch the teacher's mouth very closely while he or she says the words. Occasionally, it is beneficial to produce the movement pattern with no sound. After the child sees a difference between the movement patterns of the oral mechanism, the teacher says the words and asks the student to indicate whether he or she can hear the difference.

A third option is tactile or kinesthetic stimulation. The child's attention is drawn to the vibrations of the larynx on voiced sounds or to the air that is expelled when producing certain plosive sounds. Closely related to this is the option of auditory-motor production. Children are encouraged to imitate the words as precisely as possible in order to obtain better auditory feedback.

At other times the teacher may use the printed word. Rather than working on intrasensory auditory skills, it may be helpful to present pairs of words and ask the child to see the difference and then to listen for the difference.

Finally, rate of auditory input might be modified. Some learning disabled children are unable to process information at the expected rate. Therefore, words are said more slowly in order to detect all the features. Although many teachers may use one or more of these techniques with all children, our objective is to become as precise as possible in selecting a form of input that is in keeping with each child's style of learning.

In our comprehensive "systems analysis" approach, we believe that it is important to study more than modalities of input and output; it is necessary to examine the child's ability to process various types of information, especially that which is verbal and nonverbal. Although many people may use verbal mediation in processing certain types of nonverbal information, it may be an oversimplification to simply define a child as an auditory or a visual learner. Instead, an attempt should be made to describe the type of information that the child can or cannot process. For example, some children with severe reading disorders have superior visual nonverbal abilities. They have no difficulty with tasks requiring perception or memory of geometric designs, pictures, or block patterns. Their major problem seems to be with visual verbal learning. In contrast, there are children and adults with severe problems in visual nonverbal functions who have no problems in reading. Others have difficulty with both nonverbal and verbal learning.

Diagnostic assessments should include a study of a child's ability to comprehend and use both verbal and nonverbal symbols. In addition, an attempt should be made to determine whether the child can process multiple messages It is clear that people must attend to many features in any communication setting. During conversation they must listen to the words but also the vocal inflection, and they must observe many nonverbal features of the speaker. Similarly, when reading or writing, people must attend to multiple features.

Finally, in our "systems analysis" we attempt to determine the level of disturbance, that is, whether the problems result from breakdowns in attention, perception, memory, symbolization, or conceptualization. We recognize the difficulty in attempting to draw such distinctions because of the overlap and interrelationships between these functions. Furthermore, we need better measures to assess many processes. Nevertheless, research and clinical experience indicate that further investigation of the following processes is needed in order to understand the needs of the learning disabled child.

Attention

Many studies pertaining to the development and disorders of attention have been completed during the past decade (Bakan, 1966; Dykman, Ackerman, Clements, & Peters, 1971; Hallahan & Kauffman, 1976). The significance of attention for all learning and living cannot be minimized. Cobb (1948) stated that attention is necessary for all learning, if not for self-preservation and life itself. Attention improves with maturation, socialization, and environmental controls. Most preschoolers are somewhat distractible, but they gradually improve in their ability to select certain information and to inhibit that which is irrelevant.

Problems of attention have been observed in many learning disabled children. Strauss and Lehtinen (1947) and Cruickshank, Bentzen, Ratzeburg, and Tannhauser (1961) reported that distractability, disinhibition, and perseveration were common symptoms among "brain-injured" children. Consequently, they recommended a highly structured environment so the children could perform more effectively. Kaliski (1959) indicated that it was necessary to structure the child's world spatially, temporally, contextually, and socially. Johnson and Myklebust (1967) reported that it was beneficial to structure the environment, materials, and presentation of the materials. They emphasized, however, that it is important to keep a fluid structure and to expose children to more natural settings as soon as they are able to integrate the experiences.

Research on the effectiveness of highly structured environments is somewhat limited. Cruickshank et al. (1961) used the Strauss and Lehtinen (1947) procedures in a special classroom with a group of hyperactive children and found that at the end of one year the subjects were better able to withstand distractions. However, at the end of the second year without the structured environment, the children lost the advantages they had gained. Thus, long-term planning for children with these behavioral tendencies may be needed.

The role of pharmacology in the management of children with attention disorders also is important (Connors, 1973; Grossman, 1966). Although some studies indicate improvement in the child's ability to attend with medication, more comprehensive long-term studies are needed.

Although not all the parameters of attention have been delineated, Gardner (1966) stated that disturbances may occur in selective attention, maintenance of attention, momentary span of attention—the ability to hold several things in mind at one time—and in attention deployment—the scanning that an individual engages in before making a decision. This last factor is related to the research on impulsivity and reflectivity conducted by Kagan (1965b). Kagan studied these behaviors by asking the child to select a picture from an array that was the same as the model. He defined as "impulsive" those children who responded quickly and made many errors. "Reflective" children were those who took longer and made few errors. Several researchers who used Kagan's procedures found that learning disabled children were more impulsive and less reflective than normals (Keogh & Donlon, 1972; Nesbitt, 1974).

The implications for learning and early reading instruction are apparent. Children who have difficulty selecting relevant information or maintaining attention may have many problems in school. Some perform below the level of their potential. For example, we found that an impulsive 6-year-old made 15 errors on an auditory discrimination test when it was given in standardized form. Later, using a different form, the examiner held the child's hand, encouraging him to look at all the pictures before responding, and the child made only one error. The same child scored at a 4-year level on a picture vocabulary test when no structure was provided, but he achieved at a 6-year level when controls for impulsivity were used. Group-administered reading tests should be analyzed carefully, because some learning disabled children impulsively mark choices without attending to all the questions and possible responses. Similarly, the hasty scanner makes errors when reading and may fail to comprehend.

Information overloading also may be considered to be a part of an attention disorder, though other factors may be involved. By *overloading,* I refer to situations in which children are unable to integrate multiple messages and in some instances to monitor their performance. One of the situations where we observe overloading in some children is during oral reading. Some children seem unable to perceive and assimilate the visual material, retrieve auditory responses, and monitor their performance. They may be thinking of one word while saying something else. For example, a student read a passage in which the word *nuclear* occurred several times. Each time he substituted the word *muscular,* yet he never corrected himself. After completing the passage, we asked him to listen to a tape recording of his oral reading of the story, and the printed material was removed so he only listened. The boy was quite surprised that he made the error and asked, "Did I really say 'muscular'? I was thinking 'nuclear' the whole time." We have observed similar tendencies in other learning disabled children and have found that a systematic program of monitoring is very beneficial. Children are asked to read passages; then they listen to themselves on tape and try to detect meaning errors. Next, they listen to the tape with the printed passage before them and underline or note the errors. Many students have made marked progress with these techniques.

Although disturbances of attention may be found in many learning disabled children, we also believe it is critical to examine attention with regard to the nature of the cognitive task. Kagan (1965a) stated that attention is best when the material is in keeping with the child's cognitive structure. Attention may wane when the content is either too difficult or too easy and uninteresting. Every teacher is aware of this fact, but it becomes more crucial for children who have uneven patterns of development. Careful observation and diagnostic teaching is needed to determine which conditions and procedures foster maximum attention.

Perception

Research on the topic of perception is so vast that it is not possible to review the many findings. Therefore, only a few areas are discussed as they relate to early reading instruction and learning disabled children.

The first pertains to the active search for critical attributes, as discussed by Gibson and Levin (1975). Although this is an important factor in the perceptual development of all children, it appears that the nature of the search among learning disabled students needs extensive study. This need became apparent during some of our investigations on cross-modal perception. During the haptic portions of the studies, we noted that the learning disabled children exhibited less exploratory behavior than normals of the same age. They tended to be more passive (Johnson, 1975). Therefore, we designed a study that involved videotaping the hands of preschool normal and learning disabled children while they were engaged in the active exploration of familiar and unfamiliar objects. We analyzed the number and type of movements, the part of the hand and fingers used during exploration, the length of exploration, and various verbal responses. In general, the learning disabled children demonstrated more fixating movements, more pressing, and less edging and searching for critical attributes (Johnson & Jans, 1973). They also had more difficulty attending to the intrasensory task. Frequently, they tried to pull the object from behind the screen in order to see it. The examiners found that they had to say "Don't peek" to the learning disabled children many more times than to the normals.

Further evidence of faulty exploratory behavior among learning disabled children came from parent interviews. Blalock and Johnson (1974) designed a questionnaire to investigate various aspects of play behavior among preschool learning disabled children. The results indicated that the parents of the learning disabled children observed less spontaneous exploratory behavior and that their activities appeared to be more random than other children within the family.

More studies of both haptic and visual search behavior are necessary to confirm these preliminary findings. In addition, studies of listening behavior, though much more difficult to design, are needed. Many tests of perception assess the product of perception; our goal is to determine more about the search and hypothesis-testing behaviors of children who are suspected of having learning disabilities. It may be that the teacher should foster better exploration and provide more explicit statements regarding relevant features to which the child should attend.

Phonemic Discrimination. Phonemic discrimination, one aspect of perception, involves the ability to detect differences between paired words or syllables that are minimally contrasted. The teacher needs to know whether the child can distinguish between those sounds that signal a meaning change in our language and those that do not. Several investigators have studied this skill in relation to reading, but the results are inconclusive. Harris (1970), Wepman (1960), and others have reported that children who fail to detect differences in sounds of words may have difficulty with the printed symbol. Flynn and Byrne (1970) found that retarded readers had more difficulty with auditory discrimination of words, nonsense syllables, and musical pitches than did advanced readers in the third grade. Atchison (1975) compared the performance of first-grade normal and learning disabled children on several phonemic discrimination tasks. She constructed tests to explore various factors, including the number of phonemic contrasts in words, position of the contrasting phoneme, and familiarity of stimulus items. Learning disabled children performed significantly below the normals, but she found that a small subgroup contributed to most of the difference. Thus, one must always be cautious when interpreting group results with such heterogenerous populations. Phonemic discrimination performance did not correlate significantly with reading achievement for either group of children. Both normal and learning disabled children performed better with lexically familiar words than with unfamiliar items. This factor is particularly important to note if children have a limited vocabulary. Position of the phoneme contrast also was significant in Atchison's study. She found that both normal and learning disabled children were more successful in distinguishing words that differed in initial sounds than in final sounds.

Another process emphasized by Gibson and Levin (1975) is auditory analysis or segmentation. This involves the ability to separate words into syllables or phonemes. The authors stated that "fragmentation and recombination of sounds appear to be essential for mastery of the speech system and for decoding it to written symbols.... The child must develop the ability to hear *segmentation* in what is spoken to him before we can reasonably expect him to learn to map the written code to speech or vice versa [p. 228]." But, according to Gibson and Levin, "young children do not automatically analyze the phonemic information in speech. Before five or so, they do not even always hear words as subordinate units [p. 228]."

The importance of segmentation also has been stressed by Liberman, Shankweiler, Fischer, and Carter (1974), who stated that before children can map a visual message on the spoken word, they have to be consciously aware that a word such as *cat* has three elements. Savin (1972) stated that in his experience "everyone who has failed to learn to read even the simplest prose by the end of the first grade has been unable to analyze syllables into phonemes [p. 321]." These observations are in keeping with our clinical experience. Some cases of very severe language impairments cannot even segment words in sentences; they give evidence of this by writing *up here* as one word. We also have seen many adolescents and young adults with severe reading disorders who could not segment words into syllables. In some instances this problem affects spelling more than reading. For example, a 17-year-old read the months of the year correctly, but he spelled them as he segmented them—"Sep-ter." At times, some students find that the presence of the visual pattern (the word) may facilitate perception of all the syllables or phonemes. Thus, the teacher must decide whether to work on intrasensory auditory segmenting or to combine the work with the printed word, perhaps by presenting the word in syllabic units or in phoneme patterns. In our lab, we attempt to assess the most efficient strategies during 3 weeks of diagnostic teaching.

Blending is another auditory process that is required for reading, particularly if a synthetic phonic method is being used. Although we have not completed the data gathering and analysis on learning disabled children's blending ability, our clinical experience and initial inspection of the data indicate that this is not as great a problem for poor readers as is segmenting. Both processes, however, should be investigated, since decoding requires auditory and visual analysis as well as auditory synthesis. Because of these intermodal factors, we believe that it is important to determine first whether the child can analyze and synthesize words auditorily and then bisensorially. In remediation, it is our practice to work with the modality that is easiest for the child and to progress to those skills that are more difficult.

Visual Discrimination. Visual discrimination tasks have long been included as a part of most reading readiness tests. It is assumed that children need to be able to detect similarities and differences among letters and words in order to read. Gibson (1969) and others have contributed significantly to our understanding of visual perception and its development in children. For example, Gibson and Levin (1975) reported that children continue to progress in their ability to discriminate letterlike forms up to the age of 8, but they found that children do not confuse many letters, even at 4 years of age. Calfee, Chapman, and Venezky (cited in Gibson & Levin, 1975) presented kindergarten children with various letter-matching tasks and found the major confusions were on right–left reversals such as *b* and *d*. When letter groups were tested, however, more errors were observed. The matching of letter strings and words is more difficult for kindergarten children because of the sequencing factor.

Disturbances of visual perception have been reported among learning disabled and dyslexic children (Orton, 1937; Strauss & Lehtinen, 1947). Symptons included reversals, figure–ground disturbance, and faulty sequencing. As a result of these problems, various tests have been constructed to assess some parameters of visual perception (Colarusso & Hammill, 1972; Frostig, Lefever, Whittlesey, & Maslow, 1964), and programs of intervention have been recommended. Visual problems and procedures have been examined more carefully in recent years, and there is some indication that disturbances of visual perception may be found less frequently than once assumed. More difficulties might be attributable to linguistic or graphic–sound associations than to visual processes per se. Similarly, the programs of visual perceptual training that involve practice with geometric designs and other nonverbal figures have not always proved to facilitate reading acquisition. This does not, however, indicate that research on visual perception should be minimized. Newer models of perception may be used to study visual information processing in different ways (Neisser, 1967; Sperling, 1970).

Finally, although many learning disabled children appear to have adequate visual and auditory discrimination, the special educator always must be aware that individuals may indeed have problems at this level and that intervention should be provided.

Memory

The research on memory, like that on perception, is so vast and so interrelated with other cognitive processes that a comprehensive review is impossible. One needs to consider memory in relation to various sensory modalities: immediate, short-term, and long-term memory: recognition versus recall; memory for sequence; and other parameters. In this chapter, I highlight only a few areas that have been of greatest concern in our work with children who have reading disabilities.

In a descriptive study of 60 dyslexic children, Johnson and Myklebust (1965) reported that auditory memory disturbances predominated over visual impairments. As a group, the children were particularly deficient on the Auditory Attention Span for Words subtest of the Detroit Tests of Learning Aptitude (Baker & Leland, 1958). Their performance also was poor on the Auditory Attention Span for Syllables subtest. The latter task involves repetition of sentences and therefore may assess some aspects of syntax as well as memory span. These findings may be related to the fact that over half of this group had had some problems with oral language acquisition. These findings together with the significant investigations reported to Kavanagh and Mattingly (1972) indicate the importance of studying the interrelationships between oral language and reading.

Many studies of memory also involve the retention of information in a sequence. Again, several investigations suggest that reading disabled children have problems with temporal sequencing (Vernon, 1971). In a study of good and poor readers, Burns (1975) attempted to determine whether there were differences in sequential memory according to modality of input and output. Subjects were given sets of digits auditorily, visually, and bisensorially, and with each set of inputs they were asked to give oral and/or written responses. She found that the reading disabled subjects had difficulty with memory for a series irrespective of mode of input or output.

Other indications of sequencing problems have been noted in the ability to say the days of the week or months of the year. Only 13 subjects from a group of 60 dyslexics were able to say the months in order (Johnson & Myklebust, 1965). During remediation, the majority of these children were able to learn the series when the months were said rhythmically in groups of three.

Our clinical experience with adolescents and young adults with severe reading disorders suggests that sequencing disturbances persist if remediation is not provided. Many who came for diagnosis could not say the alphabet or the months of the year. They also had difficulty with the repetition of multisyllabic words, digits, and sentences. Typically, those with sequencing disorders misorder sounds in words when they read and spell. A few, however, are aided in their temporal sequencing by seeing the printed word. They can retain the order of the sounds when they read, because they have the entire image before them. This example again indicates the need for diagnostic teaching and the selection of inputs or modalities that will facilitate learning.

Another type of memory disorder found among language and learning disabled children is the problem of word retrieval. Many children understand words but cannot retrieve them for spontaneous communication. As a result, they may use circumlocutions, substitutions, or pantomime. Some use an overabundance of nonspecific words, such as *stuff* and *what-cha-ma-call-it,* and nonspecific pronouns (Johnson & Myklebust, 1967). Although these problems frequently are associated with auditory disorders, the teacher should be aware of possible relationships with reading. Some youngsters have difficulty with oral reading, but they can read silently. Some may substitute meaningful words such as *cat* for *kitten;* others can define the words but cannot say them. For example, one student said, when looking at the word *inspection,* "I know that it means to look over something very carefully, but I cannot say it." When learning letter names or sounds, the children may quickly point to the letter when it is said, but they cannot retrieve the name or sound. These disorders have been observed among preschool children by Jansky and deHirsch (1972) and by Mattis, French, and Rapin (1975) in older children and young adults.

In remediation, we provide such children with cuing techniques such as multiple-choice questions or the first sound of the word. In reading, the children may need more opportunities for recognition and association responses. Frequently we recommend that the initial sight vocabulary be composed of nouns and verbs, so the children can have the opportunity to associate objects or pictures with the printed form.

Reading instructors also should be aware of possible problems in cross-modal learning. Birch and Belmont (1964) and Birch and Leford (1963) stimulated considerable research on the subject of intersensory learning. They reported that retarded readers performed less successfully on tasks requiring auditory–visual integration. Although some questions have been raised by Bryant (1968) and others regarding these conclusion, it is our impression that comprehensive studies of children are needed to determine whether there are disturbances in intrasensory or integrative functions (Zigmond, 1966).

Symbolization and Conceptualization

One of the most critical aspects to investigate is the child's ability to symbolize, that is, to understand that various sounds and figures can stand for something. Severe, global disorders of symbolization are detected early in childhood when a child fails to understand spoken words or sounds in his or her environment. Mild or moderate problems may not be detected until later when the child is expected to comprehend more difficult words or to read and write.

In research and diagnosis of learning disabled children, the investigator should explore the breadth of the symbolic deficit, that is, whether the child has a generalized problem or one that is specific to reading. Some research indicates that many preschool children with auditory language disorders also have problems with the use of gesture (Knott, 1974). On the other hand, some children with severe language problems develop elaborate pantomime routines and may even respond to instruction with sign language. Our clinical experience with children who were referred during the preschool years indicates that many of them later have difficulty learning to read, write, and calculate. These observations and studies indicate that one should not view any use of a single symbol system such as reading printed language in isolation. Instead, one should investigate the comprehension and use of all symbol systems.

Since reading is often considered to be a visual symbol system superimposed on auditory language, it is particularly important to investigate many aspects of auditory verbal comprehension. This includes the ability to understand single words as well as connected speech. In general, children do not comprehend what they read unless they understand the spoken word. As indicated previously, children with severe auditory disorders will usually be identified before they enter school; however, mild to moderate problems may go undetected if the children acquire enough language for general conversation. Later, these children often are referred because of reading comprehension problems. Some youngsters fail to comprehend specific classes of words such as those representing space and time (e.g., *between, below, middle, after*). Others only have difficulty with more abstract vocabulary used in social studies and science, particularly superordinates such as *appliance* or *continent*.

Initially, some of these children may be quite deceptive, because they may learn to "sound out" words rather quickly, but they do not understand them. They are word callers and are sometimes called "hyperlexic" (Huttenlocher & Huttenlocher, 1973). Echolalic children may learn to "read" words as easily as they learn to repeat them. For example, an 8-year-old scored at the 4-year level on a test of auditory comprehension but at an 8-year level on a measure of oral reading. The latter required no comprehension. His silent reading was limited to only a few words that he could match with pictures. These children appear to "transduce" from one sensory system to another without translating. When this occurs, it is very important to assess silent reading comprehension or to ask the child what the word means or what the story is about after he or she has read it.

It is interesting to note that some of these youngsters cannot inhibit verbal responses on silent reading comprehension tasks. They must respond orally. Others are "overloaded" by oral reading tasks. Their reading comprehension deteriorates when asked to read aloud, and they seem unable to monitor for meaning. In remediation, comprehension is emphasized and oral reading is reduced.

Some children with symbolic deficits have no problems understanding single words, but they have difficulty with connected language or complex syntax. Failure to understand complex sentence structure again may be reflected in reading comprehension problems or in understanding of mathematical story problems.

During the past several years there has been a surge of interest and research pertaining to syntax. The theoretical constructs of Chomsky (1957) and others stimulated many studies on language development. They also provided the basis for test construction and programs of remediation (Lee, 1969; Lee, Koenigsknecht, & Mulhern, 1975). These developments, together with new theoretical models of reading, have fostered investigations of oral syntax and various facets of reading comprehension. Comprehensive systems of error analysis have been developed that aid the teacher in planning for children with problems (Goodman & Burke, 1972).

The educator should attempt to determine which syntactic and morphological rules the child has acquired and to what extent these rules are automatized. Although most normal children enter school with good language, many with learning disabilities have delayed or deficient linguistic systems. If they are presented with reading material containing complex syntactic patterns, they may be unable to use contextual clues or to anticipate words in sentences.

Jansky (1975) reported that many young children who are "marginally ready" for school have difficulty with syntax on several levels. She said, "their sentence memory spans are short, they have some trouble following grammatically complex directions, and their own sentences are often fragmented and poorly constructed . . . The group of children we meet for the first time during the middle school years has trouble with sentences and this interferes with reading comprehension [p. 79].

Several studies confirm the relationships between syntax and reading (Golinkoff, 1975–1976; Little, 1974). Cromer and Weiner (1966) and Weiner and Cromer (1967) are among those who found relationships between reading comprehension and syntax. Using the cloze technique, they found that the responses of poor readers were less syntactically correct than those of good readers. Kass (1966) found that subjects with severe reading disabilities were marginally deficient in the grammatic closure subtest of the Illinois Test of Psycholinguistic Abilities (Kirk, McCarthy, & Kirk, 1968).

An intensive investigation of several syntactic abilities in normal and dyslexic children was completed by Vogel (1975). She selected and/or devised nine measures of syntactic ability and administered them to 20 normal and 20 dyslexic boys with reading comprehension problems. The age range was 7 years and 4 months to 8 years and 5 months. She grouped her tests into the following five categories: recognition of melody pattern; recognition of grammaticality; comprehension of syntax; sentence repetition; and syntax and morphology in expressive language. She found the dyslexics were statistically different from the normals in recognition of melody pattern, sentence repetition, and syntax and morphology in expressive language. As a result of these findings, Vogel emphasized the importance of assessing syntactic ability when selecting reading materials. She stated, "the most important implication for the teaching of reading is that meaning is conveyed primarily through the syntactic structure rather than the individual words. Syntax carries the burden of the message [p. 82]." She also stated that if "a child is having difficulty in reading comprehension, there is a high probability that his difficulty is related to syntactic deficiencies. Therefore, the assessment of syntactic ability should be included in the evaluation and diagnostic procedures [p. 82]."

IMPLICATIONS FOR INSTRUCTION

The overall program of reading instruction that we recommend is based on the child's strengths and weaknesses. Although our goal is to teach all children to read, the initial approach varies with the nature of the disability. Many fall into one of two major categories—those who are deficient in visual processes and those who are deficient in auditory processes. We have called the former group visual dyslexics. Characteristically, they have a tendency to reverse, rotate, or invert letters or to transpose letters within words. Some attend to details within words or to the general configuration but not to both. Some have a reduced rate of visual perception. Most have visual memory problems that prevent them from remembering whole words. Because they cannot perceive and remember whole words, we use a synthetic phonic approach in remediation. Letter sounds are introduced (a few consonants and short vowels), and the student blends them into meaningful words. Letter names are not used in the early stages, and few if any explicit rules are used. Rarely are associations such as "*a* for apple" used. The objective is to help the student unlock the code—to convert the graphemes to phonemes as simply as possible. The form of the letters is kept constant, since some children often find it difficult to read both upper- and lowercase print. Emphasis is given to simultaneous auditory and visual sequencing and to phoneme–grapheme relationships during the initial phase of instruction.

The basic approach to reading for visual dyslexics circumvents their basic weaknesses and capitalizes on their strengths; however, work also is done to improve the deficits. A two-pronged remedial plan is used. The objective is to assist the child in both word attack and instant recognition. In the past we found it was not beneficial to bombard the deficit or to raise all skills to a normal level at once; thus, the dual plan. However, even when working on a specific deficit such as visual perception or memory, one must consider the most effective "teaching circuit." If a child cannot perceive letters in the normal way, he or she probably will not benefit from being given worksheets designed to improve visual perception. The teacher must decide how the materials can be used so that the child can in fact see the similarities and differences. At times color cues may be used. In other instances, the size of the letters may be increased. In other cases, tracing or extensive verbalization will be used to "lead the child's looking." The techniques are not selected at random; they are chosen on the basis of the child's pattern of strengths and weaknesses.

In contrast, the auditory dyslexic usually cannot learn phonics and therefore is taught to read whole words. Characteristically, these children have disturbances in auditory perception, rhyming, blending, analysis, and memory. Although gross discrimination may be adequate, they fail to perceive sounds within words. Many have difficulty with oral reading. Because of these learning patterns, the children are taught with an intrasensory visual approach during the initial stages of remediation. They are taught a sight vocabulary that consists largely of nouns and verbs—that is, words that can be associated with an object, experience, or picture. In this way, no oral response is required. Whereas some children benefit from saying the words aloud, others cannot concentrate on the visual image if they also must call up the auditory. Therefore, even when phrases and sentences are first introduced, the assignments are arranged so the child can match them with pictures rather than reading them aloud. In some respects the approach is similar to that used in learning a foreign language. Words often are introduced in units such as foods, clothing, or transportation. Since no child can learn every word from visual memory, and since we want to help him or her with word attack, a dual approach is also used with this group. As soon as these children have a substantial sight vocabulary, every attempt is made to help them with the auditory skills so that they can decode unfamiliar words.

Our experience in recent years suggests that not all learning disabled children can be categorized in these broad groups. Hence, many variables must be considered in assessment and remediation. Various deficits interfere with the reading acquisition process, thus reducing the development of strategies that are needed for efficient reading. It is clear that the good reader has many options to identify words, including phonics, structural analysis, and context. One or more of the disturbances already described may interfere with certain aspects of reading but not with others. For example, children with auditory comprehension problems may fail to acquire meaning, yet they can decode. Some with syntax problems do not use contextual cues because they cannot anticipate words in context. Therefore, several critical questions are raised with regard to early reading instruction:

1. What is the nature of the input stimulation? Is it primarily visual? Does it combine auditory and visual stimulation? Are all sensory channels used simultaneously?

2. What is the expected response from the child? Is he or she expected to match figures or to mark something? Is the child expected to give an oral response? Does he or she need to know how to write?

3. What is the nature of the vocabulary? On what basis were the words selected? How controlled is the vocabulary? Do the words have a consistent phoneme–grapheme relationship? How many meaningful words are used (specifically, nouns and verbs)? Is the vocabulary useful to the student? Can a recognition response be used?

4. What is the nature of the sentence structure? Is it similar to the child's language? Is the sentence length beyond the range of his or her auditory memory span?

5. What is the nature of the content? Is the material in keeping with the child's level of experience and interest?

6. Does the method require deductive or inductive thought processes? Are rules learned explicitly or implicitly?

In addition to the preceding questions, the teacher should analyze reading books for other factors such as the size of print, the amount of material on a page, variations in letter case and size, spacing between words and lines, length of story, and nature of the pictures or illustrations.

These constitute but a few of the variables to consider when teaching learning disabled children. Others include the level of intelligence, language, and experience. As we learn more about children and about learning processes, undoubtedly more variables will be included in the plan. In essence, the learning disabled child may be likened to a special type of computer. The computer has a potential capacity for processing information. However, it will function properly only when programmed to satisfy the necessary criteria for production. Although there are countless variables to control and consider when dealing with something as complex as the human brain and the reading process, the years ahead can be exciting as we study these variables in a more systematic fashion.

REFERENCES

Atchison, M. Variables influencing phonemic discrimination performance in normal and learning-disabled first-grade-age children (Doctoral dissertation, Northwestern University, 1975). *Dissertation Abstracts International,* 1975, *36,* 4100A–4101A. (University Microfilms No. 75-29, 564)

Bakan, P. *Attention.* Princeton, N.J.: Van Nostrand, 1966.

Baker, H., & Leland, B. *Detroit tests of learning aptitude.* Indianapolis: Bobbs-Merrill, 1958.

Birch, H., & Belmont, L. Auditory–visual integration in normal and retarded readers. *American Journal of Orthopsychiatry,* 1964, *34,* 851–861.

Birch, H., & Leford, A. Intersensory development in children. *Monographs of the Society for Research in Child Development,* 1963, *28,* (5, Serial No. 89).

Blalock, J., & Johnson, D. *A study of play behavior in preschool learning disabled children.* Paper presented at the meeting of the Association of Children with Learning Disabilities, Houston, Texas, April 1974.

Bryant, P. Comments on the design of developmental studies of cross-modal matching and cross-modal transfer. *Cortex,* 1968, *4,* 127–137.

Burns, S. An investigation of the relationship between sequential memory and oral reading skills in normal and learning disabled children (Doctoral dissertation, Northwestern University, 1975). *Dissertation Abstracts international,* 1975, *36,* 439A. (University Microfilms No. 75-29, 592)

Chomsky, N. *Syntactic structures.* The Hague, Netherlands: Mouton, 1957.

Cobb, S. *Borderlands of psychiatry.* Cambridge, Mass.: Harvard University Press, 1948.

Colarusso, R., & Hammill, D. *The motor free test of visual perception.* San Rafael, Calif.: Academic Therapy Publications, 1972.

Connors, C. K. What parents need to know about stimulant drugs and special education. *Journal of Learning Disabilities,* 1973, *6,* 349–351.

Cromer, W., & Weiner, M. Idiosyncratic response patterns among good and poor readers. *Journal of Consulting Psychology,* 1966, *30,* 1–10.

Cruickshank, W., Bentzen, F., Ratzeburg, F., & Tannhauser, M. *A training method for hyperactive children.* Syracuse, N.Y.: Syracuse University Press, 1961.

Dykman, R., Ackerman, P., Clements, S., & Peters, J. Specific learning disabilities: An attentional deficit syndrome. In H. Myklebust (Ed.), *Progress in learning disabilities* (Vol. 2). New York: Grune & Stratton, 1971.

Flynn, P., & Byrne, M. Relationship between reading and selected auditory abilities of third-grade children. *Journal of Speech and Hearing Research,* 1970, *13,* 731–740.

Frostig, M., Lefever, D., Whittlesey, J., & Maslow, P. *The Marianne Frostig developmental test of visual perception.* Palo Alto, Calif.: Consulting Psychologists Press, 1964.

Gardner, R. The needs of teachers for specialized information on the development of cognitive structures. In W. Cruickshank (Ed.), *The teacher of brain-injured children.* Syracuse, N.Y.: Syracuse University Press, 1966.

Gibson, E. *Principles of perceptual learning and development.* New York: Appleton-Century-Crofts, 1969.

Gibson, E., & Levin, H. *The psychology of reading.* Cambridge, Mass.: M.I.T. Press, 1975.

Golinkoff, R. A comparison of reading comprehension processes in good and poor comprehenders. *Reading Research Quarterly,* 1975–1976, *11,* 623–659.

Goodman, Y., & Burke. *Reading miscue inventory.* New York: Macmillan, 1972.

Grossman, H. Psychopharmacology in learning and behavior disorders of children. In W. Cruickshank (Ed.), *The teacher of brain-injured children.* Syracuse, N.Y.: Syracuse University Press, 1966.

Hallahan, D., & Kauffman, J. *Introduction to learning disabilities: A psycho-behavioral approach.* Englewood Cliffs, N.J.: Prentice-Hall, 1976.

Harris, A. *How to increase reading ability* (5th ed.). New York: McKay, 1970.

Hebb, D. The semi-autonomous process: Its nature and nurture. *American Psychologist,* 1963, *18,* 16–27.

Huttenlocher, P., & Huttenlocher, J. A study of children with hyperlexia. *Neurology,* 1973, *26,* 1107–1116.

Jansky, J. The marginally ready child. *Bulletin of The Orton Society,* 1975, *25,* 69–85.

Jansky, J., & deHirsch, K. *Preventing reading failure.* New York: Harper & Row, 1972.

Johnson, D. Children with communicative disorders. In J. Gallagher (Ed.), *The application of child development research to exceptional children.* Reston, VA.: The Council for Exceptional Children, 1975.

Johnson, D., & Jans, R. *A study of haptic perception in preschool normal and learning disabled children.* Paper presented at the international meeting of The Council for Exceptional Children, Dallas, Texas, April 1973.

Johnson, D., & Myklebust, H. Dyslexia in childhood. In J. Hellmuth (Ed.), *Learning disorders* (Vol. 1). Seattle: Special Child Publications, 1965.

Johnson, E., & Myklebust, H. *Learning disabilities: Educational principles and practices.* New York: Grune & Stratton, 1967.

Kagan, J. Impulsive and reflective children: Significance of conceptual tempo. In J. D. Krumbolz (Ed.), *Learning and the educational process.* Skokie, Ill.: Rand McNally, 1965. (a)

Kagan, J. Reflection-impulsivity and reading ability in primary grade children. *Child Development,* 1965, *36,* 609–628. (b)

Kaliski, L. The brain-injured child: Learning by living in a structured setting. *American Journal of Mental Deficiency,* 1959, *63,* 688–696.

Kass, C. Psycholinguistic disabilities of children with reading problems. *Exceptional Children,* 1966, *32,* 533–539.

Kavanagh, J., & Mattingly, I. (Eds.). *Language by ear and by eye: The relationships between speech and reading.* Cambridge, Mass.: M.I.T. Press, 1972.

Keogh, B., & Donlon, G. McG. Field dependence, impulsivity and learning disabilities. *Journal of Learning Disabilities,* 1972, *5,* 331–336.

Kirk, S. a., McCarthy, J., & Kirk, W. *Illinois test of psycholinguistic abilities, revised edition.* Urbana, Ill.: University of Illinois Press, 1968.

Knott, G. *A study of gesture as nonverbal communication in preschool language disabled and preschool normal children.* Unpublished doctoral dissertation, Northwestern University, 1974.

Lee, L. *Northwestern syntax screening test.* Evanston, Ill.: Northwestern University Press, 1969.

Lee, L., Koenigsknecht, R. A., & Mulhern, S. *Interactive language development teaching. The clinical presentation of grammatical structure.* Evanston, Ill.: Northwestern University Press, 1975.

Liberman, I., Shankweiler, D., Fischer, F., & Carter, B. Explicit syllable and phoneme segmentation in the young child. *Journal of Experimental Child Psychology,* 1974, *18,* 201–212.

Little, L. A study of the relationship between syntactic development and oral reading substitution miscues of average and disabled third grade readers (Doctoral dissertation, University of Kansas, 1974). *Dissertation Abstracts International,* 1974, *35,* 5971A–5972A. (University Microfilms No. 75-61, 39)

Mattis, S., French, J., & Rapin, I. Dyslexia in children and young adults: Three independent neuropsychological syndromes. *Developmental Medicine and Child Neurology,* 1975, *17,* 150–163.

National Advisory Committee on Handicapped Children. *Education of the Handicapped Act.* Washington, D.C.: Department of Health, Education and Welfare, Office of Education, 1968.

Neisser, U. *Cognitive psychology.* New York: Appleton, 1967.

Nesbitt, J. A. An investigation of the generality of reflection-impulsivity in relation to the performance of third grade children on the Illinois test of psycholinguistic abilties (Doctoral dissertation, University of Kansas, 1974). *Dissertation Abstracts International,* 1974, *36,* 851A–852. (University Microfilms No. 75-17, 651)

Orton, S. T. *Reading, writing and speech problems in children.* New York: Norton, 1937.

Savin, H. B. What the child knows about speech when e starts to learn to read. In J. F. Kavanagh & I. C. Mattingly (Eds.), *Language by ear and by eye: The relationships between speech and reading.* Cambridge, Mass.: M.I.T. Press, 1972.

Sperling, G. Short-term memory, long-term memory, and scanning in the processing of visual information. In F. A. Young & D. B. Lindsley (Eds.), *Early experience and visual information processing in perceptual and reading disorders.* Washington, D.C.: National Academy of Sciences, 1970.

Strauss, A., & Lehtinen, L. *Psychopathology and education of the brain-injured child* (Vol. 1). New York: Grune & Stratton, 1947.

Vernon, M. D. *Reading and its difficulties.* Cambridge, England: Cambridge University Press, 1971.

Vogel, S. *An investigation of syntactic abilities in normal and dyslexic children.* Baltimore, Md.: University Park Press, 1975.

Weiner, M., & Cromer, W. Reading and reading difficulty: A conceptual analysis. *Harvard Educational Review,* 1967, *4,* 620–643.

Wepman, J. Auditory discrimination, speech and reading. *The Elementary School Journal,* 1960, *60,* 325–333.

Zigmond, N. Intrasensory and intersensory process in normal and dyslexic children (Doctoral dissertation, Northwestern University, 1966). *Dissertation Abstracts International,* 1966, *27,* 3534A. (University Microfilms No. 67-42, 85).

10 Curriculum, Concepts of Literacy, and Social Class

Elsa Jaffe Bartlett
The Rockefeller University

In this chapter I describe aspects of two reading programs. My remarks focus on two curriculum dimensions that interest me. The first has to do with how each program defines beginning reading. The second has to do with the kinds of reading materials the children are supposed to use. I treat them both as aspects of a larger concern having to do with the kind of literacy that a program embodies: How are children expected to use their literacy? What value can it have for them?

I chose for analysis two programs that I think offer interesting contrasts along these dimensions: the Open Court reading program (*The Foundation Program*) and the *Distar Reading I* program. Both are popular and commercially successful; both claim to teach phonics, although they define phonics in very different ways; and both rely primarily on teacher-directed group instruction. They differ, however, in two important ways. First, they were designed for two different populations: Open Court, primarily for middle-class children, and Distar (which is an offshoot of the successful Bereiter and Engelmann Head Start programs), for the so-called disadvantaged. Second, the programs make very different assumptions about the way children learn and the kinds of things that they need to know.

THE ORTHOGRAPHIES AND THEIR MAPPING RULES

Probably any program that purports to teach phonics is going to have to simplify English orthography to some extent—either indirectly, by careful sequencing so that children encounter only "regular" words, or by changing

229

the orthography itself. For the brute fact is that the letters of English do not map onto the sounds in any linear, one-to-one phonemic fashion but instead appear to be organized at the morphophonemic level and thus serve to signal information about lexical structures rather than pronunciation per se (Chomsky & Halle, 1968; Venezky, 1972). And as a result, the mapping rules usually involve relationships between groups of letters and their sounds and are generally conditional in their application—depending on position, lexical structure, and so forth (for example, the various pronunciations of *t* in *hot, nation, another, anthill*).

Although both programs present a phonics curriculum and are more or less committed to traditional letter-by-letter sounding out or blending procedures, they confront the nonphonemic character of English orthography in rather different ways. Distar seeks to maintain a simplified set of linear, one-to-one, sound–letter correspondences and as a result, is forced to modify the orthography in several important ways. Open Court adopts a more complex set of mapping rules (which include multiple sound–letter correspondences and context-dependent mappings) and as a result, is able to maintain the more adultlike orthography by using a controlled vocabulary of more or less "regular" words. I consider some of the implications of these differences subsequently, but first, some examples are useful.

Figure 10.1 shows the Distar alphabet. The program uses only these lowercase letters throughout the first and most of the second year. The typeface is somewhat unusual: There has obviously been an attempt to make certain confusable aspects of the letters more distinct. Thus, for example, the closed portion of the *d* is tilted, whereas the closed portion of the *b* is not; the curved portion of the *h* is lower and smaller than the similar portion of the *n*; and so forth. Other modifications relate more directly to establishing one-to-one sound–letter correspondences. Thus, for example, there are microns over the vowels to indicate long sounds, and digraphs are physically joined to indicate a single pronunciation. Pronunciation is also signaled through letter size. Thus, for example, in Fig. 10.2, the small *k* (in *sick, lick*) and small *e* (in *hate*) indicate that these letters are not to be "sounded."

Taken together, these alterations work rather well to produce an orthography that can be sounded out in a consistent, left-to-right sequence. There are some exceptions. These are termed "irregular" words and are handled in a way that I think epitomizes the way in which reading has been conceptualized in this program. For example, the teacher is told that

> ...[it is important for] children to learn to discriminate between the way a word is sounded out and the way it is said. It is very important for the children to learn that irregular words can be sounded out—that there is some similarity between the sounding out and the pronunciation. They must also learn to discriminate between the way the words sound when they are sounded out and the way we say them [*Distar, Reading I, Teacher's Guide*, p. 40].

FIG. 10.1.   The Distar alphabet. (From *Distar® Reading I* [2nd ed.], by S. Engelmann & E. C. Bruner. Copyright 1974, 1969, by Science Research Associates, Inc. Reprinted by permission.)

TASK 15   Children rhyme with sick

a. Touch the ball for **sick**. Sound it out.
b. Get ready. Touch s, i, c as the children say *sssiiic*.
                If sounding out is not firm, repeat *b*.
c. What word? (Signal.) *Sick*. Yes, **sick**.
d. Quickly touch the ball for **lick**. This word rhymes with (pause)
        sick. Get ready. Touch l. *lll*. Move your finger quickly along the
                                        arrow. *Lllick*.
e. What word? (Signal.) *Lick*. Yes, **lick**.

TASK 16   Children read a word beginning with a stop sound (hāte)

a. Run your finger under **āte**. You're going to sound out this part.
                Get ready. Touch ā, t as the children say *āāāt*.
b. Say it fast. (Signal.) *Ate*. Yes, this part says **ate**.
c. Repeat *a* and *b* until firm.
d. Touch the ball for **hāte**. This word rhymes with (pause **āāt**.
        Get ready. Move to h, then quickly along the arrow. *Hate*.
e. What word? (Signal.) *Hate*. Yes, **hate**.
f. Repeat *d* and *e* until firm.
g. Return to the ball. Now you're going to sound out (pause) **hate**.
        Get ready. Quickly touch h, ā, t as the children say *hāāt*.
h. What word? (Signal.) *Hate*. Yes, **hate**. Good reading. Do you **hate**
                                        monsters?
i. Repeat *g* and *h* until firm.

TASK 17   Individual test

Call on different children to do *g* and *h* in task 16.

TASK 18   Children read the words the fast way

a. Now you get to read these words the fast way.
b. Touch the ball for **lick**. Get ready. (Pause three seconds.)
                Move your finger quickly along the arrow. *Lick*.
c. Repeat *b* for the words **sick** and **hāte**.
d. Have the children sound out the words they had difficulty identifying.

TASK 19   Individual test

Call on different children to read one word the fast way.

Do not touch any small letters.

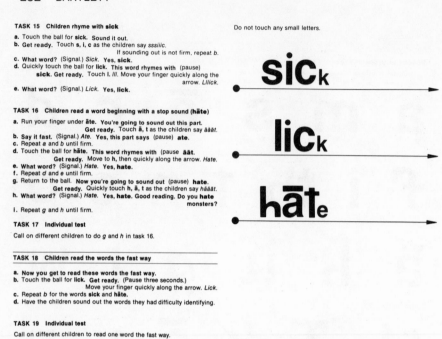

FIG. 10.2.   "Silent" letters, Distar program. (From *Distar® Reading I* [2nd ed.], by S. Engelmann & E. C. Bruner. Copyright 1974, 1969, by Science Research Associates, Inc. Reprinted by permission.)

Thus, children are instructed to sound out the word *said* as "sss-ah-id-ddd" and then to "say the word" as "sed." Similarly, if children "sound out" the word by saying "sed," the teacher is told to correct them: "You are saying the word. I told you to sound it out."

The point here, and I think it is an important one, is that the insistence on a simple, consistent set of word-recognition procedures may in the beginning lead to quick and efficient learning but may, if carried to extremes, lead to a kind of meaningless ritual that may end by confusing the child about the very relationships we are trying to teach.

In contrast, the Open Court program confronts the child immediately with a more complex orthography. There is very little simplification of the alphabet. Upper- and lowercase letters are used, and they are printed in a normal typeface. A few markings are used to indicate letter sounds. For example, microns mark the long vowel sound, a dot over the *g* indicates the soft sound, and so on. But these are used in connection with certain mapping rules, so that the markings occur only when the pronunciation is not otherwise signaled by one of these rules. (For example, the micron is used to signal the long *o* sound in *go* but not in *hope*.) Furthermore, the multiple mappings and context-dependent rules are introduced from the beginning.

For example, in the first lesson children learn two spellings for the long *e* sound (*ē* and *ee*), and in the second lesson they add a third (*ea*).

These examples are probably sufficient to illustrate the differences in these programs. I would like to consider now a few of the ways in which the simplified orthography and rules might affect the kind of reading that children learn to do.

Clearly there is an advantage in having a set of simple, consistent rules for children to follow: They are easy to practice and remember and conceivably easier to transfer to new situations. However, if one adopts the perceptual learning hypothesis of Gibson and Levin (1975), then the effects of the altered orthography can be potentially detrimental. For the hypothesis suggests that what children actually learn about the printed text depends on the kinds of choices they have to make and the context in which the choices occur. If children are consistently instructed to ignore certain letters (e.g., the small-size "silent" letters in Distar), then they may acquire no information about these letters to store as part of their sets of distinctive features, or, if you like, recognition routines for a particular word. Further, if they are taught to process information in a left-to-right sequence, they may not acquire procedures for dealing with the many right-to-left dependencies that occur in regular English. In this connection, it would be interesting to find out what information such children actually take in about the "silent" letters in Distar and whether these children have difficulty making the transition to a regular orthography in their second year. (Similar questions were raised in connection with the use of the Initial Teaching Alphabet, but as far as I know, the issues were never fully resolved; e.g., Macdonald, 1970, and Gillooly, 1971.)

But apart from potential difficulties that children may encounter in restructuring their word-recognition routines, there is another and potentially more serious drawback to the use of altered orthographies. To the extent that children are dependent on these systems, they may be unable to read materials in regular print. Superficially, this means that such children will have a limited set of opportunities to practice their skill (and pracatice is very important in developing fluency). But even more important, this kind of restriction may affect the kind of concept that such children develop about the act of reading itself: who can do it, where it can be done, and for what purpose. For one thing, if children are restricted to the material printed in their readers, they may get the idea that reading is essentially a school-based and teacher-dominated activity. Depending on their feelings about the school and their teacher, this may make reading seem more or less attractive, but it will certainly affect their notions of where and why reading can be done. For example, they may find that they cannot use their reading to show off or act smart in front of parents or siblings or even strangers outside the classroom (e.g., by reading signs, store labels, headlines, or even the printed matter on television). And as a result, reading may end up being something of a "closet" skill—quite useless to children who want to negotiate for themselves an identity of "being smart" in the outside world. The ramifications of such an attitude—particularly when children first encounter reading—may be subtle but may end by having an important effect on the uses to which their literacy is ultimately put.

I do not want to blame the whole problem of limited literacy on the use of altered orthographies; clearly that would be absurd. But I do want to suggest that the use of such systems can contribute to the problem. And I do want to point out that it is precisely in a program for the disadvantaged that we find these materials.

The Open Court program, designed as it is for primarily middle-class populations, uses a regular orthography, presumably on the assumption that most of these children can handle the complexities of the regular system without undue difficulty. As a result, reading is a potential activity in any environment and can be used to negotiate identities in a variety of circumstances.

The point that I wish to raise here is simply this: In the search for an efficient instructional system, we may arrive at something that, at least superficially, seems to make life easier for beginners but that may hinder their subsequent development, either by teaching them inappropriate word-recognition routines or, more importantly, by limiting their concept of what it is that they can use their literacy to accomplish. Furthermore, I wish to make the obvious point that the limitations lie not just in the children's expectations but also in the expectations that any such curriculum will generate in a teacher about what it is that children can learn. With its emphasis on simplistic rules and rote memory, a program such as Distar may convey the impression (no doubt, unintended) that its children cannot absorb the "real thing"—the kind of orthography, diverse mapping rules, and flexible heuristics that are used in programs intended for other children.

THE STORIES AND THEIR LANGUAGE

The vocabularies of both programs are similar in total number of words and number of high-frequency words. Distar uses 433 different words in the first year, and Open Court uses 374. In terms of frequency, about 85% of the words in both programs fall in the highest-frequency categories (A or AA words on the Thorndike & Lorge list, 1944). Similarly, the children read stories of roughly equivalent length. By the end of the first year, for example, Distar stories are presented in two 90-word episodes, and the Open Court stories run about 100 words each.

The character of the stories is, however, rather different, and it seems to me that these differences are very much related to the stated goals of the programs and particularly to the purposes for which children are expected to engage in beginning reading. In Distar, the purposes center around the notion of decoding and the careful sounding out of new words: Reading is variously defined as "blending," "sounding out," "training children to decode," and "teaching children to remember words in sentences." No other purposes are explicitly mentioned. In contrast, the stated goals of the Open Court program emphasize the notion of beginning reading as a literary experience:

> Activities and exercises suggested in the Open Court program have two main goals: to place the child in contact with many of the important ideas and achievements of the present and past times and to enlarge his capacity for effective self-expression. The stories and poems in the Readers acquaint him with the best in children's literature; they give him a bird's eye view of his cultural heritage, and they introduce him to significant ideas and concepts... [*The Foundation Program, Teacher's Guide,* p. xiv].

The differences, it seems to me, reflect more than a superficial emphasis on skills versus "reading for meaning." I think they are quite evident in the stories that children are asked to read.

As examples, consider one of the final stories presented in each program. In Fig. 10.3 is the first episode from a Distar story. The story structure is diffuse.

a fat man lIkₑd to gō fast ➤

a fat man lIkₑd to gō fast. hē went fast in his ➤

car. hē walkₑd fast and hē ran fast. hē ēven talkₑd ➤

fast. his wIfₑ did not lIkₑ him to gō sō fast. but hē ➤

went fast. ➤

hē sat down to ēat an egg and a cākₑ and a pIₑ. ➤

but hē ātₑ sō fast that the egg slippₑd and fell on ➤

his fēēt. ➤

hē bent down fast and his nōsₑ went into the ➤

cākₑ. hē went to wIpₑ his nōsₑ fast and hē hit the ➤

pIₑ. the pIₑ hit his wIfₑ. ➤

stop ➤

FIG. 10.3.   First episode, Distar story. (From *Distar® Reading I*, [2nd ed.], by S. Engelmann & E. C. Bruner. Copyright 1974, 1969, by Science Research Associates, Inc. Reprinted by permission.)

The Wolf in Sheep's Clothing

A wolf wrapped himself in the skin of a sheep and got into a sheep pen. He ate a lamb, but at last the shepherd found him.

"Do not turn me away," said the wolf. "I am one of your sheep."

"No," said the shepherd. "You are only pretending to be a sheep. I know you are really a wolf."

"How do you know?" asked the wolf. "I look like a sheep."

"Yes," said the shepherd. "But you act like a wolf." He beat the wolf with a stick and drove him away.

FIG. 10.4. Open Court story. (From *The Foundation Program* [5th ed.], "Reading and Writing." Copyright 1975 by Open Court Publishing Company. Reprinted by permission.)

For example, one would like to know why the hero is called a "fat" man. How does his fatness relate to the story? And why did he go so fast? And more important, what finally made him slow down? And how does that relate to his wife? In fact, how did she get into the story in the first place? Obviously, there are a lot of loose ends.

In contrast, the Open Court story has a much tighter construction (Fig. 10.4). There is a recognizable conflict and resolution. The shepherd clearly outsmarts the wolf for reasons that are spelled out in the story; and indeed, the elements of the story seem to cohere in a logical way. I consider the structure of these texts later, but first I want to look at the comprehension questions that follow each story.

The comprehension questions for the Distar story are presented in Table 10.1. After the children read a sentence or two, the teacher asks a specific *wh*-type question about the content. The questions are apparently designed to give children practice in locating and remembering specific information in the text they have just read. Indeed, this is explicitly stated in the introductory part of the teacher's guide:

> Most of the [comprehension] questions will pose no particular difficulty for the children. If they do have trouble producing the correct answer... repeat the sentence [from the story] for them and ask the question again... [The purpose

TABLE 10.1
Comprehension Questions, Distar Story[a]

After the Children Read:	You Say[b]
A fat liked to go fast.	What is this story about? (Signal.) *A fat man liked to go fast.*
He even talked fast.	Name some things that the fat man did fast. The children respond. *He went fast in his car. He walked fast and ran fast. He even talked fast.*
He sat down to eat an egg and a cake and a pie. But he ate so fast that the egg slipped and fell on his feet. The pie hit his wife.	What did he eat? (Signal.) *An egg, a cake, and a pie.* What happened? (Signal.) *He ate so fast that the egg slipped and fell on his feet.* Tell me all the things that happened when he went to eat the cake and the pie. The children respond. *His nose went into the cake. He hit the pie. And the pie hit his wife.*

[a]*Note.* From Story 159, Task 21, of *Distar® Reading I* (2nd ed.), by S. Engelmann and E. C. Bruner. Copyright 1974, 1969, by Science Research Associates, Inc. Reprinted by permission.

[b]What the teacher says is in roman type; the children's responses are in italics.

of this part of the program is to enable them to] grow in their ability to remember the sequence [of words in the sentence] well enough to answer the simple comprehension questions that are posed [*Distar, Reading I, Teacher's Guide*, p. 56].

In Open Court, there are few specific questions and virtually none that call for children to recall a specific word in the text (see Table 10.2). There seems to be no question as to whether children can remember what they read, let alone locate specific information in the text. All of that is presupposed. Instead, the emphasis is on an integration of the meaning of the story as a whole, on discussion, and on the opinions of individual children about what is a genuinely controversial issue.

There are three points that I would like to make about the stories and comprehension activities. First, the disadvantaged child is given a simpler set of tasks: locating and remembering specific information from the immediately preceding text. In contrast, the goal for the middle-class child is to integrate and reflect on material from the entire story. The point here is not that disadvantaged children do not need practice with this particular set of skills; probably all first graders do. The point is that in the first year, the program seems to go no further. And this can be limiting in two ways: First, it can limit children's expectations about what they can do with what they read—whether they will conceive of reflecting on it, having opinions about it, arguing with it, and so forth. Second, and perhaps more important, the limited tasks can limit the teachers' expectations about the kinds of things that children are capable of doing. And this may affect not only the reading

TABLE 10.2
Comprehension Questions, Open Court Story[a]

Introducing the Problem of the Second Story: "The Wolf in Sheep's Clothing."
A wolf made himself look like a sheep in order to fool the shepherd. Ask the children if they think the wolf will be able to fool the shepherd completely.

Reading the Story
If your class is ready for silent reading, let the children read each part of the story silently before they read it aloud. Then ask interpretive questions, or ask the children to predict what will happen next. However, if the silent-reading approach causes confusion and difficulty, go on with the unison reading.

Expressing Opinions
Ask the children how the shepherd could tell that the wolf was really a wolf. Ask them what the best way is to tell whether a person is really good or bad. (Can you depend upon what he says about himself and the way he looks, or should you think about the way he acts?)

---

[a]*Note.* From *Teacher's Guide* of *The Foundation Program* (5th ed.), p. 316. Copyright 1975 by Open Court Publishing. Reprinted by permission.

curriculum, but also the kinds of questions that are used in other parts of the instructional program.

The second point is related to the way in which beginning reading is defined. In Open Court, the definition is in terms of literary experiences, and as we would expect, the program includes fables, folktales, nursery rhymes, and other poetry, aphorisms, proverbs, and riddles. In Distar, on the other hand, beginning reading is defined as "decoding," and the notion of literature is never discussed. Perhaps as a result, the reading materials contain no poetry, and the prose is similar to that shown in Fig. 10.3.

Now we can lament the lack of good writing in Distar, and we can even say that the Distar child (who is, after all, the disadvantaged child) is really denied access to a whole literary heritage. It might be argued, however, that such children will ultimately have access to everything, once they get through the beginning stages, but that the first job is to help them break the code. And for such a task, just about any text will do, provided only that it can be handled by the decoding rules.

There are two comments that I would like to make about that argument, however. The first has to do with the relative complexity and difficulty of texts. We know from the work of Kintsch (1974), Frederiksen (1975), and many others that some texts are more difficult to remember than others and that memory is related to such things as the number of propositions and the way in which these are organized within a passage. As far as I know, this work has only been done with adults.[1] But it is possible to speculate that the differences that affect recall and comprehension in adults will also affect these processes in beginning readers. If this is the case, then we may have good reason for preferring one kind of text over another. If we can show, for example, that the propositional structure of one text is more diffuse than another, we may have a basis for a preference.

But apart from complexity, there may be another reason for preferring the reading materials in Open Court: their literary quality and the fact that they provide the beginner with an opportunity to read in a variety of literary forms. My reasoning here is admittedly even more speculative, but I want to suggest (as my third point about the stories and comprehension activities) that children must learn how to read in these forms in much the same way that they learn how to use various word-recognition routines and that this kind of learning may require a lot of guided practice over a long period of time. In a sense, I want to suggest that literary forms (or more precisely, genres) can function as cognitive structures and that they can serve as powerful devices

---

[1]Since the writing of this chapter, several studies of children's comprehension and recall of stories have appeared (Stein & Glenn, 1978; Mandler, 1978; Brown, Smiley, Day, Townsend, & Lawton, 1977). On the whole, these tend to support our speculation that aspects of text organization which affect these processes in adults do so as well in children.

for organizing experience—in this case, the experience of verbal communication.

Scribner (in press) has presented impressive evidence for the effects of discourse on problem solving and reasoning in oral language. For example, in her studies of syllogistic reasoning among nonliterate, traditional peoples, she has demonstrated that failure to solve syllogisms stems, not so much from an inability to engage in valid deductive reasoning or from any inability to recall the language of the syllogism, as from the failure to interpret that language in terms of the constraints of the genre. Subjects' difficulties appeared to lie in their inability to adopt what Scribner calls a "theoretic" interpretation of the content of the syllogism, an interpretation that depends on a knowledge of the genre and of the way in which the genre constrains the kinds of interpretations that can be given to any particular word or sentence. She has also proposed a framework for describing how experience with a given genre can lead to the development of cognitive schema for organizing increasingly complex information within that genre.

In the case of written discourse, I want to suggest that such schemas, once acquired, might serve to facilitate reading in a number of ways. For example, they might increase fluency by providing the child with a set of expectations to guide peripheral search and other preattentive processes. Or they might make it easier for the child to form a context from the particular elements that he or she is actively processing at any one time. In any case, it seems to me that learning to read must involve the learning of written discourse structures that might, as cognitive organizations, serve to order various aspects of the reading process. If this hypothesis is even remotely correct, then it seems to me at least as important for a program to provide extended practice on specific discourse forms as it is to provide practice on word recognition.

It is unclear whether such practice would be appropriate in the very beginning stages of reading. But it is possible to argue that the very repetitiveness and predictability of some forms may in fact aid the beginner even more than the child with more advanced recognition skills. (Examples of such forms are certain rhyme structures in the Dr. Seuss books or the cumulative narrative structures found in stories like "This Is the House that Jack Built" or "The Gingerbread Man.")

Nor is it clear how one would arrange for such practice with beginning readers, particularly those who are able to read only a few words or phrases. Open Court attempts to solve the problem by providing extensive suggestions for poetry- and story-listening activities at the very beginning of the year. However, it may be that listening by itself will not be sufficient for developing schemas for the written mode. The most effective way for children to acquire structures of written discourse may be through some combination of listening and reading. Thus, for example, an effective curriculum might include opportunities for children to listen to stories or poems while they are simultaneously looking at a printed version of the same text. (Such a procedure is in fact advocated in several beginning programs.) But in any case, if my hypothesis is correct, then failure to provide appropriate practice with a variety of genres may in a very real way limit the range and usefulness of the literacy that a child is supposed to be acquiring.

CONCLUSION

The purpose of this chapter has been not to provide a comprehensive evaluation of these programs, but to illustrate with a few examples certain basic differences in their concepts of literacy (i.e., the way in which each defines reading, the kinds of code relationships that children are expected to deal with, and the language that children are taught to read) and to point out that these differences coincide with differences in the social class of the children for whom each program appears to be intended.

It can be argued that the differences are temporary, that the Distar children will ultimately transfer to a regular orthography and learn to read in all sorts of discourse structures later on. But even if this is the case, and it is a very optimistic view, I must also point out that the curriculum has its effect not just on the children but also on the teacher. It influences the teacher's set of expectations and assumptions about what children can do: the relationships they can perceive, the language they can use, the questions they can comprehend, and so forth. And it is possible that an emphasis on simple tasks and simplified relationships may not stop with reading but may affect the way in which the teacher approaches a number of other curriculum areas as well.

The issue is a complex one: Children must acquire certain basic facts and skills about reading before they can develop enough literacy to use for any purpose. However, it is a basic contention of this chapter that there may very well be different kinds of literacy, in the sense that different skills may be required to read different kinds of discourse structures for different purposes. In their cross-cultural studies of the cognitive effects of literacy, Scribner and Cole (1976) presented intriguing evidence to support this notion. They found that there were specific relationships between the ways in which subjects used their literacy and their performance on classification, memory, and reasoning tasks. If this is true, then it is possible that the actual reading experiences provided by these programs may lead children to acquire somewhat different sets of basic facts and skills that, in the aggregate, amount to rather different kinds of literacy. The contention is not that one group of children will be illiterate but that each group of children may be literate in different ways.

REFERENCES

Brown, A. L., Smiley, S. S., Day, J. D., Townsend, M. A. R., & Lawton, S. C. *Intrusion of a thematic idea in children's comprehension and retention of stories.* Technical Report No. 18. Center for the Study of Reading, University of Illinois, 1977.

Chomsky, N., & Halle, M. *The sound pattern of English.* New York: Harper & Row, 1968.

Distar Reading I (2nd ed.). Chicago: Science Research Associates, 1974.

The Foundation Program (5th ed.), Level 1:1. LaSalle, Ill.: Open Court Publishing, 1975.

Frederiksen, C. H. Representing logical and semantic structure of knowledge acquired from discourse. *Cognitive Psychology,* 1975, *7,* 371–458.

Gibson, E., & Levin, H. *The psychology of reading.* Cambridge, Mass.: MIT Press, 1975.

Gillooly, W. B. The influence of writing-system characteristics on learning to read. In F. B. Davis (Ed.), *The literature of research in reading with emphasis on models* (USOE Final Rep.). Washington, D.C.: U.S. Government Printing Office, 1971. (ERIC Document Reproduction Service No. ED 059 023)

Kintsch, W. *The representation of meaning in memory.* Hillsdale, N.J.: Lawrence Erlbaum Associates, 1974.

Macdonald, J. W. (*Review of I.T.A.: An independent evaluation* by F. W. Warburton & V. Southgate and *Alphabets and reading* by J. Pitman & J. St. John). *Harvard Educational Review,* 1970, *40,* 317–325.

Mandler, J. M. A code in the node: The use of a story schema in retrieval. *Discourse Processes,* 1978, *1,* 14–35.

Scribner, S. Modes of thinking and ways of speaking. In R. O. Freedle (Ed.), *Discourse production and comprehension.* Norwood, N.J.: Ablex Publishing, in press.

Scribner, S., & Cole, M. *Studying cognitive consequences of literacy.* Paper presented at the International Congress of Psychology, Paris, France, July 1976.

Stein, N. L., & Glenn, C. G. An analysis of story comprehension in elementary school children. In R. Freedle (Ed.), *Multidisciplinary perspectives in discourse comprehension.* Norwood, N.J.: Ablex Publishing, 1978.

Thorndike, E., & Lorge, I. *The teacher's word book of 30,000 words.* New York: Teachers College, Bureau of Publications, 1944.

Venezky, R. L. *Language and cognition in reading* (Technical Rep. No. 188). Madison, Wis.: University of Wisconsin, Wisconsin Research and Development Center for Cognitive Learning, 1972.

11 Computer-Assisted Instruction in Beginning Reading: The Stanford Projects

J. D. Fletcher
Navy Personnel Research and Development Center

Design and development of computer-assisted instruction (CAI) in beginning reading were undertaken by Richard C. Atkinson and his staff over a twelve-year period, 1964–1975, at the Institute for Mathematical Studies in the Social Sciences at Stanford University. Two beginning reading CAI curriculums were developed during this period, one designed for the IBM 1500 Instructional System and the other designed for the institute's Digital Equipment Corporation PDP–10 computer facility. Hereafter, these curriculums will be referred to as the 1500 curriculum and the PDP–10 curriculum, respectively.

There were three primary motivations for initiating the Stanford projects in beginning reading. First was their obvious potential for investigating hypotheses, or notions, proposed to account for the acquisition and retention of reading skills. Second was the projects' potential for demonstrating the feasibility of CAI as a medium for instruction in the primary grades. Third was the projects' potential for developing instructional strategies and techniques for CAI itself. In the 1960s there were numerous data-free polemics on the most efficacious use of CAI. The Stanford projects were major efforts to curtail these polemics with "real-world" data on the educationally powerful issues of beginning reading.

The remainder of this chapter consists of four sections. The first documents some assumptions on which the design of the curriculums were based. The second discusses the design of the 1500 reading curriculum. The third discusses the design of the PDP–10 reading curriculum. The fourth section presents some final comments on the Stanford reading projects.

ASSUMPTIONS

Few activities demand from a theory as much precision and accuracy as the translation of its precepts to computer programs. In the case of the Stanford reading curriculums, help was simply taken from wherever it was available, and linguistic notions provided the richest background for curriculum development. In many instances, of course, there was nothing to be done but to rely on the intuitions of the project staff, consultants, and participating school personnel. This mix of linguistic, psycholinguistic, pedagogic, and intuitive considerations yielded the assumptions underlying the initial reading curriculums.

In the Stanford curriculums the reading process was viewed as a translation of printed orthography to meaning in a manner paralleling that of speech perception in which the translation is from an acoustic signal to meaning, necessitating some form of analysis by synthesis on the part of the perceiver. It was assumed that there is a level of abstraction below meaning but above raw perceptual input that is common to both speech perception and reading and that this level is adjusted upward or downward depending on the ease or difficulty of the material being read.

This view of reading engendered another idea that had a lasting effect on the CAI reading curriculums. As expressed by Carroll (1964), reading can be analyzed into two processes: the construction or reconstruction of a spoken message and the comprehension of messages so constructed. Taking this cue from Carroll, the emphasis in both the CAI reading curriculums was on speech reconstruction, that being the activity more amenable to computer presentation. Carroll went on to recommend that "these two processes— speech reconstruction and the apprehension of meaning—should [not] be separated in procedures of teaching. There is evidence, in fact, that the teaching of the mechanics of speech reconstruction (techniques of word recognition) is best done with materials which are maximally meaningful to the learner [p. 338]." To a minor extent, this latter recommendation was not followed in designing either curriculum. The 1500 curriculum taught nonsense but "regularly pronounceable" monosyllables, and the PDP–10 curriculum taught meaning-free spelling patterns. Additionally, of course, both curriculums taught words. The 1500 curriculum presented only regular words, and the PDP–10 curriculum, with its more pragmatic orientation, taught regular and irregular words.

It should be noted that amenability of pedagogical notions to computer presentation was a factor in the design of these curriculums. A primary difficulty in CAI design is the translation of instructional prescriptions to computer programs. There appear to be two basic reasons for this difficulty. First, most instructional prescriptions are vague relative to the precision required by computer programming. In one sense, CAI represents the *reductio ad absurdum* for a behavioral objectives approach to instructional design. It is difficult to incorporate in CAI objectives that cannot be expressed as behaviors measurable at a computer terminal. Second, despite all its capabilities and promise, the state of the art in computer technology has manifest limitations for instruction. These limitations are particularly noticeable for instruction in natural language skills. Currently there are genuine capabilities for speech understanding by computers and for comprehension of text, but it is doubtful that these capabilities are sufficiently powerful for CAI in beginning reading.

Both of the CAI curriculums were designed to supplement whatever reading instruction occurred in the classroom. It was assumed to be far easier to adjust and modify the computer programs used for instruction than to adjust and modify the established practice of classroom teachers. The supplemental nature of the Stanford curriculums, with their requirement for activities that could complement any classroom reading instruction, combined with their requirement for relatively precise instructional prescriptions to effect a major emphasis in both curriculums on decoding, that is, the ability to synthesize, or "sound out," an acoustic signal from orthography.

It was assumed that the linguistic skills of five to seven-year-old children could be enlisted in teaching them to read if only they could be taught to relate written symbols to the productive language capabilities they already possessed and demonstrated in their spoken language. Moreover, there seemed little reason to teach children solely to associate specific words with specific acoustic representations when a transfer capability appeared to be promised by the structure of English orthography. Orthography is a shared code based on competencies common to large communities of users, and it seemed intuitively plausible that such a sharing implies rules for associating writing with speaking. If students could be placed in situations in which they would learn these rules, they might break the code. Once the code was broken, the syntactic and semantic information associated with the acoustic information they could now synthesize from text might follow automatically. The situations appropriate for breaking this code appeared to be those in which the orthographic information bore a "regular" relationship to the acoustic information it was intended to represent—in which there would be regular grapheme–phoneme correspondences.

In the practice of the 1960s the "graph" or grapheme could be a single letter, a syllable, or a word. In the readers of Bloomfield and Barnhart (1961), Lippincott (McCracken & Walcutt, 1963), Merrill (Fries, Wilson, & Rudolph, 1966), and Behavioral Research Laboratories (Sullivan, 1967), the initial grapheme–phoneme correspondences were VC (vowel–consonant) syllables presented in words that were generally of a CVC configuration. VC words were also allowed early in these readers, and Lippincott permitted double consonant clusters (CCVC, CVCC, and CCVCC), as well as CV words. Authors of these readers evidently assumed that the basic graphic unit in beginning reading should be larger than a single letter and smaller than a whole word. Use of these units seems reasonable because of the difficulty of pronouncing consonants in the absence of vowels. In conventional practice, this difficulty is resolved by associating consonants with some "neutral" vowel such as /ə/. However, it should be noted that as useful as an association between the grapheme *b* and the phoneme /be/ may be in pronouncing *but,* it may be useless or even confusing in pronouncing *bit.* Neither of the Stanford reading curriculums taught associations between single letters and the sounds they represented.

Emphasizing that this approach was supported by Bloomfield and himself, Fries (1963) wrote:

> [This approach to beginning reading rests] upon the relation between the sound patterns of the words and the letter symbols of our alphabet but this relation is not such as to lead us to seek to match specific letters with each of the physical "sounds" of our language. Nor does it assume that the pronunciation of a word is a fusion or blending of the sounds represented by the individual letters by which the word is spelled [p. 146].

Fries' position was that "modern English spelling is fundamentally a system of a comparatively few arbitrary contrastive sets of spelling patterns to which readers, to be efficient, must, through much practice, develop high-speed recognition responses [p. 183]." Fries' statements concerning the development of high-speed recognition responses antedate recent pronouncements to the same effect by LaBerge and Samuels (1974), who based their comments on considerable empirical study.

Coming from psychology rather than linguistics, Gibson (1970) stated:

> It is my belief that the smallest component units in written English are spelling patterns. By spelling patterns, I mean a cluster of graphemes in a given environment which has an invariant pronunciation according to the rules of English. These rules are the regularities which appear when, for instance, any vowel or consonant or cluster is shown to correspond with a given pronunciation in an initial, medial, or final position in the spelling of a word [p. 329].

Spelling patterns as described by Gibson were used heavily in the Stanford PDP-10 curriculum, which incorporated substantial amounts of practice in an attempt to bring about the high-speed recognition responses recommended by Fries. The utility of this approach in CAI was demonstrated by Fletcher and Atkinson (1972) and Fletcher (1973). However, emphasis on phoneme–grapheme regularity encounters practical difficulties in curriculum design for beginning reading. One obvious difficulty is the strained vocabulary that results in choosing words to illustrate the regular spelling patterns being presented, and another is the pronunciation of orthographically regular utterances in ordinary discourse. Both of these difficulties are illustrated by Bloomfield's prototypical *Nan can fan Dan.* The sentence appears strained because *Nan* is not a particularly familiar name and because who can fan whom is not a concern of moment to beginning readers. Furthermore, the sentence may contain grapheme–phoneme irregularities in ordinary speech. For instance, *can* in this sentence would ordinarily be pronounced /ken/ or /kɪn/ in American dialects.

More serious, however, are the irregularities that occur even when spelling patterns are considered separately from ordinary speech. Students who have learned to associate /et/ with *-ut* will presumably be more likely to recognize *cut, hut, jut,* and so on. However, they may experience difficulty with *put.* As long as instruction is based on phonemic correspondences to graphemes, exceptions will be encountered.

On the other hand, English orthography may be more closely rule-governed than the number of exceptions to regular grapheme–phoneme correspondences suggest. This possibility is indicated in extensive empirical studies of English orthography by Hanna, Hanna, Hodges, and Rudorf (1966) and Venezky (1967, 1970) and in the generative English phonology of Chomsky and Halle (1968), who introduced the concept of lexical representation. The problem is to decide what is meant by regularity in the structure of English orthography and what its implications are for reading instruction. A seminal investigation was that of Venezky and Weir (1966), who demonstrated considerable regularity in the relationship of English orthography to spoken language at a level of abstraction beyond direct grapheme–phoneme correspondences. This work had a significant influence on the design of the 1500 curriculum, resulting ultimately in the idea of a vocalic center group (Hansen & Rodgers, 1968), which was assumed to be the minimal pronunciation unit rehearsed by the reader in order to build associations between orthography and oral language.

A vocalic center group was described by Rodgers (1967) as a vowel nucleus with zero to three preceding consonants and zero to four following consonants and by Hansen and Rodgers (1968) as "the optimally minimal sequence within which all necessary rules of phonemic co-occurrence can be stated [p. 74]." From Rodgers' description, then, the vocalic center group looks very much like a syllable, and in fact he suggested that the "reader will not be seriously misled if he associates the units which result from standard dictionary syllabification with the vocalic center groups [p. 16]." From the Hansen and Rodgers' description it is clear that the vocalic center group is phonologically, rather than semantically, motivated; it is expected to be the minimal orthography required to identify the sound sequence that the orthography is intended to represent. Moreover, vocalic center groups must conform to the orthographic-sound limitations of the language in which they occur: *rad, sed,* and *strempts* are all legitimate vocalic center groups according to Rodgers, whereas *slrap, tenps,* and *mealk* are not.

A serious problem with the vocalic center group notion is illustrated by its assumption that a learned association between letter sequences, for instance *map* and *ten* and their pronunciation, would facilitate association of *tap* and *men* to the appropriate pronunciation, as Rodgers (1967, p. 15) suggested. However, *map* and *ten* are vocalic center groups, and therefore they are the minimal orthographic units required for establishing the appropriate sound sequences. If they are indeed the minimal orthographic units, it is difficult to see how learning them would yield any positive transfer to the task of learning *tap* and *men*. There must be a smaller unit of orthography involved, and this distinction underlies a basic difference between the 1500 curriculum and the PDP-10 curriculum. The 1500 curriculum took the vocalic center group as the basic decoding unit to be taught, and the PDP-10 curriculum took the spelling pattern as the basic decoding unit to be taught.

Given that both curriculums were intended to increase decoding skills through the presentation of regular letter-to-sound relationships, and to supplement ordinary classroom instruction, it is notable that they differed in their selection of sight word vocabulary. The 1500 curriculum was limited to items that were either vocalic center groups or combinations of vocalic center groups. Despite considerable emphasis on spelling patterns in the PDP-10 curriculum, the complexities in English orthography and in the classroom materials the curriculum was supposed to supplement were recognized. Vocabulary items with fairly complex spelling-to-sound relationships but with high frequencies in first- through third-grade reading materials were taught in a direct paired-associate manner as "sight-words."

THE 1500 CURRICULUM

Overview

Development for the 1500 curriculum began in 1964 and ended in the spring of 1968. The system was used for two school years. About 50 first-grade students used the reading curriculum in 1966–1967, and about 70 students in grades K–2 used the reading curriculum in 1967–1968. The 1500 system supported elaborate student terminals, including three display, or output, devices—a picture projector, a cathode ray tube (CRT), and an audio system for playing prerecorded messages. The terminals also included three student input devices—a hand-held light pen, a modified typewriter keyboard, and the audio system for recording messages. The picture projector provided random access to 1,024 16 mm film frames that were displayed on a 7- by 9-in.

screen. The CRT displayed alphanumeric characters on a 7- by 9-in. screen with 16 lines of 40 character positions each. A limited number of prepared line drawings could also be displayed on the CRT. The audio system provided random access to messages that could vary in duration from 1 to 15 sec and were stored on a tape cartridge containing about 2 hours of prerecorded messages. The light pen was the principal input device used by the reading program. It was activated by being pressed against one of the CRT character positions, which was then sensed as a response and recorded. The typewriter keyboard was used occasionally by the reading program in a straightforward way. The recording capability of the audio system was seldom used. Early studies indicated that students preferred to use this capability for recording messages of their own devising that incorporated a vocabulary more distinguished by its colorfulness than by its utility in reading pedagogy. The computer system and its terminals were located at an elementary school in a predominantly black, economically depressed neighborhood. More complete descriptions of this system were provided by Atkinson and Hansen (1966) and Atkinson (1968).

The architecture of any computer system intended for CAI is notable not primarily for the curiosity that may be occasioned by the bits, bytes, and lights of a new technology but for the boundary conditions it imposes on curriculum design. The 1500 system was an impressive technological innovation, but, like any instructional medium, it imposed limits on the instructional presentations it could support. There was, for instance, no direct way to check by computer a student's ability to produce the sound sequence represented by displayed orthography, yet this ability was the principal objective of the program. Both the audio and the photographic random access mechanisms were based on serial access devices (tape and film reels, respectively), making the positioning mechanism quite slow relative to the random access speeds currently available from digitized speech and videodisc technology. Arithmetic operations within the Coursewriter II language were cumbersome (no floating point was available), and the optimization techniques discussed by Atkinson (1972, 1974), or the student modeling techniques based on parameter estimation discussed by Suppes, Jerman, and Brian (1968) and by Fletcher (1975) could not have been implemented. Preparation of line drawings for display on the CRT was a slow process, and facile illustration of a point with a graphic presentation such as a classroom teacher might easily improvise using a blackboard was out of the question. The point of these remarks is that computer system design has direct implications for CAI. The design of the Stanford CAI reading curriculums was shaped both by the body of assumptions concerning initial reading instruction discussed earlier and by the nature of the computer systems used. The former is often noted in comments on the Stanford developments; the latter is usually neglected.

The instruction presentation strategy of the 1500 curriculum was "tutorial" and based on the intrinsic branching approach to programmed instruction recommended by Crowder (e.g., 1959). Many, if not all, responses to items in this approach were analyzed to determine if a student needed remediation, should proceed to the next item, or should skip several items ahead. Most lessons in the 1500 curriculum were preceded by a screening test on the basis of which a student could pass over large amounts of information in the lesson. On the other hand, many items in the "mainstream" of the lessons were associated with remedial material so that a student who performed poorly could be given extra practice on those aspects of the material with which he appeared to be having difficulty.

The curriculum was divided into three categories of material: decoding, comprehension, and motivation. A description of these categories follows.

Decoding Materials

The decoding materials included four activities: letter identification, word matching, matrix building, and compound word identification.

Letter Identification. No direct attempt was made to teach the names of letters. It was assumed that letter names are at odds with the dominant sound they represent and that teaching letter names would confuse students who were being taught to decode. Three tasks were typically presented: (1) single letter matching, in which the student indicated with a light-pen response which of two or three letters on the CRT was the same as a letter displayed by the projector; (2) letter string matching, in which the student indicated with a light-pen response which of two or three letter strings on the CRT was the same as a letter string displayed by the projector; and (3) a same–different task, in which the student indicated if two letters or letter strings displayed on the CRT were the same or different.

Word Matching. The section on word matching consisted of paired-associate tasks in which the stimulus was the verbal pronunciation, orthography, and/or pictorial representation of a word, and the response was the identification of the appropriate word in a list displayed by the CRT. The student indicated a choice by touching it with the light-pen. The layout for word matching is shown in Fig. 11.1. A cue-fading technique was used for this activity, and four problem types were developed to correspond to the following arrays of cues: (1) picture, orthography, and audio (as in Fig. 11.1), (2) picture and audio, (3) picture only, (4) audio only. Even though there was no voice recognizer on the system, students were told to "touch and say" pronounceable responses. Because the system responded only to "touch" and not to "say," students, quite reasonably, stopped making oral responses to these instructions early in the curriculum.

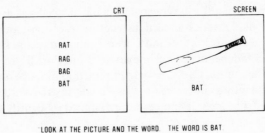

LOOK AT THE PICTURE AND THE WORD. THE WORD IS BAT.
HE HIT THE BALL WITH THE BAT. TOUCH AND SAY BAT.

FIG. 11.1.   1500 curriculum word-matching display.

Matrix Building. The core of each lesson was the matrix-building activity. Alliteration patterns, that is, initial consonants, were presented in rows, and rhyming patterns, that is, final units, were presented in columns, as shown in Fig. 11.2. A matrix was constructed one cell at a time. The initial consonant(s) of a word were called the initial unit, and the vowel and the final consonant(s) were called the final unit. The intersection of an initial unit row and a final unit column determined the entry in any cell.

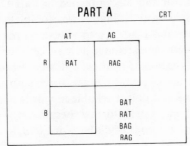

TOUCH AND SAY THE WORD THAT BELONGS IN THE EMPTY CELL.

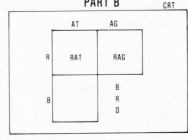

TOUCH THE INITIAL UNIT OF THE EMPTY CELL.

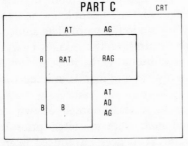

TOUCH AND SAY THE FINAL UNIT OF THE CELL.

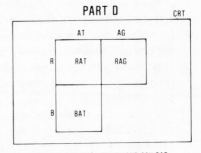

YOU HAVE PUT BAT IN THE CELL. TOUCH AND SAY BAT

FIG. 11.2.   1500 curriculum matrix displays.

The problem format for the construction of each cell was divided into four parts: Parts A and D were standard instructional sections, and Parts B and C were remedial sections. Parts B and C were branched to and from Part A and were presented independently or in combination. Part B provided remedial practice on initial units. Part C provided remedial practice on final units. In Part A, the student was instructed to "touch and say the word that belongs in the empty cell." The answer choices were designed to identify three classes of errors:

1. The inital unit was correctly identified, but the final unit was not (e.g., *BAG* in Fig. 11.2, Part A). The student was branched to Part C and then back to Part A.
2. The final unit was correctly identified but the initial unit was not (e.g., *RAT* in Fig. 11.2, Part A). The student was branched to Part B and then back to Part A.
3. Neither the initial unit nor the final unit was correctly identified (e.g., *RAG* in Fig. 11.2, Part A). The student was branched to Part B, then to Part C, and then back to Part A.

If the student's answer was correct, he or she was branched to Part D.

Individual cell building was continued until the matrix was complete. The matrices in the lesson material contained from six to twelve words and nonsense syllables. Nonsense words were considered legitimate cell entries if (1) they were occurrent English syllables; (2) they did not represent unconventional spellings for common monosyllabic words—for example, *sed* represents a regular spelling for the initial English syllable in words such as *sediment*, but it was not presented in matrix format because it was a nonstandard spelling for the homophonous monosyllabic word *said*; and (3) they comprised less than 40% of the total cell entries.

Compound Word Identification. The approach to compound words assumed a learning-transfer process in which the student knew how to read one of the two elements that formed a compound word. The student was expected to review the known word and learn both the unknown part of the compound and the compound itself. Additionally, the student studied the conventional meaning of the compound word and its role in a semantically rich sentence.

Compound words initially introduced were composed of two known monosyllables—for example, *bat* and *man* were mastered prior to the presentation of the compound *batman*. Sequences introduced later were composed of five compound words in which only one of the elements was known. Compound words were selected according to three criteria: (1) frequency in initial reading materials, (2) imaginative possibilities yielding semantically rich context sentences, and (3) opportunity to vary the known word in initial and final position in the five compound words (e.g., *hat*box, fire*hat*, *hat*band, etc.).

Comprehension Materials

The comprehension materials focused on the understanding of sentences and included four sections: usage, form class, inquiries, and sentence initiators.

Usage. The usage section was intended to cue an appropriate set of semantic associations for the lexical items presented. A list of words was displayed by the CRT. Definitions were given auditorally, and the student was expected to identify the word that matched each definition with a light-pen response. The definitions were chosen under two constraints: (1) If the word appeared in *The Rainbow Dictionary* (Wright, 1959), all the meanings defined in that dictionary were used. (2) If the word did not appear in *The Rainbow Dictionary* but appeared in the *Thorndike-Barnhart Beginners' Dictionary* (Thorndike & Barnhart, 1964), at least one of the definitions, depending on frequency and usefulness, was used. If the word did not appear in either dictionary, it was not included in the usage section nor used in succeeding lesson materials.

A strict "dictionary definition" format was avoided in defining word items. Standard definitions were reconstructed to stress functional meanings. For example, the word *bat* might have the following dictionary definition: "a stout wooden stick or club, used to hit the ball in baseball, cricket, etc." In the lesson materials this definition was reformulated: "Touch and say the word that means something you might use to hit a baseball."

Form Class. The form class section was intended to cue an operational knowledge of syntactic associations for the lexical items presented. A typical item of this sort is shown in Fig. 11.3. The student was to indicate with a light-pen response ("touch and say") which word "made sense" in the sentence.

FIG. 11.3.   1500 curriculum form class display.

Usually, one word was correct, one was of the correct form class but semantically inappropriate, and one was inappropriate both because of its form class and its semantic associations.

Inquiries.　In the inquiries section, the student was asked to identify lexical items in a displayed sentence that answered a given question. For instance, there might be two items based on the sentence *John hit the ball.* One item might require the student to indicate with a light-pen response ("touch and say" again) who hit the ball. Another item might require the student to indicate what John hit.

Sentence Initiators.　The section on sentence initiators was intended to teach students timing, pitch, and stress contours so that they could read sentences with intonation patterns commonly found in speech. High-frequency sentence initiators (*It's a, That's a, They're*) were selected from Carterette and Jones' (1968) list of multiword units uttered by six-year-old children during free discussion. These initiators were combined with words already presented to form sentences which were then displayed to the students. The idea was to use the timing features of the computer system in the following sequence: (1) A sentence was displayed by the CRT, and the student was given 2 sec in which to attempt an oral reading and record it on the audio device; (2) the audio device played a reading of the sentence; and (3) the student was given 2 sec to repeat the reading of the sentence.

Motivational Materials

Motivational materials consisted of games, rhymes, and stories. Games were sequenced into each lesson and were intended to exercise developing competencies. Rhymes were presented as listening activities to illustrate the rhyming and alliterative sounds of words and to demonstrate the rhythmic use of language. Stories were read to the students using the audio device. The stories were displayed by the CRT, sentence by sentence, so that students could follow print as it was being read.

Tenets

Rodgers (1967) listed some tenets of the 1500 curriculum that are repeated here by way of summary:

1. Reading and spelling should be taught independently. This tenet was adopted on the assumption that most reading obstacles are unrelated to spelling obstacles.

2. Reading should be initiated with a decoding or transfer stage during which the student learns to associate graphic patterns with speech sequences. This tenet led to the next.

3. The association of sight to sound is initially effected between letter patterns and vocalic center groups and is independent of meaning.

4. The sequence of items to be presented for association learning should be determined primarily by a difficulty scaling of vocalic center groups as documented by Hansen and Rodgers (1968). Four principles for ordering vocalic center groups were enunciated by Rodgers:

    a. Groups containing single consonant elements should be introduced before those containing consonant clusters (*tap* before *trap*).

    b. Groups containing initial consonant clusters should be introduced before those containing final consonant clusters (*trap* before *tarp*).

    c. Groups containing short vowels should be introduced before those containing long vowels (*tap* before *tape*).

    d. Single vocalic center group sequences should be introduced before multiple sequences (*trap* before *trapper*).

Notably, principles (a) and (b) are at variance with results later documented by Fletcher (1973), which indicated that in a pronunciation task CVC and CVCC items are of about the same difficulty and that both are significantly easier than CCVC and CCVCC items which, in turn, are of about the same difficulty.

5. Every graphic pattern should be presented as a member of a rhyme (final unit) set and an alliteration (initial consonant) set, the distinguishing characteristics of these sets being displayed in a matrix format.

6. Word items presented in matrix format should be immediately introduced in sentence contexts that emphasize their morphological, syntactic, and semantic functions.

7. Patterned word items should appear in poems, stories, essays, and descriptions in which the features of pronunciation, grammatical function, and meaning are shown to function together to convey the writer's intention to the reader.

THE PDP-10 CURRICULUM

Overview

Development of the PDP-10 curriculum began in 1968 and ended in the spring of 1975. The computer system was located at Stanford University and communicated with student terminals in participating schools over dedicated telephone lines. The system was used for six school years, beginning with the same school used for the 1500 development and about 200 first-grade students in 1969–1970, expanding to four schools and about 700 students in grades K–3 in 1970–1972, and cutting back because of funding limitations to the original school in 1972–1975, with about 400 students each year, primarily in grades K–3, although some students in grades 4–6 also participated as remedial readers. The PDP–10 supported relatively simple student terminals consisting of 10-character-a-second KSR "Model 33" teletypewriters equipped with headphones for digitized audio output. The teletypewriter provided hard-copy displays and the principal means for student input. Students received prerecorded messages from the digitized audio capability, which permitted prerecording on magnetic disks of up to 6,000 digitized messages .5, 1.0, 2.5 sec in length. The messages could then be rapidly (32 msec) accessed at random, assembled together in computer memory, and, after digital-to-analogue conversion, played to a student through headphones. There was no graphic or photographic capability at the terminals, and the teletypewriter printed only upper-case letters. This system was described more completely by Atkinson and Fletcher (1972), Atkinson, Fletcher, Lindsay, Campbell, and Barr (1973), and Atkinson (1974).

The student terminals in the PDP–10 curriculum were obviously restrictive. Teletypewriters are noisy and slow (10 characters a second is an annoying rate of display when mildly sophisticated use of alphanumerics is necessary), but their price was right and they provided printouts for review by students, proctors, and teachers. Notably, there was an effort to design a curriculum sufficiently inexpensive for schools to purchase. It is also notable that in comparing the 1500 curriculum to the PDP–10 curriculum, the limitations of teletypewriters were compensated for by the digitized audio capability and by the power of the computer timesharing system itself. The audio output system had more capability and flexibility than did the 1500 audio system, and the operating system provided more on-line computational capability than the curriculum designers needed. However, the computer operating system flexibilities required were not all available as "off-the-shelf" items. An entirely new disk file system was developed to support student data recording and the audio system. Capabilities were also developed for system-level character editing, student-mode program execution, high-speed line multiplexing, and for generating reentrant codes from the higher level languages available.

The instruction presentation strategy was "drill and practice" and based on the strands approach to CAI developed and described by Suppes (e.g., 1967). The program was divided into the seven parts or strands shown in Table 11.1.

The term *strand* was used to identify a basic component skill of initial reading (with the exception of Strand 0). Students moved through each strand in a roughly linear fashion. Branching or progress within strands was criterion dependent; students proceeded to a new exercise or new material

TABLE 11.1
PDP-10 Curriculum Strands

Strand	Title
0	Use of Teletypewriter
I	Letter Identification
II	Sight-Word Vocabulary
III	Spelling Patterns
IV	Phonics
V	Word Comprehension
VI	Sentence Comprehension

within a strand only after they had attained some (individually specifiable) performance criterion in the current exercise or material. Branching between the strands was time dependent; students moved from one strand to take up where they left off in another after a certain (again, individually specifiable) amount of time, regardless of what criterion levels they had reached in the strands. Within each strand there were two to three progressively more difficult exercises that were designed to bring students to fairly high levels of performance. The criterion procedure generally required two consecutive correct answers for each item and one errorless pass through the list of items constituting an exercise.

Entry to each strand depended on progress in earlier strands. For example, the letter-identification strand started with a subset of letters used in the sight-word strand. When a student in the letter-identification strand exhibited mastery over the set of letters used in the first several words of the sight-word strand, he or she entered the sight-word strand. Entry into both the phonics and spelling pattern strands was similarly controlled by the student's placement in the sight-word strand. Thus, a student could work in several strands simultaneously. Once he or she entered a strand, however, advancement within that strand could be independent of progress in other strands.

Most students spent 2 min on each strand, and the length of their daily sessions was 10 min. The time each student spent on any strand and the session length were parameters that could be uniquely specified. Sufficient information was saved in student restart records to assure continuation from precisely those conditions that existed at sign-off.

The strands were comprised of sets, or sections, of three curriculum items, and it was in these sections that a student needed to reach criterion before progressing in the strands. Each section was presented in either two or three separate exercises. In each exercise the three items of the section were presented in random order until the student achieved criterion. A student who already knew the material of a particular exercise could leave that exercise after only six responses, which could take as little as 30 sec. Students made five to twelve responses a minute on the program.

Students received instruction for the exercises by means of the digitized audio system. The student would input responses on the teletypewriter. After completing the response, he or she pressed the space bar, which returned control of the terminal to the computer for response evaluation. If the student discovered an error in the response, he or she could press the rub-out key before pressing the space bar, and the entire problem was presented again for a second trial. If a student pressed the rub-out key more than three times before entering a response, a "too many rub-outs" message was printed. Time-outs were also used. If a student took more than 10 sec to type any character in the response, he or she was given a "too much time" message and the answer was treated as incorrect. Students received a printed record of the work completed at the end of each session. Classroom teachers also received daily a printed report on progress achieved by their students. Kindergarten and first-grade children adapted quickly to use of the keyboard and had no difficulty in typing the relatively short responses (maximum of eight characters) required.

Description of the Strands

Strand 0—Machine Readiness.   Readiness materials were prepared to acquaint students with the manual skills required to interact with the program. The readiness strand attempted to teach students to sign themselves on the program without proctor supervision. To sign on the reading program, a student typed R (for reading) and an assigned student number. He or she then typed a space followed with his or her first name and another space. The program responded by typing the student's last name. If the last name was correct, the student typed a space and the program proceeded with the lesson. To leave the readiness strand, a student was required to perform the sign-on procedure with no more than one error. The readiness strand differed from the other strands in that branching from it was criterion dependent rather than time dependent.

Strand I—Letter Identification.   Each letter was presented twice in the letter strand. For the first pass through the alphabet, grouping of letters in three-letter sections was designed to minimize visual confusion. For the second pass through the alphabet, grouping was designed to maximize visual confusion. In all cases, sections were designed to minimize auditory confusion.

Three types of exercises (copy, recognition, and recall) were used throughout the letter-identification strand. These exercises are illustrated in Fig. 11.4. In the first exercise, a letter was typed and the student was requested

DISPLAY AUDIO

	EX. 1 (COPY)	A	TYPE A
FIG. 11.4. PDP-10 curriculum	EX. 2 (RECOGNITION)	C B A	TYPE A
letter identification exercises.	EX. 3 (RECALL)	(NO DISPLAY)	TYPE A

FIG. 11.4. PDP-10 curriculum letter identification exercises.

to type the same letter. Random presentation of the three letters in a section continued until the student reached criterion for Exercise 1, at which time he or she was advanced to Exercise 2 of the letter strand. After each presentation in the second exercise of the letter strand, the order of the three letters in the display was randomly changed, and the exercise was repeated for another target letter. Upon achieving criterion for each of the letters, the student proceeded to Exercise 3. When the student achieved criterion on the three letters in the section in Exercise 3, he or she returned to Exercise 1 with a second set of three letters.

Throughout the curriculum, if the student responded correctly, he or she proceeded to the next presentation. If the student responded incorrectly or exceeded the time allowed for a response, the teletypewriter displayed the correct response and proceeded to the next presentation. When the student responded correctly, randomly scheduled audio reinforcement messages were presented. The usefulness of variable-interval reinforcement has been established as a method of achieving performance that is stable and highly resistant to extinction. The effect of the audio reinforcement messages in the PDP-10 curriculum was unclear. It is doubtful that they comprised the principal reinforcement mechanism operant in the curriculum. Be that as it may, they continued to be used and included messages like "fabulous," "outstanding," and recorded clapping and cheering. They were at least entertaining.

When a student met criterion on a specific number of letters (i.e., those required for the first words in the sight-word vocabulary of Strand II), he or she began Strand II and continued to work simultaneously in both Strands I and II but at different levels of difficulty within each strand.

Strand II—Sight-Word Vocabulary. Strand II provided practice on a vocabulary that was introduced and taught in the classroom and contained words common to several basal reading texts and sight-word lists. The vocabulary was presented in sections of three words presented in two different exercises (copy and recognition), which are illustrated in Fig. 11.5.

When the student achieved criterion in Exercise 1 for each of the three words forming the section, he or she began Exercise 2. As in Exercise 2 of the letter strand, the order of items that comprised the display was random in each presentation in Exercise 2 of the vocabulary strand. After meeting

DISPLAY   AUDIO

| EX 1 (COPY) | CAT | TYPE CAT |
| EX 2 (RECOGNITION) | SAT CAT BAT | TYPE CAT |

FIG. 11.5. PDP-10 sight-word vocabulary exercises.

criterion for each new word in each of the two exercises, the student proceeded to the next section of three words and began again on Exercise 1. The selection of items for review and presentation in the vocabulary strand grew progressively more complex. As Atkinson (1974) showed, the curriculum was evolving toward a presentation strategy that was based on optimization notions of control theory. Discussion of this process is a feast-or-famine proposition, and famine is the option selected here. The interested reader is referred to Atkinson (1974) and Atkinson et al. (1973) for discussions of this process in the vocabulary strand.

Strand III—Spelling Patterns. The spelling pattern strand was designed to provide direct and explicit practice with English spelling patterns. Although all the spelling patterns presented in this strand were chosen from those taught in the phonics strand, new words were used. A section for this strand consisted of three monosyllabic words, such as *cat, bat, rat,* each of which incorporated the same (final unit) spelling pattern. Copy and recall exercises were used in this strand and are illustrated in Fig. 11.6.

Strand IV—Phonics. Exercises in the phonics strand concentrated on initial and final consonants and medial vowels. Students were never required to rehearse or identify consonant or vowel sounds in isolation. The smallest unit of presentation was a dyad, that is, a single vowel–consonant or consonant–vowel combination. Copy, recognition, and word-building exercises were used in the phonics strand and are illustrated in Fig. 11.7. As in the preceding strands, students worked with a section of three units and had to meet criterion for each spelling pattern in each of the exercises before proceeding to the next section.

The audio reinforced the sound values of the spelling patterns with randomly selected examples from three samples—two monosyllabic and an easily identifiable polysyllabic word. However, the word to be typed by the student in Exercise 3 (word building) was always one of the two monosyllabic exemplars.

DISPLAY   AUDIO

| EX 1 (COPY) | CAT | TYPE CAT |
| EX 2 (RECALL) | (NO DISPLAY) | TYPE CAT |

FIG. 11.6. PDP-10 curriculum exercises in spelling patterns.

FINAL UNITS

	DISPLAY	AUDIO
EX. 1 (COPY):	—AT	TYPE AT AS IN CAT
EX. 2 (RECOGNITION):	—AT —AD —AB	TYPE AT AS IN CAT
EX. 3 (WORD BUILDING):	—AD —AT —AB	TYPE CAT
	C— —	

INITIAL UNITS

	DISPLAY	AUDIO
EX. 1 (COPY):	CA—	TYPE CA AS IN CAT
EX. 2 (RECOGNITION):	CA— FA— BA—	TYPE CA AS IN CAT
EX. 3 (WORD BUILDING):	FA— CA— BA—	TYPE CAT
	— —T	

FIG. 11.7. PDP-10 curriculum phonics exercises.

The PDP-10 curriculum was unusual among spelling pattern curriculums in two respects. First, other curriculums present spelling patterns implicitly. Spelling patterns that are not themselves words (*-ab*) are presented only as components of words (*cab, tab, slab*); they are never presented explicitly by themselves. The Stanford PDP-10 curriculum presented spelling patterns both implicitly in the spelling strand and explicitly in the phonics strand. Second, the spelling patterns chosen for other curriculums are usually final consonant, or final unit, patterns; they are syllable endings (*-ab, -an, -at*) rather than syllable beginnings (*ba-, na-, ta-*). The Stanford PDP-10 curriculum presented both initial unit and final unit spelling patterns. (In contrast, the 1500 curriculum initial units consisted only of consonants or consonant clusters and were not spelling patterns.)

The spelling patterns in the PDP-10 curriculum were grouped into four categories: -VC, CV-, -VVC, and CVV-. Each of the categories was divided into subcategories according to vowels. For example, category CV- consisted of subcategories Ca-, Ce-, Ci-, Co-, and Cu-. Category -VC also included the spelling patterns -VCE, where *E* denotes a silent *e* at the end of a word. The students studied only one subcategory of spelling patterns at a time. Each item was successively presented in the exercise formats described. When the requisite number of items within a subcategory passed criterion for Exercise 3, a decision was made to determine which category and subcategory the student should study next. The student began in category -VC, and when the criterion was met, he or she was transferred to one of the categories CV-, -VCC, or CVV-, with probability P_2, P_3, or P_4, respectively, or was retained in category -VC, with probability P_1. The student always transferred back to category -VC when he or she finished one of the other categories.

Branching between vowel subcategories within each category occurred in a round-robin fashion. The branching scheme emphasized the -VC category.

Usually $P_1 = 1/2$, which meant that the student studied items in the -VC category for 2/3 of the total instructional time allocated to the phonics strand. This emphasis reflected results documented by Fletcher (1973), indicating that practice with final units (-VC) produces better performance than does practice with initial units (CV-). Branching in the phonics strand is discussed more fully by Atkinson (1974) and Atkinson et al. (1973).

Strand V—Word Comprehension. Strand V provided practice on the meaning of words introduced in the sight-word strand. A section consisted of three groups of three words. Each word was associated with one of several categories. The presentation displayed three words followed by a request to type a word of a particular category. The strand used a single exercise format illustrated in Fig. 11.8. The order of the three words presented was random, and the target word, with its associated category, was randomly chosen from those displayed.

DISPLAY   AUDIO

HOUSE CAT GREEN   TYPE THE WORD THAT IS AN ANIMAL

FIG. 11.8. PDP-10 curriculum word comprehension exercise.

Strand VI—Sentence Comprehension. A section in the sentence comprehension strand consisted of three sentences (or phrases) with one word missing in each. Displayed with each sentence were three words—two were distractors and one correctly completed the sentence. As in the 1500 curriculum, one of the distractors was of the correct form class, but it was either semantically or syntactically unacceptable in that it broke a subcategorization rule. The second distractor was unacceptable both semantically and syntactically. The strand used a single exercise format illustrated in Fig. 11.9.

DISPLAY   AUDIO

MAD DRIVE SWIM   TYPE THE WORD THAT CORRECTLY

TIM WILL — — — THE CAR   COMPLETES THE SENTENCE

FIG. 11.9. PDP-10 curriculum sentence comprehension exercise.

FINAL COMMENT

This chapter briefly discusses 12 years of CAI development in beginning reading. Some of this development met with substantial success, as evaluation studies by Atkinson (1968), Fletcher and Atkinson (1972), Jamison, Fletcher, Suppes, and Atkinson (1976), and others have shown. However, the use of computers to teach beginning reading may only have begun. By way of summary, then, it seems appropriate to list a number of observations on this development that might be usefully considered by future investigators. These observations follow in no particular order.

1. Both curriculums were intended to supplement ordinary classroom instruction. The fanfare that greeted the introduction of CAI anticipated a minor revolution in classroom practice as a result of its appearance. Despite extensive workshops, individual conferences, and daily reports on the progress of individual students, very few changes in the practice of classroom teachers were observed that could be attributed to CAI. Student achievement increased under CAI, but the impact on classroom practice was minor. Therefore, a supplemental role appears appropriate for CAI in beginning reading.

2. There was a shift in instructional strategy away from a tutorial approach toward a drill-and-practice approach. In beginning reading, as in other curriculum areas, it was difficult to anticipate and prespecify what problems a student might have with the material presented and what remedial material would help the student. It was apparent that CAI has a unique capability for bringing about the rapid, automatic reading responses discussed by Fries (1963) and by LaBerge and Samuels (1974), and the Stanford curriculum increasingly emphasized these responses. *Drill-and-practice* may be a regrettable term, evoking images of school as a sweat shop, but it describes the approach taken, and it was impossible to avoid the observation that the students enjoyed the CAI presented.

3. There was no discernible drop in student achievement resulting from the reduction in CAI terminal capabilities experienced in shifting from the 1500 instructional system to the PDP-10 system. The detailed instructional theory telling how best, or even optimally, to use the full capabilities of the 1500-system student terminals simply did not and does not exist. It is possible that the best instructional ideas available applied to both systems would make relatively little difference in instructional outcome and would fail to justify the great differences in their costs. For that matter, the necessary attention to each letter in the typed responses required by the PDP-10 curriculum may have been responsible for some of its success, whereas the facile light-pen responses used in the 1500 curriculum may have reduced its instructional effectiveness. There is a tendency in CAI development and in the development of instructional systems in general to equate the elaborateness of the materials and procedures required with the instructional value of the system. Experience with the Stanford beginning reading projects indicates that some tempering of this tendency is in order.

4. Techniques of optimized instruction were increasingly used. Promising trends in the development of the reading curriculums were experimental applications of control theory (Atkinson, 1972), quantitative models of

memory (Fletcher, 1975), and techniques of inequality aversion (Jamison et al., 1976). As Atkinson's (1974) overview indicated, work in this area was barely begun, but the utility of these techniques and the initial research issues appear to be well established.

5. Curriculum development became less theory driven and more pragmatic. This trend was particularly evident in decoding instruction: Letter names were not used in the 1500 curriculum, but they were in the PDP–10 curriculum (although neither curriculum presented letter sounds in isolation); spelling was not taught in the 1500 curriculum, but it was taught in the PDP–10 curriculum; only "regular" words and nonwords were taught in the 1500 curriculum, but "irregular" words were presented as vocabulary items in the PDP–10 curriculum and nonwords were not taught.

6. Use of games, stories, and other motivational materials decreased. The computer system was increasingly viewed as an expensive, valuable resource, and techniques for its efficient use gradually increased in relative value. This trend was aided by the students' enthusiasm for CAI, which did not appear affected by the increasing emphasis on efficiency in the curriculum.

7. An emphasis on decoding skills was maintained throughout the development. Literal and interpretive comprehension instruction can be presented by computer, as the fourth- through sixth-grade CAI reading curriculum documented by Fletcher and Suppes (1972) illustrates, but it was never the judgment of the Stanford group that the proportion of comprehension instruction to decoding instruction should have been increased in the beginning reading programs. Notably, Fletcher and Atkinson (1972) found that their sample of CAI beginning reading students scored significantly higher on the paragraph meaning subtest of the Stanford Achievement Test than did a control sample of non-CAI students.

8. From an operational standpoint, it was simpler to schedule CAI in a central location for all members of a classroom at one time than it was to present CAI to one student at a time, using single terminals installed in classrooms. The setting for the Stanford curriculums consisted of a single room in which all the computer terminals used by the school were installed and which was staffed by an experienced CAI proctor. For older children, it might have been reasonable to distribute terminals to individual classrooms, but it was not reasonable for the students in grades K–3 who used the Stanford CAI.

9. Beginning reading achievement was about the same for boys and girls under CAI. This result was first announced by Atkinson in 1968, and it persisted throughout the history of the development. To some extent, this result was presaged by McNeil's (1964) finding of superior reading achievement by boys over girls in kindergarten using programmed reading materials, but it was still surprising given well-established (e.g., Maccoby,

1966) expectations or superiority in primary-school girls over boys for verbal intellectual functioning.

10. A favorable economic argument can be made for CAI. Using computer cost data of the late 1960s and assuming system support for 1,000 terminals, Jamison et al. (1976) were able to present a favorable argument for the cost effectiveness of the Stanford PDP–10 beginning reading curriculum. With the recent, dramatic reductions in the costs of computer processing and memory, it seems likely that a stronger economic argument could be made for CAI, assuming a much smaller computer system.

11. Computer operating systems have fundamental implications for the type of CAI they can support. Although considerable effort has been expended in the design of programming languages for CAI, little attention has been paid to the design of computer operating systems for CAI. Some preliminary notions were documented by Fletcher and Schulz (1973), but considerably more should be done to identify appropriate specifications for CAI operating systems.

12. Although the strands approach was originally developed for arithmetic CAI, it is a powerful and relevant technique for beginning reading instruction as well. Some general discussion of the strands approach was presented by Suppes (1967), and it was the approach used in the PDP–10 curriculum described above. The approach appears to be of significant, general utility in the design of CAI and deserving of attention from educational researchers.

One conclusion from the Stanford projects might be that CAI has genuine possibilities for the improvement of beginning reading instruction and that the work of the Stanford development should be continued. Like many research efforts, the projects raised more questions than they answered. However, if the central problem in beginning reading instruction is to make it sensitive, on a moment-to-moment basis, to the individual needs of students, then CAI may be the most cost-effective alternative for large-scale solution of this problem.

ACKNOWLEDGMENTS

Most of the work discussed in this chapter was funded by the Office of Education, which was the principal agency for support of the IBM 1500 curriculum, and by the National Science Foundation, which was the principal agency for support of the DEC PDP–10 curriculum. Both the Carnegie Foundation, which provided initial funding for CAI curriculum development at Stanford, and the Office of Naval Research, which has provided steady support for basic research in CAI at Stanford, should also be acknowledged for their contributions to work discussed in this chapter. Sincere appreciation is expressed to E. G. Aiken, D. J. Chesler, and T. M. Duffy for their comments on early versions of this chapter.

REFERENCES

Atkinson, R. C. Computerized instruction and the learning process. *American Psychologist,* 1968, *23,* 225–239.

Atkinson, R. C. Ingredients for a theory of instruction. *American Psychologist,* 1972, *27,* 921–931.

Atkinson, R. C. Teaching children to read using a computer. *American Psychologist,* 1974, *29,* 169–178.

Atkinson, R. C., & Fletcher, J. D. Teaching children to read using a computer. *Reading Teacher,* 1972, *25,* 319–327.

Atkinson, R. C., Fletcher, J. D., Lindsay, J., Campbell, J. O., & Barr, A. Computer-assisted instruction in initial reading. *Educational Technology,* 1973, *13,* 27–37.

Atkinson, R. C., & Hansen, D. N. Computer-assisted instruction in initial reading: The Stanford project. *Reading Research Quarterly,* 1966, *2,* 5–15.

Bloomfield, L., & Barnhart, C. L. *Let's read: A linguistic approach.* Detroit: Wayne State University Press. 1961.

Carroll, J. B. The analysis of reading instruction: Perspectives from psychology and linguistics. In E. R. Hilgard (Ed.), *Theories of learning and instruction.* Chicago: University of Chicago Press, 1964.

Carterette, E. C., & Jones, M. H. Phoneme and letter patterns in children's language. In K. S. Goodman (Ed.), *The psycholinguistic nature of the reading process.* Detroit: Wayne State University Press, 1968.

Chomsky, N., & Halle, M. *The sound pattern of English.* New York: Harper & Row, 1968.

Crowder, N. A. Automated tutoring by means of intrinsic programming. In E. E. Galanter (Ed.), *Automatic teaching: The state of the art.* New York: Wiley, 1959.

Fletcher, J. D. *Transfer from alternative presentations of spelling patterns in initial reading* (Tech. Rep. No. 216). Stanford, Cal.: Stanford University, Institute for Mathematical Studies in the Social Sciences, 1973. (ERIC Document Reproduction Service No. ED 083 534).

Fletcher, J. D. Models of the learner in computer-assisted instruction. *Journal of Computer-Based Instruction,* 1975, *1,* 118–126.

Fletcher, J. D., & Atkinson, R. C. Evaluation of the Stanford CAI program in initial reading. *Journal of Educational Psychology,* 1972, *63,* 597–602.

Fletcher, J. D., & Schulz, R. W. Providing software support for computer-assisted instruction. *Journal of Educational Data Processing,* 1973, *10,* 14–18.

Fletcher, J. D., & Suppes, P. Computer-assisted instruction in reading: Grades 4–6. *Educational Technology,* 1972, *12,* 45–49.

Fries, C. C. *Linguistics and reading.* New York: Holt, Rinehart & Winston, 1963.

Fries, C. C., Wilson, R. G., & Rudolph, M. K. *Merrill linguistic readers.* Columbus, Ohio: Merrill, 1966.

Gibson, E. J. The ontogeny of reading. *American Psychologist,* 1970, *25,* 136–143.

Hanna, P. R., Hanna, J. S., Hodges, R. E., & Rudorf, E. H., Jr. *Phoneme-grapheme correspondences as cues to spelling improvement* (U.S. Office of Education Publication No. OE-32008). Washington, D.C.: U.S. Government Printing Office, 1966. (ERIC Document Reproduction Service No. ED 003 321).

Hansen, D. N., & Rodgers, T. S. An explanation of psycholinguistic units in initial reading. In K. S. Goodman (Ed.), *The psycholinguistic nature of the reading process.* Detroit: Wayne State University Press, 1968.

Jamison, D., Fletcher, J. D., Suppes, P., & Atkinson, R. C. Cost and performance of computer-assisted instruction for education of disadvantaged children. In J. Froomkin, D. Jamison, and R. Radner (Eds.), *Education as an industry.* Cambridge, Mass.: National Bureau of Economics Research, Inc., Ballinger Publishing Company, 1976.

LaBerge, D., & Samuels, S. J. Toward a theory of automatic information processing in reading. *Cognitive Psychology,* 1974, *6,* 293–323.

Maccoby, E. E. Sex differences in intellectual functioning. In E. E. Maccoby (Ed.), *The development of sex differences.* Stanford, Cal.: Stanford University Press, 1966.

McCracken, G., & Walcutt, C. C. *Basic reading.* Philadelphia: Lippincott, 1963.

McNeil, J. D. Programmed instruction versus usual classroom procedures in teaching boys to read. *American Educational Research Journal,* 1964, *1,* 113–119.

Rodgers, T. S. *Linguistic considerations in the design of the Stanford computer-based curriculum in initial reading* (Tech. Rep. No. 111). Stanford, Cal.: Stanford University, Institute for Mathematical Studies in the Social Sciences, 1967. (ERIC Document Reproduction Service No. ED 012 688).

Sullivan, M. W. *Reading.* Palo Alto, Cal.: Behavioral Research Laboratories, 1967.

Suppes, P. Some theoretical models for mathematics learning. *Journal of Research and Development in Education,* 1967, *1,* 5–22.

Suppes, P., Jerman, M., & Brian, D. *Computer-assisted instruction: Stanford's 1965–66 arithmetic program.* New York: Academic Press, 1968.

Thorndike, E. L., & Barnhart, C. L. (Eds.), *Thorndike–Barnhart beginning dictionary.* New York: Scott, Foresman, 1964.

Venezky, R. L. English orthography: Its graphical structure and its relation to sound. *Reading Research Quarterly,* 1967, *2,* 75–105.

Venezky, R. L. *The structure of English orthography.* The Hague: Mouton, 1970.

Venezky, R. L., & Weir, R. *A study of selected spelling-to-sound correspondence patterns* (U.S. Office of Education Cooperative Research Project No. 3090). Washington, D.C.: U.S. Government Printing Office, 1966. (ERIC Document Reproduction Service No. ED 010 843).

Wright, W. W. *The rainbow dictionary.* Cleveland, Ohio: World Publishing, 1959.

DISCUSSION

12

Harmony and Cacophony from a Theory–Practice Relationship

Richard L. Venezky
University of Delaware

The chapters in this volume, especially when viewed under the aegis of a theory–practice relationship, bear many similarities to catching tigers in the desert. For this latter activity, we have no dearth of theoretically sound positions. One, for example, posits the placing of a hunter in a cage in the middle of a desert and then doing an inversion of axes. This of course places the hunter outside the case and the tiger (along with, incidentally, the desert) inside the cage. Unfortunately, the relationship between such theoretical positions and the three-dimensional world of tiger hunting, just as that between theories of reading and the activities of reading instruction, has so far eluded rational explication. The following comments are concerned with this relationship, or the lack thereof, in the chapters of this volume and are organized like a concerto.

First, there is an opening movement, an andante, dealing with theory; then a somewhat slower movement, a largo, although not totally lugubrious, dealing with practice; and finally a very quick presto dealing with the relationship between the two.

When the baton is put down, I'll add some didactic comments—a brief verbal coda—similar to the way Leonard Bernstein does when he finishes with *Peter and the Wolf* and then proceeds to play melodies on the bassoon and various other instruments to show the audience which animals are represented by which sounds.

THEORY: DISORDER OR ORDER?

In discussing theory, I want to touch on what theory is, to mention theories we have now that are relevant to reading—and especially to reading for compensatory education children—and then to discuss the difficulties in dealing with theories in relation to reading instruction.

The literature on the epistemology of science, especially that by Karl Popper (1959) and Abraham Kaplan (1964), portrays modern experimental science as progressing from observation through cycles of hypotheses and experiments until a theory emerges that can predict, to someone's satisfaction, the observable phenomena in question and, equally important, that is no longer seriously challenged. A true theory must not only account for observable phenomena; it must also have wide acceptance.

The field of reading has never been at a loss for hypotheses or theories. In the beginning there was, for example, the rhythmic eye movement theory. Javal (1878) found from observation that eye movements during reading were not continuous but occurred in jumps, or saccades. Javal (and others) concluded, furthermore, that these movements were rhythmic. This theory was fairly well accepted for about 20 or 30 years, but with the introduction of the corneal reflection technique for measuring eye movements, data emerged that were not compatible with this notion, and therefore alternative theories were formulated.

Related to a theory is a model. *Model* is a term that is used quite loosely by nearly everyone today, perhaps as loosely as the term *system*. However, a model typically is a complex set of theories constructed to deal with a phenomenon in which every single element or component cannot be probed individually. A model is constructed from what is known, the gaps are filled in with hypotheses, and the resulting device used as a framework for predicting outcomes that are experimentally verifiable.

Kleene (1956) set out, probably better than anyone since, the idea of a model being justified when we are dealing with something quite complex— too complex to keep track of all the separate components. We would not, for example, call Fechner's law a model in the same sense as when we use this term in relation to word-processing models. We might in a loose sense, but we certainly wouldn't want to add that level of sophistication to something as seemingly simple as Fechner's relationship. Models growing out of theories are very common in the physical and biological sciences. There is, for example, the Ptolemaic model of the universe, which is still a reasonably good approximation to observable phenomena and certainly was in its time a good predictor of celestial behavior. There is also Bohr's model of the atom and the Crick and Watson double-helix model for DNA.

All these models have served useful functions by holding together complexes of theories, filling in gaps with hypotheses, and eventually instigating further experiments that led to changes in the models. If a model does not predict something we can test, that is, if a model cannot and does not lead to its own modification or destruction, it is a useless model. We don't have much use for models of complex phenomena that don't allow us to build improvements on the models.

In reading, there are theories and models of the processes of reading (whether in the child or the adult), theories and models of the learning process (either learning in general or the acquisition of literacy itself), and theories and models of instruction and the instructional environment. However, I tend to agree with Gibson and Levin (1975) that we probably don't know enough to build useful models of the total reading process and that we are truly chasing after the wind in doing so. As I look at the current attempts to model the total reading process, with a "psycholinguistic" box here and a "morpheme" box there, I think of a comment commonly attributed to Bertolt Brecht: "When you have everything in the wrong place, that's disorder; when you have nothing in all the right places, that's order." Order in this sense is what we tend to find in most, if not all, of the general models of reading.

Where, though, we do seem to gain profitably in experimenting with models of reading is where we have models of specific and usually quite limited processes in the overall reading process. For example, Hochberg (1970) developed "The Guided Eye Movement Model." From his own and other studies, he hypothesized that readers, while focusing on one part of the text, could look quite far ahead in the periphery and interpret enough of the visual information to decide where to focus next. Included in this model were various types of search mechanisms. The work of McConkie and Rayner (1975), however, in showing extreme limitations on what the eye can do with information in the periphery, casts considerable doubt on the validity of this model. Nevertheless, this was an interesting model that led to interesting experimentation.

In the Smith and Kleiman chapter and in the Juola, Schadler, Chabot, McCaughey, and Wait chapter there are rather good discussions of the most sophisticated and useful models we have of reading processes—those for information processing during word recognition. It is useful to remember in relation to these efforts, however, that the earliest information-processing model for word recognition did not originate with Sperling (1963) or Neisser (1967) but with Quantz in 1897. Quantz's model included stage-by-stage processing, with iconic storage, read-out into immediate memory, and short-term memory components. This model developed from a concern for measuring the speed of various mental events, a concern that was fundamental to experimental psychology at that time. Quantz's model is quite interesting in its own right and surprisingly similar to many of the current word-processing models.

Smith and Kleiman describe how a model is built and then used to derive experiments that themselves lead to changes in the model. The authors stress three problems that must be resolved and that still require improvements in the model: (1) the problem of units of interpretation; (2) the problem of lexical access; and (3) the problem of context effects. The utility of models for building better models is further exemplified in the Juola et al. chapter with a discussion of word-recognition studies that used fixed sets of target letters. The apparent ability of subjects in such paradigms to use the features of the target letters to reduce response time necessitates changes in the authors' model to account for possible overt control by readers of their own reading strategies. Reading models require a control mechanism to account for changes in behavior based on the input. The reader (or subject) seems to say in certain reading situations, "Let's try a new strategy, let's do something different," and somehow the model has to account for this. Such a mechanism can be found in models of reading inspired by artificial intelligence notions (see Rumelhart, 1977).

This same control mechanism can probably also be used to account for what we are calling inside-out factors. [Eds. Note: See Smith's chapter.] An approach to this was suggested over a decade ago by Broadbent in relation to the frequency effect in word recognition. Broadbent (1967) suggested that when we have a high expectation for a particular input, we are willing to make a decision with less visual information than when we do not have such a high expectation for the input stimulus. So in effect we could account for expectation within an information-processing model in terms of either shifts in criterion levels or shifts in the processing strategy that would allow attention to fewer visual elements.

There are, however, alternatives to the stage-by-stage models that are not presented in this volume. Turvey (1973), for example, hypothesized a complex model based on neurological concepts in which information in different forms travels at different rates through the system. Thus, gross outlines of figures would be available for matching and decision making before finer visual details would be available. Time-varying transmission will of course also allow a shift in criterion level, as was just suggested for a control mechanism in stage-by-stage models.

Turvey's model, as many other models including Massaro's (1975), incorporated parallel processing at an initial stage. Turvey also raised an anomaly that I think merits further attention in discussions of information-processing models. Although we think in terms of features like lines and curves building up into wholes, Turvey pointed out that perception must also include processes that work in the opposite direction. We don't know whether we have a straight line or a curve until we have the whole. What could be a straight line in one type of figure might be a curve in another. Only when retinal images are translated into whole units can the extraction of features from the whole take place for recognition.

Another area that is not discussed in any of the chapters in this volume is that of developmental models for reading. For information-processing approaches, the work of Haith (1971) and his colleagues seems particularly relevant. What is important about their work, even though it deals with geometric figures and not letters, is that it explores the initial stages of information processing and demonstrates where children do and do not differ from adults in visual processing. One of the results of this work, if the data are being properly interpreted, is that in the earliest stages of processing, including the building up of an iconic image, the recognition of a single figure, and the recognition of images in the periphery of the visual field, are almost identical for the 5-year-old and the adult. The two age levels begin to perform differently only when a number of objects must be retained in immediate memory prior to the selection of a response. One hopes that this line of inquiry can be pursued with letters and words, because it seems especially promising for building developmental models of word recognition. (Another line of inquiry that I believe is important for building developmental models is exemplified by the work of Golinkoff, 1974, and of Rosinski and Wheeler, 1972, which examined the development of the recognition of orthographic regularity. Their methodology usually involved judgments by children of which of a pair of synthetic words is more like a real English word.)

Although information-processing viewpoints are motivating most of the word-recognition studies today, there is a caution that should be made that I think was best stated in Tennyson's (1911) version of the Arthurian legend. Arthur, on his death bed, states: "The old order changeth, yielding place to new, and God fulfills himself in many ways, lest one good custom should corrupt the world." What I mean is that there is always room for alternative approaches, whether for convergence or for simply ensuring that a particular explanation is not ignored. Certainly the approach used by Gibson and her colleagues in their original studies of spelling units would be a good alternative (Gibson, Osser, & Pick, 1963; Gibson, Pick, Osser, & Hammond, 1962).

When we turn to models and theories about learning to read, the air becomes considerably more murky, and what we hear often sounds like noises from a shroud, to borrow from the Ancient Mariner. We have, for example, Piaget's (1935/1970) theories, which don't attend directly to reading at all but have been interpreted by Furth and Wachs (1974) and others to imply that reading is a rather low-level skill and that reading pedagogy should center on discovery procedures, so that children will find on their own what reading is all about. However, many reading skills, such as attending to the orientation of letters, are abilities that children could rarely discover on their own. If there is anything children discover in initial stages of perceptual learning, it is the invariance of labels for objects with orientation change. A cup is a cup whether the handle goes one way or another. Letters and numbers are the first objects, and probably among the only objects, that children ever encounter in their early schooling in which orientation makes a difference for labeling. The attempts by Piaget's followers in the United States to induce children to discover these types of relationships, both in the verbal domain and in the sound domain, have been unsuccessful.

Another set of theories about learning to read can be teased out of the futile arguments over the relative efficacies of instructional methods. The conflict between so-called whole-word instruction and phonics instruction boils down, not to differences over the value of letter–sound learning (both methods accept it), but instead to theoretical differences over the variables that are important for introducing reading. The whole-word people claim that letter sounds are too abstract and too complex for children to manipulate in their initial encounters with reading. Therefore, instruction is started with whole words and sentences to build up motivation, interest, and sensitivity to the task. The hard-core letter–sound people, on the other hand, deny the importance of affective variables.

Another example where practice implies theory is found in programs like *Distar* that carry implicit assumptions about learning to read and particularly about information loads that children at different stages in their development and from different backgrounds can handle. [Eds. Note: See Bartlett's chapter.]

From schooling theorists like Stephens (1967) come theories that are very different from the views in this volume. According to Stephens, the teacher's role is not really to teach very much but to give children an idea of what is important, so that in their natural exchanges with other children and with adults outside of the classroom they will attend to those elements in the environment that are important to acquire.

And finally, a new set of theories on reading instruction are emerging from studies by Weber (1971) and by the New York State Education Department (1974), which suggests that the most important variables for success in reading are such matters as instructional organization, teacher attitude, and building-level leadership and not the basic skills of the child or the particular instructional method that the teacher uses. I think that these studies should be taken seriously. Certainly the Clay chapter takes a rather strong view on what the important variables for reading success should be by stressing teacher training and teacher-centered instruction as opposed to the early CAI views described by Fletcher that wanted the teacher as far away from the child as possible.

PRACTICE: MAKING SENSE

Having displayed how variegated reading theory is, I will now turn to the difficulties of defining reading practice. One problem in discussing reading practice is that we do not have a clear task definition for reading instruction.

Many who have developed reading programs are aware of the complexities of the instructional task, but few have attempted to treat instructional decisions overtly. It is refreshing, therefore, to see the attention given to the instructional process by Bartlett, who reviews two reading programs: Chomsky; Liberman and Shankweiler; Fletcher; and Calfee and Drum, who discuss particular kinds of assessment tests.

I'll use letter–sound learning to give an idea of the number and complexity of decisions that must be made in instructional design and also to give an example of what we would have to attend to if we wanted all classroom practice to derive from theory. In doing this, I am assuming that reasons exist for teaching letter–sound correspondences. One of the first decisions that has to be made is how to teach them. Do we use inductive or deductive approaches? Perhaps there is some theory we can draw on here. Many people argue that inductive approaches are considerably better than deductive approaches at the early grade levels. But what if we were teaching letter–sound correspondences to adult illiterates? Would we teach rules, or would we not teach rules? What empirical base would we draw on to make that particular decision?

How many and what types of exemplars would we use in introducing letter–sound patterns? A recent study on letter–sound learning indicated that this latter question is quite important (Venezky, 1974). For example, children in grades 1 and 2 are introduced to the patterns for the letter *c* in initial position. In this position, *c* has a soft sound if followed by *e, i,* or *y*; otherwise, it has a hard sound. Children in the lower grades usually do not encounter exceptions to this rule. (*Cello* is probably the only word that most people ever see in their lifetimes that is an exception.) What tends to happen, regardless of reading program, is that children don't learn this particular pattern as well as many patterns that are much more complex. They develop a strong response bias toward the hard sound /k/ in early reading and don't completely overcome this bias by the end of letter–sound instruction. In fact, adults don't generally do better than 70% to 75% correct on the soft pattern when tested with synthetic words (Calfee, Venezky, & Chapman, 1969; Venezky, 1974).

If we look carefully at what children are trained on when they learn the *c* pattern, we see that in the most popular reading programs, about 95% of the intial *c* words that are introduced through third grade have the hard pronunciation. Perhaps three or four words in these readers begin with soft *c*. This bias in exemplars seems to have an effect on what is acquired, regardless of whether a rule is verbalized or not..

Beyond the question of exemplars lies another question concerning *c* and *g* and the five vowel letters. Do we introduce the alternate pronunciations concurrently or successively? Levin and Watson (1963) raised the possibility of concurrent introduction, and Williams (1968) and some of her colleagues tried experimentally to compare the two approaches, as did the Cornell

Reading Project (Robinson–Mitchell, 1968). The conclusions from the Cornell project confirm what I suspect most reading teachers would say on this matter, namely, that the bright children profit from concurrent presentation but the slower children are confused by it.

Another question concerns word position. Do we introduce letters for patterns in initial position because that is the easiest position to attend to, or do we introduce them in other positions so that children will not overattend to beginnings of words? Hill (1936) showed that one of the major effects of early instruction in reading was to shift the child's attention from various parts of the word to the beginning of the word. Reading programs place major emphasis on the initial part of a word and thereby distract the child from attending carefully to the remainder of the word.

Do we use contrast in instruction or don't we? Do we take phonetically similar items, like *pet* and *pat,* and present them together to help the child make discriminations, or do we keep them apart to avoid confusions?

How do we relate letters to sounds? Do we present sounds in isolation, or do we believe Bloomfield (1942) and Fries (1963)—that this is contrary to the dictates of nature—and present them only in context?

Do we associate letters directly to sounds, or do we use letter names to mediate between letters and sounds, or do we use objects to mediate? And which prereading skills should we teach before formal reading instruction begins?

Liberman and Shankweiler and Chomsky suggest prereading exercises that would bring the child's attention to the phonic nature of the spelling system. Johnson, in discussing learning disabilities and the diagnosis of intrasensory before intersensory abilities, also touches on this particular problem. We have a large literature, including studies by Elkonin (1963), Zhurova (1963), Bruce (1964), and others, that attends in a misleading way with this problem, as I discuss shortly.

Do we use only meaningful words, or do we use nonsense materials?

How do we sequence letter–sound correspondences? Do we introduce overtly all of the consonant clusters that exist in English (as does at least one commercial program), or do we depend on transfer to shorten the training period.

And what kind of assessment do we do? This is a question attended to in part by Calfee and Drum. How much assessment do we do? What kinds of assessment instruments do we use? Do we need highly reliable ones with large numbers of items, or can we teach teachers to do informal assessment?

It is clear that we cannot and probably should not research all of these questions. As Fletcher points out in describing the Stanford CAI project, building a reading program requires making many arbitrary decisions. Where classroom experience is not available, you make the best judgment you can, observe what happens, and make modifications if necesary. It is in a sense trusting that Francis Bacon was correct in saying that truth will emerge more rapidly from error than from chaos.

FUMBLING FROM THEORY INTO PRACTICE

Whatever might be the difficulties of building sound instructional programs, the task of finding practical implications from reading theory is exceedingly more difficult. The gap between the two is the La Brea tar pit of education and mires many well-intending people. For example, Liberman and Shankweiler ask us to "consider what we know about our writing system—namely, that it is alphabetic and not ideographic. From this, it would seem to follow that instructional procedures should inform children early on that the printed word is a model of the components and phonemes and their particular succession in the spoken word."

As sound as this statement seems at first glance, I can find, upon reflection, neither logical nor empirical support for it. Instructional decisions have to be based on a large number of issues such as the entry level skills of the child, the instructional methods the teachers can use and their relative complexity, and the available resources. It is incorrect to argue that a desired terminal behavior is the sole determinant of the instructional process. A number of strategies exist for teaching letters and sounds, yet there is not experimental justification for claiming that the best way to teach these is to make the alphabetic nature of our writing system clear to the child from the beginning of instruction.

Premature leaps from theory to practice represent one problem. A second problem is represented by good experimental evidence that fails to influence practice. Singer (1970), in a paper called "Research That Should Have Made a Difference," mentioned four or five studies that attended to issues that are important for reading instruction, yet little that was discovered in these studies ever got into practice. For example, he cited one study that demonstrated that choral reading—that is, reading in unison—is almost worthless for beginning readers. Children in the early grades read at different rates and in general cannot adjust their reading rates easily; therefore, they have difficulty reading along with others. Yet in at least one program in this country and in the teaching of reading in Mexico, this practice is still favored.

The history of reading instruction in this country shows a pervasive similarity between reading practice and religion. Both reading methods and religion tend to be charismatically based. We have in religion, of course, the charismatic individual, the hero with the thousand faces: Moses, Jesus, Peter, Joseph Smith, and so on. In reading we have an exact parallel: Parker, Gates, Flesch, Pitmann, and the other purveyors of the ultimate instructional methodology. Educators justify particular practices on the authority of the particular reading god they worship. And when reading becomes a problem, they throw out one god and bring in a new one. "The king is dead, long live the king." There is truly a belief here in the one best method, which derives, I suspect, from the American belief in the pastoral dream. There is one best way to teach reading, and we must constantly search for this holy grail of education. This seems to be more befitting of Dr. Pangloss than it does of educational research, yet it seems to go on and on and on.

Some of this attitude is attributed to the role that publishers play. The reading market in the elementary grades alone is rumored to be over $300 million a year. One publisher supposedly invested over $8 million in developing its latest reading system. No matter what new evidence is revealed about reading instruction, this particular publisher will not be changing its reading program very soon, not with $8 million already invested in it.

Finally, I want to return for a moment to the studies by Elkonin (1963), Zhurova (1963), Bruce (1964), and others to discuss the limits on what we can learn from a laboratory. Elkonin, Zhurova, Bruce, and various others proved conclusively that children before some magic age—6 in Bruce's study, 7 in Zhurova's, and so on—could not perform certain tasks that involve manipulating abstract sounds. The children in these studies couldn't segment words, or repeat the first sound of a word, or do other sound processing tasks before 6 or 7 years of age. Here was quite convincing evidence from reasonably well designed studies. However, most of these studies involved 15 or 20 training trials on some small set of stimuli and 15 or 20 transfer trials. And from that evidence, the authors generalized to whole theories about reading, or about sound segmentation, or about the development of certain abilities in children.

The great shock comes when you take these tasks, or slight modifications of them, into a classroom with the same age children and start doing these things day after day. You soon discover that almost all kids from kindergarten up can be taught all these taks without tears or frustration, given repeated practice and appropriate sequencing of tasks. There is a world of difference between the ongoing, day-by-day activities of the classroom and the laboratory. One of the most pressing needs today in reading research is for improved methodologies for experimentation in the classroom.

Perhaps one brief example will summarize these last few points. The role of letter names in reading instruction is problematic. There are references to letter names in instruction in the Fletcher chapter, the Liberman and Shankweiler chapter, and the Chomsky chapter. Fletcher notes some well-known correlational studies that show that letter names are good predictors of reading success, but he also states that the experimental attempts to show facilitation by letter naming of any reading task have not been successful.

Based on this review of the literature, no direct attempts to teach letter names were made in the 1500 curriculum, but letter–name instruction mysteriously appeared in the PDP-10 curriculum.

Liberman and Shankweiler say, on the other hand, that we should begin reading instruction, as many so-called phonics programs do, by teaching the child to associate the shape of the letter with its name and the sound it makes. There are some empirical data relevant to this issue, yet none answers the questions in a satisfactory way, mainly because the experimental designs employed did not control for many important classroom variables. We also have data on the use of labeling in discrimination of objects by adults using geometric figures, fingerprints, and other patterns. We also have the studies that Fletcher points out on the effects of letter names on word and letter discrimination.

The main advocate of using letter names for mediators in letter–sound learning is Durrell (1958). But Durrell must not have looked very closely at the relationship between letter names and letter sounds. Three of the letter names (*w, h,* and *y*) don't even contain the sounds for which they are supposed to mediate. Seven others (the five vowels, *c,* and *g*) do not contain the sound that is typically taught first for the letters they represent, and of the others, seven are made up of vowel–consonant combinations, and the rest are made up of consonant–vowel combinations.

In addition, anecdotal evidence from Russia, Israel, and the United States indicates that confusions often arise when the letter name is stressed along with the letter sound. The child often perseverates on the name and uses it to respond to the letter when the sound is sought.

FUTURE DIRECTIONS

There are other problems in relating theory to practice, but perhaps it's time to conclude by asking where should we go from here. The first direction I think we have to take is to refocus attention on the school, the classroom, and the teacher. We have to begin by defining problems that exist at these levels and then work back to the laboratory. That is the first step.

Second, it's clear, as Conant (1963) stated years ago, that major changes in teacher training are needed. Courses on reading methodology in colleges and universities do not prepare teachers for making their own instructional decisions. In many cases, these courses prepare teachers only for locating and following the teacher's guide in a published program. We also need to develop efficient in-service training methods, and as Rosner suggests in his chapter, we need a better dissemination network. This country seems to have so much money for education that 5,000 groups of teachers around the country every summer can sit down and reinvent objectives for kindergarten through 12th-grade reading without anyone knowing what the other is doing. Perhaps it would be helpful to circulate some of these.

Third, I think we should follow up both the studies of school organization, such as the Weber (1971) study and the New York State Education Department (1974) study, and a study done by Barton and Wilder (1964) for the Carnegie Corporation a number of years ago on the training of college-level specialists. This study examined, among other things, who the reading specialists were, what and how often they published, and how their attitudes about reading instruction differed from those of practitioners.

Fourth, I think we need a new science of experimentation in the classroom. Piaget (1935/1970) hinted over 40 years ago how this might be done with what he called "experimental pedagogy." Ongoing classroom programs would be examined, small changes would be made in the instructional methods, and measurements would be made of marginal gain or loss. This process would be repeated with other program components to build up an understanding of how instruction works.

At the same time, however, we need to continue basic research. Good researchers must be encouraged to pursue problems related to human processing to provide the fundamental information that is essential for understanding complex phenomenon.

We need, though, to improve the communication among researchers. We have now in the word-recognition area something that approaches the high level of communication that is found in Watson's account of the new development of the DNA model and in the literature from the turn of the century on the experimental study of reading. At that time communication seemed important. The laboratories where work was going on were well identified, and researchers visited back and forth and referred to each other in polite tones, as was the tendency in the literature of that period. It would be a pleasure to see this going on again in reading research rather than seeing, as we do outside the word-perception area, a myriad of isolated researchers scattered in cluttered obscurity around North America (and abroad), doing very often the same things with almost no communication among them.

REFERENCES

Barton, H., & Wilder, D. E. Research and practice in the teaching of reading: Progress report. In M. B. Miles (Ed.), *Innovation in education*. New York: Columbia University, Teachers College Press, 1964.

Bloomfield, L. Linguistics and reading. *Elementary English Review*, 1942, *19*, 125–130; 183–186.

Broadbent, D. E. Word-frequency effect and response bias. *Psychological Review*, 1967, *74*, 1–15.

Bruce, D. J. The analysis of word sounds by young children. *British Journal of Educational Psychology,* 1964, *31,* 158–169.

Calfee, R., Venezky, R., & Chapman, R. *Pronunciation of synthetic words with predictable and unpredictable letter-sound correspondences* (Tech. Rep. 71). Madison, Wisc.: Wisconsin Research and Development Center for Cognitive Learning, 1969.

Conant, J. B. *The education of American teachers.* New York: McGraw-Hill, 1963.

Durrell, D. D. Success in first grade reading. *Journal of Education,* 1958, *140,* 2–6.

Elkonin, D. B. The psychology of mastering the elements of reading. In B. Simon & J. Simon (Eds.), *Educational psychology in the U.S.S.R.* London: Routledge & Kegan Paul, 1963.

Fries, C. C. *Linguistics and reading.* New York: Holt, Rinehart & Winston, 1963.

Furth, G., & Wachs, H. *Thinking goes to school.* New York: Oxford University Press, 1974.

Gibson, E. J., & Levin, H. *The psychology of reading.* Cambridge, Mass.: MIT Press, 1975.

Gibson, E. J., Osser H., & Pick, A. D. A study of the development of grapheme–phoneme correspondences. *Journal of Verbal Learning and Verbal Behavior,* 1963, *2,* 142–146.

Gibson, E. J., Pick, A., Osser, H., & Hammond, M. The role of grapheme–phoneme correspondence in the perception of words. *American Journal of Psychology,* 1962, *75,* 554–570.

Golinkoff, R. M. *Children's discrimination of English spelling patterns with redundant auditory information.* Paper presented at the meeting of the American Educational Research Association, Chicago, April 1974.

Haith, M. M. Developmental changes in visual information processing and short-term visual memory. *Human Development,* 1971, *14,* 249–261.

Hill, M. B. A study of the process of word discrimination in individuals beginning to read. *Journal of Educational Research,* 1936, *29,* 487–500.

Hochberg, J. Components of literacy: Speculations and exploration research. In H. Levin & J. P. Williams (Eds.), *Basic studies in reading.* New York: Basic Books, 1970.

Javal, L. Essai sur la physiologie de la lecture. *Annales D'Oculistique,* 1878, *82,* 242–253.

Kaplan, A. *The conduct of inquiry.* San Francisco: Chandler, 1964.

Kleene, S. C. Representation of events in nerve nets and finite automata. In C. E. Shannon & J. M. McCarthy (Eds.), *Annals of Mathematics Studies* (No. 34). Princeton, N.J.: Princeton University Press, 1956.

Levin, H., & Watson, J. The learning of variable grapheme-to-phoneme correspondences. In *A basic research program on reading* (Final report, Project No. 639, U.S. Office of Education). Washington, D.C.: U.S. Government Printing Office, 1963.

Massaro, D. W. *Understanding language: An information processing analysis of speech perception, reading, and psycholinguistics.* New York: Academic Press, 1975.

McConkie, G. W., & Rayner, K. The span of the effective stimulus during a fixation in reading. *Perception & Psychophysics,* 1975, *17,* 578–586.

Neisser, U. *Cognitive psychology.* New York: Appleton-Century-Crofts, 1967.

New York State Education Department. *Reading achievement related to educational and environmental conditions in twelve New York City schools.* Albany, N.Y.: State Education Department, 1974.

Piaget, J. [*Science of education and the psychology of the child*] (D. Coltman, trans.). New York: Orion Press, 1970. (Originally published, 1935.)

Popper, K. *The logic of scientific discovery.* New York: Basic Books, 1959.

Quantz, J. O. Problems in the psychology of reading. *Psychological Monographs,* 1897, *2*(1, Whole No. 5).

Robinson-Mitchell, J. First grade reading study. In *Project literacy reports of research in progress* (No. 9). Ithaca, N.Y.: Cornell Univeristy Press, 1968.

Rosinski, R. R., & Wheeler, K. E. Children's use of orthographic structure in word discrimination. *Psychonomic Science,* 1972, *26,* 97–98.

Rumelhart, D. Toward an interactive model of reading. In S. Dornic (Ed.), *Attention and performance VI*. Hillsdale, N.J.: Lawrence Erlbaum Associates, 1977.

Singer, H. Research that should have made a difference. *Elementary English*, 1970, *47*, 21–24.

Sperling, G. A model for visual memory tasks. *Human Factors*, 1963, *5*, 19–31.

Stephens, J. M. *The processing of schooling*. New York: Holt, Rinehart & Winston, 1967.

Tennyson, A. *Idylls of the king* (W. D. Lewis, Ed. and introduction and notes), New York: Merrill, 1911.

Turvey, M. T. On peripheral and central processes in vision: Inferences from an information-processing analysis of masking with patterned stimuli. *Psychological Review*, 1973, *80*, 1–52.

Venezky, R. L. Theoretical and experimental bases for teaching reading. In T. A. Sebeok (Ed.), *Current trends in linguistics* (Vol. 12). The Hague, Netherlands: Mouton, 1974.

Weber, G. *Inner-city children can be taught to read: Four successful schools* (Occasional Papers No. 18). Washington, D.C.: Council for Basic Education, 1971

Williams, J. P. Successive versus concurrent presentation of multiple grapheme–phoneme correspondence. *Journal of Educational Psychology*, 1968, *59*, 309–314.

Zhurova, L. E. The development of analysis of words into sounds by preschool children. *Soviet Psychology and Psychiatry*, 1963, *2*, 17–27.

13

Old and New Routes from Theory to Practice

Sheldon H. White
Harvard University

This volume is intended to foster translations from theory to educational practice. The "theory" side of it deals mostly with psychological studies of information processing; the "practice" side deals with the teaching of beginning reading. The volume is specialized. It does not deal with all the reearch that might be presumed to bear on education, nor does it deal with all the subjects and goals contained within schools. However, one kind of theory that education obviously needs is theory about how humans learn. And one kind of practice that is central and archetypal in education is the teaching of beginning reading.

I was asked to discuss a linkage between research and practice that ought to be important, if any is, and to seek out and bring up for discussion the central issues of the volume. One of the things this led me to do was to look for small signs of tension or discomfort in order to try to identify the topics and the issues that create excitement. The following are some events that seemed to me to be "critical incidents" during the conference at which earlier versions of the chapters were presented.

The first occurred when one of the speakers was outlining his recent research on word perception. The report was technical and detailed, because much current work on information processing depends on rather refined experiments directed toward the differences among rather sophisticated theories. There was a break in the presentation for some discussion, and Shirley Jackson, a practitioner, asked, "Why are you telling me this? What does any of this have to do with the classroom?" The question had an immediate impact. As soon as it was asked, one did suddenly wonder what, exactly, teachers were supposed to get from a blow-by-blow portrayal of the technicalities of cognitive research. The question was aimed at a specific speaker, but it raised doubts about a major assumption governing the meeting as a whole. How do teachers and researchers benefit when each listens to an account of the other's very different activities? Teacher-researcher conferences are common and commonly polite. Blunt, confronting questions are not often heard in the midst of them. Why not? The intimidation of the professional by the academic? The fear that if the question is asked, some kind of bubble will be burst?

The first critical incident led one to wonder about how meaningful theory is for practitioners; the second critical incident was even more direct and forceful. Frank Smith said flatly that he was skeptical about whether theory can be translated into practice in any genuine way. He pointed out that attempts to translate theory into practice usually rest on forced and oversimplified reasoning: "egregious overgeneralization," "the overlooking of important issues," and "the confusing of causes with consequences." It is quite common nowadays, as we all know, for researchers to proclaim that they have derived a principle for education or, alternatively, for innovators in education to declare that their new procedures rest firmly on current research. Smith, in effect, argued that if we examine many of the advertised linkages between research and practice, we will often find that they are unreal. The translation is invalid on the research side, on the educational side, or both. Do researchers offer only convenient rhetoric for practitioners? Is there an alive and vital connection between research and practice in education?

A third sort of perturbation arose twice during the conference when instances were given of research work that seemingly had implications for education but that had been somehow ignored in practice. Dexter Fletcher spoke as the "ancient mariner," recounting his experience with the development of a computer-assisted method of instruction in beginning reading. That development program had achieved less than fond fantasy might have imagined at the beginning. But nevertheless, it did have some success, and what reward it received for its success was that it was disbanded. There are not, apparently, continuations and explorations of development efforts in the practice of education. Why not? And Douglas Ellson, a conference participant, presented his survey of innovations in education that had shown proven positive effects in evaluation studies. There have been many, many efforts to put forth innovative or compensatory educational programs in recent years. These programs have been evaluated, and the general, easy summary that most people carry around in their heads is that "nothing works." Yet Ellson has carefully sifted through evaluation reports, and he found a small body of studies where the evaluations were of acceptable scientific quality and where the data seem to say that something did indeed work. Now in these cases, we seemingly have instances of research work that was not remote from education, off in the cloudlands of theory, but that consisted of demonstration and development efforts in educational practice. The work shows signs of success, but somehow nobody seems to care. Why not? Isn't innovation in education a real issue? Isn't better education an issue?

Fourth and last, we heard remarks that suggest that we may all be fiddling while Rome burns. Frank Smith stated that he had deep doubts about the ultimate consequence of the spectrum of efforts represented at the conference. He argued that even if we were somehow to solve all the problems that had been raised at the meeting, it might not make much difference for American literacy. To solve our national reading problems, we might have to think about questions other than those of cognition, instructional design, and classroom practice. We might have to address questions of social status, social distribution, politics, and society.

And Elsa Bartlett presented a disturbing analysis of current innovative curricula in beginning reading. She sees a tracking structure built into the educational innovations, a higher level of instruction for the more well-off child, and a lower level of instruction for the child of lower social status. Embedded in these remarks there appears to be a kind of "higher criticism" of the conference, arguing not that its methods are limited but that its goals are empty or even slightly mischievous. The weaker version of this higher criticism would assert that the technicalities of bettering reading instruction are largely irrelevant to the improvement of education. Teachers know how to teach reading and have been proving that for centuries. When they don't succeed, there are problems with access to instruction, not with method. A stronger version of the higher criticism would argue that the "reading problem" in American schools really arises out of poor social arrangements, perhaps as a result of political arrangements that create a conspiracy of the haves against the have-nots. Conferences such as this one are diversionary. They seduce one into obsessing about technicalities rather than worrying about social injustice. They are part of the problem, not part of the answer. Science is the opiate of the scientist.

The foregoing four items constitute my private list of the "critical incidents" that arose during the meeting. They seemed critical because they were all denials, in smaller and larger ways, of the basic and optimistic premise on which the meeting and this volume were established—that basic research is relevant and helpful to education. In selecting these incidents, I have undoubtedly magnified them. After all, if individuals were really and totally persuaded that this kind of interchange is irrelevant or harmful, it is doubtful that they would have consented to participate. But the incidents do bring to the surface doubts, and I try to explore what they mean in this chapter.

OLDER ASSUMPTIONS
OF EDUCATIONAL PSYCHOLOGY

Clay's chapter is helpful in that in two distinct ways, she sets forth what one might call a developmental perspective embodied in her work. One important feature of a developmental perspective is the recognition that the work of the psychologist is directed toward organized systems. Organized systems maintain their integrity through a strategic balance of vital processes. They are not free to learn, adapt, or change in any old way. They can only modify their behaviors in some way consistent with that vital strategic balance (White, 1976). Clay notes at the outset of her chapter that psychologists approaching a group of teachers do not confront a group of people sitting there idly waiting for some wise words. They confront an organized educational system, teachers managing a complex body of educational routines and goals. The psychologists' advice and suggestions must be such that teachers can fit it in among all the other things they have to worry about. Then Clay notes a somewhat similar problem in the teaching of reading. Children have a functioning spoken language system. Part of the problem of teaching them reading lies in the fact that this preexisting organization interferes with the proposed new treatment of language. The teaching of reading must be such that children can fit it in among all the other things they have to worry about.

A somewhat analogous problem confronted us as a conferring group. We talked about the necessity of moving ideas from research into practice. Weren't we all aware that that's all been arranged for? There is a field called educational psychology, well represented in the American Psychological Association and organized separately in the American Educational Research Association. There are textbooks in educational psychology, and until very recently, every single teacher in this country had to pass a course in educational psychology to be certified. All this forms part of a system that is intended to move theory into practice.

Why did we try the conference as a method of moving from theory into practice? We were in some way expressing a belief that the established system is not complete in its scope or efficacy. Maybe the older system, established in the first decades of this century, is very roughly laid out. Maybe the older system is limited; it lays out one path from theory to practice, but there is some need to consider other arrangements to provide more paths. We ought to consider briefly the nature of educational psychology as traditionally conceived. We may see more clearly what our traditional lines of communication have been.

Educational psychology was established as a discipline in the first two decades of this century. Edward Thorndike published one volume on educational psychology in 1903 and a three-volume series, *Educational*

Psychology, in 1912–1914. His early work on learning and his later work on testing set the pattern for the empiricism of an ensuing discipline of educational psychology. The scientific figures who espoused or promoted the development of that educational psychology at around Thorndike's time are reasonably well known—Dewey, Hall, Cattell. The establishment of this educational psychology was not a simple fruition of scientific inquiry. It was a response evoked from the academic community to social movements that invited some specific kinds of cooperation.

Tyack's (1974) recent book, *The One Best System,* gives a history of American urban education in the last century, with particular emphasis on the collaboration between social leaders and academics. The book describes the growth of a centralized professional "scientific" coordination of American education, which bound together the idiosyncratic educational practices of a set of small, locally managed, community-controlled school systems. The idea of a "one best system" was the creation of reformers who sought to establish a more unified body of practice and standards in American education. American schools were in the hands of local groups of varying competence; professionalization would bring a uniform high standard based on scientific knowledge and management. Tyack assigned a slogan to the movement, "the one best system," somewhat satirically. The movement had its positive and negative aspects. It addressed some real problems of the turn-of-the-century American school. Teachers were poorly paid, poorly educated, and had low status. (Read Thorndike's summary descriptions of American teachers and students in his *Education: A First Book,* published in 1912.) The 19th-century American colleges were bewildering in their heterogeneity of admissions standards. Local schools were irregular in their facilities, curricula, and standards. So a reform movement began, stimulated in part by some genuine needs in the system and quite conceivably in part by a conspiracy of a WASP elite that sought to establish an overarching political control over schools that were more and more coming under the governance of local groups of ethnics. Political movements are like that; the holy and the unholy are mixed together. The problems that precipitated the movement were "solved"; and our conspicuous educational problems today are, in important part, problems of overstandardization—the overuse of standardized testing, the overreliance on SAT scores for college admission, and overstandardized management, leading to manifold pressures for community relevance, community control, and pluralism in the organization of schooling.

People like Nicholas Murray Butler, Robert Thorndike, and G. Stanley Hall were active in the political movement described by Tyack—Butler extremely so. The movement had direct relevance for them. If education was to be scientifically managed, there had to be a source of that science somewhere. And so some leading universities began absorbing teachers' colleges or creating them, creating centers where research on education would take place and teachers would receive training based on the fruits of such research.

At the turn of the century, American psychologists were pretty much bottled up in philosophy departments, growing more and more restless as their brass instruments carried their interests and theories further from the normative philosophy of their time. Beginning in the 1890s, many Americans made an obligatory pilgrimage to Wundt's laboratory, and they brought back the procedures and the special concerns of an empirical epistemology. The imported German laboratory of Wundt and Titchener held sway for only a relatively short time in this country. Then wholly American-trained psychologists (people like Thorndike and Watson) quickly established new trends. One of the things that enabled them to turn in new directions was the establishment of schools of education.

At the turn of the century, there were hopes that psychology would lead to a scientific substrate for education, social work, child guidance, mental health, and social progress. These hopes fostered and conditioned the growth of psychology. Places and resources were given to psychologists who sought to loosen the restrictions of the philosophy departments. The price they had to pay, of course, was they they had to give some kind of coherence and form to the general idea that there ought to be a scientific basis for education. And so we find Cattell, Thorndike, and Dewey in Nicholas Murray Butler's Teacher's College, setting the pattern for what was to become educational psychology. And at the same time, off on the side, we find G. Stanley Hall pulling together a Child Study Movement. This movement, more of a coalition than a discipline, was short-lived. But something much like it came to life as the Child Development Movement of the 1930s, fading away and then reviving to become the developmental psychology that impinges on education today.

The institutional form of that time that lasted and grew was the discipline of educational psychology. The normative work of the discipline expressed a definite idea about the way theory moves into practice. The general idea was this: Scientists would sit in a laboratory, and they would discover laws of learning. Teachers made aware of those laws should be more scientific and better teachers.

That's a vision that many of us still live with today in a slightly modified form. Most of us have abandoned the notion that there exist simple, general, widely applicable laws of learning that can be taught to teachers for the benefit of their practice. The behavior modifiers still believe this and practice it. (More people on both sides of the line should worry about the limited success that the behavior modifiers have achieved with their strategy.) But most of us believe that we are going to need more than a few principles of shaping and rate modification to explain learning; and so we say, "Don't ask us now, but sooner or later we are going to come up with laws and principles that will help us in schools. We can help you to think in different ways about learning, children, schools, development, socialization, motivation, behavior problems, and so on. We can give you new ideas and cause you to reflect on your old ideas. But we are still at the drawing board, still building theories of cognition and learning. When we have the science, we'll apply it."

WHAT IF WE APPLY SCIENTISTS
RATHER THAN SCIENCE?

The older educational psychology is an organized system. It has institutional structure. There are jobs, buildings, journals, a professional society, book publishers, test publishers—much social paraphernalia organized around or adapted to a recognized entity. And that entity embodies the central idea that theory is made in universities and delivered to teachers to be embodied in practice. The idea is old but not completely inflexible. If we began in the early 1900s with the idea that researchers would develop learning theory and norm-referenced tests, we can modify that premise to believe that researchers should develop information-processing theory or psycholinguistic theory or developmental theory and criterion-referenced tests or stage-referenced tests. We can make changes within the traditional system while maintaining its integrity as a system, provided that the changes are not too "radical." What is a radical change? A radical change, I think, is one that challenges the theory of human communication envisaged in and expressed by the institutional form of the system. The rather strong questions I noted at the beginning of this chapter arise out of a relatively radical feature of recent communications between theory and practice. Instead of working through "channels"—sitting within the ivory tower and passing papers out to those who live in applied settings—researchers have taken to walking out of the ivory tower, entering as participants in the applied settings.

People are walking out of the laboratories and standing in the schools and working beside the practitioners. We find this in schools and in hospitals. And I suspect that this is a movement that is going to grow in the years to come. There is a movement, not of science, but of scientists, between the laboratory and applied settings.

A number of the contributors to this volume have moved back and forth between the two ecologies, and many of the chapters draw on the transitional experiences that people have had in the course of that movement. The special issues are expressed in the chapters by Fletcher, Clay, Chomsky, and Johnson.

Fletcher expresses well the gaps in theory that become apparent when one tries to rationally specify a computer system of instruction. He writes about immense amounts of improvisation and guessing, about quick judgments on issues that might take a century or so to settle properly. There is no safe and solid way to move from theory to practice. He also gives a good sense of the practical compromises that are made when you try to do something in the real world. We in the laboratory tend to address ourselves mostly to basic principles, ideas, and relationships. But it's really rather surprising how much of practical intervention gets conditioned by small things—like the programming quirks of a 1500 or a PDP-10. What Fletcher says, in short, is that you can't address an applied setting without some willingness to transcend the state of your own art and without making some generous concessions to the art of the possible.

Clay says that if you continuously interact with an educational system, if you try to bring your point of view to the system, you are addressing a dynamic structure that has laws and constraints of its own; you have to study that structure and understand it in order to know how to act on it. We generally conceive of an applied scientist as a person who is scholarly about science and concerned about practice. We rarely concede that an applied scientist might have to be a scholar about practice. There is much to be known about schools; they are much more complex structures than they appear to be on the surface (White, 1977). And many academic proposals and prescriptions for the betterment of education fail because they are based on simplistic stereotypes; they are irrelevant, incompetent, and immaterial with respect to the complex reality. (Anyone who thinks that defining "good education" or "better education" is easy might try asking the next 10 people he or she meets to define the notion.) By living within the functioning educational system, the sensitive researcher passes beyond the legendary and the stereotypic. The researcher begins to see what the educator sees. And conversely.

Clay writes that a significant value of the scientist is in "perceptual training of the teacher." She writes about the value of the scientist not so much in offering theoretical truths as in framing and organizing reality. Then Jerome Rosner, in a not unmixed appraisal of the practical value of researchers, said, "One nice thing about researchers, they can describe things fantastically well." Not so long ago I heard Gregory Anrig, chief state school officer in Massachusetts, appraise the value of the researcher in something like the following terms: I don't necessarily need people who can bring me answers. I can use people who bring me questions.

So researchers and practitioners working with each other begin to see things they way each other does and begin to think like each other. At a conference on the relation of science to policymaking, I once heard Wolfgang Edelstein of the Max Planck Institute of Education offer a symbolic interactionist view of the transmission between scientist and policymaker. The fundamentally productive aspect of the relationship, he argued, lies in what Freudians might call the transference relationship or what George Herbert Mead might call the identification with the other. The scientist becomes a bit of a practitioner, and the practitioner becomes a bit of a scientist. In this volume a similar view emerges repeatedly. Maybe this is the ultimate reason that we have begun to send scientists rather than science into the arenas of practice. Information is not enough. Maybe we need a learning theory based on empathy or a model of identification processing.

The chapters by Chomsky and Johnson illustrate a kind of emergent creativity that one can find in applied work. What Chomsky found were new patterns of phenomena. She was trying to teach reading through writing, and she came upon invented spelling patterns that seemed to be regular and lawful, that showed order, and that in a sense begged to be figured out. What Johnson discusses are striking dyslexic dissociations of visual, auditory, graphic, and linguistic processes. Such dissociations lead one to think about the nature of thought and knowledge in new and interesting ways.

For the researcher, the move to practice can often be a vist to another laboratory. New phenomena appear, new patterns of order in nature are seen. The movement out of the laboratory need not be a move away from fundamental inquiry. It can be a movement toward it. Most psychologists are, I think, insufficiently aware of a long-standing argument in the history of psychology revolving about the questions of whether laboratory work is sufficient for—some would say even necessary to—the scientific study of psychology. A distinguished lineage ranging from Wilhelm Wundt through Lev S. Vygotsky to Urie Bronfenbrenner in our own time has argued that one cannot fully develop a science of psychology by experimental work in a laboratory. Part of what we need to know must be sought in natural settings. So conceivably the psychologists of today are not moving into educational settings solely for the sake of social welfare. They might be doing so for the sake of science.

SOME CONFLICTS OF SCIENTISTS IN PRACTICE

After scientists have paid the costs and reaped the benefits of entry into practical settings, some special conflicts arise. Scientists represent, by role definition, professional values of science. But they have assumed some additional responsibilities. The scientists have become, if you like, a little bit like engineers and/or a little bit like teachers. They adopt other values that must be balanced against their scientific values.

The chapters in this volume again and again touch on sensitive questions of the ultimate practicality of practical work, of the relevance of relevant research. The questions are new questions that might not be likely to be raised in an ivory tower, but they are striking and salient when one tries to make something happen in schools.

For example, let's suppose that you have been working on an educational project. Inevitably you have had to do this in a local setting. You can't work on the system as a whole, so you set up a project in Gary or Peoria or

Pittsburgh. You are ingenious or lucky. You get a strong positive effect of the intervention. You know it, the teachers know it, *mirabile dictu,* the formal evaluation says so—cases randomly assigned to treatment and control conditions, simple statistical effects with no messy higher-order interactions, differences so sizable that they seem practically as well as statistically significant. You submit your paperbound report to Washington, which is quite likely to reward your success with a refusal to continue funding the project and which will in any case sooner or later proceed to forget that the project ever existed. Your final report will become part of what has been called the "fugitive literature." Some concerned scholar, such as Douglas Ellson, may fish it out of ERIC and ask why nobody has ever done anything about it. Those who hear the question will look a little confused—educators, professors, bureaucrats—sensing that it is a perfectly reasonable question, but it is not their question. It is somebody else's, or it ought to be somebody else's.

So you are a scientist who has made the commitment to practice, who has gone out and tried to make a change, and ultimately nothing seems likely to happen. What do you do? The problem you face is that the world of education contains very few ways for transmitting innovations, and there are significant internal mechanisms for resisting their introduction. This is the Achilles heel of the contract mechanism so much favored in Washington these days.

You can describe the local operation in a paperbound report, with the fate that I have discussed. You can write academic journal articles, or you can write in some journals that go to teachers. But you can't write much, and you can't show much. Or you can hope somehow to connect with the market mechanism. Some kinds of developments that are appealing to publishers or to educational hardware manufacturers get picked up and get carried around the system this way.

This limited, uncertain path to educational usage puts some delicate questions to the scientist-innovator. When you invest years and time and effort on a development project, then you have to care. Do you drop the innovation, implicitly conceding it to be an empty gesture, or do you accept the task of "selling" it? Doing the latter assumes that you have capabilities that are outside the scope of research work. You turn into a marketer or a guru or a preacher, or you at least have to find ways to coordinate the work of such people. Scientists who preach or market are doing something outside the role of the scientist. So there is a kind of "Catch-22"; they regularly come to choice points where they must consider relinquishing either the scientific or the practical. And traditional conceptions of the scientist's role do not offer either personal or legal safeguards for an essential aspect of practical work, namely, that one deals directly with possibilities of benefit or harm to a child.

A second issue arises in the form of value questions that inevitably occur whenever one tries to depart from or transcend the normative. In the traditional scientist's role, the scientist's findings are translated to teachers, who in turn translate them in working with children; the children are two steps removed from the scientists. Now, the scientist-innovator deals directly with children and sets about changing the conditions of their existence. What do the children need? What's the real problem? What's good? What's bad? Teachers, pediatricians, social workers, and reading specialists consider such questions every day. But all follow socially accepted professional definitions of function that are by convention good. Whether or not these professionals in fact do a child any good, their work is accepted as good as long as they properly adhere to the accepted canons of their professional practice. The researcher who introduces innovations in practice must consider questions of harm or benefit in a wide-open way.

Notice that questions about what's good and what's bad for children are always handed to researchers when they are asked to make an evaluation. Evaluations are demanded for educational innovations today. Major bills coming out of the Congress demand them. Administrative funding of research or demonstration projects now routinely incorporates the requirement for evaluation. These legislative and administrative demands are almost never accompanied by statements of what, exactly, the values to be evaluated are. Researchers, in the course of executing an ostensibly technical function, must introduce judgments about what constitutes good education, good social or cognitive development, good family, good community environment. It is somewhat surprising how easily researchers do this. Child development researchers, for example, often take on the task of assessing "good child development" or "optimal child development" by using tests and assessments that contain buried value principles—"older is better," "middle class is better," "not visibly perturbed is better," and so on. These are buried evaluational principles, and if they are exhumed and brought up for explicit discussion, one finds that developmental psychologists are uneasy and disunited about their scope and authoritativeness. Yet individual researchers apply such principles, presumably on their professional authority as developmental psychologists. In fact, the "games" of developmental psychology are not designed to bring about consensus and group agreements about values. When scientists make judgments about values, they do so as individuals, *ex cathedra*. The fact that practitioners and politicians today regularly delegate value choices to scientists constitutes a significant contemporary problem in the relationships between sciences and social action (Rein & White, 1977).

In many instances, scientists do not have to engage in deep brooding about the practical thrust of their work. They are able to accept what one might call the "simple engineering role." Some educational practice with socially understood and accepted objectives is to be reformed. The scientist accepts those objectives as targets, perhaps asking for or offering some behavioral definitions, not in order to challenge the goal but rather to seek translations that will allow for better estimations of the goal in the course of the research. Simple engineering looks like a reasonably safe way for the scientist to become practical without stepping into the quagmires of ethical and political disputation. But how large is the safe ground on which one can stand with assurance?

Surely nothing could be better socially understood and accepted as an objective than better reading. Here, there is some safe ground. Some of us have apparently accepted the goal of better reading in simple engineering terms, and we are proceeding toward reasonable analyses of terms in the teaching of reading—human information processing, the processes of teaching, the nature of available curricula. But some have come to believe this offered goal is chimerical; they adopt what one might call the "complex engineering approach." They try to examine the manifest problem as something that arises out of a complex social context. They try to look at the broad sociological system of which the symptom of poor reading is an expression. And they arrive at arguments that say that one might have to work on something other than the teaching of reading in order to solve the manifest problem of "poor reading."

There are costs and benefits of either the simple or complex approach. The simple engineers are able to enter into active work on the problem, but their work may be futile. The complex engineers have the presumptive advantage of a broader and more sophisticated view of the problem, but they may have tied their own hands. The dilemma, whether to take a simple or complex view, is not particularly unique to psychologists working on education.

There is a third and final consequence of the movement out of the laboratory to which I would like to call attention. Psychological laboratories in the univeristy are nicely self-contained in a way that natural environments cannot be. Psychologists who deal with issues of cognitive development have to deal with issues that are philosophical, biological, sociological, and anthropological. Conventions (crippling conventions, I think) dictate that only the boldest or more foolhardy will cross disciplinary lines and try to do so. But there are no neat boundaries in a natural situation; scientists who go toward such a situation revisit the broad matrix of reality out of which their specialized work has grown. As they become more and more aware of the breadth of the matrix, as they become more and more scholarly about practice (as responsible activists ought to be), they become more and more aware of the breadth of the causative systems out of which psychological problems arise. Another "Catch-22": The psychologist who engages in a complex engineering analysis of a problem in education may well decide that the *real* problem does not require a psychologist for solution.

SOME SUMMARY REMARKS

The "critical incidents" that I have chosen for discussion are of a kind that arises frequently nowadays at discussions of psychology and education. They arise, I believe, because of a transition in institutional forms. An older vision of the interface between psychology and education is reasonably understood by most people on both sides and is embodied in the normative practices of universities, journals, professional societies, and government funding. Knowledge made in laboratories will be transmitted to practitioners in education, who will translate theory into practice. There is nothing fundamentally wrong with this vision; it is alive and well. But another kind of normative practice is appearing, resting on the cooperative activity of the scientist and the educator and other scientists in the development of innovations in practice. Institutional embodiments of this newer form of interaction are to be found all around—the development of educational laboratories and centers, contract houses and research institutes, the shift in government from grants to contracts, the general movement in psychology toward a greater investment in research in the natural human environment in place of that in the laboratory environment.

As with any developmental process, there arise tensions between an older and comparatively well put-together organization and a newer, more complex, not-so-well organized system. Problems arise that are not covered by the norms of the scientist's role and the traditions of the scientist–teacher relationship. Teachers given legitimate scientific material ask blunt questions about what it is all supposed to mean to them. Looking at some of the educational psychology textbooks to which they have been exposed for decades, I can only marvel that it has taken them so long to ask. Social scientists find that they, or someone, have to be something other than scientists in order for their work to move toward practical use. They find themselves confronted with disconcerting value questions. And they find that greater and greater exposure to the natural contexts out of which their research arises leads them toward serious reflection on the efficacy and limitations of their role as scientists.

Psychology began, not so long ago, with some borrowed assumptions about the constitution of its research as "scientific." Based on those assumptions, it arranged its traditional alignment with practice. What seems to be evolving now, with experience, is a more informed view about where and how psychologists build knowledge and where and how they can be practical.

In the light of that informed view, the unanalyzed assumptions of the past have come to seem more and more inadequate. The expressed difficulties and deep questionings of these meetings and volumes are all, it seems to me, positive signs, signs of learning.

REFERENCES

Rein, M., & White, S. H. Policy research: Belief and doubt. *Policy Analysis,* 1977, *3,* 239–271.

Thorndike, E. L. *Educational psychology.* New York: Columbia University, Teachers College Press, 1903.

Thorndike, E. L. *Education: A first book.* New York: Macmillan, 1912.

Thorndike, E. L. *Educational psychology: Vol. I. The original nature of man; Vol. II. The psychology of learning; Vol. III. Mental work and fatigue and individual differences and their causes.* New York: Columbia University, Teachers College Press, 1912–1914.

Tyack, D. B. *The one best system: A history of American urban education.* Cambridge, Mass.: Harvard University Press, 1974.

White, S. H. Developmental psychology and Vico's concept of universal history. *Social Research,* 1976, *43,* 659–671.

White, S. H. The paradox of American education. *Principal,* 1977, *56,* 7–13.

14

Implications for Compensatory Education Drawn from Reflections on the Teaching and Learning of Reading

Edmund W. Gordon
Columbia University

INTRODUCTION

It was the ubiquitous and persistent problems of poor reading competence, especially prevalent in low-status populations, that motivated this collection of papers—an attempt to pool what is known about the initial learning of reading, in order to understand better how that knowledge can inform compensatory or special programs of education for the children of the poor. In developing this chapter, I have sought to mine the 40 papers prepared for these volumes with a view to identifying their implications for compensatory education—that is, for improving the acquisition of reading competence by children from low-status families.

This chapter considers two large issues related to compensatory programs in reading. The first surrounds the concept of compensatory education itself—how this concept came into being, the varying assumptions upon which it is based, and what is known or thought to be known about the children toward which it is directed. The second issue concerns what is known about the processes of becoming a competent reader and about reading instruction. The first section of the chapter examines the first issue; against this background, the second section considers the implications of various chapters in these volumes for teaching the children of the poor to read.

THE NATURE OF COMPENSATORY EDUCATION

The Historical Development of Compensatory Education

The education of large numbers of children from diverse backgrounds and with a variety of personal characteristics can be said to be a problem peculiar to modern societies. Before the 20th century, there appears to have been little concern for universal education. In fact, it was not until the 19th century that public schools became available throughout the United States. During most of that century, schooling remained unavailable to large numbers of children, and not until the end of that century were schools made available to most black children. It was during the nation's experience with large-scale industrialization and immigration that the schools' inability to equalize their output began to be obvious. Industrialization placed great demands for literacy on the society and its schools. The new immigrants looked to the schools to make them literate (and in English to boot). Blacks, recently freed from slavery and beginning to congregate in the urban centers, also turned to the schools for help. From the time that these two groups began to present special problems for the public schools, increasing attention has been given to the development of special remedial programs, forerunners of today's compensatory programs. These programs usually provided a slower presentation rate, involving a good bit of repetition, and had generally lower standards and goals than other programs. The programs were introduced into schools to accommodate individuals who did not fit into regular school programs. Despite these special programs, however, the newcomers to public education often did not fare well. Underachievement, failure, and dropping out were not uncommon. Nevertheless, illiteracy and lack of education did not preclude entry into the labor force; many of the schools' failures were absorbed into the society either through low-level, unskilled jobs in commerce and industry or through return to the farm.

As the 20th century progressed, the society's need for better educated persons and the demands of ethnic minority and other low-status people placed on the schools a new responsibility—that of making school achievement independent of social origins. This growing concern for equality of educational opportunity was focused initially on equal salaries for black and white teachers. It evolved into a concern for equal facilities. In a brief period, the demand for equal facilities and resources had shifted to a demand for the same (i.e., shared, integrated facilities). In 1954, the Supreme Court ruled segregated facilities illegal. But neither equal educational opportunity nor school desegregation was achieved as a result of that decision. Ten years after the decision the nation was still struggling with inequality in education. The concern for equality of educational opportunities now had a dual focus: school desegregation/integration, and education of high quality.

During this time, a great number of special programs directed at the educational problems of disadvantaged children were developed under the auspices of the Office of Educational Opportunity and the Office of Education. In the 1950s and 1960s, these programs were primarily directed toward the poor and emphasized remedial work and cultural enrichment. The addition of activities defined as *culturally enriching* probably provided the clearest distinction between previous remedial educational programs and the broader view of compensatory education. These efforts also included a variety of in-school programs, including specialized guidance services designed to make schooling more effective. New instructional programs, which were outside of the remedial tradition in that they were designed to make the learning experience more appropriate to the characteristics of the learner, were also offered. Recent developments in the teaching of math and social studies were represented in these emerging programs for the poor. Probably the most consistently effective new method was the use of the computer to assist or supplement instruction (Jamison, 1976). This method combined the characteristics of earlier programmed instruction and learning machines with the capabilities of computer systems to provide fairly systematic instruction and drill with immediate feedback and review in an independent study format.

Chronologically, the next major expression of compensatory education involved the adaptation of nursery-school and day-care programs to the education of the poor. These adaptations were based on the assumption that if youngsters were arriving at school poorly prepared, one way to improve their education was to begin their schooling earlier. During the late 1950s and the early 1960s, a good bit of experimental work aimed at creating enriched nursery and day-care programs to better prepare youngsters from low-income families for public school was conducted. This culminated with the federally supported Head Start program, which gave great emphasis to learning how to learn; to language development, socialization, routinization (helping children to learn and adjust to school routines), attendance, health, and nutrition; and to aiding parents in their roles as supporters of early learning.

A third major development in compensatory education was the emergence of anti-dropout programs devised to increase the "holding power" or magnetic capacity of secondary schools. A variety of work and study programs, guidance services, and more relevant course work were introduced into urban high schools. To further enhance these programs, indigenous persons were hired as staff members to provide adult models with whom students could more easily identify. The effort to retain youngsters in school was not, until the 1960s, matched by an effort to increase the options for such youngsters after they completed high school. By this time, school retention programs had begun to give a heavy emphasis to vocational and occupational training. These school retention programs, funded by the Economic Opportunity Act of 1964, had come to be primarily focused on job development and training and on the transition from high school to jobs for noncollege-bound students.

Several instructional improvement projects were also initiated. With the passage of the Elementary and Secondary Education Act of 1965, public schools became major centers for attacks on the educational problems of the poor. Under this act, school districts with high concentration of low-income families were allocated funds with which to supplement and enhance their programs for economically and educationally disadvantaged children.

Approaches to Compensatory Education

During the years that such programs have been in operation, schools have taken several different approaches to developing compensatory education programs. One of these has been based on the assumption that providing alternative experiences would enable children to circumvent so-called deficits in their home environments and thus reduce academic retardation. Compensatory education has also been thought of as reparations: Minority groups have requested that special funds, resources, and opportunities be channeled to their communities as reparations for earlier societal neglect. A third conceptualization of compensatory education has been derived from the field of special education. That is, compensatory education programs have utilized uncommon materials, devices, and techniques to correct, offset, or counterbalance specific malfunctions or disabilities in disadvantaged children. Another approach to compensatory education involves utilizing the individual characteristics or experiences of the learner as a basis for the design of learning experiences. In this approach, curriculum becomes the focus of compensatory efforts. Deficiencies or inadequacies in instructional methods are modified so that they are more appropriately matched to the needs, styles, and characteristics of the learner.

Most of these conceptions of compensatory education have grown out of what can be referred to as a "deficits" concept. Circumvention of insufficient environment, reparations for neglect, special education to compensate for malfunction—all these approaches involve the underlying assumption of a deficiency. Comparisons of poor and minority children with the so-called "mainstream" children have revealed areas in which the former function differently from the latter. These differences have been considered deficits. If readiness for traditional academic experiences is taken as the criterion, then poor and minority children do have deficits, since they lack the characteristics and behavior associated with successful academic learning. Since these characteristic differences have been shown to be related to early experiential deprivation and to other factors associated with poverty and low social status, schools developed educational programs to attempt to compensate for this deprivation—hence, "compensatory" education.

Thus, in the traditional views of compensatory education as circumvention, reparations, or special education, early deprivation was assumed to have reduced the possibility for equal educational opportunity. It was out of a concern for reducing inequalities that Congress commissioned the 1964 study of equality of educational opportunity. In reporting the results of the study—that family background accounted for the greatest amount of the variance in school achievement—Coleman and his colleagues (Coleman, Campbell, Hobson, McPartland, Mood, Weinfeld, & York, 1966) asserted that, in a democracy, school achievement could and should be made independent of social circumstance. This concern with equalizing educational opportunity, and particularly Coleman's assertion, which was reflected in the increasing demands of the poor and minority groups, placed on the schools the responsibility to make schooling effective, regardless of social circumstance. This responsibility greatly influenced the direction of compensatory education programs.

The purpose of the equality in educational opportunity study was to investigate the problems of racial separation in the schools. Since this issue had already been settled by the Supreme Court, more relevant questions might have been asked: What is the status of equal educational opportunity? What is required to achieve equality of educational opportunity?

To answer such questions, one must define equal educational opportunity. Does it involve equalizing the *opportunity* to learn or equalizing the *effectiveness* of schooling and the quality of learning? When Coleman wrote about making schooling independent of social circumstance, what he was really saying was that the schools should be made equally effective for all segments of the population. When that becomes the standard, the responsibility for ensuring that all categories of youngsters leave school with equal degrees of educational competence is placed on the school. This conceptualization of the issue, however, ignores the fact that there are individual differences in children's capacity to benefit from schooling. Consequently, the idea that children should leave school with equal competence should apply to groups, not individuals. Coleman understood this. What Coleman was suggesting is that the schools have the responsibility to ensure that no *category* of youngsters—poor children, rich children, white children, black children, Spanish-speaking children—leaves schools with inadequate levels of achievement. He was *not* suggesting that every individual should leave the school with the same level of learning and achievement.

A New Definition of Equal Education Opportunity

In a related effort at defining equality of educational opportunity (Deutsch, 1960, in Gordon, 1972), I have asserted that education should, at a minimum, result in survival level achievement for all pupils, except perhaps for about 5% of the student population who are truly intellectually defective. There should be no upper limit placed on the achievement of the remaining 95%, however. In other words, all individuals should be free to exceed the minimal standard by as much as their capabilities and motivations will permit. To the extent that the schools ensure such base-line achievement and to the extent that all individuals choosing to, and capable of, going beyond this level are availed of the opportunity to do so, educational opportunity would be equalized.

What I am calling for, then, is equality of achievement at the survival level and equality of opportunity to exceed that level. In this context, it may be more appropriate to talk about good, or quality, education rather than compensatory education. And in this context, the concept of compensatory education applies not only to poor or minority group children but to all youngsters in the school.

If society takes as a guide the Coleman or Gordon version of equality of achievement and opportunity, then the school has the responsibility for: (1) enabling those youngsters who come to school ill prepared or handicapped for existing school programs to circumvent these obstacles to learning; or (2) removing the obstacles. The school would thus remediate the discrepancy between the learner and the school by building upon the learner's individual strengths, learning characteristics, and capacities to achieve the criterion level of survival skills. If any one wants to call that compensatory education, I will not argue. But it begins to sound like that which may be thought of as simply a system of educational programs designed to provide all youngsters with an adequate education, regardless of the level at which they enter school.

This broader conception of compensatory education has not been widely accepted. Most programs have, as indicated earlier, focused on a deficit model. Head Start and other preschool programs directed at the remedial preparation of youngsters for admission to school, programs directed at increasing the holding power or schools, and programs aimed at increasing access to educational opportunity (such as desegregation plans) have all been based on this assumption. At a second level of priority, attention has been given to a variety of in-school activities and programs designed either to improve the quality of schooling or to speak to special disabilities or special needs of youngsters. These programs range from special reading, guidance, and cultural enrichment programs, to nutrition and health programs. It could be accurately said that from 1964 to 1979, just about every idea for improving education that has surfaced in this country has been tried in some fashion. Few of these programs, however, have departed from the primary concern with correction of and/or compensation for deficiencies. So pervasive has been this view of deficits that even programs directed at parents have had an emphasis on expiation.

For many years, the parents of low-income and minority group youngsters were thought to have little interest in the education of their youngsters or to have low levels of educational aspiration for their children. As a consequence of this commonly held view, considerable attention was given to finding ways to motivate these parents to increase their interest in the education of their youngsters and to raise their levels of aspiration. However, more careful examination of this problem reveals that the real issue is not one of lack of interest or aspiration but one of low levels of competence in those parenting skills that support academic learning.

The evidence seems to indicate that large numbers of these parents have high aspirations for their children. In fact, some evidence indicates that the aspirations of some of these parents may be higher than the reality of the situation is likely to justify. An example of inappropriately high aspirations of parents can be found in the experiences of the Mississippi Child Development Group, one of the more successful Head Start projects. The Head Start classes, which were largely under the control of this Mississippi parents' group, were probably more skill-oriented than is beneficial for preschool children. These parents wanted their children to learn how to read. They insisted that the Head Start program give heavy emphasis to preliteracy skills and actual instruction in reading at a time when most researchers in child development were arguing that preschool programs should emphasize socialization and preparation for learning rather than basic skill mastery. These parents certainly were not uninterested in their children's schooling. Their interests were so high that they were impatient with the potential products of schooling and emphasized a set of learning activities that were inappropriate to the age group being served.

If one looks at what happens to these parental aspirations from the beginning of school to the end, one frequently sees parents' exaggerated hopes, as their youngsters enter school, completely diminished by the time their children reach high school. Some persons have suggested that this is a function of what happens, or does not happen, to the child at school. Parents enroll their youngsters in school expecting that schooling will enable the children to do things that they never had an opportunity to do, only to discover that schools are relatively ineffective in educating their youngsters. Even after successfully completing a school program, these young people often are still noncompetitive and unskilled with respect to entry into the mainstream. These circumstances have resulted in what would appear to be a lack of interest in education. This might be more correctly thought of as high initial expectation interacting with frustrated aspiration and low-level supportive skills to produce a depressed interest.

Who Needs Compensatory Education?

Although most compensatory programs are based on an assumption of deficit, compensatory education does come in several varieties. Among them are programs of early intervention (preschool) designed to enrich the developmental and "learning to learn" experiences of the child, to better prepare him or her for subsequent school experiences. Early intervention also directs effort at enhancing the parenting capabilities of the child's primary caretakers. Within the school experience, we find attention given to a long list of educational strategies including remediation, tutorials, specialized programs in reading and math, experiential enrichment, behavior modification, computer-assisted instruction, open and informal learning, and highly structured design and delivery. None of these characteristics, however, sets compensatory education apart from other forms of education as much as the populations toward which it is directed.

Several populations have been identified as the targets for compensatory educational services. Most prominent in legislative concern have been children from poverty-stricken families. The educational programs of the Office of Economic Opportunity were directed at that income group, and eligibility for participation in services and programs under Title I of the Elementary and Secondary Educational Act is limited to children from low-income families. There are problems, however, in the use of family income as the indicator of eligibility. Although it is true that the incidence of educational disadvantage and underachievement is high in this group, the two conditions are not perfectly correlated. Some families that are as poor as church mice nonetheless produce children whose academic achievement is quite good. Conversely, some children who come from families with income adequate to or in excess of survival needs are educationally disadvantaged. Further, given the income formulae in current use (community averages rather than individually determined), help goes to communities with high concentrations of low-income families rather than to specific families with low income. It is clear that low income is indicative of risk with respect to educational disadvantage, but income is not a very specific indicator of compensatory educational need.

Membership in a low-status ethnic minority group has also played a major role in the politics of identifying group need. Blacks, Puerto Ricans, Chicanos, and native Americans are most often singled out as special targets for compensatory educational services. With a high degree of consistency, these populations have been shown to have high incidences of educational disadvantage. Like low income, however, low-status ethnic group membership does not necessarily indicate educational disadvantage, nor does high-status group membership preclude such handicaps. At best we can assert that low-status group membership in the United States is indicative of high risk of educational disadvantage, but it tells us little about the needs of the individual for compensatory education.

Characteristics of the Disadvantaged

Since compensatory education has, as we have seen, most often meant education for the poor, it is important to understand the way in which this population has been viewed in the literature and the way in which the problem of educating the poor has been viewed by society. Basically, compensatory education was introduced to serve a population that was thought to be inferior, increasingly burdensome, and useless to the society.

Society's response to the problem of the education of the poor has reflected one of two views of human nature. Social reformers and the more humanistically oriented members of society have taken the more tractile or plastic view of human nature, which suggests that intervention can result in changed quality of function. This view is associated with a humanistic concern with individual and civil rights and with the recognition, by some factions in society, that improving the condition of the poor is incompatible with maintaining the status quo. The opposing, and more popular view— which has influenced education and social organization for the past three to five centuries—is that little can be done with the have-nots in society, because their condition is pre-ordained and hardly anything will modify it. This view leads to a welfare or reformist approach to the problem of the poor rather than a revolutionary approach. The reasoning goes like this: If in fact these people are poor, uneducated, and disorganized, it is because fate has deemed it so; one need not feel guilty about doing far less than is otherwise indicated, since intervention will not change their conditions. This view leads to missionary-type efforts, which are designed to make the doer feel better but are not necessarily designed to change the fundamental condition of the recipients.

Within this second point of view, the culturally disadvantaged or minority-group child has been perceived as a prototype that does not vary from group to group or from individual to individual. This has resulted in a description of the disadvantaged child as a low-status, low-income underachiever, exhibiting inadequate language and insufficient moral development. All of the characteristics that have been identified in any group of disadvantaged persons have been brought together to collectively characterize an undifferentiated disadvantaged child.

This composite description of the disadvantaged child, which has dominated work in this field, is based on early research that compared disadvantaged children to more privileged children, or black children to white children, or migrant children to less mobile children. In each instance, the research, ranging from comparative developmental psychology to educational psychology, took a mainstream child as the norm and examined ways in which youngsters in special groups deviated from that norm. This approach, which also came to dominate the approaches to service, placed a very heavy emphasis on the differences between the mainstream or normative group and the special group in question—differences that, as we have seen, were considered deficits. Research attention was also directed to the home environments and family circumstances of the disadvantaged group. These studies provided us with a catalogue of factors present in homes and environments of the disadvantaged population that interfere with normal school and societal achievement.

Furthermore, the study of the characteristics of disadvantaged populations has received more attention than any other aspect of the education of socially disadvantaged children. In an earlier period, the studies of disadvantaged children followed the example of the research relating to children in general— that is, an emphasis on emotional or individual social development. More recently, this work has been supplemented by studies emphasizing intellectual or cognitive development. In both cases, however, less attention is given to developmental sequences than is devoted to comparing the status of emotional, social, or intellectual development in the disadvantaged population with that in a more privileged population.

It must be noted that the discovery of differences between two distinct populations may not enable us to specify the nature of the learning problems involved. The aversive conditions found in the disadvantaged nexus merely present the scientist with the challenge and responsibility of discovering the sources of these conditions, the mechanisms through which they have arisen, and the extent to which they are modifiable. We must remain forewarned that a catalogue of the characteristics of a disadvantaged population, as opposed to those of an advantaged population, without a serious analysis of their origin, validity, and modifiability, is not helpful pedagogically. With this caveat in mind, we can now review some of the research done to identify the characteristics of disadvantaged children.

Home Environment and Family Characteristics. Research conducted on environmental factors has been described largely in negative terms, with little attention directed toward positive aspects of the environemnt or aspects that could be used to the educational advantage of these disadvantaged children. Generally the environment has been described as noisy, disorganized, and austere and lacking in many of the diverse cultural artifacts associated with the development of readiness for schooling. Adult models to which the children are exposed have been interpreted as representing incongruous values in relation to the demands of the schools and the larger community.

Few of these studies represent systematic long-term investigations conducted in naturalistic settings. Much of this work tends to be speculative and is based on relatively small and unrepresentative samples. The findings, nonetheless, point to the importance of environmental factors. Interpretation of such findings, however, will be greatly limited until single enumeration and description of environmental factors are replaced by ecological investigations designed to show the relationship between certain features of the environment and certain behavioral characteristics.

Language, Cognition, and Intelligence.   Nowhere is the relationship between environmental encounters and subsequent behavior in greater need of study than in the area of the devleopment of language and cognitive function. Although great effort has been spent in identifying patterns of function in these areas, little of this work has led to meaningful concepts of the causes of dysfunction or to clear directions for remediation.

Data from several studies suggest that children from disadvantaged backgrounds show weaknesses in using normative abstract symbols to represent and interpret their feelings, their experiences, and the phenomena of their environments. Nevertheless, there exist in these populations quite complex language systems. The form in which the language is expressed may not be syntactically correct nor may the specific symbols be consistent with those normally used by the dominant culture, but this language is adequate to the needs of the culture in which it has developed. When this fact is recognized, the important question becomes whether and to what extent a given language system may be utilized in understanding and managing complex technical problems. If the facts, the relationships, and the ideas of science and philosophy cannot be expressed in the language system in question, then that language is inadequate for the demands of contemporary education. To date, investigations into this question, which could be called the *utilitarian dimension of divergent language patterns,* have not been conducted. Conclusions about deficits in symbolic representation and language development are reflected in studies of concept development in disadvantaged children, whose concept formation has been described as content-centered rather than form-centered and whose reasoning has been described as more inductive than deductive. The connection between language development and concept development has been stated in this way: If a high level of language development is a prerequisite to advanced concept formation and problem solving, the dominant lower-class pattern of restricted rather than elaborated language usage is likely to be associated with serious limitations in conceptual function.

Intelligence and Sociological Status.   Several researchers have strongly asserted that intelligence is not primarily a genetically determined entity but rather a function that develops in, and through interaction with, the environment. This position is reflected in much of the work on intellectual function in disadvantaged populations. Although many studies show differences in intelligence—differences that favor more advantaged groups—much effort has been directed toward establishing determinants of these differences in the differing social experience of the groups. Most research in this area has determined a relationship between intelligence and socioeconomic status. This relationship, however, is not seen to be permanent or irreversible. In addition, the cultural bias of intelligence tests, which may result in children from deprived backgrounds receiving scores that do not accurately reflect their basic intelligence, has often been noted. On the other hand, more psychomotor and behavioral disorders and greater reading disability have been found in disadvantaged populations than in more privileged groups. These findings, which are based on a study of the relationship between income, health, and school adjustment, suggest a continuum of reproductive errors or developmental defects. The incidence of error is greatest in the population for which medical, nutritional, and child care are poorest, and the incidence is least where such care is best. This formulation, when applied to the question of social class or racial differences in intelligence, has led to the general feeling that racial IQ differences are a result of environmental deprivation rather than of limited inherent potential. In the definitive review of this problem, Klineberg (1963) found no scientifically acceptable evidence for the view that ethnic groups differ in innate ability. More recently, Jensen (1969) has strongly asserted the position, also held by others, that intelligence-test score differences between blacks and whites can be attributed to genetic differences in the quality of intellect. His analyses led him to conclude that 80% of the variance in test scores can be explained by heritability and 20% by environmental factors. The issue, however, continues to be the subject of debate with inconclusive evidence offered by adherents of both sides. Personal preference and ideology appear to currently guide policy and practice.

Perceptual Styles and Patterns of Intellectual Function.   Disadvantaged children have been noted by several investigators and observers (e.g., Deutsch, 1960; Riessman, 1962) to demonstrate styles and perceptual habits that are either inadequate or irrelevant to the demands of academic efficiency. Probably the most significant finding in this area is the characteristic absence of any high degree of dependence on verbal and written standard English for cognitive cues. Many of the children have not adopted receptive and expressive modes traditional to and necessary for success in school. Socially disadvantaged children have also been found (Riessman, 1962) to be inferior to control groups of middle-class children on tasks requiring concentration and persistence, and evidence of a lack of involvement with, attention to, and concentration on the content of academic experience has been found.

Motivation and Aspiration.   Several different conclusions can be drawn on the motivational problems of the disadvantaged from a theoretical perspective, since the research literature lacks substance. Disadvantaged children have been found to have self-centered, immediate, and materialistic–utilitarian characteristics not alien to our culture. But, in light of the limited horizons and opportunities of the child, these characteristics may function as depressants on motivation, aspiration, and achievement. In addition, disadvantaged children are seen to lack appropriate sources of immediate satisfaction and immediate feedback available to their more advantaged cohorts. This lack of informal instruction on how to overcome obstacles that are part of everyday school situations may be an added impairment to a disadvantaged child's already low motivational drive. Attitudinal factors are closely related to motivational factors and are frequently a source of problems in educational planning for disadvantaged children. There has been a tendency to think that disadvantaged youth view education and learning in terms of job market value and seek the job that requires the least amount of schooling necessary, a situation that is further encouraged by parental reinforcement. This trend remains somewhat illusory, however, as both the children and parents have been shown to be very involved in the school experience when it does not exhibit purposes that are incongruous with their needs and purposes. At the same time, what some researchers have explained as disadvantaged children's inability to delay gratification may only be a response on the part of these youngsters to a situation with few alternatives and sources of immediate gratification. Banks and McQuater (1976) have advanced a new conception. They find that, controlling for the interest of the task across ethnic groups, there is no difference associated with ethnicity in the ability to delay gratification, and suggest that results of earlier work on this question reflected differential task interest.

The Advanged, the Disadvantaged, and Educational Planning

Most of the investigators upon whose work our knowledge of the characteristics of socially disadvantaged children is based have developed their data against a background of experience with children from the homes of middle-class white families. They have tended to describe these characteristics in terms of their deviance from the norms of this group and to view these behaviors and conditions as deficits. Little attention has been given to viewing the behavior and conditions of socially disadvantaged children as information that schools might use to design meaningful and appropriate learning experiences. By implication, these studies suggest that the language, cognitive styles, and values of disadvantaged children are negatives to be overcome. There is not doubt that in many instances upward mobility may not otherwise be possible; however, to demean everything with which the child is identified may produce only immobility. This concern is seldom represented in work directed at identifying and understanding the socially disadvantaged child.

Even if the primary characteristics of this population were essentially unwholesome, the research done to establish these observations would still be inadequate. Although this research is not exceptionally good, it is very likely that if these studies were replicated today many of the same patterns would be found. Nevertheless, if we were to do within-group studies of patterns of deficit and facility, we would probably find that within any one of these groups—disadvantaged or advantaged—we would find comparable ranges of characteristics. What we are dealing with in the literature on the disadvantaged is the tendency of certain kinds of characteristics to occur in high frequency in certain groups. With few exceptions, we are talking about differential frequencies of characteristics that both groups share.

This distinction has important implications for planning school programs. For example, if we are going to be working with a large number of poor children, then we ought to anticipate a medley of health problems. Moreover, the number, diversity, and intensity of said problems will be greater than we would expect to encounter in a more affluent population. This does not imply, however, that in a population of affluent youth we will not have some serious health problems; rather, the realm, magnitude, and degree of the impairments among disadvantaged youngsters will be markedly greater. What this suggests for education—getting back to our earlier point about good education—is that an adequate program must accommodate itself to the variety of characteristics that are likely to be encountered in a varied population of children in our society. Furthermore, one doesn't need to seek recourse in a deficits approach to the characteristics of the poor in order to justify programming for them. In other words, we know that the range of characteristics, functioning, and disabilities that we have tended to associate with the poor are likely to be present in any group of youngsters—with a higher incidence in the poor population, but nevertheless present in other groups. A good system of education has to be prepared to beat these problems. We could also expect to find, in our population of disadvantaged, some children who have not been handicapped by this condition. These children appear to function quite well and seem capable of continuing to do so. If we use the deficits model as the primary approach to developing programs, then we are not prepared to meet the needs of this group of youngsters who are poor, of low status, and in many ways disadvantaged but who are not handicapped. Clearly we are left with the implication that identifying the generic characteristics of the disadvantaged—or the advantaged—serves little purpose when one begins to think in terms of the design of an adequate educational program.

On the other hand, there are some characteristics and conditions in the lives of individuals that may be pedagogically important. As I indicated earlier, the functions served by one's language and the facility with which it is used have important implications for education. These characteristics may differ for individual learners as well as for groups of learners. Group differences in attitudes toward learning may have particular relevance for education, especially in a society where some groups perceive themselves as powerless and less likely to gain access to rewards and resources. (Ogbu, 1978, has described the relationship between black pupils' perceptions of unequal reward for equal work and their attitudes toward involvement in academic learning tasks.) Where cultures foster affective and cognitive habits that are dysfunctional in academic settings, these habits must be recognized in designing educational programs. But in planning educational interventions for individual learners, characteristics associated with group membership may not be as important as the learning behavior of the individuals. It may well be that ethnicity, social class, and income level are not precise enough as indicators of learning function or dysfunction to be used in educational planning. In other words, a widely varied group such as the disadvantaged may be too diverse for that designation to be meaningful in educational decisions. What may be necessary is much more customized approach to education based on adaptive, or diagnostic and prescriptive, intervention.

What then is meant by *the disadvantaged?* I believe that we'll end up by disclaiming both the "disadvantaged" label and the "compensatory education" label, or perhaps by suggesting that they are in a sense misnomers. Insofar as all good education ought to be compensatory, they are misnomers. Both labels may also be dysfunctional for eduction. The pedagogically relevant question involves the functional characteristics of those individuals who are to be educated. If education is seen as fostering the development of individuals, then individual differences become the focus, making discourse on disadvantaged status superfluous. I guess what we are really talking about is the "sizing up" of the nucleus of characteristics that a person brings to a particular educational situation and of how to best utilize this complex of traits in his or her education. Of course, sets of characteristics may vary among people and, on certain tasks, within a person. Depending on the task, our manner of leaning may set us at a disadvantage or advantage. Seen in this light, disadvantage/advantage is unimportant, since what we are really talking about is what is appropriate to the education of this individual given this particular complex of characteristics.

READING INSTRUCTION
FOR COMPENSATORY EDUCATION

Given the rather nebulous nature of compensatory education and the multitude of essentially negative characteristics thought to be peculiar to disadvantaged children, one cannot be sanguine about the possibility of finding solutions to the problems of educating the poor by examining what is known about the teaching and learning of initial reading. Nevertheless, a review of the collection of papers presented at these conferences reveals several conceptions and issues that can throw light on some of the problems of compensatory education.

Stages of Reading Development

Chall identifies five stages in the development of reading competence. Stage one involves decoding—the learning of arbitrary sets of letters and the association of these with the corresponding parts of spoken words. The developmental task at stage two is confirmation of what is already known, the elaboration of complex phonic elements, and the use of generalizations and redundancies. Most of this occurs through stories listened to and read. According to Chall, stages one and two involve the mastery of print. Stage three involves the mastery of ideas. The developmental task is to learn, through reading, content facts, concepts, and how to do things. In stage four, the reader learns to deal with more than one point of view and adds layers of facts and concepts to those acquired earlier. In stage five, the task is to develop a world view and involves the ability to use reading as one of many ways of knowing and experiencing.

A mental contrast of the ways in which life styles and life conditions facilitate or frustrate mastery of each of these stages should quickly reveal the advantage held by children from more affluent homes over children of the poor. As I indicated in an earlier commentary (Vol. 1), it may be said that the conditions and characteristics of life for low-status people in our society do not afford them the richness of literacy experiences necessary to confirm decoding skills and to develop fluency in using them. In addition, each stage requires a support system that facilitates mastery, in the absence of which it becomes the burden of the formal education system to compensate. Since these stages appear to be sequential in their natural occurrence, the problem for compensatory education is to promote their sequential mastery at ages for which existing materials and models may not be appropriate and in situations for which school and academic mastery provide insufficient motivation.

Diagnosing the Reader as Information Processor

Johnson draws heavily on psychological and systems theory for her approach to diagnosing reading problems. Her orientation is to view the child as an information processor who has multiple modalities for input and output of information and who has potential for a variety of complex integrative networks. In this approach, the reading diagnostician is concerned with finding out whether a child has a disturbance of input, integration, or output—that is, whether the child has difficulty receiving and assimilating information, or whether he or she is unable to retrieve and express what he or she knows. These concerns lead to a diagnostic process that considers three psychological processes (intrasensory, intersensory, and integrative functions) and three conditions (overloading, information processing, and level of disturbance). This highly specific, technical approach to diagnosis reflects the work that is being done with children with neurological insult; it may nonetheless be appropriate for a wider range of children. The population that is the target of compensatory education, for example, is known to be at risk of developmental disorders associated with poor health and nutritional conditions. Even in the absence of organic defects, Johnson's approach makes sense because mental processes may be dysfunctional from lack of appropriate stimulation or cultivation or from temporal disturbances in the sequence of their development. Despite the logic of such a diagnostic approach, however, some of us would consider it inappropriate on the grounds that our intervention strategies do not yet match our diagnostic conceptualizations. There are very few facilities capable of doing the kind of diagnostic work implied by Johnson's approach, and even fewer school or clinic settings capable of providing necessary treatments for the conditions diagnosed.

Assessment of Mastery

In a more immediately practical vein, Calfee and Drum also stress the importance of diagnostic information. They argue that classroom assessment should aim toward the precise measurement of specific reading skills for short-term instructional decisions. The goals of such assessments are: (1) optimizing instructional sequences; (2) measuring immediate response to instruction; (3) regrouping for instruction for specific purposes; and (4) deciding on selection and allocation of resources. Whereas Johnson is concerned with more basic mental processes, Calfee and Drum are concerned with criterion mastery: What are the functional competencies and limitations of the children being assessed? What children need what instruction and materials? These questions provide the data for what Bloom calls "mastery learning," in which children are constantly monitored to determine who has mastered a competency and is ready for the next step and who needs additional exposure to achieve mastery.

Matching Traits and Treatments

Neither the Johnson nor the Calfee and Drum approach to assessment meets the Bateman call for greater attention to the potential payoff to be gained in manipulating trait/treatment interactions. Drawing from a special education model, Bateman sees the potential importance of educational designs influenced by the special characteristics and needs of the learner. Assessment procedures sensitive to these characteristics will need to go beyond the Calfee and Drum task- or criterion-centered approach and will not generally require the probes for neuropathology peculiar to Johnson's work. Rather, such assessment will need to be sensitive to cognitive and affective styles, learning rate, sources of motivation, degrees and directions of aspiration and interest, and idiosyncratic response tendencies (Fisher), as well as to contingencies (Holland) and context known to influence behavior. On the other hand, Williams rather doubts the utility of these efforts at diagnostic and prescriptive instruction. She calls attention to the fact that there is no convincing evidence that matching instructional treatments to diagnostic category will enhance learning. She is not alone in this pessimism. All of the reviews of the trait/treatment research have concluded that the theoretical promise is greater than is supportable by the empirical evidence. Yet some of our ablest empirical and theoretical scholars hold on to the belief that such matching has promise. The lack of evidence to support this position may be due to the relatively low level of current assessment and intervention technology. We do not yet have sensitive and valid measures of many of these personal and ecological variables, and we certainly don't have treatments to match them.

Functional Mismatching

Much has been said about the mismatch between the indigenous language of low-status pupils and the standard dialect. Shuy and Smith, writing independently, offer insightful observations. Rather than emphasizing differences in the structures of the languages, they focus on their functions. Shuy asserts that a functional mismatch between standard English and the student's language is probably more important than a phonological or grammatical mismatch. Smith argues that:

A largely neglected theoretical issue that may play a considerable role in the apparent inadequacy of much of our reading instruction is the fact that language as it is normally encountered and employed outside the classroom has a variety of functions.... The language children first hear and use always has a function, and language and function are probably learned simultaneously. Children learn to talk while learning that language can be used to satisfy needs, express feelings, explore ideas, ask questions, obtain answers, assert oneself, manipulate others, and establish and maintain specific interpersonal relations. But children may have acquired ability in one or two functions of language without being able to comprehend all its functions. Sometimes it may be thought that children lack language ability, when they are merely unfamiliar with certain functions.

Now consider this concern with the function of language within the context of Chall's developmental stages. Disturbance in the learning of the functions of language can occur at the acquisition stage, at the consolidation stage, or at the stages where facility, expansion, and flexibility are the task. On the other hand, since different situations and cultural settings emphasize different functions of language, the functions learned in one setting may not be those needed in another. This confusion or mismatch with respect to the functions of language may lie at the heart of difficulties in second- or multiple-language mastery and of reading dysfunction for culturally or linguistically displaced persons.

Decoding as Something to Fall Back On

Another compelling contribution by Smith is the notion that word and letter recognition are fall-back functions called into play when the dominant function in reading—grasping concepts and relationships that reflect and elaborate what one already knows—fails. (Smith's conception is consistent with Frederiksen's top–down conception of reading fluency.) What is it that skilled readers do? Most of us agree that it is not simply rapid decoding. Rather, it appears that the letter and word symbols and configurations stimulate thought. It is only when these stimuli fail to maintain the thought flow that we slow down or stop to register and translate letters and words. For example, when we read unfamiliar foreign or highly technical material, we fall back on decoding. It appears that familiarity with orthographic patterns (Venesky & Massaro, and Samuels) leads to automaticity (LaBerge & Samuels, 1974), which together with practice and experience enable the skilled reader to virtually skip through printed material, having his or her thinking guided by the stimulation provided by printed symbols. This view of decoding and reading suggests that persons with limited familiarity with the content to be read and limited related experience and knowledge will have greater difficulty reading than will others. To be more precise, such persons will be more dependent on decoding skill. The problem is compounded by the fact that those persons with limited experience and knowledge are also, usually, the persons with poor decoding skill. This compound problem is, of course, the problem of most of the target population for compensatory education. Since remedial decoding instruction moves so slowly, and since skill in reading also involves skill in thinking based on accumulated knowledge, it may be that developing alternatives to reading as sources of information is indicated—not as a substitute for reading but as an aid to improvement in reading.

What Needs To Be Done

Other chapters in these volumes provide additional contributions to our understanding of the teaching and learning of reading and the relation of that understanding to the problems of compensatory education. The chapters discussed above are sufficient, however, to establish two points. First, the extensive work directed at identifying the characteristics of low-status children not only provides few good leads for intervention; this work also appears to have developed quite independently of the extensive body of reading research, appears to be uninformed by it, and seems to have had little impact on reading research. Second, despite the limitations of the "characteristics-of-the-disadvantaged" research and the lack of meaningful interaction between that body of work and research on reading, the potential for reciprocal contributions from one field of study to the other is not at all modest. The history of scientific and professional knowledge is rich with examples of how our general knowledge of the human condition and human functions has been enriched by the study of special populations that are at greater risk or in which the frequency of dysfunction is exacerbated. Systematic investigation of the problems of reading in disadvantaged populations can contribute greatly to our understanding of the problems of the teaching and learning of reading in the total population.

The generalizability of findings from special populations to broader populations may, in part, be a function of the generality of the characteristics of populations defined by social status rather than by functional or learning-process characteristics. With the possible exception of home, family, and language characteristics, a review of the research on the disadvantaged suggests that there are no affective, cognitive, motivational, or aspirational characteristics that clearly set ethnic minority or low-SES children apart from their more privileged peers. Rather, it is more likely that affective, cognitive, and other characteristics vary within these status groups as much as between them and higher-status groups. It may well be that the low pay-off of our work with disadvantaged populations is in part a function of our having given too much attention to their status and insufficient attention to the learning process.

In the more promising work reported in this collection of papers, concern for process identification and process analysis is quite prominent. In all six categories of findings or positions discussed earlier, promise for improved work seems to be associated with efforts at linking up process characteristics of learners with process demands of learning tasks. This is not to suggest that disadvantageous status, deprivation, and the denial of opportunity are unimportant concerns in our effort to improve the education of the poor. These conditions are powerful deterrents to effective learning and optimal development, and if compensatory education is ever to succeed, it will only be by reducing these handicapping conditions. But even the elimination of these adverse social, economic, and political conditions is not likely to eliminate learning dysfunctions as long as schooling is not adaptive to the wide variations in the learning behavior of our pupils. It is my considered judgment that this is the pedagogical problem that has not been dealt with in compensatory education. It is, however, beginning to receive attention in some of the better work on the teaching and learning of reading. This work could receive a mighty boost forward if more of the resources and energy that go into compensatory education were combined with the best of our research and practice related to the teaching and learning of reading.

REFERENCES

Banks, W. C., & McQuater, G. V. Achievement motivation and black children. *IRCD Bulletin,* 1976, *11*(4), 1–7.

Coleman, J. S., Campbell, E. Q., Hobson, C. J., McPartland, J., Mood, A. M., Weinfeld, F. D., & York, R. L. *Equality of educational opportunity.* Washington, D.C.: U.S. Government Printing Office, 1966.

Deutsch, M. *Minority group and class status as related to social and personality factors in scholastic achievement.* Ithaca, N.Y.: Society for Applied Anthropology, 1960. (Monograph No. 2) [Gordon, E. W. Toward defining equality of educational opportunity. In F. Mosteller & D. P. Moynihan (Eds.), *On equality of educational opportunity.* New York: Random House, 1972.]

Jamison, D. Computer assisted instruction and compensatory education. In Educational Testing Service, *The ETS/Los Angeles Unified School District Study.* Princeton, N.J.: ETS, 1976.

Jensen, A. R. How much can we boost IQ and scholastic achievement? *Harvard Educational Review,* 1969, *39,* 1–123.

Klineberg, O. Negro–white differences in intelligence test performance: A new look at an old problem. *American Psychologist,* 1963, *18,* 198–203.

LaBerge D., & Samuels, S. J. Toward a theory of automatic information processing in reading. *Cognitive Psychology,* 1974, *6,* 293–323.

Ogbu, J. U. *Minority education and caste.* New York: Academic Press, 1978.

Riessman, F. *The culturally deprived child.* New York: Harper & Row, 1962.

15

Theories and Prescriptions for Early Reading Instruction

Lauren B. Resnick
University of Pittsburgh

Are some ways of teaching beginning reading more effective than others, especially for children in compensatory educational programs? What does the research say? Do the research findings agree with what experts in the field say about the theory of reading? These are the questions addressed in these volumes. The aim of the volumes is to clarify points of agreement and disagreement as a basis for advising educators and the public on the approaches to instruction most likely to be effective for hard-to-teach children. I attempt in this chapter to summarize the major points of view expressed here and to relate these positions to outcomes of evaluation studies comparing various reading approaches. On the basis of these twin sources of evidence, I draw implications for current practice in compensatory education and for new approaches to instruction that need systematic development and trial.

There is little doubt that those closely involved in questions of reading instruction—either as researchers or as practitioners—believe that what is taught, and how it is taught, matters. The intensity of discussion, over the course of decades, is enough to convince us of this. But are these advocates of one or another approach right? Is there any basis at all for deciding among programs? Or is it the case, as some people continue to claim, that it doesn't matter how reading is taught as long as there is commitment to learning on the part of the teacher and the school; or that different children learn in such different ways that there is simply no way of choosing among competing programs on a general basis?

To respond to these questions, I begin by characterizing what I perceive as the two main strands of theory concerning the nature of reading and learning to read. I then consider such empirical evidence as is available on the relative effects of programs that appear to embody these two views of reading. On the basis of this evidence, I (a) recommend an aspect of current practice in early reading, and (b) suggest new kinds of program development that hold promise for improving other important aspects of reading instruction.

COMPETING POSITIONS ON THE NATURE OF READING

Two main strands of theory concerning the nature of reading can be identified, both in the various chapters of these volumes and in a perusal of as much as a century of research literature on teaching reading. For the sake of simplicity, I call these the *reading as translation* and the *reading as language* positions.

Reading as Translation

One view considers reading to be essentially a process of translating printed symbols into some approximation of oral language and then letting already developed oral language abilities take over. In this view, reading is largely "parasitic" on speech. The most important thing that must be done in learning to read is to learn what the printed symbols "say" (i.e., what sounds they correspond to). No other activity is unique to reading; everything else is shared with speech. In addition, because the ability to comprehend speech is already present in any individual who is learning to read, only word recognition needs to be taught directly. Once words can be recognized, practice in this new (visual) mode of receiving language symbols will produce the fluency and response to meaning that characterizes skilled readers.

The reading as translation view generally leads to a predominant, or even exclusive, preoccupation with mastery of the alphabetic code. It suggests that whatever else is done early in instruction, the code must be taught. From this derives the notion that instructional materials should be organized so as to highlight predictable aspects of the print–sound code. In research, the translation position is associated with a concern for word recognition processes, with the role of the alphabetic code in recognition, and with the role of fast or "automatic" word recognition in facilitating reading comprehension. (See, for example, Perfetti & Lesgold, Vol. 1, this series.) People who characterize reading in terms of print–sound translation freely admit that many people learn to read—that is, master the code so that they can use it automatically—without much direct instruction. But they often express special concern for the "hard-to-teach," including children in compensatory programs. They assume that the difficulty these individuals have in becoming competent readers is primarily a difficulty in mastering the code. They look for—and demonstrate—difficulties in skills they consider prerequisites to learning the alphabetic code, such as segmenting the speech stream (Liberman & Shankweiler, Vol. 2; Rozin & Gleitman, 1976). They tend to advocate prereading activities that teach these prerequisites or methods of reading instruction that teach them in the course of teaching the code (see also chapters by Rosner, Vol. 2; and Wallach & Wallach, Vol. 3).

Reading as Language

The second strand of theory holds that reading is a separate, autonomous language process. Understanding the written word is in certain important ways different from understanding spoken language. Written language is organized differently from spoken language. It also fulfills different social functions. Although written material *can* be read aloud, it is not primarily intended for this use. Furthermore, there are important differences in the ways in which speech and print are mentally processed. Because it is an autonomous language process, reading cannot be taught as if it were parasitic on speech. That is, we cannot assume that because people know how to translate print into sound (recognize words), they will be able to understand and use written language in functional ways. Instead, reading instruction must focus quite directly on the functional use of written language, preferably from the outset of instruction.

The instructional views of people who interpret reading as an autonomous language system are varied. None deny, for example, that the alphabetic code must be learned, but they vary widely in their view of the amount and timing of direct instruction that should be devoted to it. All agree that reading instruction, essentially from the outset, must focus on deriving meaning from written language and on functional use of the written word. For this, they are prepared to sacrifice, if necessary, some rigor and speed in acquiring knowledge of the code. In general, people with this view of the nature of reading do not believe that learning the code is very difficult or that not knowing it is the major cause of reading failure. But a problem in characterizing this group of reading theorists is that they agree more on what learning to read is not—that is, it is not simply mastering the code—than on what it is.

A variety of approaches to reading instruction have been advocated by people who view reading as an autonomous language process. Probably the oldest and still most widely used is the "look–say" approach to word recognition, generally embodied in basal reading instructional programs prior to the late 1960s. "Look–say" or "whole-word" teaching methods arose in the first half of this century as a reaction against the dry, dull, and not very successful methods of reading that had predominated earlier and that focused on oral reading and on learning the alphabetic code. (See Resnick & Resnick, 1977, for a characterization of these earlier methods and of the success rates associated with them.) The essence of the philosophy underlying basal reading approaches was that reading should, from the outset, focus on extracting meaning rather than on "mechanics," the latter to be acquired later and with as little instruction as possible.

This basic view is shared by proponents of various "language-experience" approaches to reading instruction, although these people (e.g., Goodman & Goodman, Vol. 1) believe that for reading to become a functional communication system, it is necessary for it to be rooted in the communication needs and processes of the learner. For this reason, the basic "material" of reading ought to be text actually produced by the learners or their peers. Special variants of language-experience approaches have been proposed by those immersed in work with people from illiterate communities and from cultural backgrounds sharply divergent from dominant Western ones—for example, Ashton-Warner (1963) working with Maori children in New Zealand, and Freire (1970) working with illiterate adults in Brazil. In each of these cases, a key observation was that to make the effort to become literate, people of any age needed to recognize that their own concerns—not only those of an outside, and perhaps oppressive, culture—could be expressed in writing.

A similar argument is made by those who propose variants of language experience for compensatory education populations in America today. People who are concerned with these groups and who espouse the autonomous language system view of reading argue that failure to learn to read stems primarily from learners' not recognizing the relevance of school-related reading to intrinsically important events outside of school. The problem is a failure to recognize reading and writing as functional tools within their own culture, not an inability to perform the component skills such as decoding. Two prescriptions for instruction follow: for beginners, immediate and continuing focus on meaning through the medium of written materials produced (directly or through dictation) by the learners; and for those in need of remedial help, a focus on the reading and discussion of intrinsically interesting material rather than on "skill building." With respect to basic research, the autonomous communication system definition of reading leads to a concern with the ways in which meaningful written language is processed. Sentences are the smallest units of concern, and recently longer texts have been studied. The study of discourse processing is a relatively new area of study for psychology, and particularly for the psychology of reading, and therefore is developed much less thoroughly than is word recognition research. (See Just & Carpenter, 1977, for a collection of current work in this field.)

THE EMPIRICAL EVIDENCE CONCERNING READING INSTRUCTION

Evidence clearly favoring one reading instructional approach over another in school settings is difficult to find. Most studies fail to show significant differences, and those that do show differences are often attacked on one or another fine point of research methodology. Nevertheless, a consistent pattern of findings can be detected concerning both program effects and general style of instruction. This pattern can be summarized briefly in the following way. Concerning programs, when skill in word recognition is the primary dependent variable, code-oriented programs tend to be advantageous over language-oriented programs. This is especially true for children from low-socioeconomic-status (SES) groups and for low achievers in general. However, when comprehension beyond the very simplest levels is the criterion, there is no clear advantage for either code- or language-oriented programs. Concerning instructional style, direct instruction and well-structured curricula used under direct teacher control have a clear advantage, again especially for low-achieving or low-SES groups. I draw these conclusions on the basis of the evidence discussed in the following paragraphs.

Follow Through. Follow Through is a national experiment in primary education that has allowed comparisons of several different instructional approaches for poor children of varying cultural backgrounds. We now have data from several cohorts of Follow Through students (Stebbins, St. Pierre, Proper, Anderson, & Cerva, 1977). In none of the evaluations are the different instructional programs compared with each other in a strict experimental design. Instead, each program is compared with its own control group, which received the "standard" program of the school district. This means that the program to which the control group is exposed is not strictly specified. Nevertheless, patterns can be detected in which groups instructed with certain programs, used in a number of different school districts and over a number of years, often show reading achievement test scores superior to their control groups, and groups exposed to other programs rarely show such an advantage. These patterns suggest that the most structured Follow Through model—the University of Oregon's, which uses *Distar*, a program developed explicitly for Follow Through and other compensatory use—more regularly shows advantages over its control group than do the less structured models.[1] This pattern is strongest in first and second grades; it is present but

---

[1]*Distar* stresses systematic code learning. Instruction in the program is teacher led, and children are taught in small groups. Activities for both the teachers and the students are prescribed in detail by the program.

weaker in third grade. By fourth grade, the advantage has disappeared. This summary is based primarily on data from the reading subtest of the Metropolitan Achievement Tests. From fourth grade on, this test stresses comprehension tasks. Data collected by the Oregon model sponsors on their own school suggest that when a test is used that stresses word recognition (such as the WRAT, the Wide Range Achievement Test), the advantage of the program is maintained even into the upper elementary grades.

To interpret this pattern, it is necessary to know that the Oregon and other structured Follow Through models use direct instruction approaches to reading and that their programs are code oriented rather than language oriented. Furthermore, these programs tend to include careful and individualized record keeping and a focus on a mastery of identifiable and measurable "components" of reading competence. The child-centered or less structured Follow Through models tend to use language-oriented instructional strategies. There is considerable variety with respect to specific programs and instructional styles, but there is—in keeping with the child-centered philosophy that governs most of these programs—substantial emphasis on embedding reading in naturally occurring language settings and relatively little emphasis on structured, direct instruction. The range of activities that might be considered "reading" or "reading related" in these programs is very wide; by contrast, only formal reading and writing activities would be so considered in the structured programs. Thus, children in structured programs probably spend more time actually engaged in activities involving written materials.

Why is the advantage for the structured programs strongest at the lowest grade levels? It could be because the programs have been in use longer at those levels, and therefore both the materials and their implementation are more refined. However, the difference might also reflect a gradual shift in characteristics of the reading tests over grade levels. Although texts must be read and questions answered at all levels, the complexity of the texts and the inferential demands of the questions become progressively greater in higher grades. Children who were very good (for their age and grade) at word recognition could excel on the lower-grade tests because the linguistic complexity is low. At higher grades, more sophisticated language competence is required to do well, although the ability to recognize words is still needed. Therefore, the drop-off in advantage for the structured Follow Through models at higher grade levels probably reflects the structured programs' relative strengths. They are especially good at teaching word recognition but not especially good at teaching comprehension. The continued high performance of Oregon's children on the WRAT lends strength to this interpretation. Notice, however, that the structured, code-oriented programs are not *worse* at teaching comprehension than are the child-centered, language-oriented models; they are just not any better.

Chall's "Great Debate" Book. The Follow Through findings, based on national samples and a common set of measurements for various programs, mirror an older finding based on a review of research literature on reading instruction conducted up to about 1965. Jeanne Chall's book, *Learning to Read: The Great Debate*, published in 1967, reviewed a very large collection of studies comparing code, basal, and language-experience methods. She concluded the following:

> Early stress on code learning, these studies indicate, not only produces better word recognition and spelling, but also makes it easier for the child eventually to read with understanding—at least up to the beginning of the fourth grade, after which point there is practically no evidence. . . . The experimental research provides no evidence that either a code or a meaning emphasis fosters greater love of reading or is more interesting to children. . . . There is some experimental evidence that children of below-average and average intelligence and children of lower socioeconomic background do better with an early code emphasis. Brighter children and those from middle and high socioeconomic backgrounds also gain from such an approach, but probably not as much. Intelligence, help at home, and greater facility with language probably allow these children to discover much of the code on their own, even if they follow a meaning program in school [pp. 83–84].

Chall concluded that code emphases foster reading with understanding, but her evidence is virtually only for the primary grades. We do not know, on the basis of the older literature, whether the early gain with code-oriented programs is maintained later. Chall herself speculated that whether the advantage would be maintained would depend on whether reading in the higher grades contained enough stress on language and vocabulary growth and provided sufficiently challenging materials for reading. She apparently believed, although she did not directly state it at that time, that reading programs needed to shift from a code to a language emphasis after a certain level of code competence had been reached.

Guthrie's Study of Reading Problems. Guthrie and his colleagues (Guthrie, Samuels, Martuza, Seifert, Tyler, & Edwall, 1976) reviewed research on the nature and locus of reading problems. They report comparisons of good and poor readers, as measured by a standardized reading comprehension test, that show: (a) no difference in the grammatical or semantic acceptability of words substituted in the course of "misreading" a text; but (b) a greater tendency on the part of good readers to make errors based on graphic similarity. These findings are contrary to what proponents of language approaches to reading often predict—namely, that emphasis on learning the code will produce a tendency to attend *too much* to the spelling and *not enough* to the meaning of words and therefore will interfere with comprehension. Guthrie et al.'s summary also shows that poor readers in the intermediate grades tend to be about as deficient in word knowledge as they are in comprehension, again contrary to what language proponents predict. Poor comprehenders are both poor decoders (i.e., they make more errors) and slow decoders (even when they do decode accurately). They are also weaker in using semantic and syntactic cues of language (e.g., they are less bothered by syntactic variations) both when reading and when listening. The general pattern seems to be one in which good decoding skills are quite clearly associated with good comprehension and in which syntactic and semantic difficulties are associated with oral as well as written language. This evidence, although correlational, seems to support those who view reading as translation to speech and to suggest that code-oriented early instruction is likely to be the most successful in overcoming difficulties in learning to read.

Guthrie's group also reanalyzed data from two major earlier investigations to determine whether instructional practices make a difference along the lines that I have suggested in this chapter. The first reanalysis was of the Bond and Dykstra (1967) first-grade studies. Using a word-reading subtest as a measure of knowledge of the code, this reanalysis showed a skills-oriented method (either linguistics or phonics) to be superior to a language-oriented method. The addition of a phonics program to a basal reading program also increased the basal's apparent effectiveness. On a paragraph-meaning test, no clear difference between skill-based and language-based approaches could be detected. The authors concluded that comprehension is not a problem in first grade and that it is therefore not surprising that instruction oriented primarily toward language comprehension has no strong effect. On the other hand, direct instruction in the code does seem to have positive effects on the aspect of reading that requires instruction at this stage.

The second reanalysis was done on the Educational Testing Service study of compensatory reading programs. The programs were classified as either high or low in instructional time and high or low in skill (code) emphasis. In addition, sex and three levels of SES were distinguished. Analyses of covariance (controlling for differences in autumn achievement test scores) on various dependent variables were then calculated. Clear patterns with respect to instructional emphasis are difficult to detect; however, more instructional time, especially for low-SES and compensatory instructional groups at both second- and sixth-grade levels, was found to be a clear benefit.

The California Teacher Study.   The import of time and its relation to type of instructional program can be understood best by considering the work of Berliner and others on the California Teacher Study (Berliner & Rosenshine, 1977; Fisher, Filby, & Marliave, 1977; Rosenshine, 1976). According to these studies and literature reviews associated with them, increased time and direct teaching produce the strongest learning results. Most observable "direct teaching" tends to be focused on code aspects of reading. This may be partly because observers can easily agree on when "reading instruction" is taking place in the case of word recognition but are less certain of what constitutes "instruction" in comprehension. Whether a result of observational methodology or a real effect, this finding confirms a frequently noted correlation between a code orientation in reading and direct instructional strategies. The correlation is evident too in some chapters in these volumes (e.g., Bateman, Vol. 1; or Wallach & Wallach, Vol. 3; as against Goodman & Goodman, Vol. 1), although there are some exceptions (e.g., Chomsky, Vol. 2, on a child-centered approach to early appreciation of the code). The correlation raises some questions for us: Is the apparent effectiveness of code approaches to teaching due to their direct instruction characteristics or to the content of what is taught? If the former, might a language-oriented program using direct instruction be equally or more effective? I return to these questions as I address the question of what new instructional approaches warrant development and trial in the schools.

A RECOMMENDATION FOR CURRENT PRACTICE

I have distinguished, on the basis of these volumes and related literature, between two broadly defined approaches to reading instruction: a code orientation and a language orientation. The review of field research in reading has suggested an advantage for code-oriented teaching roughly through the primary school years, the period during which tests demand relatively unsophisticated language processing and give a clear edge to those who can recognize printed words accurately and quickly. This advantage is especially marked for children in compensatory programs. After the primary grades, there is no clear evidence supporting either code or language approaches to instruction. What does this suggest for formulating policy regarding reading in compensatory education programs?

As a matter of routine practice, we need to include systematic, code-oriented instruction in the primary grades, no matter what else is also done. This is the only place in which we have any clear evidence for any particular practice. We cannot afford to ignore that evidence or the several instructional programs already in existence that do a good job of teaching the code. The charge—made by some who espouse language-oriented approaches and who view reading as an autonomous communication system—that too early or too much emphasis on the code depresses comprehension finds no support in the empirical data. On the other hand, neither is there support for a radical claim that once the code is well learned, other reading problems will disappear. Thus, there is no evidence that code-emphasis programs alone will "solve" the reading problem.

What appears to be needed is systematic code teaching together with attention to language-processing (i.e., comprehension) aspects of reading.

But to say this is hardly to have completed a prescription for compensatory reading instruction. Virtually every reading program today claims to be providing just such a combination—yet we lack many smashing successes. Where does the difficulty lie?

It lies in part in a fundamental competition between code and language demands in early reading. Learning the code requires a controlled vocabulary—but language processing requires a rich language with which to work. This conflict cannot be wished away. Beck and Block (Vol. 1), in their comparative program analysis, pointed out how an "add-on" phonics program might lose its power when the spelling patterns taught are not given extensive practice in the reading materials that immediately follow. And no one has yet demonstrated empirically, with a compensatory education population, a successful way of teaching the code entirely on the basis of student-generated stories or words drawn from students' natural environments. The strongest claims for success along these lines come from certain proponents of "alternative education." Despite the absence of formal evidence, I have seen enough of these programs to believe that many students who would resist reading in conventional programs become good readers in them. But in most successful cases, there is some largely "unsung" systematic code teaching, at least for a while, for most students. (For a systematic "alternative teaching" approach, complete with a diagnostic procedure and rather clear instructional plans, see Kohl's [1973] *Reading, How To*.)

The problem facing those who would design reading instruction for compensatory education, then, lies in great part in finding a balance of emphasis and timing between code and language aspects of reading. At the same time, substantial attention to *how* to address the language-processing aspect of reading is needed. We have a number of good code-oriented programs available, but we have no strong success to report for a language-oriented program. This does not argue for teaching the code and letting language take care of itself. It argues, instead, for using what we have in the way of successful code-teaching approaches and meanwhile focusing intensively on developing language-teaching approaches that are as effective in their own domain. In the next section, I consider some of the possibilities for language instruction and for combining code and language teaching.

TOWARD SOLVING THE REST OF
THE READING PROBLEM:
NEW APPROACHES THAT SHOULD BE TRIED

In this section I consider two issues: (a) how to teach language aspects of reading, and (b) how to combine language and code teaching.

Teaching Language Processes

Oral Versus Written. A first question in considering how to teach language-processing skills is whether it will be most effective to teach them in an oral mode or in a written mode. A not infrequently made proposal—by those who favor a strong code orientation for early reading—is to focus beginning reading instruction largely or exclusively on the code while providing separate instruction in oral language comprehension. This approach assumes that those who do not comprehend what they read, even though they know the code, are deficient in general language-processing skills and further, that reading comprehension is not a significantly different process from listening comprehension. It adopts, in other words, a "translation" definition of reading. A proposal of this kind has been made most explicitly by Sticht, but no serious empirical test has been made. Sticht himself, in his chapter (Vol. 1), describes a program of reading instruction in which considerable oral work takes place; but the written and oral activities are not clearly separated. A systematic effort to test Sticht's model ought to be made.

An important aspect of such a test should be attention to the possibility that separate instruction in oral comprehension may be effective in improving reading for certain kinds of materials or up to a certain level of complexity, but that beyond that point, the oral approach may become cumbersome or even totally ineffective. The existence of such a point would be strongly predicted by anyone espousing the notion of reading as an autonomous communication system. Arguments supporting this position can be made on the basis of skilled readers' ability to process written material far faster than people can speak. There is also evidence that skilled readers reading complex materials engage in a fair amount of "checking back" to earlier text, something not possible with oral presentations. These behaviors suggest different processes for reading than listening, at least in part. In addition, analyses by Olson (1977) and others of differences in the structure of written texts and oral communications suggest that written messages may be different enough in structure to require different processes than speech messages. If different processes are involved, then instruction in comprehending written material would be called for; transfer from oral comprehension could not be depended upon. These considerations suggest that we also ought to develop and test strategies for teaching written language-processing skills.

Direct Versus Informal Teaching. This brings us to our second question—what role direct instruction should play in teaching language skills. As already mentioned, there appears in these volumes a correlation of opinions: Those who advocate a focus on the code tend to advocate direct instruction; those who advocate a language-processing emphasis advocate looser, learner-directed instructional approaches. So widespread is this correlation of beliefs that we rarely question its appropriateness. Yet there is nothing inherent in a language-processing emphasis that requires informal teaching styles. To break free of the current, rather unproductive, confrontation between language and code advocates, one of the things we have to do is mentally "uncouple" informal teaching and language orientation. It may be that only learner-directed, informal teaching styles can bring about the functional uses of reading that language-oriented people stress. But it may be the case that direct instruction will work as well or better, especially if the processes involved in language comprehension, whether oral or written, can be better specified than they are currently. What we need to do, in the tradition of American pragmatism, is to "try it and see."

There are, then, two approaches to instruction in language processes to be explored: informal and direct. Consider the informal or child-centered method first. It might appear that this approach has had its chance and failed. Our look at the evidence from field research suggests no outstanding reading successes among child-centered programs or language-experience methods except for the quickest learners and high-SES groups. These data provide no recommendation for informal teaching styles with children in compensatory programs. Yet I think it is the case that we have not yet seen a real trial of learner-centered methods. Such a trial would require using the best aspects of informal teaching systematically enough and in enough classrooms that we could find out both whether the approach is usable by a significant number of teachers and whether, when used, children learn to read well. The current state of informal education ideology and methodology precludes such a test. Programs and teaching strategies are described in the loosest terms; relatively few opportunities for extended apprenticeships exist; and teachers are thus forced to invent for themselves a good deal of what they do. Not all teachers are good inventors; few have enough years on the job to permit them to grope toward success. A first requirement then is that proponents of informal language-teaching approaches make their methods more accessible by specification, systematic training, and the like.

A serious test of the power of an informal, language-oriented approach to reading will also require sustaining the program over a relatively long period, at least several years. This may be difficult, especially in communities that have become used to watching test score data as indicators of the success of their schools, because the growth in language competence brought about by informal approaches may not be reflected in scores on tests now in use. A trial of informal approaches, therefore, may require use of achievement tests that are more sensitive to growth in language competence than our current ones appear to be. In other words, I am suggesting that child-centered, language-experience approaches to reading have not yet had a real trial in this country. To have such a trial, we would need both sustained commitment to it and attempts by those who believe in the power of these teaching approaches to develop more explicit ways of helping teachers implement them and measure their effectiveness.

The alternative approach is to develop systematic, direct instruction approaches to teaching comprehension and language-skill aspects of reading. Once we disengage the language-processing orientation from informal teaching methods, this becomes a prospect that can at least be considered. Such direct instruction in comprehension was the aim of the early basal reading systems. But the basal reading systems we inherited from the 1930s did not meet their originators' aspirations. Today's series reflect the successive waves of disenchantment with the basals in the variety of "add-on" activities that they incorporate—phonics units, language-experience activities, and so on. The possibility of direct instruction in comprehension apparently needs rethinking. Proposals for developing direct instruction approaches to teaching comprehension and writing deserve serious consideration at this time, as do proposals for expanding the knowledge base that might guide this development along profitable new lines.

Combining Language and Code Teaching

I have stated here that both code and language teaching will be required in successful reading instruction. How are they to be combined? The basic choice is whether to teach code and language simultaneously or successively. That is, both code and language aspects of reading can be the focus of instruction from the outset, or one can be emphasized first and then the other.

Successive Teaching. Successive strategies have been the most popular in the past and still dominate most thinking about teaching reading. Which should come first, in a given theorist's or practitioner's opinion, is very much a function of that individual's preferred definition of reading. Translation proponents—even when they recognize the need for some instruction and practice in language aspects of reading—want to emphasize the code at the outset and for as long as it takes for fluency to develop. Autonomous language system proponents want to begin with a meaning emphasis and let the code come later—if instruction in it is needed at all. Empirical evidence appears to support the code-first position. Initial emphasis on the code in a direct instruction program produces initial advantages and no long-term disadvantages. A language-first emphasis, at least in the versions tried up to now, has not shown a clear advantage at either stage. Therefore, if a successive timing strategy is to be chosen, the current evidence argues for focusing first on the code. This sequence is in agreement with the stage theory of reading development outlined by Chall (Vol. 1), in which the first two stages of reading are concerned largely with learning the code and developing fluency and confidence in word recognition. (These stages follow a period of developing readiness, which includes attention to the function and meaning aspects of written language.) A code-first sequence also agrees with Adams, Anderson, and Durkin's (1978) recent position paper on cognitive processes in early reading. The authors argue that word recognition, word meaning, grammatical interpretation, and interpretation of logical interrelations among parts of the text are all active at all stages of reading but that at the beginning of reading, the new and most difficult task—and therefore the preoccupying one—is word recognition. Focusing instruction on the code, then, is a way of helping children at the beginning stages with their most difficult task.

Simultaneous Teaching. Is simultaneous attention to code and language-processing aspects of reading possible? Might it alter the course of reading acquisition? We don't know the answer to either question, since a carefully documented simultaneous teaching strategy does not exist. Nevertheless, we can consider some possibilities and assess the likelihood of their being successful. I have already discussed the inherent difficulty of combining language and code emphases that derives from the code teacher's need for a carefully controlled vocabulary. But most code programs develop large recognition vocabularies relatively quickly, and the "conflict" might not have to last more than a few months. Elsa Bartlett (Vol. 2) suggests that one code-oriented program, *Open Court,* may be an example of successful early introduction of a rich variety of written materials. If materials of this kind can be used as the basis for direct instruction in language processing, then a very minimal delay between code and language foci can be envisaged. Bartlett's analysis of the program does not suggest how systematically or effectively the materials are used, but this is a case worth investigating, particularly because the program involved is coming into increasingly wider use with hard-to-teach populations (Bateman, 1977). According to Bartlett's analysis, *Open Court* is able to introduce richer-than-usual reading selections in part because it introduces elements of the code quickly and relies on children to be able to handle variability in print-to-sound translation. Many contributors to these volumes believe that a slower, more deliberate pace is needed for the hard-to-teach children in a compensatory education population. If they are right, then a long delay in language instruction might be required for these children. But a recent report (Bateman, 1977) suggests that *Open Court* is being used successfully with many hard-to-teach groups (compensatory, learning disabled, etc.). Certainly this trend should be monitored closely over the next few years.

Another alternative for simultaneous language and code emphases is to use informal, language-experience methods for language development simultaneously with a structured, code-oriented program. Strict code advocates are likely to claim that this will confuse children, who will encounter irregularly spelled words in the course of their informal work and who will be encouraged to guess and otherwise depend on cues other than orthography in their early reading attempts. We have no firm data on this, but informal observation suggests that most children are quite good at recognizing the different demands of different situations and would attend to the code during the formal instruction. A greater impediment, in my opinion, lies in the difficulty of school and classroom organization that the simultaneous use of direct and informal teaching seems to imply. Observations of classrooms in which a combination of direct and informal teaching is being tried suggest that one or the other aspect tends to be ignored, or at least given short shrift. Teachers complain about competing demands on their time, although they usually recognize that the children have plenty of time in the school day for both. My personal observation is that individual teachers, by temperament or training, seem to be good at one or the other kind of instruction and attendant classroom management, but rarely at both.

These observations lead me to propose, as an instructional approach worth development and trial in the schools, a reorganization of the school program so that informal instruction and direct instruction both take place but in clearly separated times and places and under the direction of different teachers. Various models for this separation are possible. For example, the school day might be divided into two halves—one for formal instruction, the other for informal. Or the "home" classroom could be organized along informal lines, with children assigned on a rotating basis to a skill center staffed by teachers who are proficient at teaching code and those language skills that seem to improve most through direct instruction. Whatever the particular arrangement, it is clear that seriously combining formal and informal teaching may require extensive reorganization of staff, time, and space allocations within schools. The effort may have some surprising side benefits, however, because it may solve problems of homogeneous versus heterogeneous grouping, "mainstreaming," cost-effective use of special reading teachers, and other problems that are difficult to contend with in the context of self-contained classroom organizations.

SUMMARY AND CONCLUSIONS

On the basis of the chapters included in these volumes, it is possible to identify two main strands of theory about the nature of reading. These are: (1) *reading as translation,* a view that holds reading to be essentially the translation of printed symbols into an approximation of oral language, so that already developed capabilities for understanding and using speech can be applied to written language; and (2) *reading as an autonomous language process,* a view that understanding the written word is in certain important ways different and separate from understanding spoken language. The two views of reading lead to different kinds of prescriptions for early reading instruction. Reading as translation suggests predominant attention to helping children master the alphabetic code. Reading as autonomous language suggests that reading instruction must focus quite directly on the functional and meaningful use of written language right from the outset of instruction. Both basal "look–say" methods and informal "language-experience" methods of teaching are attempts to meet this requirement in instruction.

Evidence clearly favoring one instructional approach over another in field settings is difficult to find. Nevertheless, a repeating pattern of findings concerning both what is taught and how it is taught can be detected if we examine several decades of applied research. This pattern can be summarized roughly as follows: When skill in word recognition is the outcome being studied, code-oriented programs tend to show up better than language-oriented programs. This is especially true for low-socioeconomic groups and for low achievers in general. However, when comprehension beyond the very simplest levels is the criterion, there is no clear advantage for either code- or language-oriented programs. Concerning instructional style—direct instruction, teacher-controlled use of time, and well-structured curricula have a clear edge—again especially for low-achieving or low-SES groups. These conclusions are drawn on the basis of evidence from: (a) several cohorts of Follow Through children; (b) Jeanne Chall's book, *Learning to Read: The Great Debate,* which reviewed studies conducted up to about 1964; (c) research reviews conducted by Guthrie and his colleagues for the National Institute of Education's compensatory education evaluation studies: (d) reanalyses of data from the Bond and Dykstra first-grade studies and the Educational Testing Service study of compensatory reading programs; and (e) the California Teacher Study.

These findings suggest several lines of action for national reading policy and for further development and study of reading instruction. First, as a matter of routine practice, we need to include systematic code-oriented instruction in the primary grades, at least for hard-to-teach children, no matter what else is also done. This is the only place in which we have any clear evidence for a particular practice. We cannot afford to ignore that evidence or the several instructional programs already available or nearly ready for use that do a good job of teaching the code. There is no empirical evidence that too early or too much emphasis on the code depresses later comprehension. On the other hand, there is no evidence that code-emphasis programs alone will "solve" the reading problem. Such programs succeed well in teaching word recognition skills. They show no advantage, however, once comprehension becomes the main criterion of success (starting at about third or fourth grade). For this reason, we need to work on developing programs that do a good job of teaching the meaning and functional aspects of reading. Two possibilities for such programs should be pursued. The language-experience approach, which builds on children's own writing and dictation, should be specified by its proponents precisely enough that it can be given a serious try in schools. Despite widespread interest in learner-centered, language-experience approaches, these methods have not been adequately described. Much is left to teacher invention, but not all teachers are well prepared for this task. A real trial of the language-experience approach will require a precise specification of the approach, its sustained use over several years, and quite probably, tests that are more sensitive to students' ability to use written language than our current ones appear to be. The second possibility for language-oriented reading instruction that should be investigated is direct instruction. For a decade or more, language-oriented approaches and informal, learner-centered methods of teaching have tended to be linked in educators' minds. This is not a necessary relationship, however. Just as we need to further develop and test language-experience approaches, we also need to explore direct instruction in comprehension. Such instruction may begin with oral comprehension skills, as is advocated by several of the experts who contributed to these volumes, or it may work directly on the comprehension of written material, as others advocate. In either case, success will probably depend on the emergence—now more than a vague promise, given new psychological research on language processing—of a detailed theory of the mental activities that take place during language comprehension. Thus, investment in "basic" research on how people understand written language can be expected to yield practical results for reading instruction within some reasonable, if not immediate, period of time.

Finally, attention will have to be paid to how to combine code and language aspects of instruction. A successive strategy in which code is emphasized first and language follows, or vice versa, is the most common today. The practical successes of code programs at the earliest grade levels, especially with compensatory education children, suggest that code should precede language if a successive strategy is used. However, simultaneous teaching of code and language aspects of reading may be even more effective, and several possibilities for such simultaneous teaching are suggested.

ACKNOWLEDGMENTS

This paper was supported by a grant to the Learning Research and Development Center from the National Institute of Education (NIE), United States Department of Health, Education, and Welfare, for a series of conferences on the Theory and Practice of Beginning Reading Instruction, Contract #400-75-0049. This paper was presented at the fall meeting of the National Academy of Education, New York, October 1977.

REFERENCES

Adams, M. J., Anderson, R. C., & Durkin, D. Beginning reading: Theory and practice. *Language Arts,* 1978, *55*(1), 19–25.

Ashton-Warner, S. *Teacher.* New York: Simon & Schuster, 1963.

Bateman, B. Personal communication, May 1977.

Berliner, D. C., & Rosenshine, B. The acquisition of knowledge in the classroom. In R. C. Anderson, R. J. Spiro, & W. E. Montague (Eds.), *Schooling and the acquisition of knowledge.* Hillsdale, N.J.: Lawrence Erlbaum Associates, 1977.

Bond, G. L., & Dykstra, R. The cooperative research program in first-grade reading. *Reading Research Quarterly,* 1967, *2* (entire issue).

Chall, J. S. *Learning to read: The great debate.* New York: McGraw-Hill, 1967.

Fisher, C. W., Filby, N. N., & Marliave, R. S. *Instructional time and student achievement in second grade reading and mathematics.* Paper presented at the meeting of the American Educational Research Association, New York, April 1977.

Freire, P. *Pedagogy of the oppressed.* New York: Seabury Press, 1970.

Guthrie, J. T., Samuels, S. J., Martuza, V., Seifert, M., Tyler, S. J., & Edwall, G. *A study of the locus and nature of reading problems in the elementary school* (Final report, 2 sections). Newark, Del.: International Reading Association, 1976.

Just, M. A., & Carpenter, P. A. (Eds.). *Cognitive processes in comprehension.* Hillsdale, N.J.: Lawrence Erlbaum Associates, 1977.

Kohl, H. *Reading, how to.* New York: Bantam Books, 1973.

Olson, D. R. From utterance to text: The bias of language in speech and writing. *Harvard Educational Review,* 1977, *47*(3), 257–281.

Resnick, D. P., & Resnick, L. B. The nature of literacy: An historical exploration. *Harvard Educational Review,* 1977, *47*(3), 370–385.

Rosenshine, B. Classroom instruction. In N. L. Gage (Ed.), *The psychology of teaching methods: The 75th Yearbook of the National Society for the Study of Education.* Chicago: National Society for the Study of Education, 1976.

Rozin, P., & Gleitman, L. R. The structure and acquisition of reading. In A. S. Reber & D. Scarborough (Eds.), *Reading: Theory and practice.* Hillsdale, N.J.: Lawrence Erlbaum Associates, 1976.

Stebbins, L. B., St. Pierre, R. G., Proper, E. C., Anderson, R. B., & Cerva, T. R. *Education as experimentation: A planned variation model* (Vol. IV-A: An evaluation of Follow Through). Washington, D.C.: U.S. Department of Health, Education and Welfare, 1977.

Author Index

Numbers in italic indicate the page on which the complete reference appears.

A

Ackerman, P., 212, *225*
Adams, M. J., 13, *26,* 334, *338*
Adelman, H., 191, *204*
Aderman, D., 96, 103, *106*
Ames, L. B., 139, *148*
Anastasi, A., 177, *203*
Anderson, J. R., 34, *42,* 72, *87*
Anderson, R. B., 325, *338*
Anderson, R. C., 72, *87,* 334, *338*
Arnold, R. D., 174, 196, *203*
Ashton-Warner, S., 324, *338*
Atchison, M., 215, *225*
Atkinson, R. C., 97, 98, *106,* 173, *203,* 246, 249, 256, 260, 262, 263, 264, 265, *266, 267*
Austin, M. C., 197, *203*

B

Baddeley, A. D., 71, *87*
Bakan, P., 212, *225*
Baker, H., 218, *225*
Banas, C., 178, *203*

Banks, W. C., 311, *319*
Barnhart, C. L., 245, 253, *266, 267*
Baron, J., 75, 81, 83, *87,* 96, *106*
Barr, A., 256, 260,262, *266*
Barr, R., 196, *203*
Barton, H., 282, *282*
Bateman, B., 334, *338*
Baumal, R., 85, *90*
Beardsley, M., 163, *170*
Beers, J., 46, *64*
Bell-Berti, F., 120, *131*
Belmont, L., 219, *225*
Bentzen, F., 212, 213, *225*
Berliner, D. C., 328, *338*
Berlyne, D. E., 153, *170*
Bever, T. G., 72, *87,* 116, *131*
Biemiller, A., 154, *170*
Bijou, S. W., 113, *131*
Birch, H., 219, *225*
Bissex, G., 43, 44, *64*
Bjork, E. L., 77, *87,* 94, 96, *106*
Blalock, J., 215, *225*
Block, J. H., 200, *203*
Bloom, B. S., 177, *203*
Bloomfield, L., 245, *266,* 278, *282*
Bobrow, D. G., 73, 86, *89*

339

AUTHOR INDEX **343**

Subject Index